The Critical Response
to Gloria Naylor

☙

Recent Titles in
Critical Responses in Arts and Letters

The Critical Response to Gloria Naylor

☙

Edited by
Sharon Felton
and Michelle C. Loris

Critical Responses in Arts and Letters, Number 29
Cameron Northouse, Series Adviser

Greenwood Press
Westport, Connecticut • London

Library of Congress Cataloging-in-Publication Data

The critical response to Gloria Naylor / edited by Sharon Felton and
    Michelle C. Loris.
        p.   cm.—(Critical responses in arts and letters, ISSN
    1057–0993 ; no. 29)
        Includes bibliographical references (p.) and index.
        ISBN 0–313–30026–7 (alk. paper)
        1. Naylor, Gloria—Criticism and interpretation.   2. Feminism and
    literature—United States—History—20th century.   3. Women and
    literature—United States—History—20th century.   4. Afro-American
    women in literature.   5. Afro-Americans in literature.   I. Felton,
    Sharon.   II. Loris, Michelle Carbone, 1946–   .   III. Series.
    PS3564.A895Z65   1997
    813′.54—dc21   97–21977

British Library Cataloguing in Publication Data is available.

Library of Congress Catalog Card Number: 97–21977
ISBN: 0–313–30026–7
ISSN:1057–0993

First published in 1997

Greenwood Press, 88 Post Road West, Westport, CT 06881
An imprint of Greenwood Publishing Group, Inc.

Printed in the United States of America

The paper used in this book complies with the
Permanent Paper Standard issued by the National
Information Standards Organization (Z39.48–1984).

10 9 8 7 6 5 4 3 2

Copyright Acknowledgments

Sharon would like to offer a personal thank you to those who continue to believe in her--Bill, her family, and a few others.

Michelle dedicates this volume to Victoria, Salvatore, and Teresa--with love.

Contents

Linden Hills

Mama Day

Bailey's Cafe

Contents

Series Foreword

Critical Responses in Arts and Letters is designed to present a documentary history of highlights in the critical reception to the body of work of writers and artists and to individual works that are generally considered to be of major importance. The focus of each volume in this series is basically historical. The introductions to each volume are themselves brief histories of the critical response an author, artist, or individual work has received. This response is then further illustrated by reprinting a strong representation of the major critical reviews and articles that have collectively produced the author's, artist's, or work's critical reputation.

The scope of *Critical Responses in Arts and Letters* knows no chronological or geographical boundaries. Volumes under preparation include studies of individuals from around the world and in both contemporary and historical periods.

Each volume is the work of an individual editor, who surveys the entire body of criticism on a single author, artist, or work. The editor then selects the best material to depict the critical response received by an author or artist over his/her entire career. Documents produced by the author or artist may also be included when the editor finds that they are necessary to a full understanding of the materials at hand. In circumstances where previous isolated volumes of criticism on a particular individual or work exist, the editor carefully selects material that better reflects the nature and directions of the critical response over time.

In addition to the introduction and the documentary section, the editor of each volume is free to solicit new essays on areas that may not have been adequately dealt with in previous criticism. Also, for volumes on living writers and artists, new interviews may be included, again at the discretion of the volume's editor. The volumes also provide a supplementary bibliography and are fully indexed.

While each volume in *Critical Responses in Arts and Letters* is unique, it is also hoped that in combination they form a useful, documentary history of the critical response to the arts, and one that can be easily and profitably employed by students and scholars.

Cameron Northouse

Acknowledgments

Both editors wish to thank the staff at Greenwood for their assistance. Sharon owes thanks as well to Carol and other library staff from Austin Peay State University (Clarksville, Tennessee), to Paige at Belmont University (Nashville, Tennessee) and to the various contributors and permission editors who have cooperated with us from around the globe.

Michelle notes: I am fortunate in the friends and colleagues I have the pleasure of thanking for their support of this project. A primary debt of gratitude is due to the Department of English and the University Research and Creativity Committee of Sacred Heart University for their grant of the release time which enabled me to begin and to complete this project. I want to thank Carol Clarke, Carolyn Tanski, and Christina McGowan, librarians at Sacred Heart University for their research assistance, and Beverly Boehmke, Department Secretary, for her invaluable clerical help. I am especially grateful to Julie Holt and Denise Discepelo for their continued assistance throughout the project. I want to express special thanks and regards to Sharon Felton, my collaborator on this project. For her superb editorial skills, meticulous scholarly attention, and for her genuine spirit of collegiality, I count myself fortunate. This entire project extends many thanks to Gloria Naylor whose continued interest and generous cooperation provided a special contribution to our work and our deepest gratitude is to her for the art and vision of her work.

Chronology

1950	Gloria Naylor born
1968	Naylor becomes Jehovah's Witness
	Begins work as switchboard operator
1981	B.A. in English from Brooklyn College
	Begins graduate work at Yale University
1982	*The Women of Brewster Place* published
1983	American Book Award
	M. A. in Afro-American studies from Yale University
1985	*Linden Hills* published
1988	*Mama Day* published
	Becomes a member of Book-of-the-Month Club selection committee
1989	Film version of *The Women of Brewster Place* shown on ABC
1990	Begins One Way Productions
1992	*Bailey's Cafe* published
1993	*Gloria Naylor: Critical Perspectives Past and Present*, critical collection published by Henry Louis Gates, Jr., and K. A. Appiah, New York: Amistad Press
1994	Stage production of *Bailey's Cafe* performed by Hartford Stage Company, Hartford, Connecticut
1996	*Gloria Naylor,* critical work published by Virginia Fowler, Boston: Twayne Publishers

Introduction

Gloria Naylor offers one of the most powerful and promising voices in contemporary American literature. In just over a decade she has produced a body of work enormously diverse in its literary appeal and extensive in its vision. Beginning with her first novel, *The Women of Brewster Place*, which was published in 1982 and which won the American Book Award for first fiction in 1983, Naylor's appeal can be traced throughout an impressive range of critical scholarship. Current criticism is largely divided among five categories: the examination of Naylor's work

- as a production of an African-American writer,
- as an example of work positing a feminist or women's studies agenda,
- as a focus of influence studies or intertextual comparisons,
- as a study in narrative and/or rhetorical methods, and
- as an exponent of popular culture.

Whereas these critical viewpoints commonly overlap, this overview consciously seeks to separate these scholarly perspectives into smaller units to facilitate their discussion. We emphasize in this introduction the first two perspectives--Naylor's work as representing African American and feminist concerns. The other issues, while they are indeed salient critical perspectives, are often subsumed under the more comprehensive explorations of African American and/or feminist views. Some of the essays selected to appear in this volume, however, do engage in depth the other three critical perspectives.

African American scholars have embraced Naylor's work for its authentic representations of a cross-section of both native African lives and the lives of all classes of African Americans. Naylor's characters have not escaped the burden of their race, and critics have found fruitful material in Naylor by which to trace the history of race relations in America. Beginning with Sapphira Wade, a slave whose bill of sale from 1819 is provided as a frontispiece to *Mama Day*, and ending perhaps with *Linden Hills'* Laurel Dumont, a young black woman who holds a corporate position at IBM, Naylor has depicted a range of roles available to African Americans in our society. Race will be tainted, upon occasion, with class in Naylor's fiction, for the most affluent among her cast of characters--for instance, Luther Nedeed--will demonstrate the least moral value, whereas those with the fewest material possessions--like Miranda Day--will be the most spiritually developed.

Feminist scholars and those interested in women's studies have also found Naylor's work especially noteworthy. Naylor's women accomplish remarkable deeds and demonstrate an enormous strength of character. From the mundane--Mattie Michael's offering a piece of homemade angel food cake to another woman--to the miraculous, the birth of George to Mariam, a virgin mother, Naylor's women are all survivors, blessed with talents that make them extraordinary women.

A third focus of much Naylor scholarship involves influence studies. Several scholars have established convincing readings of Naylor's work as including parallels to and/or revisions of Shakespeare's canon. Other critical work links Naylor's *Linden Hills* to Dante's *Inferno*, and Naylor herself has confirmed this use of Dante. A scholar in this volume establishes and argues successfully for a critical link between Naylor's fourth novel and yet another classic--Chaucer's *Canterbury Tales*. Additionally, Naylor's work takes its place among a notably diverse legacy of major American authors, including Walt Whitman, William Faulkner, Ralph Ellison, Toni Morrison, Alice Walker, and Zora Neale Hurston just to name a few. The notion of influence studies, however, sometimes implies comparisons between or among works, and under this category, scholars have offered fruitful comparisons between Naylor and a spectrum of American and world authors: Charles W. Chesnutt, Edith Wharton, Willa Cather, Jean Toomer, Ann Petry, Nella Larsen, Jessie Fauset, Bessie Head, Paule Marshall, Ntozake Shange, Audre Lorde, Eudora Welty, up to and including Lee Smith.

Furthermore, considerable scholarship has been devoted to Naylor's rhetorical and narrative methods. *The Women of Brewster Place,* for instance, is identified as "a novel in seven stories." This paradoxical designation confirms the innovative structure and style of Naylor's book. Rather than being judged as seven distinct stories, Naylor's work insists upon a vision of unity. The first six stories each feature the narrative of a different female protagonist, and the seventh inscribes the women in a collective union, the block party. Naylor's work exhibits the cohesiveness of a novel, but it is indeed a novel with a contemporary cinematic feel. Naylor's later productions continue to garner additional critical inspection regarding her narrative techniques. Like Faulkner's Snopes and Sartoris clans, characters will reappear from one Naylor novel to the next, sometimes in a slightly different guise. Also, like Faulkner, Naylor consciously plays with chronology: for instance, George from *Mama Day* (1988) is actually born in a later novel, *Bailey's Cafe* (1992). There is a critical initiative that suggests Naylor's first four novels might be seen as a holistic collection, a consciously-designed quartet much like Lawrence Durrell's *The Alexandria Quartet*. The argument for quartet design will be more definitively established once Naylor's future literary works are offered and assessed. Other successful analyses of Naylor's rhetorical and narrative methods link her work to specialized storytelling techniques such as magical realism or writing through women-centered prose.

Naylor's cinematic narrative method is responsible, no doubt, for her first novel being turned into an enormously popular television movie. Thus, scholars who embrace popular culture have readily adopted Naylor's work, for no less esteemed a popular culture icon than Oprah Winfrey starred in the television adaption of *The Women of Brewster Place*. Winfrey served as the guiding force behind getting studio executives to pursue the project, and as a result of these efforts, Naylor's work reached a huge audience and received significant critical acclaim. Other issues portrayed in popular culture--such as female genital mutilation, the Holocaust, and hoodoo/folk medicine--find expression throughout Naylor's canon.

In short, any reader--young or old, black or white, male or female--will find something of value in Naylor's powerful compositions. Naylor's work illuminates: it provides an insight into places we may or may not have lived, violences we may or may not have experienced, lessons we may or may not have learned. Most of all, she illuminates for us the deepest places of our human selves and the dilemmas of our own human ways. Naylor's work forges **connections**, connections among other African American writers, other female writers, other classic literary figures. Equally important are the connections she makes within the canon of her own texts. This volume utilizes that central notion--connections--as a thematic ground for the essays selected herein for inclusion. A more specific preview of each essay will be offered at the end of this introduction.

An African-American Voice

As an African American writer, Naylor's work stands alongside the history of the best fiction produced by African Americans this century. Charles W. Chesnutt, W. E. B. Du Bois, Jean Toomer, Zora Neale Hurston, James Baldwin, Ralph Ellison, Richard Wright, and Toni Morrison have all been identified as voicing concerns and issues vital to an understanding of African American life, giving voice to experiences that are similarly reflected in Naylor's fiction. Two of the women who live on Brewster Place have, like Ellison's Invisible Man, migrated from the oppressive society of the South in hopes of locating a more promising future up North. Mattie Michael was banished from her family because of her out-of-wedlock pregnancy. Likewise, Etta Mae Johnson was forced to leave her Rutherford County, Tennessee home because the Southern community could not deal, in 1937, with her feisty attitudes. Whereas life in the North will present challenges of its own, Mattie, Etta Mae, and Ellison's Invisible Man will embrace their residence in the North--they will find a place from which they can grow--and they will consider the move a displacement that finally results in personal progress.

Similarly, the street itself--Brewster Place--will demonstrate the limited success available to African Americans even in the more receptive North. The housing project of Brewster Place is built on "worthless land"; moreover, once the brick wall is erected, the community becomes enclosed, a dead end, left to determine its own prosperity or decline. The block community is, at least to some degree, knitted together by the presence of Ben, a poor, old black superintendent who lives in the damp basement apartment. Again, like Ellison's Invisible Man or Richard Wright's "The Man Who Lived Underground," the grim basement view provides Ben with an unusual perspective of this community. His hole is not only a place from which he can observe the goings-on of the block, but also it is a place from which he can retreat to drink himself into an alcoholic stupor. The residents know that when they hear him, early in the morning, singing "Swing Low, Sweet Chariot," he is returning from the haze of too much alcohol. As a result of Ben's death (and the rape of one resident), the community loses its focus, its stability. The women are forced to take steps to assert a new sense of solidarity in their neighborhood and in their sense of identity, joined in a common goal--as African Americans and as women who refuse to be vulnerable.

African American concerns have formed a primary consideration in Gloria Naylor's other novels as well. *Linden Hills'* Luther Nedeed is, in one sense, the epitome of success: coming from a clearly-defined patriarchal heritage, this fifth generation Luther Nedeed has inherited a veritable kingship over which he rules. Owner of the Tupelo Realty Corporation and therefore overseer of an entire community, the power he wields is considerable. The community is geographically situated in concentric circles, and the closer one moves to the bottom of the hill, the more prestigious the address--and the more domination one may expect Luther Nedeed to enact. Not only does Naylor reverse the reader's expectations over the notion of class ascendancy--which, in the case of *Linden Hills*, means descending the hill (an observation that led to the critical link to Dante's *Inferno*)--but also she portrays Luther Nedeed with bitter irony. The man who could be a marvelous role model, an immensely successful black businessman, property owner, and wielder of power, is in fact reprehensible.

Much like *Song of Solomon's* Macon Dead, who is an equally heartless and shrewd businessman, Luther Nedeed has lost his spiritual center. He attends his ten-year class reunion with the active intention of locating a woman who has become desperate, a woman disillusioned with her prospects of happiness and eager to secure a husband at whatever cost. He finds such a woman, and the relationship more resembles a business arrangement than a marriage. His treatment of her, as well as the expectations he holds for his tenants, establish him as a totalitarian power broker, ruthless and diabolical.

Readers should notice that the lack of a spiritual center extends beyond just Luther Nedeed. Indeed, members of the entire community sell themselves out just for the prestige of living in Linden Hills. Barbara Christian has said that every upwardly mobile resident has to "erase" a part of him- or herself for the opportunity of living here. Because virtually every resident pursues the same variety of wealth and power that Luther Nedeed embodies, Naylor presents a sharp social and class critique of all African Americans who sell themselves out.

Furthermore, as if Naylor wanted her thematic lesson regarding African Americans who sell themselves out to be abundantly clear, she offers two or three other portraits of individuals in *Linden Hills* who lose their spiritual centers, and we see the traumatic or ridiculous ends to which they come. The first is that of Winston Alcott, a young man on his way to an "establishment" version of success by his skill as an aspiring lawyer. His dirty little secret, the obstacle to his unfettered success, is that he has been pursuing a homosexual relationship for some eight years with David. He has decided to give up his homosexual lifestyle, however, and in fact to marry Cassandra, a socialite, in order to improve his chances at promotion, at rising through the corporate partnership more quickly. The marriage is *the* social event of the season, notable for its display of ostentation. But despite the fur capes, the expensive caviar, and the cordial festivities, readers understand the inauthenticity of this union: this marriage is for show only; it holds no potential for success.

Laurel Dumont is married to Linden Hills' ambitious district attorney, and she herself holds an equally prestigious position at IBM. Yet in order to achieve her material successes, she has deliberately distanced herself from her African American heritage, from any sense of self she has known. After she entered college, Laurel never quite found the time to visit her grandmother (Roberta) who raised her, so when she finally does return to her grandmother--Laurel is thirty-five--her desire to reconnect with her past is staggeringly difficult. As Laurel listens to classical music, Roberta suggests that perhaps she might listen to blues singers such as Billie Holliday, Bessie Smith, and Muddy Waters in order to recapture her heritage. Laurel fails to forge a connection between herself and Roberta (or among her other black female acquaintances), however, and her suicide depicts the dire consequences of losing touch with one's past.

The third portrait Naylor offers in *Linden Hills* of an individual obsessed with control is much more comic, but under the comedy lies a ridiculously futile objective. As Assistant to the Executive Director at General Motors, Maxwell Smyth has allowed his ambition totally to negate his humanity. He changes the spelling of his last name from the common "Smith" to the rarer "Smyth," a move that makes a public statement of sham erudition. But Maxwell attempts to control his most private functions as well: he never sweats, and he regulates his diet to such a degree that he no longer requires the use of toilet paper. Naylor makes the point through Winston, Laurel, and Maxwell that once an African American denies his or her most basic impulses--sexual, emotional, or physical-- the result will inevitably be problematic. Her point is underscored by the portraits she offers of the few "good" people in *Linden Hills*. The ones who are most humane don't live in Linden Hills at all and they own very few material possessions, but they are spiritually rich.

Mama Day is the novel set, geographically and perhaps psychologically, closest to Africa: the island of Willow Springs represents the portion of the United States that juts out into the Atlantic Ocean towards Africa; moreover, it is not claimed by either neighboring state. Those who live there embrace the powerful magic of the conjure woman Miranda Day. Miranda's magic comes to her from a rich ancestry of conjure women, the most important being Sapphira Wade. Sapphira's ties to Africa are clearly present; her bill of sale opens the text and it is due to her actions that the island of Willow Springs was deeded to its current residents. Lineage, ancestry, and heritage are privileged in this novel; few African American novels offer such a careful rendering of history, and it is a precedent that adds not only tradition but dignity to the lives of *Mama Day*'s characters.

Another source of dignity must be noted in Miranda Day herself--in her extraordinary ability to bridge the gap between the culturally different worlds of the mainland and the island. For example, at one end of the medical spectrum is shifty Dr. Buzzard (and the spiteful Ruby as well) whose attempts at the invocation of magic and/or "spell-casting" always seem to benefit Buzzard or Ruby more so than the patient. While there is comedy in their portraits--Dr. Buzzard is a laughable character with his rooster-tail hat and his necklace of bones--the reader remains necessarily nervous regarding these two; Buzzard and Ruth wield their variety of power irresponsibly, allowing it to be tainted by narrow personal motives. At the extreme other end would be traditional medicine, the mainland's way, the established Western form, clearly represented by Dr. Brian Smithfield. Miranda's way occupies a more central position; she retains the conjure woman's secrets of beneficial roots and herbs, and she is blessed with an intuition, a sensitivity to subtle physical signals, not often found in Western medicine. Like Pilate, the most natural of women from Morrison's *Song of Solomon*, Miranda is constantly associated with the natural symbol of eggs. Similarly, she serves as a bridge between Cocoa, who has immersed herself deeply in the mainland world--specifically, New York--and the island's traditional ways. Although Miranda is firmly entrenched on the island, she still watches Phil Donahue to expand her horizons all the way to a New York studio audience. In many manifestations, Miranda Day serves as a balancing force, a nexus that successfully negotiates between two very different worlds.

Inherent in the above sketch of *Mama Day* is the sense that Naylor's African characters are beginning to assume a wider variety of portraits. That idea is significantly fleshed out in *Bailey's Cafe*: not only is there a large number of characters in Naylor's fourth novel, but also the portraits they occupy are notable for their breadth and their diversity. *Bailey's Cafe* gives voice to an Ethiopian jew who has become pregnant despite her claims of virginity, a Stanford graduate who cross-dresses, a woman who is prostituted because of her brother's demands, a plethora of lost individuals who seek a way out of their misery. Counterposed to these characters are several more, including the reader him/herself, who will compassionately listen to the endless litany of emotional pain they reveal.

A Feminist Voice

Feminist concerns are so intricately woven into the fabric of Naylor's fiction that one might point merely to Naylor's statement that her goal as a writer is to give a voice to the voiceless--and that many times the voiceless one is a black woman, an individual for whom, at the time Naylor began writing, few authors had spoken. In the exclusive interview included in this volume, she calls herself a transcriber of lives; she expresses a similar sentiment in the classic interview with Toni Morrison published in *Southern Review* and with a number of other interviewers. Moreover, Naylor is careful now to define her brand of feminism as social, economic, and political equality for all humans. What is perhaps most interesting to note is the manner in which her feminist concerns have evolved throughout her career.

In *The Women of Brewster Place*, Naylor admits her stance was essentially romantic: the black women she gave voices to were largely victims, and their united attempt was to break through a wall--recall the closing pages of the work--of social, and particularly male, entrapment. Mattie Michael is betrayed in some sense by Butch Fuller, by her father, by the justice system, and clearly by her well-loved, ungrateful son. Etta Mae, Lucielia, and Cora Lee are all, despite their various stages of commitment, ultimately used and discarded by their men. Whether the women have achieved any progress by the end of the novel is a question left unanswered: the women strive to tear down the wall separating Brewster Place from the rest of society--in effect, leveling the playing field between themselves and mainstream society--but their effort occurs only in a dream. These women may be moving towards social equality, but the final words affirm that Brewster Place ambiguously "waits to die." In any case, the women of Brewster Place continue to come up short regarding issues of economic or political clout.

No greater social or political clout is awarded to any woman in *Linden Hills*. Willa Prescott Nedeed, like generations of other Nedeed wives before her, is physically entrapped in a basement; thus, she is entirely stripped of her voice. Only one individual, Willie, can hear the eerie strains of her haunting wails permeating through the neighborhood, and he does not yet understand the meaning of these cries. The opening lines of the poem he creates--"There is a man in a house at the bottom of a hill. And his wife has no name" (277) suggest at least the potential for change, but just like Brewster Place which waits to die, this poem has not yet been written; it exists only in the shadowy edges of Willie's sleep. Furthermore, only through a fabulous set of circumstances does Willa have the opportunity to be released from her prison, from her entrapment as a "madwoman in the basement."

One might argue that *Linden Hills* offers at least a portrait of a woman, Laurel Dumont, who has achieved economic progress. But the effectiveness of her portrait must be tempered by the personal demons that accompany her success. She has discarded her heritage in her drive to achieve economic status, and her terminal encounter with Luther Nedeed teaches her the cruelest truth of all: that despite her efforts, despite all she has given up, she is still nothing. Laurel has fought a history of "ingrained male assumptions that she didn't count" (246). This encounter, however, is too much to bear. The interpersonal bonds that sustained and supported the women's collective efforts in *The Women of Brewster Place* have failed to provide Laurel with a reason to survive. Laurel's facelessness at the time of her suicide speaks to her loss of identity, just as the face of Priscilla McGuire Nedeed disappears throughout her successive photographs.

Perhaps the purest validation of the male's unyielding grasp of social, political, and economic power in *Linden Hills* is demonstrated by a conversation between Maxwell Smyth and Xavier Donnell. Maxwell explains "some hard cold facts [about black women]: there just aren't enough decent ones to choose from. They're either out there on welfare and waiting to bring you a string of somebody else's kids to support, or they've become so prominent that they're brainwashed into thinking that you aren't good enough for them" (108). He continues with the observation that there is "a whole mass [of black women] that are coming out of these colleges with their hot little fists clenched around those diplomas. . . . They no longer think they're women, but walking miracles. They're ready to ask a hell of a lot from the world then and a hell of a lot from you. They're hungry and they're climbers. . . . Hook up with one of them and . . . [y]ou get your balls clawed off" (109-110). Clearly, the playing field has not yet achieved equality or balance here, for educated and motivated black women remain undesirable in the patriarchal framework of Linden Hills.

Naylor extends her feminist framework in what is perhaps her best novel to date, *Mama Day*, which wrestles with the problem--and the power--of romantic love. The novel defines that problem as a struggle for both self-identity and mutuality (mutual recognition). The terms of such love, the novel declares, are steep and may not be met in a world limited by a patriarchal system. The vision of the novel challenges us to a radical suspension of disbelief: if we are to be transformed by the power of love we must know how to listen; we must be able to see with the heart.

Naylor uses the love story of Cocoa and George to illustrate her feminist vision of love. Both Cocoa and George struggle with each other to maintain their self-identity, but both are defensive, fearful to be vulnerable, to express their feelings and needs. Cocoa, however, eventually lets down her guard: she wants George to see her true self. She invites him home to the magical, matriarchal world of Willow Springs where he can see who she is by understanding where and who she comes from. Cocoa's true self descends from a long line of Day women--conjure women, women with special spiritual powers. Cocoa's ancestry begins with Sapphira Wade, a woman who could "grab a bolt of lightning [and turn] the moon into salve." Sapphira Wade, a slave who took her freedom, gives the Day line its name and forges a family of powerful women.

The power of the Day women currently resides in Cocoa's great-aunt Miranda Day, the ruling matriarch of Willow Springs, a conjure woman whose healing powers challenge George's rationalist, masculinist ways of seeing and understanding. George, "a good hearted boy with a bad heart" as Mama Day defines him, must learn that love, "the power greater than hate," requires that he break through his resistance to Miranda's female, intuitive, irrational, and emotional world. He cannot. George knows only "the facts" and what he can see right in front of him. George's maps, his ways of knowing, are useless in Willow Springs.

Challenging George to a central condition of romantic love--an act of mutuality--Miranda requests George's "hand in hers--his very hand--so she can connect it up with all the believing that had gone before. . . . So together they could be the bridge for Baby Girl to walk over" (285). George refuses. He violently resists by destroying the hen house. George would rather die for love of Cocoa than live loving her in the terms of mutual recognition set forth in the novel.

Naylor's compelling feminist vision then offers us this lesson about love: because of our common human nature both men and women have a similar motivation to experience love, but the capacity to fulfill this desire is confounded by a difference in gender. For Naylor, love--a balance of self and other--can be transformative and magical only if we are willing to transcend the limitations of our gendered reality.

Bailey's Cafe furthers Naylor's discourse on the complications and implications of a gendered reality. Her account, framed by the Holocaust and Hiroshima, connects the collective burdens of sexism, racism, and anti-Semitism that drive us to the despair at the "edge of the world." In this novel, Naylor includes women worldwide in her vision, and, indicative of her growth as a writer, she includes men such as the fatherly narrator Bailey, whose character she endows with fullness and substance.

Re-envisioning the stories of Biblical women--stories written by men-- Naylor offers her most compelling portrait of female sexuality. Beginning with Eve, a woman whose sexuality would, in traditional patriarchal terms, define her as a "whore," but who instead "choose[s]" who she is, and culminating with Mariam, the mutilated virgin who, at Christmas, gives birth to George, the baby whose birth is meant "to bring in a whole new era," Naylor unfolds for us her reconstruction of the female condition. She presents to us women who have been violated and scourged by male violence and male menacing. She presents to us women who are themselves victimizers of other women. But transcending the mutilation and degradation, Naylor's women have hope, compassion, and the power to bring forth new life.

Naylor's feminist concerns have deepened and matured in both *Mama Day* and *Bailey's Cafe*. The women in these novels are powerful and important even when they have been oppressed and violated. These women are often mothers, caregivers, healers, or just plain survivors of the violence done to them. No longer offering a one-dimensional portrait, the women and the men in *Mama*

Day and *Bailey's Cafe* are multi-leveled, complex, polyphonic, even as they may be disturbing; these characters demonstrate the author's increasing maturity as a writer. Naylor said in the interview included here that she wants her work to present a community of people who are both saints and sinners. An authentic portrait of African Americans--male and female--necessarily includes both light and shadow, and in these last two novels, signifying Naylor's accomplishments, readers see a more complex portrait of humanity.

A powerful vision obviously shapes Naylor's works. Her stories illuminate for us the complexities of human character. Her stories, which we love to read, are tales of women, like Mattie Michael or Cocoa Day, who fall in love and are betrayed or transformed by the experience. Her stories are tales of men, like Luther Nedeed whose lives are consumed by greed and a thirst for power; or men like Bailey, who are somewhat indifferent guardians and guides to humanity's search for meaning; or men like George Andrews, who would give his life--but not his soul--for love.

The moral geography of Naylor's stories is central in all her works. "Where" her stories take place illuminates for us the moral meaning of these common lives. *The Women of Brewster Place*, set on a dead-end street, depicts the struggles and survival of seven poor black women whose lives are dead-ended by an oppressively male world. *Linden Hills*, a tale of class and money, power and greed, unfolds a grim allegory of material success and spiritual bankruptcy that must be read in conjunction with its progressively-entrapping geography. *Mama Day* gives voice to a storm of love and magic and the magical transformation wrought by human compassion, and it portrays a place--and a mood--not easily located on any traditional map. Finally, *Bailey's Cafe*, a novel set both everywhere and nowhere, transcribes a metaphysical place with an apocalyptic vision: it is "the last place before the end of the world" (68).

Naylor's work, in short, forges connections--between love and loss, hope and despair, between the sacred and the mundane, security and fear, light and shadow. To paraphrase a line from *Bailey's Cafe*, no one we meet through the artistry of Naylor's pen comes in with a simple story. Every one is multifaceted; each can be viewed from a variety of critical perspectives. Therefore, "plan to stick around here and listen while we play it all out" (35).

The essays collected here represent some of the best scholarship being produced and published on Gloria Naylor. Please note that we have departed slightly from the usual *Critical Responses* series format by omitting reviews of Naylor's work. Because several fine reviews were included in the well-known Henry Louis Gates, Jr. and K. A. Appiah volume on Naylor, we have decided to avoid any possible duplications and to concentrate instead solely on scholarly articles.

Upon occasion, we have also departed slightly from the straightforward manner of reproducing critical articles exactly as they were published. On a small number of essays, in order to assist future scholars in their own research, we have purposely constructed a Works Cited bibliographic entry wherein none existed in the original manuscript. We have clearly included a notice if the Works Cited entry was constructed by us, and we certainly take full responsibility if there are any errors present in such a constructed entry.

Scholars, please take advantage of the Naylor bibliography included before the general index.

Presenting a diversity of critical responses has certainly been one of our goals as editors; however, another goal has been to include essays that demonstrate the thematic idea of *connections* suggested earlier in this introduction. We offer here the perspectives of new and established scholars, domestic and international, black and white, male and female, and views both critically embraced and uncommon. Each scholar has made his or her own unique connection to Naylor's works, and we are confident that the inclusion of our exclusive interview with Naylor will offer a base from which additional fruitful scholarship will develop. For quick reference, then, here is a brief survey of the essays selected for inclusion in *The Critical Response to Gloria Naylor*.

Ebele Eko's essay connects Naylor's work--especially an examination of Kiswana Browne--with the work of other black female writers. Eko includes a treatment of two other novelists, Bessie Head's *Maru* and Paule Marshall's *Browngirl Brownstones*, along with an exploration of Ama Ata Aidoo's play, *Anowa*. An examination of the ways in which language usage characterizes individuals is the focus of Cheryl Lynn Johnson's dissertation excerpt. While Johnson's work pursued her thesis--a "womanist way of speaking"--through fiction by Toni Morrison, Alice Walker, and Naylor, we have included here just her focus on Mattie Michael's and Butch Fuller's relationship. Jacqueline Bobo and Ellen Seiter's essay on *The Women of Brewster Place* offers a nicely synthetic view of the feminist emphasis of both the text and the television adaptation. Their essay will be of interest not only to feminist scholars but also to those interested in exploring narrative versus screen versions of works and to those pursuing popular culture issues. Maxine L. Montgomery's article explores the supportive relationships between the female characters; she notes that Mattie Michael plays a pivotal maternal role. Finishing out the discussion surrounding *The Women of Brewster Place*, James Robert Saunders' essay pursues some commonly critically-unexplored territory. He looks at a few of the religious and spiritual figures found throughout Naylor's first three novels: *Brewster Place's* Reverend Moreland T. Woods, the Reverend Michael Hollis from *Linden Hills*, and several of the spiritually-connected characters of *Mama Day*.

Five essays comprise the discussion on *Linden Hills*. Mary F. Sisney offers a powerfully creative reading of *Linden Hills* as an example of the rarely seen black "novel of manners." She also includes important comparisons between Naylor's work and that of Nella Larsen and Jessie Fauset. Offering a critical connection between *Linden Hills* and *Mama Day* is Nellie Boyd's essay. Boyd looks at the importance of place and leadership in these two novels. Grace E. Collins' article, as its name implies, counterpoints the differing narrative strategies Naylor employs in her depictions of the similarly-named characters Willa and Willie. Charles P. Toombs discovers that Naylor employs food tropes throughout *Linden Hills*; he argues that a character's choice of foods helps to delineate his/her character in this novel. The fifth essay, commissioned for inclusion in this volume, is by Christine G. Berg; it establishes Naylor's usage of a specific Walt Whitman poem. This poem, recited at the occasion of Winston Alcott's wedding, represents virtually the only white voice in the novel, according to Berg, and she extends with conviction the observation that Whitman is among the best-loved of poetic mentors for African Americans.

We include here a more expansive collection of criticism on *Mama Day* than has been available so far; it is fair to say that *Mama Day* is the most critically pursued of Naylor's four novels. With that in mind, we have selected criticism that represents the range of scholarship. Opening this chapter is Susan Meisenhelder's work that presents a scholarly discussion of George, Cocoa, and Miranda Day as intricately and spiritually linked to one another. Suzanne Juhasz's essay is an adaptation of a chapter from her book *Reading from the Heart: Women, Literature, and the Search for True Love*. Juhasz isolates a number of connections not only among Naylor's female characters and women's romantic fiction in general but also between Naylor's work and that of--surprisingly--Louisa May Alcott's *Little Women*. The next essay, Lindsey Tucker's "Recovering the Conjure Woman," will be of special interest to scholars pursuing a study of unique African and African American folk traditions, especially those related to medicinal issues. Conjure is a favorite trope among African American writers--male and female--and Tucker does a fine job establishing comparisons and contrasts between Naylor's and other writers' use of this mystical heritage. Hélène Christol's study examines the unusual geographic placement, Willow Springs, found in *Mama Day*. She then goes on to substantiate how geography and genealogy are combined. Gary Storhoff's essay features a strong interpretation of the Shakespearean subtext of Naylor's third novel. Storhoff's work must be considered a classic among the Naylor critical canon. Lastly, Elizabeth T. Hayes finds abundant evidence to substantiate her claim that *Mama Day* may be viewed as a narrative of African American magic realism.

The chapter on *Bailey's Cafe* demonstrates the diversity of critical perspectives that Naylor continues to attract. In her second essay included in this volume, Maxine L. Montgomery looks at the multiple voices in *Bailey's Cafe* and, coming around full circle, compares this work back to Naylor's earlier novels. Angela diPace's essay explores the underlying use of the Holocaust and World War II issues as they pertain especially to Bailey's narrative. Karah Stokes' essay isolates an important narrative technique Naylor utilizes in her depiction of a violent act, and Stokes then compares Naylor's technique with that of Charles W. Chesnutt. William R. Nash studies the issue of cultural nationalism. Philip Page, who has published a major work on Toni Morrison, pursues the images of wells and abysses in this fourth novel; he links their inclusion to Jungian archetypes. Rebecca S. Wood's work investigates the themes of universalism and nationalism throughout Naylor's fourth novel. The works by Nash and Wood--offering different perspectives on similar subjects--should be especially provocative viewed in comparison to one another.

Finally, an exclusive interview with Naylor completes this volume. This interview, we hope, will serve as an important resource in future Naylor scholarship because of the diversity of issues she discusses with such candor. Naylor talks freely, not only about her past, her concerns as a writer, but also she revisits some issues regarding her prior work. Perhaps more importantly, she offers some suggestions regarding the direction and the interests she embraces for her future work. She ends with a comment that forges an important connection of her own--between her garden and the human spirit.

The Women of Brewster Place

Eko, Ebele. "Beyond the Myth of Confrontation: A Comparative Study of African and African-American Female Protagonists." *Ariel* 17.4 (Oct. 1986): 139-152.

Times have changed since the sixties, and a new breed of black women writers in African and America are giving creative birth to a new breed of female protagonists. One of their deep concerns, a point which Hoyt Fuller has stressed,[1] is to help destroy degrading images and myths and recreate for black women images that liberate and build up self-identity. The myth of black mother-daughter confrontation, to which a whole volume of a scholarly journal has been devoted,[2] is one such.

I intend to focus on the creative process of myth destruction and recreation in two works each from Africa and America. By comparing and contrasting the confrontation of daughters and their mothers and "totems" of that tradition--the reactions, the revelation of deep-seated mother-daughter resemblances, and the challenge the daughters become to those around them--I hope to prove a number of things. First that, far from being selfish, spoiled, and pugnacious, these daughters are budding activists, products of the times (all four works are published between 1959 and 1983). Second that their mothers too experienced similar frustrations in their youth but lacked a voice and silently conformed. Third that their conscious choice achieves a double goal: raising the level of their awareness, and challenging others to greater black consciousness. Fourth, these daughters are their writers' mouthpieces, used to address pressing problems in African and African-American communities. In a sentence, I will try to show the crucial importance of female determination to stand for equity and choice.

The characters I discuss--Anowa in Ama Ata Aidoo's play, *Anowa*; Kiswana Browne in Gloria Naylor's novel, *The Women of Brewster Place*; Margaret Cadmore in Bessie Head's novel, *Maru*; and Selina Boyce in Paule Marshall's novel, *Browngirl Brownstones*--reveal many bonds and parallels, despite obvious separations of time, space, and even genre. "You got to take yuh mouth and make a gun," says Silla Boyce, Selina's mother,[3] a statement which finds ironic fulfillment in each of these four daughters under study. There are astonishing resemblances in their defiant utterances, their self-assertion, their committed and courageous opposition to the oppressive status quo. Each struggles to break free, to be herself, to be different from her mother's expectations. Nevertheless, each discovers in herself a mere extension of her mother's personality. They are similarly unified in their expressing and dramatizing what I may call "creative rebellion" against oppressive institutions and traditions. Their capacity for personal sacrifice and the challenges they pose to others demand that they be looked at seriously as catalysts for social, economic, and political changes.

An exciting starting point is the deceptive lull before the dramatic moment of confrontation over cultural and ideological values. A critic has summarized the situation thus:

> The conflict is basically between the idealists (the daughters) and the pragmatists (the mothers). . . . [T]hey are grieved to see their children making choices that they do not understand, turning their backs on the things the mothers have struggled to attain.[4]

In *Anowa*, Anowa's mother Badua, a village woman of Ghana, wants her daughter to become a full woman in the village, "happy to see her peppers and onions grow."[5] In *The Women of Brewster Place*, Kiswana's middle-class mother swears to whatever gods will listen to "use everything at her disposal to assure a secure future for her children."[6] In *Maru*, Margaret's foster mother, the missionary Margaret Cadmore senior, who rescues and nurtures the orphan child of a dying Masarwa woman, raises her with great care to prove her pet theory that "heredity is nothing, environment is everything."[7] Selina's mother, Silla Boyce, an ambitious Badjan immigrant to New York, labors and saves so that she can buy a brownstone house to pass on to her daughters. All of them are well-meaning mothers, who like Janie's grandmother in *Their Eyes Were Watching God*, long for them "to pick from higher bush and a sweeter berry."[8] They wish for their daughters what they missed, because in the words of the poet Tagore, "when you feel sorrow, grief and joy for someone you enlarge yourself, you enrich yourself."[9]

Ironically, the daughters refuse to conform. They rebel against their mothers, not *as* mothers but as representatives of societal authority and expectations. Bell Hooks explains this universal psychological phenomenon in terms of her personal experience with her mother:

> She is also always trying to make me what she thinks it is best for me to be. She tells me how to do my hair, what clothes I should wear. She wants to love and control at the same time. . . . I want so much to please her and yet keep part of me that is my self my own.[10]

The daughters want to be themselves. Anowa wants to choose her own husband in a conservative society where one's parents do the choosing. Her stubborn independence is nothing short of radical. In a language shockingly disrespectful in context, she declares her stand: "I don't care mother. Have I not told you that this is to be my marriage and not yours" (17). Adding shock to shock, she proceeds to do what she pleases, leaving home with a promise not to return. Anowa's rebellion is a challenge to her entire community and evokes prompt reaction, not only from her parents but also from the elders of the village.

Her mother's warning carries the potency of a collective curse: "It's up to you, my mistress who knows everything. But remember, my lady--when I am too old to move, I shall still be sitting by these walls waiting for you to come back with your rags and nakedness" (17). Her father, Osam, wants her apprenticed to a priestess to curb her spirits. The village old woman laments that the age of obedience has run out, while the old man blames it all on fate, remarking that Anowa has the "hot eyes and nimble feet of one born to dance for the gods" (20). Regardless of threats and curses, Anowa leaves with her head held high, promising to make somebody out of the husband they had ridiculed as a cassava man or a worthless fellow.

Just as Anowa's haughtiness shocks the entire village community, Kiswana in Gloria Naylor's *The Women of Brewster Place* shocks her middle-class parents with her inflammatory denunciation of their status symbols and values: "I'd rather be dead than be like you--a white man's nigger who's ashamed of being black!" (85). Matching action to words in the vogue of black activists in the sixties, Kiswana chooses an African name (instead of Melanie), blows her hair into an afro, quits college, moves out of her bourgeois neighborhood to a low-income project, decorates it with African artifacts, and gets a boyfriend in dashiki. The reaction she gets is as sharp as it is forceful. Her mother's lone voice carries with it the moral superiority and confidence of the self-made black middle class, whose hard-earned security has come under fire. She taunts Kiswana about her misguided zeal and mocks her foolishness:

> Where's your revolution now, Melanie? Where are all those black
> revolutionaries who were shouting and demonstrating and kicking
> up a lot of dust with you on that campus? Huh? They're sitting in
> wood-paneled offices with their degrees in mahogany frames...
> (83-84)

She adds, "There was no revolution, Melanie, and there will be no revolution" (84). The battle rages back and forth, each pointing to concrete actions to defend her stance. Denouncing her parents as "terminal cases of middle class amnesia," Kiswana declares that she is now physically near her people (the poor blacks) and their problems. Mrs. Browne counters by pointing to the solid achievements of the NAACP, which she supports, as opposed to the futile dreams of those she calls "hot heads."

In the remote Botswana village of Dilepe, Margaret Cadmore in Bessie Head's *Maru*, like Kiswana, has to face a crisis of choice. She is alone, a new teacher in a strange village; her white foster mother has retired and gone back to England. She has been brought up like an English girl, with Western manners and impeccable English. Everyone who meets her assumes she is a colored, a status not without prejudice in Botswana but certainly much better than that of the Masarwa, who are considered the lowest of the low, condemned to perpetual servitude to Botswana people. Against that background, Margaret Cadmore's firm and cool declaration in answer to her colleague's simple question, and later to the headmaster's inquiry, "I am a Masarwa" (24), sends waves of shock the length and breadth of Dilepe village. With her one-sentence identification, Margaret confronts herself, her past, her upbringing, her future, and her society. She defies all assumptions, bursts out from the walls of her white foster mother's protection, and stands proud, aloof, and vulnerable.

Compared to Anowa and Kiswana, Margaret is like a lamb thrown to ravenous wolves. Pete, the school principal, Morafi, a cattle chief, and Seth, another totem in the community, all band together against the woman whose identification with Masarwa slaves has sent "thrills of fear down their spines" because they all own slaves. Margaret is seen as "a problem"; her statement is "a slap in the face" (44), and their response is therefore a vicious counter-offensive. Pete organizes Margaret's pupils to taunt her into resigning. "You are a Bushman" (46), they chant to their teacher's face. Quiet but resolute, Margaret, with the aid of her friend Dikeledi and Maru, the brother, thwarts all of Pete's attempts to have her disgraced and dismissed.

Unlike Anowa, Kiswana, and Margaret, whom the reader meets at about the same age and comparable maturity, Selina's stubborn spirit grows slowly throughout Paule Marshall's *Browngirl Brownstones.* Even as a little girl, her mother sees her as "her crosses," mischievously in league with her day-dreaming father, a disobedient and difficult child. Selina's total indifference to her mother's ambition of acquiring a brownstone house in New York culminates one day in her screaming rejection: "I'm not interested in houses." But her mother's dreams are only part of a larger community dream. Selina simultaneously deflates and demeans these aspirations by the hammer-blow criticisms she levels against the entire Badjan Association when given a chance to make a few remarks: "It [the Association] stinks . . . because it's a result of living by the most shameful codes possible--dog eat dog . . . it's a band of small frightened people. Clanish. Narrow-minded. Selfish. . . " (23). Her dramatic storming out after her speech, like Anowa's precipitous departure from the village and Kiswana's move to a lower-class neighborhood, leaves her mother shaken. Her announcement of her imminent departure for Barbados, the land her mother and the Badjan community had fled for New York, is a final slap in their faces. Unlike Badua and Mrs. Browne, Silla is drained by the confrontation. She pouts about her two daughters: "Gone so! They ain got no more uses for me and they gone. Oh God, is this what you does get for the nine months and the pain and the long years putting bread in their mouth . . . ?" (306). Unlike Badua, who sends Anowa away with a curse, or Mrs. Browne, who fights back, Silla resigns herself to the inevitable with some dignity and impatience:

> "G'long," she said finally with a brusque motion.
> "G'long! You was always too much woman for me anyway, soul. And my own mother did say two head-bulls can't reign in a flock. G'long!" Her hand sketched a sign that was both a dismissal and a benediction. "If I din dead yet, you and your foolishness can't kill muh now!" (307)

And yet, despite what appears on the surface as the open rebellion of daughters against their mothers, each mother, like Silla Boyce, somehow glimpses in her daughter "the girl she had once been." The daughters in turn discover that they are not "way out" after all, but extensions of their mothers, the "bridges over which they have crossed." Mary Washington has suggested that all blacks must find a way to their true identity through the community, and she believes that "for Black women, the mother is often the key to that unity."[11] Anowa's boldness is clearly inherited from her mother Badua, who argues with her husband and gets her way most of the time. In obvious reference to her mother's strong powers, Anowa asks Badua to remove her "witches" mouth from her marriage. Ironically, her husband and the village old woman later accuse her of "witchcraft" to explain her extraordinary strength of character. The tragedy of Anowa is her husband's weakness. Where Anowa's father argues with and respects his wife, Kofi Ako feels threatened by Anowa's boldness and sound advice. His moral weakness is their undoing, bringing about the double suicide that more than fulfills Badua's curse.

Kiswana no doubt believes herself the epitome of radicalism until she listens to her mother's theatrical recounting of her proud heritage and commitment to the black cause. Suddenly, she comes to understand and appreciate the source of her own dynamism, idealism, and dedication: her mother. The generation gap is finally bridged when Kiswana notices her mother's red painted toenails and realizes that they share similar tastes. It dawns on her that she is indeed a part of her mother:

> . . . she looked at the blushing woman on her couch and suddenly realized that her mother had trod through the same universe that she herself was now traveling. Kiswana was breaking no new trails and would eventually end up just two feet away on that couch. She stared at the woman she had been and was to become. (87)

To an even greater extent, Margaret Cadmore can be seen as her foster mother's programmed alter ego. The missionary gives the orphan her own name and proceeds systematically to fill her mind with "a little bit of everything." Much of her personality--her common sense, logic, resourcefulness, and resilience--filters into Margaret, enabling her to survive in the closed and prejudiced environment of Dilepe, much like the one the missionary had worked in. Her charm, her education, and her talent are all a heritage from her mother. Even their artistic abilities are similar: "The styles of both artists were almost identical, almost near that of a comic-strip artist in their simplicity, except that the younger disciple appeared greater than the master" (87). Despite the success of Margaret's environmental upbringing, she does not lose her identity as a Masarwa. It is this that gives originality to her art and upholds her commitment to common people. In a startling and ironic way, Margaret, whose mother has prepared her to help her people, fulfills that destiny not only through her symbolic paintings but also by her marriage to Maru, heir to the Dilepe chiefdom.

Even Selina, whose alienation from her mother starts early in *Browngirl Brownstones* and is underlined through her addressing Silla as "the mother" and associating her with winter colors, comes to acknowledge a union with Silla. She confesses that despite her love for her father, "there was a part of her that always wanted the mother to win, that loved her strength and the tenacious life of her body" (133). Slowly but certainly, through exposure and some bitter experiences, the young rebel comes to understand, in Gloria Gayle's words, that "in the world of racism the mother is a fellow victim rather than a natural enemy."[12] It is not till the end of the novel, however, that Selina identifies with her mother instead of her father as her source of inspiration, strength, and idealism:

> "Everybody used to call me Deighton's Selina, but they were wrong. Because you see I'm truly your child. Remember how you

used to talk about how you left home and came here alone as a girl
of eighteen and was your own woman? I used to love hearing that.
And that's what I want. I want it!" (307)

The mother's anger fizzles out because for her too it is a moment of truth. She
has come to glimpse in Selina the girl that she once was.

Beyond the confrontations with and resemblances to their mothers, these
daughters are seen by others as abnormal. They are ahead of their time, and
they act as catalysts for changes that affect not only those around them, but the
larger society. They are, in Kofi Ako's words of complaint against Anowa,
"looking for the common pain and the general good," issues he believes should
not concern any normal woman. But these are not ordinary women. Anowa's
uniqueness is underlined throughout. Her father declares categorically: "Anowa
is not every woman." Kofi Ako repeatedly echoes him: "You are a strange
woman, Anowa. Too strange" (36). In despair he asks if she cannot be like
other women. Like a stone in a pond, Anowa sends ripples around her. She is a
stumbling stone to many. Her parents often quarrel over her, taking sides with
her in turns. The magic that seems to permeate everything she touches and,
above all, her adamant moral and ideological stance against any form of slavery,
shows her as a revolutionary, championing the cause of the common man,
pleading for freedom and justice for the oppressed everywhere. She continues
in the independent tradition that makes her reject an arranged marriage and with
it other restrictions and oppressive traditions and taboos. She must be free to
be herself. In a sense, Anowa is a political activist. She upsets her family,
shakes the community out of its sleepy complacency, and the women especially
out of their stupor of resignation. Her courageous, lonely stance reveals the
spiritual dimension of her character. The village old man's comments (after her
open accusation of impotence precipitates Kofi Ako to shoot himself and Anowa
to drown herself) sum up her true significance and the importance of the self-
criticism her life provokes in others: "She was true to herself. She refused to
come back here to Yebi, to our gossiping and our judgements" (64). From
indignation to self-justification to self-criticism, Anowa's village community is
forced to initiate significant adjustments to its whole system of thought.

That cycle repeats itself in case after case. Mrs. Browne would never
have narrated the highlights of her life to Kiswana had she not been frightened
by the degree of determination and commitment she senses in her. She knows
that despite her taunts, the Black Arts Movement of the sixties did give birth to a
new breed of black men and women, "strange," zealous and, like Kiswana,
concerned with the "common pain and the general good." Because of her
choices and theirs, things can never be the same again in Kiswana's family, nor
among middle-class blacks. The movement represented here by Kiswana has
forced her parents and others like them to re-evaluate their lives, to see what
they have lost and gained, to come to grips with crucial issues of unity and
cooperation in the black community. Her actions are a direct challenge to her
parents, telling them that there is much more than just making it in a white world.
She challenges them to bridge the schisms along class lines. She calls for what
W. E. B. Du Bois and other Pan Africanists have called for, a moral responsibility
that blacks prevent their leadership from becoming as oppressive as that of
whites. The cultural symbols of Kiswana's African name, hairdo, dress, and
artifacts are her way of warning the upward-moving blacks not to forget their

roots nor the bridge over which they have passed, that human bond and link to mother Africa that makes them a people. Nothing could be more political.

For African Totems of Botswana, who know their roots but cling selfishly to oppressive traditions and prejudices, Margaret Cadmore's embarrassing defiance causes an even greater political upheaval and challenge. Her quiet and placid surface hides a resilient and creative woman who is able to withdraw within herself from the he fierce storm of love that she unleashes. Her strong influence on all the characters in the novel is decisive. The scheming Totems, Pete, Seth, and Morafi, who oppose her vehemently, are hounded out of town because of her. Maru, the heir, and Moleka, his powerful and sensuous friend, both fall in love with her at first sight, despite near-suicidal implications for their status in society. Margaret turns two best friends into fierce rivals, vying for her sake to outdo each other in their generosity towards their Masarwa slaves, forced for the first time to come to grips with issues like Masarwa humanity, social responsibility, and the future of their community.

The sudden change in Moleka, that untamed human energy associated with solar images, may better illustrate the significance of Margaret's influence. At their very first meeting, the reader is told that: "Something in the tone, those soft fluctuations of sound . . . had abruptly arrested his life. . . . He had communicated directly with her heart. It was that which was a new experience and which had so unbalanced him" (32). He thinks, "I have come to the end of one road and I am taking another" (33). For Moleka, as for Margaret, the result of their meeting is psychologically crucial. Margaret secretly falls in love with Moleka, and this love, which tames Moleka, unleashes and feeds her creative embers, giving life to her artistic vision in a vital and lasting manner. Through her canvas, Margaret reaches out to common people and things, touching them with her art. Women engaged in their daily common chores, a white goat and her black kid, the makorba tree, the village huts and scenery: these are the subjects of Margaret's paintings. The desire to please the one she loves is the driving force that puts an authentic stamp on her art.

Ironically, it is her influence on Maru, the man with a vision of a new world order, that proves socially and politically far-reaching. Maru, who, like Moleka, had blatantly exploited the young women of Dilepe, quickly comes to a new beginning upon meeting Margaret. For the sake of her love, he readily renounces his chiefdom, abandoning "the highway of life" for the dusty and lonely footpath that leads to a horizon of possibilities. Just as Margaret infuses life and vitality into the women she paints, symbolically freeing them from all bondage and exploitation, even so Maru dreams of a possible world with freedom and equity. Just as art recreates for Margaret her fragmented sense of self, even so Maru sees in Margaret's love a potent force for recreating his dissipated energy and the fragmented vision of his life. The beauty and possibility of these dreams are symbolized by the sunny daisies Maru envisions lining the footpath of the home he has prepared for his Masarwa bride. The disturbing fact that Maru's dream kingdom is physically far from Dilepe may be explained as part of the dream-like quality of his vision, a quality that their dramatic departure and wedding share. As the heartbroken Margaret lies dying emotionally from the shock of her friend Dikeledi's marriage to Moleka, Maru appears and carries his bride away to his "magic kingdom," transforming her melancholy into love and joy. Fortunately, her occasional tears convince both the reader and Maru that her love for Moleka has not simply evaporated.

Nonetheless, Margaret's marriage to Maru, like a climax to a musical performance, ushers in a quiet revolution of its own, the political awakening of the Masarwa:

> When people of Masarwa tribe heard about Maru's marriage to one of their own, a door silently opened on the small, dark airless room in which their souls had been shut for a long time. . . . As they breathed in the fresh, clear air their humanity awakened. . . . They started to run out into the sunlight, then they turned and looked at the dark, small room. They said: "We are not going back there." (126-127)

Margaret Cadmore's resourcefulness and personal achievements help to destroy the myth of Masarwa inferiority. Her cultural pride gives identity to her people, and challenges the myth of racial superiority. Her calm defiance forces those around her into self-examination. Above all, her symbolic marriage suggests the unlimited potential of love even in the most racist and oppressive of societies. It offers her people a choice.

Even Selina, a loner through much of *Browngirl Brownstones*, comes to understand, through her experiences, the bane of racism, and to identify with the pains of her mother, her community, and all oppressed peoples. The racist and condescending comments of her white friend's mother about her and her people revolt and radicalize her, finally sealing a bond between her and "Miss Thompson, the whores, the flashy young men and the blues, the Association, her mother, the Badjan women, all of them. She feels their pain and their rage at this illusion" (291). This sudden growth in awareness is a double-edged challenge, for herself and for those around her. On her part, she repents of her dishonest plans to exploit the Association and refuses the scholarship she has won. She makes an attempt to evaluate the past honestly. She purges herself of her contempt for her mother over her father's deportation and suicide, lays his memory to rest, and frees herself at last from the bondage of memory in readiness for her departure to Barbados in search of what she calls the "centre of life." Her choice of values and her search for her roots and identity are like challenges thrown to her community, symbolized by the bangle she throws to them before her departure. In her Afterword to *Browngirl Brownstones*, Mary Washington captures her significance to her community in the following words:

> In making her choice to return to Barbados, to begin with, Selina symbolizes the community's need to reorder itself, to recognize the destruction of human values in the community devoted to money, ownership and power. . . . it assigns even to an oppressed people the power of conscious political choice. They are not victims. (322)

Selina's spiritual and intellectual values challenge the narrowness, exclusiveness, and selfishness of a Badjan community consumed by its passion for possession, despising all other blacks who are not of their stock. Young Selina becomes larger than life, acting as a historical, cultural, and political bridge between Badjans and other blacks of African descent. With one bracelet thrown to her people and one on her arm, the link remains unbroken as she starts on a quest that will take her through other books and in the guise of other protagonists to England, the Caribbean, South America, and finally back to Africa, connecting all blacks in the Diaspora, linking them all, with myriads of thin strong threads, to the navel of Mother Africa.

I have come to the conclusion that there have been Anowas and Kiswanas in every generation. However, like their mothers, whom they resemble (at least before society molded them into acceptable patterns), they have generally been treated very lightly in literature, denied an authentic or serious voice until the emergence and rediscovery, in the 1970s, of black women writers. What is superficially interpreted as daughter/mother confrontation only camouflages deep-seated frustrations that occasionally explode against those who are closest--the mothers.

Despite differences in milieu and circumstance, the four protagonists I discuss are fearlessly dynamic in articulating their concerns. Together they lift the veil on female experience, denouncing and rejecting those unquestioned ideas and assumptions that bind and oppress the weaker elements in society. They use their "mouths as guns" to confront forces and face issues regarded as taboo for them. Their courage is an example for others trapped in similar situations. Their decisions to speak, act, move, work, or paint--aspects of their creativity and resourcefulness--transform them. In helping others, these women find their lives enlarged and enriched.

This study reveals greatest affinity between the two African protagonists, Anowa and Margaret Cadmore. Both face strong traditional prejudices and taboos. Since necessity is the mother of invention, one is not surprised to see in them comparatively more resourcefulness and resilience than in their American counterparts. The fact that Anowa dies does not diminish her dynamism or moral strength. If anything, she seems the strongest of all the characters. On the other hand, Selina and Kiswana are faced with the subtle racism of the United States and the devastating effects of eroded cultural values and lack of identity for blacks. Naturally, these two characters emphasize more the need for awareness, selfhood, and cultural roots. These women demonstrate a high degree of sensitivity, a deep awareness of the critical need for psychological wholeness as a prerequisite for successful survival in a dominating Western culture.

Finally, each protagonist scores her marks on the political chart in direct proportion to her commitment, resilience, and creativity. In this regard, Margaret Cadmore, the least loud and articulate of the four, probably achieves the most, thanks to the enduring quality of her artistic talent. Of greater significance, however, is the new collective voice of dynamic young women who are not circumscribed in their vision nor limited in their commitment and who have used their mouths as well as their guts effectively. Their sacrificial engagement to a vision of a better world order is, in the final analysis, the only valid measuring rod of their effectiveness as social, cultural, and political missiles within fiction.

Endnotes

[1] "The New Black Literature: Protest or Affirmation." *The Black Aesthetic,* Addison Gayle, Jr., ed., (New York: Doubleday, 1972): 348.

[2] *SAGE: A Scholarly Journal on Black Women,* 1.2 (Fall 1984)

[3] Paule Marshall, *Browngirl Brownstones,* (New York: Random House, 1959). Subsequent references are to this edition.

[4] Mary Helen Washington, ed, *Black-Eyed Susans: Classic Stories By and About Black Women* (New York: Anchor, 1975): 24.

[5] Ama Ata Aidoo, *Anowa,* (London: Longman, 1970): 20. Subsequent references are to this edition.

[6] Gloria Naylor, *The Women of Brewster Place,* (New York: Penguin, 1983): 86. Subsequent references are to this edition.

[7] Bessie Head, *Maru,* (London: Heinemann, 1972). Subsequent references are to this edition.

[8] Zora Neale Hurston, *Their Eyes Were Watching God,* (1937; rpt. Urbana: U of Illinois P, 1978): 28.

[9] Qtd. in Chabani Manganyi, *Looking Through the Keyhole,* (Johannesburg: Raven, 1981): 9.

[10] "Reflections of a 'Good' Daughter from *Black is a Woman's Color,*" *SAGE* 1.2 (Fall 1984): 28-29.

[11] Mary H. Washington, "I Sign My Mother's Name," in *Mothering the Mind,* eds. Ruth Perry and Martin Watson (New York: Holmes & Meier, 1984): 157.

[12] "The Truth of Our Mother's Lives: Mother-Daughter Relationships in Black Women's Fiction," *SAGE* 1.2 (Fall 1984): 10.

Works Cited

This Works Cited entry has been constructed by the co-editors from citations noted in the original manuscript; it did not appear as part of the published essay.

Aidoo, Ama Ata. *Anowa.* Longdon: Longman, 1970.

Fuller, Hoyt. "The New Black Literature: Protest or Affirmation." *The Black Aesthetic.* Ed. Addison Gayle, Jr. New York: Doubleday, 1972. 346-369.

Gayle, Gloria. "The Truth of Our Mothers' Lives: Mother-Daughter Relationships in Black Women's Fiction." *SAGE* 1.2 (1984).

Head, Bessie. *Maru.* London: Heinemann, 1972.

hooks, bell. "Reflections of a 'Good' Daughter from *Black is a Woman's Color,*" *SAGE* 1.2 (1984): 28-29.

Hurston, Zora Neale. *Their Eyes Were Watching God.* 1937. Urbana: U of Illinois P, 1978.

Manganyi, Chabani. *Looking Through the Keyhole.* Johannesburg: Raven, 1981.

Marshall, Paule. *Browngirl Brownstones.* New York: Random House, 1959.

Naylor, Gloria. *The Women of Brewster Place.* New York: Penguin, 1983.

Washington, Mary Helen, ed. *Black-Eyed Susans: Classic Stories By and About Black Women.* New York: Anchor, 1975.

_____. "I Sign My Mother's Name: Alice Walker, Dorothy West, Paule Marshall." *Mothering the Mind.* Eds. Ruth Perry and Martine Watson-Brownley. New York: Holmes & Meier, 1984. 142-163.

Johnson, Cheryl Lynn. "A Womanist Way of Speaking: An Analysis of Language in Alice Walker's *The Color Purple*, Toni Morrison's *Tar Baby*, and Gloria Naylor's *The Women of Brewster Place*." Excerpt from Ph.D. dissertation, University of Michigan, 1988.

Gloria Naylor's first novel, *The Women of Brewster Place*, continues the tradition set by other contemporary black women novelists. Like its precursors, it obliterates traditional stereotypes and images of black women by telling the story of these women, and uses their voices in the social and cultural context of the black community. Although this novel has assumed a firm position in the tradition set by black women writers, it has its own unique features that allow it to be not merely a continuation of, but also a significant addition to, this tradition.

Gloria Naylor describes *The Women of Brewster Place* as "a novel in seven stories"; however, the structure of this novel seemingly belies the novelistic tradition. *The Women of Brewster Place* has no clearly discernable character, theme, or setting. Each chapter focuses on a different woman who experiences and endures conflicts within herself and as a result of her interactions with others. One may argue, then, that Naylor's literary work is not a novel but a collection of short stories. One may also posit another perspective: that the central character and theme of *The Women of Brewster Place* are fused into one entity, black women, and that the novel characterizes the struggle of not one, but seven black women who, in a common setting, have different versions of their confrontations with racism and sexism. These seven women constitute the major character or protagonist of this literary work, and their struggles against the two "isms" comprise the theme of this novel. This analysis, then, adopts the second perspective: that Naylor's work is a novel, not a collection of short stories.

The setting is Brewster Place: a dead-end street with four double housing units that is described by the author as "the bastard child of several clandestine meetings between the alderman of the sixth district and the managing director of Unico Realty Company" (1). The first occupants of Brewster Place were Irish, then Mediterraneans, and then blacks. Because Brewster Place is a dead end street and the blacks who live there are poor, powerless, and ignored by others in the city, it exists independently of the outside world and perpetuates its own values and mores according to the needs of its inhabitants and the limitations imposed on them from the larger society. This setting creates a unique social environment. Its physical structure insulates its residents from interference from the outside world; thus, they are able to formulate and maintain their own social rules of behavior and to condemn those who, because of their lifestyle or background, do not adhere to a prescribed pattern. Within this rather limited environment, the residents exist under similar circumstances.

As stated earlier, the focus of *The Women of Brewster Place* is the black women who live in this community. In the novel's prologue, Naylor describes the "colored daughters" of Brewster Place, a description that establishes the economic and social positions of these women: poor, uneducated black women who, despite challenging conditions, cling tenaciously to their need to survive and their "womanishness." All of these women have different stories to tell about their lives and the limited choices that are available to them as a result of their race, gender, and economic status. Although many of the women share similar problems such as their relationships with men and with other members of their community, each woman faces a unique situation that calls for responses related not only to the situation itself, but also to the personality of the woman and her perception of herself and the mores of the community. By placing each woman into a different situation, the author creates different voices and social contexts; Naylor shows how the language and worldview of these black women varies according to the situations in which these women find themselves. As the context shifts, so does the language. Within the context of Brewster Place, seven women tell stories of passion, disappointments, tragedies, and triumphs.

Mattie Michael is the first woman to tell her story. She is an unwed mother whose son skips bail, an action that results in the loss of her home. Mattie's story begins, however, in her hometown in Tennessee, thirty-one years ago, when she is seduced by Butch and becomes pregnant as a result. The language here is southern and rural, with many images of nature. She recalls what brought her to Brewster Place when upon moving into her apartment, she smells "freshly cut sugar cane." And sugar cane, its taste, smell, and texture, figures prominently in her early life.

Mattie's interaction with Butch communicates much about male-female language, formal and informal language, and social attitudes. His mode of address in the opening scene shows his ability to use language to gain her attention and interest. His light and easy greeting, "Hey, gal," suggests an air of familiarity that the reader learns is not authentic (8). Her response, "I heard you the first time, Butch Fuller, but I got a name, you know," alerts the reader to Butch's violation of social rules, as her language seems formal in comparison to his. Butch, however, refuses to adhere to a language that would reflect their relationship. Instead, he responds in a manner that mocks the formality that she tries to establish between them: "Well, 'cuse us poor, ignorant niggers, Miz Mattie, mam, or shoulds I say, Miz Michael, mam, or shoulds I say Miz Mattie Michael, or shoulds I say Miz Mam, mam, or shoulds I . . . " (8). Butch's feigned formality, consisting of exaggerated use of black vernacular such as "'cuse" and "shoulds," the constant repetition of "mam" which is usually used to address an older black woman, and the various formal representations of her name, shows his mockery of the social distance between them. He uses language to try to establish an informal relationship between them by exaggerating the modes of address that show social difference. Butch wants to seduce Mattie; however, he realizes that his intention would not be served if he were to address Mattie according to their status in the community. Mattie is cautious because she realized "she was being drawn into a conversation with a man her father had repeatedly warned her against. That Butch Fuller is a no-'count ditch hound, and no decent woman would be seen talkin' to him" (9). Mattie is a "decent woman" according to the standards of her community. She lives quietly with her father and mother, obeys their rules, and is active in church-related activities. She socializes only with those of whom her family approves. Butch Fuller understands how their different social positions in the community make him a *persona non grata* in Mattie's world. Hence, he resorts to various language strategies to lessen the social distance between Mattie and himself.

One strategy he employs to disarm her is through use of innuendo. He uses seemingly innocent language that, nevertheless, suggests sexual meanings. For example, after he has teased her about her formality with him, Butch states: "'Now that I done gone through all that, I hope I can get what I came 'for,' he said slowly, as he looked her straight in the eyes." Mattie immediately suspects that his statement has a sexual connotation: "The blood rushed to Mattie's face, and just as her mouth dropped open to fling an insult at him, he slid his eyes evenly over to the barrel at the side of the house. 'A cup of that cool rain water.' And he smiled wickedly" (9).

His "innocent" request for a cup of water serves three purposes. First, it seemingly restores the conversation to a socially approved level. Mattie cannot claim that he has spoken to her in a disrespectful manner. Secondly, his request and her subsequent embarrassment suggest that any sexual meaning is in *her* mind, not his. This would reverse their social roles of lascivious male and innocent girl. Third, and perhaps most important, his statements are designed to create sexual tension between them. Butch's language cloaks his real intentions while it simultaneously sets the context for an intimate relationship between them.

Mattie's reaction to Butch's language game shows her understanding of his real meaning, and also her embarrassment at being tricked by his words: "'Here's your water.' She almost threw it at him. 'I couldn't even deny a dog a drink on a day like today, but when you done drunk it, you better be gettin' on to wherever you was gettin' before you stopped.'" Mattie's response indicates that Butch has succeeded in shortening the distance between them. She no longer displays the polite behavior that is appropriate for their different social roles. Instead, she shows anger because she has unwittingly allowed him, through his clever use of language, to trespass social boundaries.

Another strategy Butch Fuller uses to seduce Mattie is to make her defensive. Butch challenges Mattie to accompany him to the sugar field by suggesting that she is afraid to be independent. He realizes that a simple request to her would be ineffective, as he anticipates her reservations and challenges her to deny them: "'Of course, now, if a big woman like you is afraid of what her daddy might say?'" (10). Mattie is, indeed, afraid of what her father would say, knowing that "her father would kill her if he heard she had been seen walking with Butch Fuller." Mattie responds defiantly: "'I ain't afraid of nothing, Butch Fuller.'" Her following statement, however, belies her courage: "'And besides, Papa took Mama to town this afternoon.'" Hence, her courage, her willingness to disobey the social rules that separate them, surfaces only when she feels safe to do so

The relationship between speech style and social context is sharply revealed when Mattie and Butch encounter Mr. Mike, a deacon of her church. The conversation between Mattie and Butch as they go to the sugar field is light and easy. The tone and manner of Mattie's speech shifts, however, when she sees Mr. Mike. She realizes that she has violated social rules by being with Butch; thus, she feebly tries to create a context that Mr. Mike, a representative of the respectable people of her community, would find acceptable. After greeting Mr. Mike (both Mattie and Butch acknowledge the deacon's status by using the formal "Mr." in their address to him), Mattie tries to give an explanation for being with Butch: "'Going to cut cane, Mr. Mike,' Mattie chimed up loudly and give the machete an extra swing to underscore her words." When Mr. Mike responds suspiciously, "'Ain't you all taking the long way to the levee, though?',", Butch circumvents any indication that he and Mattie were engaged in any wrongdoing by shifting the focus and meaning of the deacon's remark. "'Too much sun on the main road,' Butch said easily. 'And since black means poor in these parts-- Lord knows, I couldn't stand to get no poorer'" (12). Both Butch and Mr. Mike laugh at Butch's remark, indicating a lessening of tension between the two men and acceptance of Mattie's explanation for being with Butch. Butch cleverly ignores the implied meaning of the deacon's question by shifting the focus of the conversation to a larger realm, that of racism, thereby diverting attention from the immediate situation. By addressing a topic with which Mr. Mike can readily identify, Butch demonstrates his ability to use appropriate language according to the social situation. He also displays his ability to manipulate language in order to disguise his intentions. His knowledge of language and social roles and contexts allows him to achieve his ultimate goal: the seduction of Mattie.

Mattie's inability to manipulate language is shown not only in her interaction with Butch, but also when she reveals her pregnancy to her father. His pain and anguish over her pregnancy intensify to a feverish level when she refuses to tell him the identity of the father of the child. Their relationship is based on his superior role in the home; his daughter must never defy him. When she refuses to obey him, he feels his power in the home dissolving:

> Her silence stole the last sanctuary for his rage. He wanted to kill the man who had sneaked into his home and distorted the faith and trust he had in his child. But she had chosen this man's side against him, and in his fury, he tried to stamp out what had hurt him the most and was now brazenly taunting him--her disobedience. (23)

Mattie understood the consequences of not adhering to the social hierarchy within her home: her father would never forgive her for not obeying him. Mattie, unlike Butch, refuses to use language that would maintain a social relationship between her and her father because she cannot lie to him nor reveal the truth for such would bring harm to him. She disobeys the established rules of language conduct within her social context and is estranged from her family as a result.

Works Cited

This Works Cited entry has been constructed by the co-editors from citations noted in the original manuscript; it did not appear as part of the published essay.

Christian, Barbara. "Trajectories of Self-Definition: Placing Contemporary Afro-American Women's Fiction." *Black Feminist Criticism: Perspectives on Black Women Writers*. New York: Pergamon, 1985. 171-186.

Naylor, Gloria. *The Women of Brewster Place*. New York: Penguin, 1983.

Bobo, Jacqueline and Ellen Seiter. "Black Feminism and Media Criticism: *The Women of Brewster Place*." *Screen* 32.3 (Autumn 1991): 286-302.

That black women are writing and talking about their history, their politics and their socioeconomic status is not a recent occurrence, though it has sometimes been treated as if it is a 1980s phenomenon. Hazel Carby, in *Reconstructing Womanhood*, documents the fact that black women have long used the mechanisms available to them to attain a "public voice," Whether in writing, public speaking, or establishing national networks among a wide spectrum of black women, black feminists have worked diligently to comment upon and improve their social condition.[1] Other recent research by black women has recovered a wealth of literary and political work written by black women and used this as the basis for formalizing a body of thought concerning black feminist theory.[2] This archaeological work was necessary, notes Valerie Smith, because black women had been structured out of the writings of others.[3] The consequences of this neglect were that black women were misrepresented in the theoretical writings of others, if not omitted entirely. For cultural critics this was a particularly vexing problem, in that one of its consequences has been a limited access to works created by black women: now, however, the groundwork has been laid by literary scholars for an analysis of a range of cultural products. No longer can a text constructed by a black woman be considered in isolation from the context of its creation, from its connection with other works within the tradition of black women's creativity, and from its impact not just on cultural critics but on cultural consumers. As we witness the aggressive move towards adapting black women's literature for film and television, a similar effort directed at film and television criticism is now needed. Of course, different considerations must be brought to bear on a work of literature and on its media transformation; which suggests that some theoretical work needs to be done. Film studies has in large part shunned the study of adaptations as too literary, too traditional, and too uninformed by developments in film theory. But, in the case of black women's fiction, adaptations to film and television are the primary, if not the only, source of black feminist thought available to a large audience.[4] Works such as *The Color Purple* (Steven Spielberg, Warner Bros, 1985) and *The Women of Brewster Place* (Donna Deitch, ABC, 1989) represent a particularly vital area of popular narrative film and television today, and have the potential to challenge existing conventions of representation and characterization of women in ways that can also attract a broad, mass audience.

This article begins with a consideration of the ways in which black women and other women of colour have been either neglected or only selectively included in the writings of feminist cultural analysts: we consider the responses by women of colour to this omission, the ramifications for feminist studies, and some ways in which this neglect might be redressed. We then turn to an analysis of the television version of *The Women of Brewster Place*, which was based upon the novel by the black American writer Gloria Naylor. Examining the insertion of *The Women of Brewster Place* within a range of political and social appropriations can provide a necessary intervention in the struggle over the meaning of black women's artistic work. This analysis assesses the programme from the perspective of its usefulness for feminist cultural criticism in general and of its position within the politics of popular cultural representations.[5]

The politics of feminist cultural criticism

The problematic relationship between the feminism of middle-class white women and issues affecting other women, in particular women of colour, has been documented in several well-known works which examine differences between women from historical and social perspectives.[6] For example, Hazel Carby, a black feminist cultural critic, has looked at the historical, social and economic conditions governing the lives of black and white women, emphasizing that oppression manifests itself differently in black and white women's lives. A crucial difference arose from women's roles during the slavocracy: white women were used (in part) to produce heirs to an oppressive system; black women functioned as breeders to produce property that added to the capital accumulation of the plantation system. The continuing divergent material circumstances would later affect the production of black and white women's texts about the status of their various oppressions.[7]

Aïda Hurtado, writing about the different ways patriarchy has affected white women and women of colour, notes that white women in the US have responded with the notion that the personal is political. Hurtado stresses that the political consciousness of women of colour "stems from an awareness that the public is *personally* political."[8] Her conclusion that the public sphere contains the elements of political thought and activity for women of colour is especially important for white feminist critics to recognize:

> the public/private distinction is relevant only for the white middle and upper classes since historically the American state has intervened constantly in the private lives and domestic arrangements of the working class. Women of Color have not had the benefit of the economic conditions that underlie the public/private distinction. White feminists' concerns about the unhealthy consequences of standards for feminine beauty, their focus on the unequal division of household labor, and their attention to childhood identity formation stem from a political consciousness that seeks to project private sphere issues into the public arena. Feminists of Color focus instead on public issues such as affirmative action, racism, school desegregation, prison reform and voter registration--issues that cultivate an awareness of the distinction between public policy and private choice.[9]

White feminist film and video critics can learn from the writings and experiences that have characterized fiction and literary criticism by women of colour. However, greater effort needs to be devoted to making this work available. Michele Wallace--a black feminist cultural critic who has taken some difficult stands against impediments to black women's progress--addresses a significant aspect of the problem. Her book *Black Macho and the Myth of the Superwoman* (1979), along with Ntozake Shange's choreopoem *for colored girls who have considered suicide when the rainbow is enuf* (1978), are considered pivotal works in contemporary debates about the racial "correctness" of black women's cultural works. Wallace has criticized Adrienne Rich in her role as an intermediary between black women's writing and the public dissemination of their work. In her review of Rich's *Blood, Bread, and Poetry* (1986) for the *New York Times Book Review*, she chronicles Rich's political evolution, noting that when Rich won the National Book Award for poetry in 1974, she insisted that the honour be shared between herself and the black women who were also nominated, Alice Walker and Audre Lorde.[10] Wallace writes that even though Rich might have the best of intentions, she "pretends to sponsor that which is not in her power to sponsor, that which she can only silence: a Black feminist voice and/or theory." Wallace explains that Rich exercises control over the works of black women and other women of colour in that she is a gatekeeper for those works that will appear on the "essential reading list." She adds: "When I say reading list, that's a euphemistic way of referring to book contracts, book sales, teaching jobs, tenure, publication in anthologies and journals, without which it is now impossible to be a writer, much less a black feminist writer."[11]

The gatekeeping function of certain strains of white feminist thought extends beyond being a filter through which designated works are sifted: it limits the kinds of issues that can be written or thought about. Because much of the creative and theoretical work written by black women is available only through alternative outlets, some mainstream critics remain ignorant of, and uneducated in black feminist thought. Wallace writes that the problem at present represents

> a critical juncture at the crossroads of a white mainstream academic feminism, which is well paid, abundantly sponsored and self-consciously articulate, and a marginalised, activist-oriented Black feminism, which is not well-paid, virtually unsubsidized and generally inarticulate, unwritten, unpublished and unread.[12]

In the face of these shortcomings, feminists working within cultural studies need to rethink their writing. Jane Gaines, a white feminist cultural critic, has assessed the inadequacies of contemporary feminist criticism (Lacanian psychoanalysis and Marxist feminism) in its practice of examining creative works only for their significance to white, middle-class heterosexual women. Gaines chastises mainstream feminists for their token gestures towards the inclusion of different perspectives, stating "our political etiquette is correct, but our theory is not so perfect."[13]

In a similar critique, Coco Fusco details the political expediency within the current "crisis of conscience." Fusco criticizes avant-garde art institutions and the individuals who operate them for their selective inclusion of works by people of colour and for the assumption that a "single event" series can serve as a corrective to decades of racism and sexism. Since these serve as mediators between works by people of colour and public knowledge of their existence, Fusco feels that the avant garde needs to look to its own practices and reexamine its perspective on "the other."[14]

A survey of the opinions of many feminist media analysts in the recent special issue of *Camera Obscura* on "the spectatrix" makes clear the lack of substantial theorizing about issues around class or race and cinema. After summarizing the terrain of female spectatorship, the editors admit that there is a difficulty in redressing this omission: it is easier, they say, to recognize that spectator positions involving race, class, age, and so on need to be taken into account than it is "to arrive at satisfactory methods for doing so, or even more simply, to understand what it is that we want to know, and why."[15]

What we want to know and why we as cultural commentators need to know it is exemplified in the problem of sampling currently confronting researchers in cultural studies, audience studies and ethnographic work. Recently there has been a surge in empirical work in reader/audience studies, especially relating to women's genres such as romance, melodrama and soap opera. In cultural studies work on audiences (as in much of the mass communications research it seeks to oppose), samples have tended overwhelmingly to be white. This fact deserves a closer look: it is too frequent an occurrence to be shunted aside or excused by the brief apologies which attribute white samples to limited funding or scope. It is not something that "just happens," not simply a case of sampling error, nor of the failure of individual researchers to be sufficiently diligent in making contacts, although these are certainly factors that contribute to the problem.

This situation has partly to do with the demographics of the academy in the United States: who the researchers are (predominantly white), where they live (in segregated white neighborhoods), and where they work. Occupational segregation has been durably established in US universities: whites filing professorial ranks and senior positions, and people of colour relegated to service and clerical positions, or assuming faculty positions in small numbers and at untenured, junior levels. This structure remains in place even as many institutions pay fashionable lip service to their efforts toward diversity in faculty and student population. It also, and less obviously, has to do with the trend towards interviewing respondents in their homes. Women of colour will probably be less likely to welcome white researchers into their homes than will white women. As long as the state so often interferes in their private sphere under the guise of a range of seemingly innocuous ventures, women of colour will be wary of intrusions into their domestic space by white middle-class professionals. Thus, while theoretically sound, the increased emphasis of late on the crucial role of the domestic sphere in shaping media consumption must be scrutinized in terms of the limitations it may set on the kinds of participants available for studies involving the home as both site and object of research.[16]

James Clifford, among others, has called attention to the unequal power relations inherent in the ethnographic enterprise and to the "objectification" of the subject in ethnographic discourse.[17] While many white social scientists are only now considering these issues, people of colour have long been aware of the possibilities of being ripped off by researchers, and of the ways in which academic studies are often used in the long run to legitimate various forms of oppression. While it would be wrong to dismiss ethnography as a valuable method, it has to be recognized that it produces knowledge which circulates in influential ways within the disciplines in which it is used. Thus, for example, many of the notions of gender difference deriving from ethnographic work with all-white samples in current circulation are reified and ethnocentric: the experiences of women of colour with the media remain unheard, unstudied, untheorized.

Nevertheless, some recently published research by women of colour promises to change the way researchers consider media audiences. Jacqueline Bobo's work with black women's responses to the film *The Color Purple* has demonstrated how black women, because of their low expectations of the media (and their expectation of encountering racism) can read around and through a Hollywood text.[18] Minu Lee and Chong Heup Cho's work with middle-class Korean soap opera fans in the United States similarly points to a much wider range of reactions and uses than has been imagined in theorizing the (white) spectator.[19] It can be predicted with certainty that other work by women of colour will not only alter the pool of empirical findings in cultural studies, but also challenge, redefine, and renovate the theoretical agenda in ways white academics cannot at present imagine. White researchers must work harder to consider the problems of racial and ethnic difference, scrutinize their research designs and their methods of contacting respondents, and bring to their work a high degree of self-consciousness about racism and the power relations inherent in research.

Ultimately, however, substantial improvement in the situation awaits bringing more women of colour into the field of cultural studies and its descriptions of media audiences. There is an unfortunate tendency to consider as a separate agenda--one set apart from theoretical work--issues of affirmative action, diversification of academic faculties, recruitment of students, and equitable entrance requirements. Experience also demonstrates that far too often graduate students of colour lack academic advisors who are strong advocates for them or for their course of study. It is no accident that there are few black, latino, native-born Asian and native American doctoral students or PhDs in the United States--and with numbers especially small in media studies. Problems range from a curriculum and canon which are overwhelmingly white to a lack of precedent for students to do research relating to their experience--and a lack of encouragement from advisors.[20] A rewriting of the canon and the curriculum must take into account popular films and television programmes, as well as independent and experimental work by black filmmakers. White feminists must recognize that, as an area of academic interest, feminist cultural studies is likely to appear trivial to women of colour until white academics connect more strongly with the politics of the public sphere and the university.

The Women of Brewster Place

The Women of Brewster Place is the story of seven women who live in the rundown black neighborhood of Brewster Place, located in an unnamed American city. A brick wall at the end of the block, erected as a result of political and economic machinations, separates the residents from the rest of the world. It comes to stand for racism, and its effects are felt daily in the women's lives. Both Gloria Naylor's novel and the television programme are composed of six interconnected stories which detail the lives of seven women. This structure gives characters an individuality that rescues them from the fate of being viewed as anonymous "female heads of households." At the same time, according to Barbara Christian, the interrelationships of the women's lives is given full play, establishing "...Brewster Place as a community with its own mores, strengths and weaknesses."[21]

The first and longest story follows Mattie Michael from her parents' home in the rural South, through her struggles to survive on her own in a northern city with her young son Basil and finally as a middle-aged woman forced to move to Brewster Place after losing her home to bailbondsmen when her son is accused of murder. Etta Mae Johnson is an aging femme fatale who has existed by her ability to attach herself to successful men: she comes to live with her lifelong friend Mattie when she runs out of men to take care of her. Ciel, Mattie's "adopted" daughter, lives a desperate life waiting for the father of her child to return after each of his abrupt departures: during an argument about his current exodus, their child accidentally dies. Kiswana Browne is a starry-eyed civil rights activist from a financially secure family, now living in Brewster Place because she feels the need to be close to "the people." She organizes the residents of the neighborhood for a rent strike against the owners of the squalid buildings in which they live. Cora Lee, the poorest and most isolated character, is a young woman with seven children: her children are the terror of the neighborhood and everyone tries to persuade her to stop having more. Lorraine and Theresa have arrived in Brewster Place after living in other, better, neighborhoods around the city. They have been forced to move on when the other residents have learned they are lesbians, because Lorraine is fearful she will lose her job as a schoolteacher. Theresa refuses to move again because, as she puts it, there is no place left to run; Brewster Place is the end of the line: she does not care how their neighbors on Brewster Place treat them. Lorraine, on the other hand, ostracized by her family and fired from a teaching job, yearns to be part of the community. She wants to be embraced within it, but encounters cruel rejection when she tries to participate in the newly-formed block organization. Alienated from the other women, Lorraine ventures out along one night and is raped in an alley by a group of young black men (in the television version there is only one rapist).

The Women of Brewster Place was heavily promoted on US network television, on early morning talk shows, and in magazine articles about Oprah Winfrey, its prime mover, star and executive producer: it was only on Winfrey's insistence that ABC executives agreed to air the programme. In spite of all the advance publicity, it generated a conspicuous lack of critical attention. Those publications which did review it made the now obligatory observation that the novel was yet another written by a black woman with an unflattering depiction of black men: but even these comments lacked the fervour or bite of those directed against The Color Purple. More forceful were reviewers' complaints that the programme was simply a black soap opera, that it was formulaic melodrama at its worst, and that it had the look of a situation comedy.

Audience response, however, was phenomenal: over its two-part broadcast the programme easily outdistanced competing offerings. Given the current decline in audience for network television, the Nielsen ratings (23.5/36 the first night; 24.5/38 the second) also indicate that people who normally do not watch network television tuned in specifically to watch this programme.[22] The series was given a full rerun during prime time within a year of its original broadcast--a privilege reserved for only the most popular mini-series. A double VHS cassette of The Women of Brewster Place is currently available for rental in most large video stores in the United States.

Although it has received little critical attention, The Women of Brewster Place was quite unlike anything on commercial network television in the US. This obviously had to do with the unique set of circumstances enabling its production: Oprah Winfrey has made productive use of her stardom as a talk show host to gain economic and creative control over her own television projects, which she sees through many different phases. (Winfrey has also been the subject of an extraordinary amount of negative publicity from many sources, from the National Enquirer to The New York Times, which cast her acquisition of production facilities, capital and so on in the melodramatic light of neurotic greed and obsession with power).[23]

An additional element which helped distinguish The Women of Brewster Place was its maker, Donna Deitch, an independent director best known for the feature film Desert Hearts (1985), a lesbian love story. Deitch produced Desert Hearts on a shoestring, and the film went on to enjoy a moderate success on the art cinema circuit in the United States. Deitch was probably selected to direct The Women of Brewster Place because of her past focus on relationships between women and her handling of the lesbian romance using the techniques of commercial mainstream cinema: it is in fact precisely on this point that Deitch has been criticized--for her prettification of the *Desert Hearts* story and its treatment as conventional Hollywood romance.[24] Deitch's work on *Brewster Place* could similarly be criticized for its glamorous visual treatment of the character Lorraine. However, the television series, like the novel, does focus on the violence of homophobia and its far reaching and destructive effects on the everyday lives of the characters.

The selection of Deitch as director is noteworthy also in that it marks the first time a woman has directed a media adaptation of the work of a black woman author; a vastly more promising situation than Steven Spielberg's self-selection as director of Alice Walker's *The Color Purple*. Deitch and screenwriter Karen Hall said they attempted to remain very faithful to the original novel and to Naylor's vision of the lives of the black characters, in order to compensate for the fact that they themselves are white.[25] Naylor herself, who lost control of the screen rights for the book in her publishing contract, had originally envisaged an adaptation of her novel for the non-commercial Public Broadcasting Service-- circumstances which might have made more likely the hiring of a black woman as director. With the exception of Euzhan Palcy (*A Dry White Season*, 1989), no black women directors have succeeded in making commercial feature films in the US, although independent filmmakers such as Julie Dash, Debra Robinson and Zeinabu irene Davis, or television directors such as Caroll Parrott Blue, M. Neema Barnette and Debbie Allen certainly had the qualifications to take on such a project.

Significantly, the novel probes subject areas similar to those explored in other works from black women writers, such as Toni Morrison, Paule Marshall, Alice Walker, and others, through the 1970s and 1980s. A few of these topics--a sense of community, female bonding, overcoming adversity--are especially significant because they brought to the project elements not normally found in television plots. *The Women of Brewster Place* runs close to the codes of the television melodrama (especially of soap operas and made-for-television movies), but at the same time is very different. There are three notable features appearing in the television adaptation that the novel *The Women of Brewster Place* shares with other works by black women writers and which are critical to the present analysis: an exploration of the sense of community among black women, an indictment of sexism, and an emphasis on the importance of black women supporting each other. In *The Women of Brewster Place*, the black community is used for survival rather than individual advancement and upward mobility. Although the programme tells the story of seven women, the first and longest story establishes Mattie Michael (the Oprah Winfrey character) as a pivotal figure--functioning much as the "tentpole character" does in soap opera. Mattie's story covers about eighteen years, beginning with her first and only pregnancy. Through good fortune, hard work and the friendship of an older woman, Mattie achieves one of her dreams of success: she becomes a home owner. Miss Eva's and Mattie's house is represented neither as a cold and alienating bourgeois prison in the tradition of family melodrama on film (and of avant-garde feminist films such as *Jeanne Dielmann* [Chantal Akerman, 1975]), nor as the flimsy, obviously artificial, temporary set of American soap operas. Rather, the characters' aspirations to the comforts and the aesthetics of cozy domestic space are dignified with many lingering takes of interiors in which an absence of dialogue focuses attention on the sounds and the rhythms of life within the home. These images contrast sharply with the cramped rooms without views on Brewster Place. At the end of the first episode, Mattie loses the house when her son, on a murder charge, skips bail and disappears. The rest of the story traces Mattie's descent, her fall from economic grace and her arrival at Brewster Place. By the end of the programme, we realize that Mattie's personal fall has permitted her move into a nexus of women friends and neighbors, and thus the beginning of community--troubled though it may be--of Brewster Place.

This is a strikingly different structure from that of most Hollywood film narratives, in which images of community are for the most part entirely lacking, and narrative conventions are typically based on the autonomous, unconnected individual.[26] *The Women of Brewster Place*, though, does not offer a utopian image of community: poverty, violence, and bigotry are permanent features, and these are shown to deform personal relationships and threaten women. Yet it contains striking instances of deeply held values that are starkly opposed to the values of the mainstream white culture and economy. For example, after Mattie has left her rat-infested apartment and searched futilely for another place to live, she and her infant son are taken in by Miss Eva to share her home. Miss Eva rejects the money that Mattie offers her for board, refusing to translate into market relations her gesture of help to a woman in need. Mattie, bewildered by this generosity, puts money in the cookie jar every week, but Miss Eva never takes it. Miss Eva shares all her material wealth and comfort with Mattie-- literally a stranger off the street--without hesitation. It is almost impossible to conceive of this kind of act towards a person unrelated by blood in the universe of the white family melodrama. Miss Eva also shares her home with her granddaughter Ciel, and cares for and raises Mattie's son Basil just as though he were a member of her own family.

A second feature *The Women of Brewster Place* shares with the work of other writers in its tradition is a scrutiny of sexism and of violence again black women by black men. Novels such as *Browngirl Brownstones* (1959), *The Color Purple*, and *Beloved* (1987) often explore the meaning of violence in everyday life, and the costs of survival. Their frank confrontation of incest, rape and wife- and child-beating has been the most controversial aspect of these works. Although there is an attempt to put sexism in the context of the continual humiliation of black men by white people and the desperation caused by the massive denial of economic opportunities, there is at the same time a vehement rejection of violence. For example, in the television version of *The Women of Brewster Place*, Mattie's father, Sam, is played sympathetically by veteran black actor Paul Winfield. Dialogue stresses that Mattie is his pride and joy. Yet on discovering that Mattie is pregnant and will not reveal the name of the child's father, he explodes in a violent rage and beats her to the ground with a stick. In both novel and television programme, there is a graphic portrayal of the blows falling on her pregnant body. Mattie's mother (Mary Alice), a mild woman and devoted wife, picks up a rifle, points it at her husband and says: "So help me Jesus, Sam, hit my child again and I'll meet your soul in hell!" Thus, while feelings of rage and frustration are acknowledged--in this case, a father's disappointment that his dreams for his daughter's future are ruined--the violence is uncompromisingly condemned.

In the face of both domestic violence and the multiple circumstances of oppression facing black women (the triple jeopardy of sex discrimination, race discrimination, and poverty), the heroines of these novels by black women emerge as exceptionally strong and able to fight for survival. *The Women of Brewster Place*, like other novels by black women, offers distinctive portrayals of black women, in that these women fight back, get out, leave the abuse behind. They are usually assisted in this by another black woman. As Barbara Christian has argued, this process often involves a new feeling of self-worth and identity, forged through identification with another women.[27] In *The Women of Brewster Place*, the characters are paired in ways that reveal the tensions and contradictions of their positions: Mattie (celibate) and Etta Mae (lusty); Mattie (a single mother) and Ciel (struggling to keep her marriage together); Kiswana (privileged, single, do-gooder) and Cora Lee (poor, uneducated, mother of seven); Theresa (out as a lesbian) and Lorraine (in the closet to protect her job).

A third feature characteristic of much of black women's fiction, and which is developed in the television version of *The Women of Brewster Place,* with its reordering of the conventions of the television melodrama, is an exploration of a range of relationships between women: as friends, roommates, lovers, mothers and daughters. All these relationships take place outside of the nuclear family: Mattie and Ciel, for example, have one of the strongest bonds of love in the story, and they have adopted each other as mother and daughter, in much the same way Mattie and Miss Eva adopted one another. The white family melodrama has been preoccupied with ties of blood--the relentless interest in ascertaining paternity, for example, a staple of the woman's film and the soap opera--and with intense mother-daughter conflicts within the family. In novels in the black woman's writing tradition, these kinds of issues do not appear, and a more encompassing view of family takes their place.

Like *The Color Purple*, *The Women of Brewster Place* deals explicitly with sexual love between women. Its final story concerns Lorraine and Theresa, a middle-class couple who have just moved into the neighborhood. The narrative explores in detail the persecution and hostility from black women and men that lesbians face. As in *The Color Purple*, *The Women of Brewster Place* places sexual love between women on a continuum of sexual experience which includes heterosexuality and celibacy. In a key scene towards the end of the television programme, Mattie and Etta Mae discuss the relationship of Lorraine and Theresa and the vicious gossip that is circulating about them. They have witnessed the disapproval of people in the neighborhood, especially from a busybody named Miss Sophie. Miss Sophie senses before anyone else that there is "something funny" going on between "those two." When she figures out what it is, she spreads the word "like a scent," as it is described in the novel. While Mattie does Etta's hair, she is working through her own feelings about how "the two" feel about each other. She asks Etta how "they get that way" and if they are that way from birth. Etta says categorically that women like that are just different: "they love each other the way you would a man." Mattie, still uncertain, talks about her love for the women in her life, including her best friend Etta: "Ornery as you can get, I've loved you practically all my life." She tells Etta that she has loved some women more deeply than she has loved any man, "and there have been some women who loved me more and did more for me than any man ever did." There is a pause before Mattie finally adds "maybe it's not so different. Maybe that's why some women get so riled up about it, 'cause they know deep down it's not so different at all."

The idea of sisterhood as a sustaining element for black women has been discussed frequently in an abstract sense in political writing, but it became widely visible for the first time with the popularity of *The Color Purple*. For all the discussion about the novel and the film, one of the most enduring memories of that work is its portrait of the bonds that exist between the black women. In black women's writing there is a rich legacy of depictions of women supporting women: it is vividly portrayed in Harriet Jacobs's *Incidents in the Life of a Slave Girl* (1861), Zora Neale Hurston's *Their Eyes Were Watching God* (1937), and more recently in Toni Morrison's *Sula* (1972) and *Beloved* (1987). The novel *The Women of Brewster Place* looks at the ways in which black women support each other, and the potentially tragic repercussions when that support is lacking: Lorraine's rape occurs after she has been rejected from the community of Brewster Place. Gloria Naylor comments that her intent was to demonstrate how black people's survival depends on mutual support and that when this fails, the community can collapse.[28]

Barbara Christian argues that Naylor both acknowledges the remarkable achievements of writers such as Walker, Morrison and Marshall, and at the same time criticizes "women-centered communities." Along with a celebration of black women's survival instincts, Naylor feels that black women should also look towards political power. For although the community of Brewster Place holds its residents together for a time, at the end they are again displaced women.

> By presenting a community in which strong women-bonds do not break the cycle of powerlessness in which so many poor black women are imprisoned, Naylor points to a theoretical dilemma with which feminist thinkers have been wrestling. For while the values of nurturing and communality are central to a just society, they often preclude the type of behavior necessary to achieve power in this world, behavior such as competitiveness, extreme individualism, the desire to conquer. How does one break the cycle of powerlessness without giving up the values of caring so necessary to the achievement of a just society?[29]

Christian discusses two sections of Naylor's novel which offer resolutions to this question. The first is the dream-like sequence at the end of the book: in the novel, Lorraine's rape is followed by a subjective account of the thoughts, fears and nightmares, over an entire week, of each of the other women on the block. The women are haunted by the violence against another woman and their failure to stop it. After the week has passed, the block party takes place, and Mattie dreams that the women tear down the wall blocking the street as a protest against the forces that led to Lorraine's death. As Christian states, "Even as the women in the final scene of the novel chip away at the wall that imprisons them, we are aware that this is someone's dream, for such an act would be the prelude to a community rebellion, a step these nurturing, restricted women cannot take if they are to survive as they have."[30]

Much of this subtlety is lost in the television version of the novel-- indicating some of the limitations of the adaptation of literature to the small screen. In the television version, the action is compressed into a single night--in which Lorraine is raped during the block party and the women turn from discovery of the crime to an attempt to tear down the wall. The final shots of the programme are medium shots of the women from the other side of the wall. Drenched by rain and flooded by coloured lights, they tear at the wall with their hands. The strange lights, the rain and the odd camera angle represent a complete stylistic break with what has gone before. But the tendency is to take the image literally rather than as suggesting a dream state; so that the women look bedraggled and desperate, their attempts to dismantle the wall pitiful and hysterical. Earlier, Mattie's first-person voice over had offered a reflection on the events of her life. In this final scene, however, there is no visual, active equivalent to her and the other women's earlier contemplative, intersubjective reactions. The women are not seen as reflecting on the violence; rather they erupt into a burst of collective action, puzzling in its futility, on the spot. A "naturalistic" television style can render Naylor's symbolic action--the tearing down of a brick wall--only with great difficulty, and at the cost of a complete stylistic break.

The character Kiswana represents a second resolution to the question posed by Naylor about avenues to power for black women. Kiswana grew up in the upper-middle-class black neighborhood of Linden Hills. The segment of the story devoted to Kiswana focuses on her psychological conflict with her mother and her struggle for a separate identity, placing her political activity in the light of youthful rebellion (a story familiar enough in the bourgeois family melodrama). This segment also establishes that, unlike the other women on Brewster Place, Kiswana lives there by choice and can leave whenever she wants to. It is her privileged background and the fact that she has other options that enable Kiswana to organize the residents as a united political entity to work against the landlord and the city government. As Christian aptly analyzes the character, Kiswana is the only one of the women who can rebel because

> she does not risk survival, as the others would if they rebelled; nor has she yet been worn down by the unceasing cycle of dis-placement that the others have experienced. And she has a sense of how power operates *precisely* because she comes from Linden Hills, a place she leaves *precisely* because it is so focused on money and power.[31]

As Naylor constructs a range of class positions for black women, from the impoverished Cora Lee to the privileged Kiswana, she presents the need for those who struggle for survival also to develop an ability to understand and use political power. This aspect of the novel is translated with some difficulty to television. Cora Lee is reduced to an object of Kiswana's reformist zeal--Kiswana wants to get Cora Lee and her children out to see her boyfriend's staging of *A Midsummer Night's Dream*. Cora Lee seems rather too easily converted, through her one-time exposure to black people performing in a work of "high art," into a better mother: tidying up her apartment, keeping the kids clean, encouraging them to work harder at school. In the novel, Cora Lee's story is written from a point of view which allows her to react with silent suspicion and resentment to the intrusions of Kiswana, a single, middle-class woman who is unfamiliar with her problems. (This ambivalence towards Kiswana is expressed most strongly in the casting of Robin Givens, who had received a large amount of unfavorable publicity accusing her of opportunism in her marriage to boxing champion Mike Tyson. Givens's performance is broader than that of most of the other main characters, being more in the style of the situation comedy *Head of the Class*, in which she had gained most of her previous screen experience).

In the novel, Cora Lee's segment is used as a sort of reverie on the sensual aspects of mothering infants: Cora Lee loves babies, but seems unable to understand children when they grow older and create responsibilities other than nurturing. Here, the juxtaposition of Cora Lee's sensuality with creative expression (the theatrical performance) appears to be a commentary on the consequences of oppression. But on television, where we are denied her account of her own childhood and her relationship with the men who "give" her the adored babies, Cora Lee's characterization is rendered rather simplistically: she appears a creature of pure sensuality and a confused welfare recipient. She is never included in the community as an active member, and takes no part in the interplay of personal and public dramas in which the other characters are involved. In the novel, while the other women feel Cora Lee should stop having so many kids, she is still considered an integral part of the community.

Conclusion

As a novel and as a television programme, *The Women of Brewster Place* makes a strong contribution to black feminist thought as well as to feminist criticism in general. Black feminist theory has criticized, corrected and improved the understanding of feminism put forward by white critics. Novels such as *The Women of Brewster Place*, as well as *The Color Purple*, have made an admirable attempt to dramatize into an explicitly feminist narrative black feminist commentary on the material, historical, social, economic, and symbolic status of black women. If the media versions fall short of the novels, their popularity with audiences--especially with black women--shows that much more work needs to be done by feminist critics on considerations of audience and on the analysis of all works by women of colour, in whatever medium.

The Women of Brewster Place would make a productive addition to the canon of films by and about women represented in courses on melodrama, women directors, and women's representation in film and television. As a popular work written by a black woman author, adapted for the screen by a white director and screenwriter, it opens up questions around the nature of women's experience and of differences stemming from race and class. The television version of *The Women of Brewster Place* in particular violates expectations about representations of black women long familiar from movies and television series. Within the narrow range employed by the media in showing black women, three features are familiar: the black woman tends to be defined by a "natural" connection to sexuality, by her relationship to white people as domestic servant, and by her role in the nuclear family as a domineering or restraining force. The television adaptation of *The Women of Brewster Place* situates its characters in ways that challenge, complicate and politicize our understanding of these types. As in the novel, it continually violates expectations of characters' sexuality: one of the most lascivious characters is Miss Eva, a woman in her seventies; one of the most glamorous is Lorraine, a lesbian. The scarlet woman, Etta Mae, is perfectly happy to settle down with Mattie, her best friend. Mattie, who is involved in the programme's only extended love scene--a scene unusual for American television in its length and eroticism--remains celibate after her teenage pregnancy. As with the sexuality of all the characters, Mattie's celibacy is shown to be the result of a confluence of different factors--fatigue, limited time, fear of pregnancy, fear of men, lack of opportunity, enjoyment of motherhood.

For each character there are costs as well as gains from the lifestyle she has adopted.

The maternal melodrama, which has inspired important critical work by white feminists such as Linda Williams and E. Ann Kaplan, takes on an entirely new aspect when considered in terms of black women's experiences with motherhood and childrearing. *The Women of Brewster Place*, which includes a number of figures who are strong black mothers, is careful to portray the crushing limitations these women face in family life in a racist society and to investigate the hostility and resentment they incur from others who are threatened by their strength. As such, it could usefully assume a place alongside films like *Blonde Venus* (Josef von Sternberg, 1932), *Stella Dallas* (King Vidor, 1937), and *Mildred Pierce* (Michael Curtiz, 1945) as a point of comparison and as a corrective, stemming largely from the insights of black feminist sociology, to the dominance of psychoanalysis as a critical method in film theory's treatment of the figure of the mother. Black feminist sociologists offer a perspective on black women's lives which has particular relevance for commentators on "women's genres." In *The Women of Brewster Place*, the black mother's suffering cannot be located internally, because the role of the public sphere in determining the fate of mother and children is abundantly, incessantly, clear. Patricia Hill Collins notes that as black women researchers provide more information on the ways black women perceive their own mothering, a different view of motherhood emerges.[32] Black women are very connected to their biological children, as well as to those in their extended families and within the wider black community. They are also well aware of the choices available to them in "historically specific political economies." Collins directs us to Janice Hale's work, which demonstrates that black mothers see their roles in part as intermediaries between their children and institutional intervention. As Collins puts it: "Black mothers are sophisticated mediators between the competing offerings of an oppressive dominant culture and a nurturing Black value-structure."[33]

It can be seen, then, that a cultural product such as *The Women of Brewster Place* is dramatizing a psychological dynamic very different from that of the white family melodrama or soap opera. There is an emphasis on the process and survival of grief, on community and on family ties not defined exclusively by blood relation, and on women's lifelong friendships as a survival mechanism. All of these are issues missing from mainstream feminist considerations and prominent in the recent work of black feminist cultural critics. There is a pressing need for feminist media critics to acquaint themselves with the work of black feminist theorists and creative writers, and to understand the relevance of this work of ongoing considerations of female representation, melodrama, and relations between domestic and public space. Here the work of black feminist literary critics, sociologists and historians may offer a better and richer perspective on media representations and the interplay of race and gender. Finally, the creative work of black women writers, and the success of that work when adapted to small and large screens, can revitalize an interest among feminists in identifying and producing television and film which is both popular and politically challenging.

Endnotes

[1] Hazel Carby, *Reconstructing Womanhood: The Emergence of the Afro-American Woman Novelist* (New York: Oxford UP, 1987).

[2] Examples are Barbara Christian, *Black Women Novelists: The Development of a Tradition 1892-1976* (Westport: Greenwood, 1980); Mary Helen Washington, *Invented Lives: Narratives of Black Women 1860-1960* (New York: Anchor, 1987); and more recent essays about black feminist theory in Cheryl Wall (ed.), *Changing Our Own Words: Essays on Criticism, Theory, and Writing by Black Women* (New Brunswick: Rutgers UP, 1989); and Joanne Braxton and Andree Nicola McLaughlin (eds.), *Wild Women in the Whirlwind: Afra-American Culture and the Contemporary Literary Renaissance* (New Brunswick: Rutgers UP, 1990).

[3] Valerie Smith, "Black feminist theory and the representation of the 'Other'," in Cheryl A. Wall (ed.), *Changing Our Own Words*, pp. 38-57; "Gender and Afro-Americanist literary theory and criticism," in Elaine Showalter (ed.), *Speaking of Gender* (New York: Routledge, Chapman, and Hall, 1989), pp. 56-70.

[4] This point is made by Barbara Christian in "The Race for Theory," *Feminist Studies* 14.1 (1988): 67-79. This is a revision and update of an article first published in *Cultural Critique* 6 (1987): 51-63.

[5] Although much of what is written in this article concerns women of colour in the United States, we would like to think it can be more broadly applicable and useful for feminists in other countries. For a more specific detailing of black women's cultural activities throughout the world see the entry of "Black Cinema" in Annette Kuhn (ed.), *Women in Film: An International Guide* (New York: Ballantine, 1991).

[6] See, for instance, bell hooks, *Ain't I a Woman? Black Women and Feminism* (Boston: South End Press, 1981); Gloria I. Joseph and Jill Lewis (eds.), *Common Differences: Conflict in Black and White Feminists' Perspectives* (New York: Anchor, 1981).

[7] See Carby's *Reconstructing Womanhood*, and also her earlier assessment of the relationship of white feminism to the actual lives of women of colour in "White Woman Listen: Black Feminism and the Boundaries of Sisterhood," in Centre for Contemporary Cultural Studies, *The Empire Strikes Back: Race and Racism in Seventies Britain* (London: Hutchinson, 1981): 212-235.

[8] Aïda Hurtado, "Relating to Privilege: Seduction and Rejection in the Subordination of White Women and Women of Color," *Signs: Journal of Women in Culture and Society* 14.4 (1989): 849.

[9] Hurtado, p. 850.

[10] Michele Wallace, "Sexism is the least of it," *New York Times Book Review*, 17 March 1987, p. 18.

[11] Michele Wallace, "The Politics of Location: Cinema / Theory / Literature / Ethnicity / Sexuality / Me," *Framework* 36 (1989): 42-55.

[12] Wallace, "Politics," p. 48.

[13] Jane Gaines, "White Privilege and Looking Relations: Race and Gender in Feminist Film Theory," *Screen* 29.4 (1988): 12-26. Gaines succinctly assesses the difficulties of theorizing about "the other" using traditional feminist analysis.

[14] Coco Fusco, "Fantasies of Oppositionality: Reflections on Recent Conferences in Boston and New York," *Screen* 29.4 (1988): 80-93. A rebuttal to Fusco's article was presented in a later issue of *Screen*: Berenice Reynaud and Yvonne Rainer, "Responses to Coco Fusco's 'Fantasies of Oppositionality'," with reply from Coco Fusco, *Screen* 30.3 (1989): 79-100.

[15] Janet Bergstrom and Mary Ann Doane, "The Female Spectator: Contexts and Directions," *Camera Obscura* 20-21 (1989): 5-27.

[16] See, for example, David Morley, *Family Television: Cultural Power and Domestic Media* (London: Comedia, 1986); Janice Radway, *Reading the Romance: Women, Patriarchy and Popular Literature* (Chapel Hill: U of North Carolina P, 1984); and studies such as those by Rogge, Tulloch, and Seiter, in Ellen Seiter et. al. (eds.), *Remote Control: Television, Audiences, and Cultural Power* (London: Routledge, 1989).

[17] An early influential article on this topic is James Clifford, "On Ethnographic Authority," *Representations* 1.2 (1983): 118-146.

[18] Jacqueline Bobo, "*The Color Purple*: Black Women as Cultural Readers," in E. Deidre Pribram (ed.), *Female Spectators: Looking at Film and Television* (London: Verso, 1988): 90-109.

[19] Minu Lee and Chong Heup Cho, "Women Watching Together: Ethnographic Study of Korean Soap Opera Fans in the US," *Cultural Studies* 4.1 (1990): 30-44.

[20] For specific examples of this problem for students of colour in graduate programmes, see Yolanda T. Moses, *Black Women in Academic: Issues and Strategies* (Washington, DC: Project on the Status and Education of Women/Association of American Colleges, 1989). An especially frank and insightful look at the issue is given by Karen J. Winkler, "Minority Students, Professors Tell of Isolation, Anger in Graduate School," *The Chronicle of Higher Education*, 9 Nov. 1988: A15, A17.

[21] Barbara Christian, "Gloria Naylor's Geography: Community, Class, and Patriarchy in *The Women of Brewster Place* and *Linden Hills*," in Henry Louis Gates, Jr. (ed.), *Reading Black, Reading Feminist* (New York: Meridian, 1990): 353.

[22] These numbers represent the rating and share for the two nights the programme was broadcast. This means that approximately forty-seven million viewers watched the programme the first night and approximately forty-nine million the second. The share numbers indicate that more than one-third of the viewing audience was tuned in to *The Women of Brewster Place*.

[23] Barbara Grizzuti Harrison, "The Importance of Being Oprah," *The New York Times Magazine*, 11 June 1989: 28-30.

[24] See the entry on "Lesbian Independent Cinema" in Annette Kuhn (ed.), *Women in Film: An International Guide*.

[25] M. A. Gillespie, "Winfrey Takes All," *Ms.* (Nov. 1988): 50-55.

[26] See David Bordwell, Janet Staiger and Kristin Thompson, *The Classical Hollywood Cinema: Film Style and Mode of Production to 1960* (New York: Columbia UP, 1985).

[27] Barbara Christian, "Trajectories of Self-Definition: Placing Contemporary Afro-American Women's Fiction," in Marjorie Pryse and Hortense J. Spillers (eds.), *Conjuring: Black Women, Fiction, and Literary Tradition* (Bloomington: Indiana UP, 1985): 233-248.

[28] Quoted in William Goldstein, "A Talk with Gloria Naylor," *Publisher's Weekly*, 9 Sept. 1983: 35-36.

[29] Barbara Christian, "Gloria Naylor's Geography," p. 366.

[30] Christian, 358.

[31] Christian, 367.

[32] Patricia Hill Collins, "Learning from the Outsider Within: The Sociological Significance of Black Feminist Thought," *Social Problems* 33.6 (1986): 17.

[33] Collins' reference is to Janice Hale's 1980 work "The Black Woman and Child Rearing," in LaFrances Rodgers-Rose, ed., *The Black Woman* (Beverly Hills: Sage, 1980): 79-88.

Works Cited

This Works Cited entry has been constructed by the co-editors from citations noted in the original manuscript; it did not appear as part of the published essay.

Bergstrom, Janet and Mary Ann Doane. "The Female Spectator: Contexts and Directions." *Camera Obscura* 20-21 (1989): 5-27.

Christian, Barbara. "Gloria Naylor's Geography: Community, Class, and Patriarchy in *The Women of Brewster Place* and *Linden Hills*." *Reading Black, Reading Feminist*. Ed. Henry Louis Gates, Jr. New York: Meridian, 1990. 348-373.

Collins, Patricia Hill. "Learning from the Outsider Within: The Sociological Significance of Black Feminist Thought." *Social Problems* 33.6 (1986).

Fusco, Coco. "Fantasies of Oppositionality: Reflections on Recent Conferences in Boston and New York." *Screen* 29.4 (1988): 80-93.

Gaines, Jane. "White Privilege and Looking Relations: Race and Gender in Feminist Film Theory." *Screen* 29.4 (1988): 12-26.

Hurtado, Aïda. "Relating to Privilege: Seduction and Rejection in the Subordination of White Women and Women of Color." *Signs: Journal of Women in Culture and Society* 14.4 (1989).

Naylor, Gloria. *The Women of Brewster Place*. New York: Penguin, 1983.

Wallace, Michele. "The Politics of Location: Cinema/Theory/Literature/Ethnicity/
    Sexuality/Me." *Framework* 36 (1989): 42-55.
_____. "Sexism Is the Least of It." *New York Times Book Review* 17
    March 1987: 18.

Montgomery, Maxine L. "The Fathomless Dream: Gloria Naylor's Use of the
    Descent Motif in *The Women of Brewster Place*." *CLA Journal* 36.1 (Sept.
    1992): 1-11.

   The Women of Brewster Place is an experimental novel that functions as
a rare, incisive work of social criticism. Gloria Naylor's clever choice of
Langston Hughes' poem "Harlem" as an epigraph directs the reader's focus of
attention to the lives of those for whom the American dream, whether it entails
socioeconomic advancement or stability and fulfillment in the nuclear family, is
all too often indefinitely deferred. No doubt the community of Brewster Place is
a microcosm for black America, and it is comprised of marginal people who are
excluded from the social, economic, and political mainstream. Each quest for
linear progress ultimately fails on the community's rather foreboding dead-end
street. That a series of reversals precede the eventual condemnation of the
community comes as no surprise, given its questionable origins and the
assembly of residents who are forced to live there.
   Significantly, however, with the creation of the fictive world that is
Brewster Place, Naylor not only documents the failure of the American dream,
but she challenges its validity in terms that point to the formation of an intensely
private reality suspended above time and space in which dreams are fulfilled.
The novel conforms to the romantic mode, as Northrop Frye defines it, for its
action takes place on multiple levels, none of which correspond with objective
reality.[1] The descent motif that is so popular in African-American fiction figures
prominently in the establishment of this romantic world, and the motif entails a
protagonist's physical or psychological journey to a place where he or she
attains self-knowledge.[2] Of necessity, this place is outside the boundaries of the
social mainstream and demands an abandonment of money, property, and title--
in short, all of the outward trappings that signal middle-class success. What the
protagonist gains as a result of this often tortured, circuitous journey is the sense
of wholeness that life in the social mainstream inhibits. It is this journey that
constitutes the structural and thematic center of the novel.
   Brewster Place is itself an inverted world whose reality is determined by
the rich and powerful. Nothing is quite what it should be. The community is a
world apart, the product of an unscrupulous political bargain. It is designed to
fail. The omniscient narrator's description of the community's ironic beginnings
as "a bastard child" whose "true parentage was hidden" calls attention to the
particular experiences of individuals across time and space who are
dispossessed from history.[3] Bastardy serves as an apt metaphor for the
exclusion owing to race that the residents of the community experience. From
their perspective, linear history is an oppressive cycle that perpetuates their
exclusion in a world that is characteristically white and therefore off-limits.
   Animal imagery is pervasive in the novel, not in description of the rural
South, but in description of the decaying urban community environs and its

residents. Mattie Michael arrives on Brewster Place in a van that creeps "like a huge green slug" (7). The appropriately named Reverend Moreland Woods, a wolf in sheep's clothing, has "jungle-sharpened instincts" (66). C. C. Baker and his gang of social misfits travel in a pack, like wolves. Canaan Baptist Church is "a brooding ashen giant" with organ chords "barreling out of its mouth" (62). Perhaps more revealing, though, is the description of the community from Etta Mae Johnson's point of view following her disappointing one-night stand with the local minister. Her return to the community is indeed a descent of sorts, an admission of failure, for she is the victim in the primitive mating game between herself and Reverend Woods. Woods assumes the role of Satan in a topsy-turvy Eden, and Etta Mae is a fallen Eve, forever banished from the Eden of marriage and social status that would be hers as the pastor's wife. Free of all illusions of a life of respectability, security, and identity with Woods, Etta Mae sees the dark world of Brewster Place realistically: "Now it crouched there in the thin predawn light, like a pulsating mouth awaiting her arrival" (73). As she returns to the community, she is downcast and broken in spirit. Much like the wayward biblical prophet of doom Jonah, who finds himself secluded for three days in the belly of a fish, she reluctantly prepares to enter into a night world of darkness and confusion from which she, too, may never escape.

For each of the characters, a series of reversals resulting in the loss of something of value--identity or social status, for instance--precedes entry onto Brewster Place. Linden Hills, a neighboring middle-class community whose reality suggests light, ascent, and possibilities, places no such demands on its residents. Ben, the kindly janitor and resident alcoholic, typifies the dilemma that the men on Brewster Place face because the tokens of manhood--wealth, prestige, and political power--are reserved for whites and the well-to-do. Naylor uses the account of Ben's Southern sharecropper experiences as a historic frame accounting for the anonymity that the men in the community endure in the welfare system. Ben in subject to the whims of Mr. Clyde, the wealthy white landowner for whom Ben and his family work, and is powerless to protect his daughter from the landowner's sexual advances. As spokesperson for a capitalist system in which manhood is synonymous with social, economic, and political power, Ben's wife, Elvira, voices the emasculating sentiments that consign not only Ben but all the men on Brewster Place to a state of perpetual boyhood:

> "If you was half a man, you coulda given me more babies and we woulda had some help workin' this land instead of a half-grown woman we gotta carry the load for. And if you was even quarter a man, we wouldn't be a bunch of miserable sharecroppers on someone else's land--but we is, Ben." (153)

Ben is a tragi-comic figure, a permanent fixture in the community, and even as he intones "Swing Low, Sweet Chariot" during his many drunken binges, he is an ever-present reminder of the failure of America's economic system as a means to achieving upward socioeconomic mobility. It is appropriate, then, that Naylor places Ben in a setting that confirms his status as a social outcast: a damp, dingy basement apartment that is nearest to the wall on Brewster Place.

The women suffer losses that are no less dehumanizing than those which the men experience. Cora Lee, the typical welfare mother, is Case number

6348, without a valid identity.   College-educated, articulate, the lesbians Theresa and Lorraine forfeit jobs and apartments in search of a secure place free of homophobia.   Once on Brewster Place, however, they are still social misfits, living in a world without an address, labeled simply "The Two." Mattie Michael, who is forced to leave a supportive family in her familiar rural South after an unplanned pregnancy, loses a comfortable, spacious home.   Kiswana Browne, who shuns her middle-class background and her great-grandmother's name, is the community's radical but one who lacks a genuine understanding of her ancestral past.   Her mother's brief history lesson, revealing the strength of Kiswana's great-grandmother, serves as a powerful reminder of the vibrant past which Kiswana willingly suppresses.   And finally, Cora Lee's disorderly, single-parent home replaces the secure nuclear family of which she was once a part. Naylor's use of Shakespeare's classic romance *A Midsummer Night's Dream* as a thematic and structural focal point for Cora Lee's narrative is effective in calling attention to the uniqueness of the subterranean world that the characters in the novel inhabit.   The actors and actresses who participate in the play enter a dark forest, where there is confusion and chaos, but even after the drama ends, they are still unable to regain identity and unhindered spatial movement. Naylor's characters continue in a somber world without release.   After the play ends, Cora Lee returns to Brewster Place, having entertained and then abandoned her dreams of middle-class success for her seven children.   At the close of her narrative, with a great deal of hesitancy, she enters the dark and is soon surrounded by the nameless, faceless men, the mysterious shadows who frequent her home, robbing her of her self-esteem.

       Thus, the reality that those in the community face on a day-to-day basis contradicts notions of upward socioeconomic progress implicit in the novel's temporal dawn-to-dusk narrative time frame.   Because of the conflict between what society prescribes as being attainable for all of its citizens, regardless of race or gender, and what the characters actually experience, they are forced to develop what W. E. B. Du Bois refers to as double-consciousness, a sense of psychic two-ness resulting from the ongoing tensions between the black and American identities.[4]   The ultimate descent which the characters enact is one that is psychological in nature, for Naylor's novel explores the characters' collective unconscious.   Her use of oral tradition is, then, a signal narrative strategy popular in black women's fiction.   By donning the mask of storyteller, the women in the novel find themselves rooted in a specific history and culture and thus recreate the unity and self-hood that temporality destroys.   Naylor invests the spoken voice with matchless authority, as the women use the spoken voice to establish a new cosmology, an underground world in which they are agents of their own destiny while others--whites and men--are marginalized.

       This underground world is constructed around Mattie Michael, the community's larger-than-life central mother figure.   Mattie is the community's stabilizing force whose community influence is boundless, and one of the distinguishing features of African-American fiction is the presence of characters like Mattie who are "sort of timeless people whose relationship to the characters is benevolent, instructive, and protective, and they provide a certain kind of wisdom."[5] Mattie's is an ancient wisdom borne out of the hardships she has faced by virtue of being both black and a woman in a world that is white and male.   The important role that she plays as guide in the symbolic descent that the women in the community undergo is especially evident in Etta Mae's narrative. The blues originating from Etta Mae's down-home rural past pervade her narrative and suggest not only the presence of a vibrant, underground folk culture but also the women's ability to transform, and creatively so, an oppressive reality. Her narrative, like the novel itself, is what Ralph Ellison refers to as "an autobiographical chronicle of personal catastrophe expressed lyrically."[6] After her tryst with Reverend Woods in a seedy motel room and her return to the night world of Brewster Place, she finds Mattie, an avid gospel music fan, listening to Etta Mae's blues records. Mattie offers the warmth and support which Etta Mae needs at this crucial moment, and they share an important common bond based on the disappointments which each has faced in romantic relationships. The omniscient narrator describes their bond thusly:

> Etta and Mattie had taken totally different roads that with all of their deceptive winding had both ended up on Brewster Place. Their laughter now drew them into a conspiratorial circle against all the Simeons outside of that dead-end street, and it didn't stop until they were both weak from the tears that flowed down their faces. (60-61)

Etta Mae, like the indomitable, classic blues singer she epitomizes is, with Mattie's assistance, able to transcend the near-tragic night world of Brewster Place. Indeed, at the end of her narrative, her psychology is hardly one that is suggestive of the depth of gloom: "Etta laughed softly to herself as she climbed the steps toward the light and the love and the comfort that awaited her" (74).

Not only is the bond of friendship among the women in the community liberating and redemptive, but the mother-daughter bond is rejuvenating as well, for Mattie plays a pivotal role in the personal transformation that Lucielia Turner undergoes. Ciel is a grieving mother who has lost two children abruptly--one, through an abortion; the other, through an accidental electrocution. Following the funeral for her daughter Serena, Ciel is traumatized in a death-in-life state. In what is perhaps the most moving scene in the novel, Mattie bathes Ciel carefully and tenderly, as a mother would. She then rocks her backward in time, symbolically, back into the womb, thereby negating the psychologically destructive effects of temporality, the oppressive cycle that has led to the almost overwhelming calamity which Ciel now faces:

> She rocked her into her childhood and let her see murdered dreams. And she rocked her back, back into the womb, to the nadir of her hurt, and they found it--a slight silver splinter, embedded just below the surface of the skin. And Mattie rocked and pulled--and the splinter gave way, but its roots were deep, gigantic, ragged, and they tore up flesh with bits of fat and muscle tissue clinging to them. They left a huge hole, which was already starting to pus over, but Mattie was satisfied. It would heal. (104)

Ciel undergoes a mystical rebirth, not a repetition of the first, physical birth, but one that is spiritual in nature. Significantly, that rebirth takes place in private, outside the watchful gaze of a white, male society, and is oriented toward allowing her access to a new mode of existence in which she is no longer subject to the limitations imposed by time and space. The scene's reference to other bereaved mothers--those in Greek mythology, Jewish mothers during the Holocaust and Senegalese mothers--unites Mattie and Ciel with a broad community of dispossessed women who are denied the luxury of grief. In the patently unique community of women that is Brewster Place, Ciel grieves freely, however, and hers is a catharsis that is similar to the laughter that unites Mattie and Etta Mae. As if to reveal Ciel's new mode of existence, her narrative points toward new beginnings, concluding with a violation of the novel's rigid temporal time frame: "And Ciel lay down and cried. But Mattie knew the tears would end. And she would sleep. And morning would come" (105).

By bonding together in relationships among themselves--becoming families of choice--in which the mother figure is central, the women descend on a physical plane but enact, paradoxically, an ascent which is spiritual, not physical, and which is oriented toward recovering a prelapsarian, childlike innocence. They form not only a separate and distinct community but also constitute an alternative world far removed from both white and male spheres. Theirs is the creation of a mythic, timeless realm much like an Edenic, matrilineal West African past that exists outside of, indeed, prior to, the Fall, the chaotic beginnings of Brewster Place. Early in the novel, the omniscient narrator prepares the reader for this important break with temporality by drawing an analogy between the mythical phoenix, believed to be able to recreate itself from its own ashes, and the seven women who tell their tales, thereby immortalizing their own histories. The mythical bird contrasts sharply with the frail pigeon in Kiswana Browne's narrative, whose flight is arrested by the overpowering winds. Collectively, by relying upon survival strategies emanating from the black folk past, the women annul the psychologically destructive effects of linear time.

In the latter section of the novel, the dichotomy between Mattie Michael as central mother figure and Lorraine, the black-woman-as-victim, exemplifies the unresolved conflict which the women in the community experience in the search for selfhood. Lorraine, one of the community's lesbians, functions as the women's alter ego, a second self. She is the more passive in her tensed relationship with Theresa. The two are polar opposites:

> Theresa was growing tired of being clung to--of being the one who was leaned on. She didn't want a child--she wanted someone who could stand toe to toe with her and be willing to slug it out at times. If they practiced that way with each other, then they could turn back to back and beat the hell out of the world for trying to invade their territory. But she had found no such sparring partner in Lorraine, and the strain of fighting alone was beginning to show on her. (136)

Lorraine undergoes a rather sudden and dramatic rebirth as a result of conversations with Ben in his secluded basement apartment. She assumes a more forceful, aggressive posture in her relationship with Theresa. Even so, their relationship is subject to external and internal strife. The implication is, of course, that they can never find complete, unconditional acceptance in a context where heterosexual relationships are considered to be the norm. Miss Sophie, the community gossiper, serves as the clarion voice of morality, labeling the couple's lifestyle as sinful and unnatural, and the community bands together against what they consider to be the evil in their midst. C. C. Baker and his gang viciously and brutally rape Lorraine, who is a threat to their masculinity. Her resulting retreat into madness is commentary on an insane world of unresolved tensions, a world that is hopelessly polarized along race and gender lines.

Mattie Michael's ambiguous, surreal nightmare prior to the long-awaited block party is the culminating event in the novel, the ultimate expression of a night world of horror, frustration, and chaos. The nightmare reveals the suppressed conflicts underlying the women's troubled lives. Each of the women dreams that she is Lorraine, the final victim who is impossibly separated from the community. Although the women's indefinitely deferred dreams explode into social chaos and natural discord, localized in the Brewster Place community, the slogan "Today, Brewster Place, Tomorrow, America" is a veiled promise of a continuing universal dilemma not limited to the community's decaying environs. Mattie's dream is unreal, but its truth cannot be ignored, even as the dream gives way to the actual block party, heralded by morning and sunshine.

Naylor's use of the descent motif is thus revealing of the bottomless night world that is Brewster Place. The novel itself lacks closure, thereby indicating that the dilemma which the women face continues without a resolution. Unlike in the Shakespearean drama, there are not happy endings, no reassuring reunions between the opposing worlds of reality and romance. Instead, the community is condemned as casually as it is created. But the spirits of the seven women whose lives are so vividly chronicled remain inviolate, transcending the community's decaying walls. Each draws upon ancient, transforming rituals from the he black folk past and, like the ebony phoenix, finds a rare kind of survival power, thereby violating the decrees of those who are in positions of power and authority.

Still, the tension between women who dare to defy prescribed roles and the society in which they must live remains constant. The moral world of light, values, and respectability to which Naylor as novelist is subject reasserts its ascendancy at the novel's end, not only aiding in the destruction of the lesbian relationship between Theresa and Lorraine but also canceling the entire community as well. What remains in Naylor's ground-breaking fictional exploration of the difficulties involved in nontraditional lifestyles for women and the highly ambivalent, unresolved conclusion with which the novel closes: "So Brewster Place still waits to die" (192).

Endnotes

[1] Northrop Frye discusses themes of descent within the larger context of the romantic mode in *The Secular Scripture* (Cambridge: Harvard UP, 1976): 97-126.

[2] *The Women of Brewster Place* is among the many African-American novels that make use of this recurring motif. In Ralph Ellison's *Invisible Man*, the nameless hero's discovery of his ethnic past precedes his retreat into an underground coal cellar; in Toni Morrison's *Sula*, the community of the Bottom exudes the vibrant black folk culture that is essential in both Nel and Sula's quest for selfhood; in LeRoi Jones' *The System of Dante's Hell*, the urban hero's journey to a Southern community called the Bottom signals the beginnings of his symbolic rebirth. For a discussion of the nuances of this popular motif, see Jerome Thornton, "Goin' on de Muck: The Paradoxical Journey of the Black American Hero," *CLA Journal* 21.3 (March 1988): 261-280.

[3] Gloria Naylor, *The Women of Brewster Place*, (New York: Penguin, 1983). Subsequent references to the Penguin edition are included parenthetically in the text.

[4] W. E. B. Du Bois, *The Souls of Black Folk*, (1903, rpt. New York: New American Library, 1969): 45.

[5] Toni Morrison, "Rootedness: The Ancestor as Foundation," *Black Women Writers*, ed. Mari Evans (New York: Anchor, 1984): 343.
[6] Ralph Ellison, "Richard Wright's Blues," *Shadow and Act*, (New York: Random House, 1972): 76-79.

Works Cited

This Works Cited entry has been constructed by the co-editors from citations noted in the original manuscript; it did not appear as part of the published essay.

Du Bois, W. E. B. *The Souls of Black Folk.* 1903. New York: New American Library, 1969.

Ellison, Ralph. "Richard Wright's Blues." *Shadow and Act.* New York: Random House, 1964. 77-94.

Frye, Northrop. *The Secular Scripture.* Cambridge: Harvard UP, 1976.

Morrison, Toni. "Rootedness: The Ancestor as Foundation." *Black Women Writers 1950-1980: A Critical Evaluation.* Ed. Mari Evans. New York: Anchor/Doubleday, 1984.

Naylor, Gloria. *The Women of Brewster Place.* New York: Penguin, 1983.

Thorton, Jerome. "Goin' on de Muck: The Paradoxical Journey of the Black American Hero." *CLA Journal* 21.3 (March 1988): 261-280.

Saunders, James Robert. "From the Hypocrisy of the Reverend Woods to Mama Day's Faith of the Spirit." From *The Wayward Preacher in the Literature of African American Women.* Jefferson: McFarland, 1995. 105-124.

In the "Dawn" section that begins *The Women of Brewster Place*, our attention is drawn to a housing project that "became especially fond of its colored daughters as they milled like determined spirits among its decay, trying to make it a home" (4). Prior to the slow but steady arrival of these black women, the premises had been inhabited first by Irish immigrants and then by "dark haired and mellow-skinned" Mediterraneans. The women of Brewster Place are the last in a long line of lower-class citizens who have struggled to rise above the socioeconomic barriers that often press new arrivals to this country down and inhibit their attempts to enter into the mainstream. These women are not new arrivals, however; they are the descendants of slaves brought to American shores untold generations ago. It is sometimes mind-boggling to contemplate how, even today, most immigrants seem, in general, to fare better than African American counterparts who have been here so much longer.

What was the method by which blacks were so consistently left out? Of course, slavery itself was the biggest holdback. And then even after formal slavery ended, various forms of quasi-slavery--for example, sharecropping and Jim Crow laws--were instituted to perpetuate many of the conditions that had been the hallmark of the original slavery situation. Well into this twentieth century, black people as a social block were denied the opportunity that would have given them access to political and economic power. If blacks blamed white society for the predicament, they would not be entirely wrong. It is whites who have been in power from the earliest colonial days to the present. It is whites who initiated slavery as it has existed in this country. And whites, in many ways, have aided and abetted the perpetuation of racial distinctions that have almost always spelled inferior status for blacks.

Yet, particularly as we read *Brewster Place*, we must wonder about the extent to which blacks share complicity for their own degradation. Lucielia Louise Turner is largely responsible for the electrocution of Serena and the abortion of what would have been her second child. That mother made what turns out to be an unreliable man her priority over the care she might otherwise have given her children. That man, Eugene, selfishly comes and goes as he pleases, complaining, "With two kids and you on my back, I ain't never gonna have nothin'" (95). So he can leave, and, upon returning, lie with regard to his whereabouts. He counts on Ciel to sympathize with him, and she does so until profound tragedy occurs. Confronted with the loss of his children, he simply leaves once again, not particularly caring whether Ciel will be able to recover emotionally.

Naylor claims to have done all she could to avoid black male bashing. In an interview with Toni Morrison, she insisted that in *Brewster Place* she had

> bent over backwards not to have a negative message come through about the men. My emotional energy was spent creating a woman's world, telling her side of it because I knew it hadn't been done enough in literature. But I worried about whether or not the problems that were being caused by the men in the women's lives would be interpreted as some bitter statement I had to make about black men. ("Conversation" 579)

Perhaps the author's portrayals of problems caused by men were not intended to be a "bitter statement," but it cannot be denied that she is issuing a firm indictment. From the beginning of the novel, where Butch Fuller abdicates any responsibility for his part in the sexual liaison with Mattie Michael, to near the end, where C. C. Baker rapes Lorraine, we are given views of black men that run the gamut of interpersonal horrors.

Critic Larry Andrews has suggested that "most of the men in the novel may indeed be so ego-crippled by racism as to be unable to love their women" (10). Such may be the case for Butch in pre-1960s Rock Vale, Tennessee, and for C. C. in his urban ghetto environment. But the Reverend Moreland T. Woods's psychological situation is quite different. He is not an ego-crippled black man. Naylor characterizes his congregation as a group of people who "would have followed him to do battle with the emperor of the world. . . . They would willingly give over half of their little to keep this man in comfort" (66). In the minds of those followers, he is God's anointed representative. Although not as conspicuous as Divine in terms of wealth and prestige, he is nonetheless equally dangerous.

Manipulation is at the heart of Woods's intentions. On the night Etta Mae Johnson visits the church, "he glided to the podium with the effortlessness of a well-oiled machine. . . . He eyed the congregation confidently. . . . He was going to wrap his voice around their souls and squeeze until they screamed to be relieved" (65). This preacher understands the nature of his power and knows how to use it for the greatest effect.

But Etta also had manipulative power. Previously she had finagled a Cadillac out of a married man who was in the delicate position of not even being able to report the theft since the sheriff was his wife's father and not likely to think kindly of an unfaithful son-in-law. That son-in-law was powerless, and Etta knew it. Obviously, she is adept at some of the vicious games that people are capable of playing with one another. So why is it that she has no chance of winning the game she plays with Moreland?

For the church service, she wears a scarlet dress that is "too little dress" revealing "too much bosom." She accomplishes through intention what Helga Crane inadvertently achieves when she dons her red dress and wanders into the storefront church in Harlem. Just as Pleasant had been attracted to Helga, Moreland "noticed Etta from the moment she'd entered the church. She stood out like a bright red bird among the drab morality that dried up the breasts and formed rolls around the stomachs of the other church sisters" (67).

Etta stands out not only because she exudes sexuality. She stands out through the sheer force of her distinct personality. While still a young girl in Rock Vale, she had acquired the name "Tut" because she "always had her chin thrust toward the horizon that came to mean everything Rock Vale did not" (59). We have seen the word *horizon* used before as a means of portraying (im)possibility and woman. At the very beginning of *Their Eyes*, we are told that men's dreams "sail forever on the horizon" even if those wishes do not "come in with the tide" (9). There is always some precedent in the world for men's aspirations, while women have no such advantage.

But Etta is unusual. There in Rock Vale, she "was not only unwilling to play by the rules," but she even goes so far as to challenge "the very right of the game to exist" (59). She is a rebel who, though it is the 1930s, can look whites straight in the eye and treat them in accordance with what she thinks they deserve. Due to a set of rather ambiguous circumstances--in terms of their presentation in the novel--she is run out of Rutherford County. It has something to do with the tenuous situation of an interracial liaison. What we are told is that "she left one rainy summer night about three hours ahead of dawn and Johnny Brick's furious pursuing relatives" (60). We are never actually told what Etta did to Johnny, but judging how those relatives "had waited in ambush for two days on the county line, and then had returned and burned down her father's barn" (60), it can be concluded that she retaliated violently to some kind of sexual indiscretion committed by Johnny. When we learn that "Etta was sorry she hadn't killed the horny white bastard," we can speculate further that what Johnny did was attempt to rape her.

Such were the circumstances of black life in the South. However, the issue becomes why Etta's life has not changed very much, even after her escape to the North. She remains a free spirit, but like Zora Hurston herself--who had to flee Eatonville to preserve her independence--Etta is an anomaly whose freedom of spirit is threatened by men who see women only as sex objects. Etta's situation is similar to that portrayed in Ann Petry's novel *The Street* (1946), where men from every walk of life are obsessive in their efforts to seduce Lutie Johnson, who is attractive, single, black, and poor.

One would think, though, that a minister would be different, that instead of contributing to the oppression of black women, Moreland would want to help them through their timeworn dilemma. As it turns out, however, he is not much different from Hurston's Reverend Pearson in that they both are entangled in a moral contradiction. While the Bible condemns fornication and promiscuity, Moreland participates in those biblical offenses and is still capable of rising into the pulpit to "damn into hell for the rest of the congregation" the very lifestyle he himself is guilty of practicing. He understands the nature of "the game" and is very good at playing it. This is one reason why Etta, though excellent herself at playing the game, has no chance of winning this time.

We get a vivid picture of the dynamics of male/female relationships as Naylor juxtaposes the societally presumed positions of man versus woman within the metaphorical context of a card game. Moreland, the preacher, becomes Moreland, the card shark, who contemplates Etta and marvels

> how excellently she played the game. . . . And although she cut her cards with a reckless confidence, pushed her chips into the middle of the table as though the supply was unlimited, and could sit out the game until dawn, he knew. Oh, yes. Let her win a few, and then he would win just a few more, and she would be bankrupt long before the sun was up. And then there would be only one thing left to place on the table--and she would, because the stakes they were playing for were very high. But she was going to lose that last deal. She would lose because when she first sat down in that car she had everything riding on the fact that he didn't know the game existed.   (71-72)

The very name "Moreland Woods" should be a tip-off for us, particularly since we had seen how the name "Pleasant Green" was an inadequate barometer for determining character. "Tea Cake Woods," in *Their Eyes*, is one more deceptive name that, combined with the other two, helps to convey the fact that men offer no panacea for the predicament of women regardless of how responsive those men might at first seem to be.

Inside the church, Moreland speaks with Etta for only a brief moment. If he takes any longer, the congregation will grow suspicious and assume he has ulterior motives with regard to the sultry visitor. "Just let me say good-bye to a few folks here," he tells Etta, "and I'll meet you outside" (69). Mattie knows what Moreland has in mind; even Etta knows. Yet she also knows what the cards are that have been dealt to her as a woman. Moreland, with graying temples and gold-capped teeth, is no doubt older than Etta. But she is the old obsessed with the fear of growing old. Back in the "Mattie Michael" section of the novel, she had urged Mattie to go with her to New York City because of the "place called Harlem with nothing but wall-to-wall colored doctors and real estate men" (26). Note that a woman as independent-minded as Etta is not going to New York to *become* a doctor or real estate agent. She goes to that metropolis with the intent to meet and marry a man in one of those two professions. As a child in Rock Vale, the reason she was called "Tut" had nothing to do with her appearing to others to have the power of a king. She was called "Tut" because one would have thought she was the "*wife* of King Tut" (my emphasis). The distinction is important even for a baby girl who, in that Southern village, had strutted "around . . . like a bantam." The diminutive aspect of the bantam breed of chicken refers not just to the fact that Etta was, at the time, small in stature. The author's use of the bantam is a reference to how any appearance of power that Etta exuded had to be weighed against the power of men and boys in the same community.

By the time Etta encounters Moreland, it has become abundantly clear that the reinforced values of society have caused the odds to be stacked heavily against her. She counts on the preacher not knowing just how delicate her position is as a lonely, single, middle-aged black woman. She misleads herself, but the author warns the reader of Moreland's "razor-thin instinct" and we are told that he is an "alert observer." Those traits are what facilitated his rise to the top of his theological profession. With Etta, he knows "exactly how much to give" (71) and how much he can take, and he knows that in the end she will submit to his sexual desires.

In analyzing Mattie and Etta, Barbara Christian concludes that they are both in Brewster Place "because of their concept of themselves as women . . . . These middle-aged women live through others" (356). More specifically, they live through the men with whom their lives have become intertwined. It is an unquestionably profound revelation that for a woman like Etta, "even if someone had bothered to stop and tell her that the universe had expanded for her . . . she wouldn't have known how to shine alone" (60). What this means is that even if those individualistic dreams flitting on the horizon were to become probable for her, she would not be in possession of what Christian calls the "psychological resources" to achieve those dreams without a "good" man by her side.

Naylor's message about such dependency is best conveyed as we look at how Moreland's treatment of Etta steadily deteriorates. In the early stages of their game, he "helped her into the front seat of his car" (71). After the liaison is completed, he drops her off on a deserted avenue where she "got out of the car unassisted" (72). In the midst of sexual intercourse, he beats "against her like a dying walrus" with his "floundering thrusts into her body" (72). She is, for him, nothing more than a piece of meat primed for his sexual satisfaction. She was destined to be exploited in spite of her unique qualities, destined to be a pawn who will personify the struggle in which all the women of Brewster Place are engaged. Far from suggesting a solution, Moreland is a formidable obstruction intent on relegating women to a position where they will be no freer than the antebellum slave women who were vulnerable to being visited periodically by the master.

*   *   *

As we consider Naylor's second novel, Linden Hills (1985), it becomes clear that the problems prevalent in Brewster Place do not disappear just because some women have made it to an upper-middle-class neighborhood. The plight of Willa Prescott Nedeed exemplifies the circumstances of all the Nedeed wives. Willa has been cast off into the basement by her husband, Luther, who is the last in a long line of Nedeed men. Willa's offense is that she bore her husband a child who is too light-skinned.

In presenting the Nedeed family, Naylor has offered up another extreme case of male oppression, and yet as with the women in Brewster Place, we must ask to what extent the Nedeed women must bear some of the blame for their own predicaments. It is Willa herself who wants to be a Nedeed. Her husband's distant predecessor was the founder of Linden Hills and within the framework of the black community, the Nedeeds have always wielded considerable power. As we are told:

> Her marriage to Luther Nedeed was her choice. . . . She knew then
> and now that there were no laws anywhere in this country that

forced her to assume that name; she took it because she wanted
to. . . . She must be clear about that before she went on to anything
else: she wanted to be a Nedeed. After all, every literate person in
the Western world knew it was a good name. (278)

Even after she has been relegated to the basement, the power to emerge is in
Willa's hands. She was "manipulated" down into that hole, but "she Willa
Prescott Nedeed, had walked down twelve concrete steps. And since that was
the truth--the pure, irreducible truth--whenever she was good and ready, she
could walk back up" (280). We are told--from a symbolic, surrealistic
perspective--that her walk down those steps had begun "from the second she
was born" (280). She hears the deadbolt sliding into place, presumably locking
her down there. Naylor wants us to understand that any attempt at progress
under such conditions will be a difficult endeavor, but entirely possible once the
requisite willpower is summoned.
     Equally difficult, as Naylor presents it, is the more general struggle
between good and evil. The author uses the Dantean concept of descending
concentric circles to convey how as residents move down in Linden Hills to the
more prestigious houses, they are inevitably "consumed" by Nedeed whose first
name, incidentally, bears a striking resemblance to the name Lucifer, the Devil.
     Over the course of the generations, what have the Luther Nedeeds (of
each generation) been doing there at the bottom of Linden Hills? They have all
been undertakers, specializing in what we can take to be more than the mere
preparation of bodies for the grave. The Luthers deal in souls. When Winston
Alcott forsakes his homosexual lover and instead marries a woman for the sake
of appearances, there is a Luther of the Tupelo Realty Corporation who gives
the newlywed couple a mortgage on Tupelo Drive, one of the lowest and most
prestigious levels in Linden Hills. That same Luther has special praise for
Lycentia Parker, who "spent her last days working" (135) in the effort to halt the
construction of a housing project. It is not so important that she opposed the
project. The point is that in opposing it, she joined forces with the Wayne
County Citizens Alliance that, in young Willie Mason's words, "was the Ku Klux
Klan without a Southern accent" (134). What she has done, in effect, is plot with
racist whites to prevent the less fortunate of her own race from having access to
affordable housing.
     But Lycentia is dead now, and in death she has become the object of a
major confrontation between the Reverend Michael Hollis and Luther; the two
men are literally in battle for that woman's soul. Luther wants her funeral
services to be held in his own home, but Michael keeps control in this instance,
insisting that the funeral "be held in his church and not some godforsaken
funeral parlor if it was to be held at all" (165).
     The nature of the battle becomes even more crystallized as we observe
the home addresses of these two men. Luther's address is "999," which read
upside down in the sign of the Devil. Michael's address is "000," which he
argues "aren't zeros, they're O's. Three eternal circles that are quite appropriate
for a home owned by the church" (169). According to the minister, the O's in his
address signify the Holy Trinity. Michael further draws the distinction between
himself and Luther by pointing out: "You could draw a straight line from my front
door to Nedeed's down there at the bottom of that hill, there's a huge difference
between how I earn my subsistence and how he does. Why, my life is devoted

to the Lord and he's a. . . . Well, never mind" (170-171). Like the Devil, who began as one of God's angels, Luther started out with good intentions. He was a real estate entrepreneur devoted to the advancement of blacks. But as he fostered that general prosperity, the economic achievement took precedence over spiritual salvation

Michael serves as the human guardian who would prevent people from exchanging their souls for vast wealth. He warns Willie Mason:

> There are so many forces that govern our lives beyond the material, the tangible. There is to be an accounting, son, for each and every one of us. And we can't balance those books with our stock dividends. We better pay heed to that on this side, because when we get to the other side and the body is gone, we might just find ourselves with no soul as well.   (169)

Even as he preaches, however, the reverend is in conflict with himself. Long before he came to Linden Hills, "he was twelve years old, sitting in the fifth row of his grandmother's weather-beaten church" with its "sagging walls miraculously held up by the Tennessee heat" (157). A vital part of his past consisted of attending church in the rural South, where the services included "clapping and swaying" and every now and then "an unpredictable explosion of sound" (157). That was the setting where he was "called" into the ministry.

It is quite telling that now Michael cannot remember what made him want to serve in a ministerial capacity. Despite his choice, "everyone knew that in four years Michael Hollis had never even made it to chapel" (159) when he was at the University of Pennsylvania. Although his reflections on the rural South are incomplete, he is, during his college years, still aware that "going to chapel wasn't" the same thing for him as "going to church." Church means to him something other than what was available to U-Penn's Sunday chapel. The distinction has to do with cultural roots, on the one hand, as opposed to the more sterilized version of religion that an Ivy League environment is likely to provide.

John Wideman, in his autobiographical *Brothers and Keepers* (1984), talks about having been on the verge of "coming apart" as a consequence of being one of "about ten of the seventeen hundred men and women who entered the University of Pennsylvania as freshmen in 1959" (29). To maintain his equilibrium, he and another black freshman "would ride buses across Philly searching for places like home," and only after "a number of long, unsuccessful expeditions" did they finally find "South Street" (32). Those two college classmates had searched for the poolrooms, barbershops, and rib joints that would remind them of their cultural origins and allow them to return to the university and endure that alien world.

Just as had been the case in real life with Wideman and his friend, Naylor's fictional preacher is able to find refuge in South Philadelphia.

> On Sunday afternoons he quietly left the dorm and drove past the manicured lawn and Gothic stones of the Penn chapel into South Philadelphia to sit in the back of reconverted candy stores with stained-glass cellophane peeling at the windows. Where, more often than not, the altar was a scarred wooden table with an oilskin

cloth and plastic crucifix; the battered piano missing keys if not
pitch; the chairs missing leg braces if not backs. . . . Every Sunday
. . . Michael made the circuit: The Tabernacle of the Saints, The
Zionist Mission, The House of Divine Ascension. . . . Sitting in the
rear of those small rooms, he could almost see the currents racing
from back to front and back again. The presence of that type of
raw power connected up with something in his center.   (159)

While seated in the rear of those storefront churches, Michael is reunited with
the raw energy he had felt as a child at the holy roller-type church service. He is
reprieved momentarily, reenergized to the point where he can return to the
campus and continue his academic studies.

Upon completing his undergraduate work, Michael enrolls at Harvard's
divinity school while remaining committed to the style of worship that he learned
in Tennessee. In Cambridge, he scorns "what Harvard considered a 'model
sermon'" (161). After graduating from the divinity school, he concludes that his
degree is "total horse dung." As an undergraduate he made his way to South
Philadelphia. As a graduate student he leaves the campus to attend Sunday
services in Roxbury, where once again he can maintain his connection to the
pulse of the common folk. He pursues Ivy League training but never loses sight
of the source for his spiritual strength.

As he receives his pastorate in Linden Hills, Michael learns that he is
about to be tested one more time. Unlike the down-to-earth congregations he
has been affiliated with in the past, now his own congregation "stiffened under
the cashmere, silk, and beaver skins, so he had to reach over them to the
others, where he felt a supple willingness to receive, be filled, and return the
energy he needed to keep going" (162). The poorer members of his
congregation sit in the back during church service, but he preaches over the
pews of wealthy members to find those humble parishioners who are willing first
to receive the spirit and then, by way of call-and response technique, supply the
verbal feedback to keep him inspired. But those seated up front with their
"plastic postures" begin to consume more and more of the pews until Michael, in
desperation, must resort to sponsoring Christmas parties specifically for the low-
income neighborhood of Putney Wayne. Michael's object is to get Putney
Wayne residents to attend Sinai Baptist on a regular basis. They come "at first,
sitting in the back pews and the balconies, but gradually drifting away to where
they could be free to worship as they believed" (163). Thus Michael's source of
strength disappears to the point there he becomes vulnerable and finally
succumbs to the hedonistic lifestyle that he (like Moreland) nevertheless
preaches against.

Catherine Ward renders this assessment of what the reverend's moral
position. has become after a sustained period in Linden Hills: "Years spent
pursuing sensual pleasure and material possessions have isolated Hollis. He
has an endless supply of women, closets full of expensive suits, and a couple of
LTD's . . . 'and he has lost touch with his own feelings" (76). He has slid into the
world of strict materialism and fallen prey to that pervasive sin of adultery. He
gets through his hypocritical days by periodically taking shots of Scotch and
popping mints to cover the smell. At the critical juncture when he is faced with
the task of preserving Lycentia's soul, we wonder how he can ever perform this
particular mission.

"Are you ready for death?" (182) he asks those who have amassed for the funeral. Like a father confessor now himself confessing, he posits, "Will the fancy homes, fancy clothes, and fancy cars make you ready? Will the big bucks and big jobs make you ready?" (182). Michael tells Lycentia's husband that Jesus is not ready to call his wife. If not now, then when? That is when Luther takes charge of the ceremony and recapitulates the events he regards as the highlights of her life, such as her work on the Linden Hills Beautification Project and her work as secretary of the Tupelo Realty's neighborhood board. Lycentia's "good works" helped raise the status of her community, consequently causing it to be separate from the lives of the masses of blacks.

Willie, symbolic of the masses, detects something devious in how Luther closes the lid of Lycentia's coffin:

> But he hadn't seen anything. Nothing but a man closing the lid of a coffin. And there was no harm in that. . . . A man leaning over and with his hand closing the lid of a coffin. . . . It was that right hand. It moved too slowly over the top of the lid before it clicked shut . . . it moved as if Nedeed was . . . (186)

Those last ellipses are another of the author's not so subtle hints that Luther is an agent of the Devil. It is he who will take authority over the dead body as though now collecting on the terms of some previous arrangement.

As we think back to Michael's explanation for the three "O's" in his street address, we recall what he said about the numbers representing the Holy Trinity. But after Luther takes charge, it seems more appropriate to consider how the numbers might suggest a negation. And as much as Michael's lifelong struggle has been to achieve a high level of spirituality, we must ultimately conclude he has failed in that endeavor. He is like one of T. S. Eliot's hollow men whose "dried voices . . . are quiet and meaningless" (77). While Luther is claiming authority, Michael "did absolutely nothing." Separated from the source of what has been his strength, he is drained of the spiritual essence that might have allowed him to defeat the proponents of evil.

*   *   *

In *Linden Hills* we are afforded a glimpse of the woman who in the author's next novel will come to symbolize what is needed for spiritual fulfillment. This essential woman is the great-aunt of Evelyn Creton, one of the Nedeed wives who remembers that as a child she had been "ashamed of her great-aunt, Miranda Day, when she pulled up in that cab each summer, calling from the curb at the top of her voice, 'Y'all better be home'" (147). The old woman was toothless, almost illiterate, and wore loose-fitting shoes. Evelyn shunned her so she would not be embarrassed in front of her teenage friends. Even then, the future Mrs. Nedeed was focused on social mobility, and Mama Day was proving to be a persistent inconvenience.

In the actual novel, *Mama Day* (1988), we are presented again with the dichotomy of material versus spiritual success. George Andrews has his own engineering firm and his job is "to redesign the structures that take care of our basic needs: water supply, heating, air conditioning, transportation" (60). He is, quite simply, the mechanical man who is as detached from the spiritual realm as a person can get. However, his love interest is another of Mama Day's great-nieces, Ophelia, who while living in New York City is nonetheless torn between that impersonal venue and the island of Willow Springs, whose bridge connects it with the mainland right at the dividing line between South Carolina and Georgia. This is an important point because while both of those states have sought to usurp Willow Springs to be part of their individual territories, the island remains an entity unto itself with strong cultural ties to Africa.

That African connection is personified in legend through the person of the transported African, Sapphira, who married her owner, Bascombe Wade, bore him seven sons, arranged for Willow Springs to be deeded over to his slaves, and then killed him and walked right out onto the Atlantic Ocean, presumably en route back to her homeland. A similar occurrence can be seen in Toni Morrison's *Song of Solomon* (1977), where it is suggested that there were Africans brought to American shores who had the capacity to fly, if necessary, in order to return to the place of their origin. In both literary instances, we are confronted with an almost incomprehensible spirituality that is nevertheless used by the authors to criticize diluted forms of African American religiosity.

Paule Marshall's Avey Johnson (*Praisesong for the Widow*, 1983) is able only in retrospect to perceive that her and her husband's quest for the good life caused an emptiness that will not be remedied until she travels to the mysterious island of Carriacou. Similarly, Naylor's Ophelia must make the trip southward from New York City to achieve the dynamic spiritualism of her ancestral past. Mama Day lives in Willow Springs, and as an example of her powers, the author compares her to a medical doctor who is occasionally called to render services on the island. The physician, Brian Smithfield, is obliged to accept that there is

> no point is prescribing treatment for gout, bone inflammation, diabetes, or even heart trouble when the person's going straight to Miranda after seeing him for her yea or nay. And if it was nay, she'd send 'em right back to him with a list of reasons. Better to ask straight out how she been treating 'em and work around that. Although it hurt his pride at times, he'd admit inside it was usually no different than what he had to say himself--just plainer words and a slower cure than them concentrated drugs. . . . But being a good doctor, he knew another one when he saw her.   (84)

These are serious ailments that Mama Day is at least as capable of handling as the degreed practitioner. In fact, hers is the final say-so even concerning prognoses that the doctor makes. A descendant of Sapphira, Mama Day carries on the tradition of that primordial ancestor who was indeed responsible for the Willow Springs community existing in the manner that it did with so much of its cultural essence intact.

Mama Day is, more specifically, a midwife. Literally speaking, that is her function for this community. But on a symbolic level, she is more. She serves as the source for spiritual creation and regeneration in the midst of an increasingly industrialized world. While the doctor's cures, for example, are condensed for mass consumption and institutionalized convenience, Mama Day tailors her remedies more precisely to the needs of her individual patients. Moreover, since she also functions in the realm of the spiritual, her powers far exceed the capabilities of those who are limited to practical means.

Houston Baker, in *Workings of the Spirit* (1991), points out "the importance conjure has historically possessed for an African diasporic community" (79). In particular, Baker has reference to the fact that Zora Hurston was an initiate in a Louisiana hoodoo ceremony. The critic expands further on that intriguing phenomenon as he explains, "one reason the conjurer held such a powerful position in diasporic African communities, was her direct descent from the African medicine man and her place in a religion that had definable African antecedents" (79). Mama Day is a prime example of how the fields of medicine and religion were so thoroughly intertwined in African culture. I would also add the field of politics as an arena in which the historic cultural figure of the conjurer played a role.

The revolutionary Ned Cuffee in Marshall's *Chosen Place* was an obeah man.   Derived from the Ashanti word *obayifo*, *obeah* means capable of performing magic. Obviously, not everyone can lay claim to such power. But those who do, form part of a belief system where, as Roger Bastide reports in *African Civilizations in the New World* (1967), special individuals "fly through the air, suck the blood of their victims, radiate light from their anus, and turn themselves into animals" (103).

Childish superstition? Perhaps. But the mere fact that it is unexplainable is not enough to cause one to reject the possibility. Remember, Christianity itself is largely based on the acceptance of and faith in entities that are unseen and, for the practical person, totally unbelievable. Yet Christianity flourishes as one of the most pervasive modes of thought in the civilized world. Prior to the encroachment of Christianity of African soil, legitimate religious and political systems were already in place. As the wise Obierika explains in Chinua Achebe's *Things Fall Apart* (1959), "the white man is very clever. He came quietly and peaceably with his religion" (162). But religion was only the beginning. By the end of that novel, we learn how introduction of a new religion has been the means whereby a foreign people has gained political control. "We have fallen apart" (162), mourns Obierika. Indeed, the cultural patterns have been seriously altered.

But ultimately the patterns are not destroyed. Resistance is as much a factor in Achebe's novel as in the European plot to usurp Nigerian authority. Resistance is also evident in the literature about blacks in the diaspora. Squire Gensir, in Claude McKay's *Banana Bottom* (1933), reminds those who would deny the validity of obeah practice:

> When you read in your stories about the Druids, the Greek and Roman gods . . . and the Nordic Odin, you felt tolerant about them. Didn't you? Then why should you be so intolerant about Obi and Obeahmen? . . . Obeah is part of your folklore, like your Anancy tales. . . . And your folklore is the spiritual link between you and your ancestral origin.   (125)

In that novel about Jamaica, white preachers use various methods of intimidation to steer the natives away from their own distinct religious practices and toward a belief in Christianity. Again we see how the attempt to gain religious sway is the preliminary step in the process of attaining general power over a presumed primitive community. Those descendants of Africans attend the Christian church, but then secretly at night they visit the Obeahman and thereby preserve their heritage.

Susan Willis has argued that the predominant theme of contemporary African American women writers is "the journey (both real and figural) back to the historical source of the black American community" (57). We see this theory played out in Toni Morrison's *Beloved* (1987), where the former slave Baby Suggs, "accepting no title of honor before her name . . . became an unchurched preacher" who "opened her great heart to those who could use it" (87). "Uncalled, unrobed, unanointed," her sanctuary is "the Clearing--a wide-open place cut deep in the woods nobody knew for what" (87). Her tenure comes to an end only as the "big-city revivals" make their way out to the Clearing, which now is reached not by a simple, narrow pathway, but by a well-worn track signifying increased urbanization and a more formal, and thereby sterile, religious service.

Mama Day epitomizes a tradition similar to what Baby Suggs represents. The former has a supernatural understanding of her great-niece's needs and knows, for example, what type of man George is without having met him. She seems even to know of his general comings and goings without the benefit of engaging him in conversation. And of course she is gifted with the knowledge of an appropriate remedy when Ophelia is cursed by a woman who believes the great-niece is having an affair with her husband. George must facilitate the cure, and Mama Day orders him back to her own chicken coop in search of what lies beneath a formidable red hen. Mama Day insists, "You gotta take this book and cane in there with you, search good in the back of her nest, and come straight back here with whatever you find" (295). There is nothing in the hen's nest. But nonetheless in that coop a vicious battle takes place between George, the harbinger of urban ideals, and the chicken, a symbol of the old ways, specifically as they pertain to African voodoo-type ceremonies. George succeeds in nullifying the curse, but he dies in the process. What he is able to accomplish is due only to the power of Mama Day.

This female conduit of African culture does more than offer her assistance in selected problem cases. She is the thread that holds together the Willow Springs community. We see this most profoundly as she orchestrates the yearly Candle Walk which takes place not on December 25, but on December 22. Naylor does not wish to eliminate Christian themes such as sacrifice and rebirth, but she does make it clear that Mama Day's celebration is not based on the Eurocentric approach to Christianity. There are legends associated with the Candle Walk ceremony, such as the one about the origin of Willow Springs, that "the island got spit out from the mouth of God, and when it fell to the earth it brought along an army of stars. He tried to reach down and scoop them back up, and found Himself shaking hands with the greatest conjure woman on earth" (110). Is there any wonder why the old Reverend Hooper has tried his best to put an end to the Candle Walk ritual? From his perspective, the rite is sheer blasphemy. It cuts across the grain of biblical doctrine as it was imparted to him along the way toward his credentialed position.

On the other hand, that version of Willow Springs' origin can be viewed as a variation of the earth origin story presented within the first nineteen verses of Genesis. God remains the ultimate source of creation, but instead of the encounters the Old Testament describes with men such as Adam, Moses, Abraham, and David, this time the communion is with an empowered woman.

Furthermore, there is the suggestion in *Mama Day* that God is a woman. Mama Day "goes to bed to get down on her stiffened knees and pray to the Father and Son as she'd been taught. But she falls asleep, murmuring the names of women" (280).

Much has been made over how gender references in the Bible denote God as a "him" or a "he." Moreover, Genesis 1:27 specifies that "God created man in his own image." Such details are enough to convince some people that God must be a man who correspondingly gave men on earth power far beyond anything that might have been afforded to women.

But as one reads on further in that Genesis verse, one finds the basis for some controversy. The passage continues, "In the image of God created he him; male and female created he them." Nowhere in the Bible are we given a physical description of God. That entity, spirit that it is, may defy gender classification. As we take this latter section of the verse in conjunction with the former, it seems more likely that the use of male gender in reference to God was as much for the sake of convenience as anything else.

What does it mean that the word "own" is emphasized in Genesis 1:27? Shug Avery, in *The Color Purple* (1982), offers Celie that following perspective:

> The thing I believe, God is inside you and inside everybody else. You come into the world with God. But only them that search for it inside find it. And sometimes it just manifest itself even if you not looking, or don't know what you looking for. Trouble do it for most folks, I think. Sorrow, lord. Feeling like shit.   (202)

For black women to wait on a white male God for their redemption would be a ludicrous thing to even contemplate. Men, who have usually been the ones in control of biblical interpretations, have manipulated passages so that the world might be the way that they wished it to be. As one reanalyzes Genesis 1:27 in its entirety, it would seem that in creating both woman and man, God's intent was to have individuals be true to what was best in their own inner workings. The extent to which God pressed His image on them was only to inculcate morality.

It is important to note the time frame within which Mama Day prays and then unconsciously, in troubled sleep, murmurs women's names. It is when Ophelia is in the throes of the curse with her "eyes, lips, chin, forehead, and ears smeared everywhere, mashed in and wrinkled, with some gouged places still holding the imprints from [her] fingers." In a word, she has become an absolute monster with "flesh from both cheeks . . . hanging in strings under [her] ears" (276). That would certainly be enough to comprise the requisite "trouble" that Shug had in mind when she laid the conditions whereby God might be reached. It is in such dire straits that Mama Day "in her dreams . . . finally meets Sapphira" (280), who is the female equivalent of Moses, who had powers that defied any simple explanation.

Mama Day has inherited many of Sapphira's gifts. It is fitting that she be a leader in the Candle Walk where the residents of Willow Springs have in the past changed: "Lead on with light, Great Mother. Lead on with light" (111). All the marchers must bring with them some source of light (a kerosene lamp, a candle, or even just a sparkler) in reverence to the Woman who freed them. And the walk is not without practical value. Just as the Bible has one of its admonitions that "it is more blessed to give than to receive" (Acts 20:35), those who participate in the Candle Walk must give something to someone else. The nature of the walk allows people in need to accept gifts without submitting to a condescending charity. Whether walk participants give a handful of cookies or a bushel of potatoes, "it all got accepted with the same grace, a lift of the candle and a parting whisper, 'Lead on with light'" (110). Such altruism cannot be taught in religious seminaries. Nor can it be bargained for in that ongoing activity of tabulating who will receive eternal life for doing what deeds. Rather, the Candle Walk is a distinctly woman-inspired effort to achieve a morally legitimate community within which true godliness can thrive.

Works Cited

This Works Cited entry has been constructed by the co-editors from citations noted in the original manuscript; it did not appear as part of the published essay.

Achebe, Chinua. *Things Fall Apart*. London: Heinemann, 1959.

Andrews, Larry R. "Black Sisterhood in Gloria Naylor's Novels." *CLA Journal* 33.1 (1989): 1-25. Reprinted in Gates and Appiah.

Baker, Houston A., Jr. *Workings of the Spirit*. Chicago: U of Chicago P, 1991.

Bastide, Roger. *African Civilizations in the New World*. 1967. London: Hurst, 1972.

Christian, Barbara. "Gloria Naylor's Geography: Community, Class, and Patriarchy in *The Women of Brewster Place* and *Linden Hills*." *Reading Black, Reading Feminist*. Ed. Henry Louis Gates, Jr. New York: Meridian, 1990. 348-373. Reprinted in Gates and Appiah.

Eliot, T. S. "The Hollow Men." *T. S. Eliot: The Complete Poems and Plays 1909-1950*. New York: Harcourt, Brace, and Jovanovich, 1971. 56-59.

Gates, Henry Louis, Jr. and K. A. Appiah, eds. *Gloria Naylor: Critical Perspectives Past and Present*. New York: Amistad, 1993.

Hurston, Zora Neale. *Their Eyes Were Watching God*. 1937. Urbana: U of Illinois P, 1978.

McKay, Claude. *Banana Bottom*. 1933. Chatham: Chatham Books, 1970.

Morrison, Toni. *Beloved*. New York: Knopf, 1987.

Naylor, Gloria, and Toni Morrison. "A Conversation: Gloria Naylor and Toni Morrison." *Southern Review* 21.3 (1985): 567-593.

_____. *Linden Hills*. New York: Ticknor & Fields, 1985.

_____. *Mama Day*. New York: Random House, 1988.

_____. *The Women of Brewster Place*. New York: Penguin, 1983.

Walker, Alice. *The Color Purple*. New York: Harcourt, Brace, and Jovanovich, 1982.

Ward, Catherine C. "Gloria Naylor's *Linden Hills*: A Modern *Inferno*." *Contemporary Literature* 28.1 (1987): 67-81. Reprinted in Gates and Appiah.

Wideman, John. *Brothers and Keepers*. New York: Holt, Rinehart, and Winston, 1984.

Willis, Susan. *Specifying: Black Women Writing the American Experience*. Madison: U of Wisconsin P, 1987.

Linden Hills

Sisney, Mary F. "The View from the Outside: Black Novels of Manners." *Reading and Writing Women's Lives: A Study of the Novel of Manners.* Bege K. Bowers and Barbara Brothers, eds. Ann Arbor: UMI Research P, 1990. 171-185.

In 1853, when the first novel written by a black American was published in London, the novel of manners was flourishing. That year, two Elizabeth Gaskell novels--*Cranford* and *Ruth*--appeared, and a few years earlier (1848), Thackeray's *Vanity Fair* was published. But fugitive slave William Wells Brown's *Clotel* was not a novel of manners. It was a slave narrative written in the abolitionist tradition of Harriet Beecher Stowe's *Uncle Tom's Cabin* (1852).

Thackeray would no doubt have scoffed at the idea of a fugitive slave writing a novel comparable to *Vanity Fair.* Imagine Sambo as the protagonist in a novel of manners. That would be, to quote Thackeray, "entirely low" (54).[1] In the novel of manners, the lowest classes and the darker races provide background and often comic relief. They are the maids, butlers, cooks, and footmen for the middle- and upper-middle-class heroes and heroines.

Indeed, at first glance, the black novel, which usually calls for change in society--the abolition, first, of slavery, then, of Jim Crow and, finally, of racial oppression--appears to have little in common with the more conservative novel of manners, which generally accepts the mores of the society depicted and requires the individual to change in order to find her or his place in that society.

How could black Americans accept a society that rejected them? Why would they want to find their place in a social system that always placed them at the very bottom? And how could black American writers write about a society from which they were excluded? Even the characteristic tone and method of the novel of manners seem ill-suited to the black writer. Not all novels of manners follow the happy ending convention of high comedy, but the tone tends to be light--ironic, satirical.[2] And if there is political upheaval or violence, it usually takes place offstage. As Thackeray says, "Our place is with the non-combatants" (282). The only battles fought are domestic, taking place in the characteristic settings of the novel of manners--the drawing room, the opera, dances, weddings. Cruelty takes the form of slander and ostracism. There is no place in the novel of manners for the kind of bestiality--rapes, lynching--that has been part of the black American experience.

And yet, the black novel and the novel of manners share at least three fundamental and related concerns--the fight for acceptance, the loss of identity, and the sense of oppression. In the black novel, the fight against Jim Crow and other forms of racism is, in part, a fight for acceptance. For characters in the so-called Talented Tenth novels (1890-1920), being accepted by the best of white society seemed to be the primary goal.[3] Such novelists as Charles Chesnutt and James Weldon Johnson created black heroes and heroines who differed from members of white society only in the degree of their suffering and in their capacity for compassion. These characters were usually white-skinned, middle-class blacks, sometimes, as in Chesnutt's *The Marrow of Tradition* (1901), closely resembling a white half-sibling and sometimes, as in Chesnutt's *The House Behind the Cedars* (1900), and Johnson's *The Autobiography of an Ex-Coloured Man* (1912), choosing to pass as white in order to escape the brutality and oppression of racism.

"Passing" also occurs in the novel of manners. To pass is to deny one's true identity--family, heritage, class. Becky Sharp constantly attempts to pass for a lady in *Vanity Fair*. The daughter of an alcoholic artist and a French opera singer, she claims to be related to a "noble family of Gascony" (20). But passing can take more subtle forms than rewriting family histories. Becky is also passing when she assumes the role of a timid young maiden in a vain attempt to capture Joseph Sedley. And when the spirited Lily Bart, in Edith Wharton's *The House of Mirth* (1905), tries to mold herself into the image of a dull, dutiful wife so that she can attract Percy Gryce, "all on the bare chance that he might ultimately decide to do her the honour of boring her for life" (25), she, too, is passing.

In the rigidly structured, patriarchal societies depicted in novels of manners, there is only one place for a woman: beside or behind a man. And so women like Becky Sharp and Lily Bart must suppress their spirits and hide their true identities in order to trick men into marrying them. For Becky, marriage is a way to gain status and acceptance, to become a lady. For Lily, already a lady, marriage is a vocation:

> "Isn't marriage your vocation? Isn't it what you're all brought up
>   for?"
> She [Lily] sighed. "I suppose so. What else is there?"   (9)[4]

There is nothing else for the lady; she cannot work or live alone. Until she is married, a lady in the novel of manners has no security, no freedom, no identity.

Since there could be no black ladies and gentlemen in white society, the characters in early black novels had more in common with Becky Sharp than with Lily Bart. Just as Becky sought to marry a gentleman in order to become a lady, some of the blacks passing as white--the ex-coloured man, for instance--married whites in order to solidify their position in white society. There was no place in that society for any person known to be black, no matter how fair-skinned, wealthy, or genteel he or she might have been.

In the years following the Civil War, the newly emancipated and the already-free blacks who were educated and had acquired property began to form black societies. By the 1920s, close to sixty years after Emancipation, some very exclusive black societies existed in such cities as Charleston, Atlanta, New Orleans, Harlem, Chicago, Philadelphia, and Washington, DC (Frazier 196-200). These societies were generally as conservative and patriarchal as those depicted by Thackeray and Wharton. Although the black lady could work, usually as a teacher, a seamstress, or a secretary, her place in society was not secure until she married. For some of these women, marriage was the fulfillment of a dream, a long-awaited reward for a virtuous life. For others, it could be stifling and confining, even more unbearable than the life Lily Bart would lead as Mrs. Percy Gryce. But for all black society ladies of the twenties, marriage was a necessity.[5]

Although most black writers of the twenties--the Harlem Renaissance period of black literature--portrayed lower-class blacks, the so-called Rear Guard novelists focused on black society. Robert Bone describes these writers in his *Negro Novel in America* (1965):

> Fundamentally these novelists still wished to orient Negro art toward white opinion. They wished to apprise educated whites of the existence of respectable Negroes, and to call their attention-- now politely, now indignantly--to the facts of racial injustice. From these nonliterary motives certain familiar consequences flowed. Where the Harlem School turned to the folk for literary material, these novelists continued to draw their characters from the Negro middle class. . . . Where the Harlem School emphasized "racial" differences, these authors suppressed them.   (97)

Two of the more prominent members of the Rear Guard were women writers. One was Jessie Fauset, high school teacher, literary editor of the N.A.A.C.P. journal *The Crisis*, and member of the "Old Philadelphia" society; the other was Nella Larsen, nurse, librarian, wife of a physicist, and daughter of a Danish mother and black father. Both women were well educated, and both had traveled and lived in Europe. These cultured society women were the first black novelists of manners. Their novels, which focus on marriage as a means for the black woman to establish and maintain her place in society, have more in common with the works of such literary ancestors as Edith Wharton and Jane Austen than with those written by such black contemporaries as Claude McKay and Countee Cullen.[6]

Fauset, who wrote four novels between 1924 and 1933, explained her literary objectives in the foreword to her third novel, *The Chinaberry Tree* (1931):

> In the story of Aunt Sal, Laurentine, Melissa and the Chinaberry Tree I have depicted something of the homelife of the colored American who is not being pressed too hard by the Furies of Prejudice, Ignorance, and Economic Injustice. And behold he is not so vastly different from any other American, just distinctive. He is not rich but he moves in a society which has its spheres and alignments as definitely as any other society the world over. . . . He has seen, he has been the victim of many phases of immorality but he has his own ideas about certain "Thou shalt nots." And acts on them. . . . He boasts no Association of the Sons and Daughters of

the Revolution, but he knows that as a matter of fact and quite inevitably his sons and daughters date their ancestry as far back as any. So quite as naturally as his white compatriots he speaks of his "old" Boston families, "old Philadelphians," "old Charlestonians." And he has a wholesome respect for family and education and labor and the fruits of labor. He is still sufficiently conservative to lay a slightly greater stress on the first two of these four. (ix-x)

The case of the aptly named Stranges, Aunt Sal and her daughter Laurentine, illustrates the importance of family and of "Thou Shalt Not's" to black society. Both women are "comely and upstanding" (1), and there is not a black or white women in Red Brook more poised, talented, or rigidly moral than Laurentine Strange. But Aunt Sal has committed three of the most unpardonable "Thou Shalt Not's": she has borne a child out of wedlock, the child's father is already married, and he is a white man. To the respectable black citizens of Red Brook, the "sin" of miscegenation is just as objectionable as the sins of adultery and bastardy. Because of the "scandal" surrounding her birth, black children will not play with Laurentine when she is small, and she has trouble finding a suitable mate when she becomes an adult. Little Lucy Stone plays with her until Mrs. Stone intervenes: "My mumma say I dasn't. She say you got bad blood in your veins" (8). Phil Hackett, an early suitor, is also frightened away by the "bad blood" and hint of scandal. But as so often happens in the novel of manners, the virtuous woman is finally rewarded. At the end of the novel, Laurentine is marrying a doctor and entering the black society of Red Brook. Her cousin, Melissa Paul, is also rescued from scandal by marriage to a respected member of the Red Brook community. In the last sentence of the novel, the two women are compared to "spent swimmers, who had given up the hope of rescue and then had suddenly met with it . . . sensing with all their being, the feel of the solid ground beneath their feet, the grateful monotony of the skies above their heads" (340-341).

This ending is typical of Fauset's novels. Although her heroines are talented and self-sufficient, occasionally even prosperous, not one "feels the solid ground beneath her feet" until she finds the right man to love and marry. Critic Hiroko Sato describes the basic Fauset plot: "a beautiful heroine and a handsome hero are finally united after overcoming innumerable obstacles" (68). Most of those obstacles involve other handsome men, the heroes' rivals, the heroines' unworthy suitors. Before she marries the right man, the Fauset heroine must reject or be rejected by the wrong one. Thus, Laurentine Strange must be rejected by the selfish Phil Hackett before she can marry the loving Doctor Stephen Denleigh. And two other heroines fair enough to pass as white, Angela Murray in *Plum Bun* (1929) and Phebe Grant in *Comedy: American Style* (1933) must reject wealthy white suitors before they can find suitable black mates.[7]

In their depiction of marriage, Fauset's novels resemble those written by Jane Austen. The marriages are correct and proper. They bring order to the women's lives, ending long, sometimes painful, searches for love and acceptance. Through marriage, the Fauset heroine finds her place in society. She belongs.

Larsen's heroines, who also seek love and acceptance, have less success with marriage. Although it provides them with a place in society, marriage does not bring order, security, or peace to these women's lives. They have not married the right men; therefore, instead of finding themselves--their best selves--through marriage, like the heroines in Fauset's novels, these women, like Lily Bart and Rebecca Sharp, must deny their true selves. For Clare Kendry, Irene Redfield, and Helga Crane, marriage is a struggle, a trap, a dead end.

Helga Crane, the heroine of *Quicksand* (1928), the first of Larsen's two novels, has the same problem with black society as does Fauset's Laurentine Strange. Like Laurentine, Helga is the illegitimate daughter of one white parent (her mother) and one black (her father). Comparing black society to white, the narrator explains Helga's problem: "Negro society . . . was as complicated and as rigid in its ramifications as the highest strata of white society. If you couldn't prove your ancestry and connections, you were tolerated, but you didn't 'belong'" (8). Because she is more passionate and rebellious than the conservative Laurentine, Helga has even more trouble "belonging." Indeed, she is not certain that she wants to be accepted by black society since she does not completely accept its values.

When the novel opens, Helga is dissatisfied with her position as an English teacher at Naxos, a school for black girls: "Nor was the general atmosphere of Naxos, its air of self-righteousness and intolerant dislike of difference, the best of mediums for a pretty, solitary girl with no family connections" (5). She refuses to wear the subdued colors deemed respectable by the Dean of Women, "a woman from one of the 'first families'"; "'Bright colors are vulgar'--'Black, gray, brown, and navy blue are the most becoming colors for colored people'" (17-18). While the other women at the school wear "drab colors, mostly navy blue, black, brown, unrelieved, save for a scrap of white or tan about the hands and necks" (17), Helga chooses vivid colors and sensuous fabrics that reflect her more passionate nature: "dark purples, royal blues, rich greens, deep reds, in soft luxurious woolens, or heavy, clinging silks" (18). In the opening scene, she is wearing a "vivid green and gold negligee and glistening brocaded mules" (2).[8]

Unhappy as an outcast and unwilling to conform, Helga escapes Naxos, leaving before the school terms ends. Trying to explain why she must leave, she tells the principal: "But I--well--I don't seem to fit here. . . . Then, too, the people here don't like me. They don't think I'm in the spirit of the work. And I'm not, not if it means suppression of individuality and beauty" (19-20). Helga is so determined to escape the oppressive atmosphere at Naxos that she ends her engagement to fellow teacher James Vayle. Her rejection of this socially acceptable man clearly distinguishes Larsen's heroine from the women in Fauset's novels.

In a Fauset novel, James Vayle would be the handsome hero, "the right man." As a member of an Atlanta "first family," he belongs to the best of black society. And he is enough in love to risk alienating his family by marrying a socially obscure woman. Helga, however, is not impressed by Vayle. She finds him stuffy, and instead of allowing him to help her adjust to Naxos, she resents his easy acceptance of the school's restrictive environment. In fact, Helga is so certain that Vayle is the wrong man for her that she rejects him twice, once at Naxos and several years later in Harlem.

If James Vayle is the wrong man for Helga, certainly the man that she finally marries, the Reverend Mr. Pleasant Green, is not the right one. With Reverend Green, Helga finds passion, both in his sermons and in the bedroom. But she is even more out of place in "the tiny Alabama town where he was pastor to a scattered and primitive flock" (118) than she is at Naxos. The women in this town have no time to worry about the "suppression of individuality and beauty"; they are too busy cooking, cleaning, and having babies. Helga even has trouble handling these wifely duties. When her passionate nights with Reverend Green bring her three children in twenty months, she realizes that she is dying more than living, "too driven, too occupied, and too sick to carry out any of the things for which she had made such enthusiastic plans" (123). During the especially painful fourth delivery, she retreats into a weeks-long stupor: "Nothing penetrated the kind darkness into which her bruised spirit had retreated" (128). As her spirit and body recover, Helga plans her escape from the quicksand in which she is mired: "For in some way she was determined to get herself out of this bog into which she had strayed. Or--she would have to die. She couldn't endure it. Her suffocation and shrinking loathing were too great. Not to be borne" (134). But there is no escape, except perhaps through death. *Quicksand* ends with the following chilling sentence: "And hardly had she left her bed and become able to walk again without pain, hardly had the children returned from the homes of the neighbors, when she began to have her fifth child" (135).[9]

Helga's fate--slow death through painful childbirth and suffocation in an unfulfilling marriage to a fat, dirty man so egomaniacal and ignorant that he does not notice his wife's despair--is severe punishment for her failure to conform. And she is punished throughout the novel. Much of that punishment is self-inflicted, the result of ambivalence and inner conflict. As the narrator explains, Helga suffers because "she could neither conform, nor be happy in her unconformity" (7). Although she resents the restrictions placed on her by black society, she does not relish the role of rebel: "For Helga Crane wasn't, after all, a rebel from society, Negro society. It did mean something to her. She had no wish to stand alone" (107). As a wife, she is suffocated; as a single woman, she is isolated. Never at peace, Helga wanders almost literally around the world, searching for "a place for herself" (118). But there is no place for Helga Crane; she is condemned to be forever out of place.

The punishment for a woman "out of place" is even more severe in Larsen's second novel, *Passing* (1929). In that novel, Larsen contrasts two women, the very proper Irene Redfield and the very improper Clare Kendry. Each woman is fair enough to pass as white, but Irene, born into a middle-class family, has married a black doctor and become an important member of Harlem society while Clare, the daughter of an alcoholic janitor, has married a white businessman and become a wealthy, if isolated, white woman.

Irene leads a safe, morally upright life as a wife, mother, and socialite. She spends her time buying gifts for her family, having tea parties for her friends, and supporting her favorite charities by organizing such social events as the Negro Welfare League Dance. Above all else, she values security and tranquillity for herself and her family: "Yet all the while . . . she was aware that, to her, security was the most important and desired thing in life. . . . She wanted only to be tranquil. Only, unmolested, to be allowed to direct for their own best good the lives of her sons and her husband" (235). When she encounters Clare, a childhood acquaintance, Irene immediately recognizes the danger to her own security. She has "a natural and deeply rooted aversion to the kind of front-page notoriety that Clare Kendry's presence" brings (157).

Clare is, as she herself confesses, "not safe." Her life is filled with intrigue, passion, and even terror. She is terrified that her husband will discover her racial identity. During the months before her only child is born, for example, she worries about its complexion: "I nearly died of terror the whole nine months before Margery was born for fear that she might be dark. Thank goodness, she turned out all right. But I'll never risk it again. Never! The strain is simply too-- too hellish" (168). Yet, she dares to socialize in Harlem whenever her husband is out of town. And she does not hesitate to involve the clearly reluctant Irene in her schemes, sending her "furtive" letters with no return address, crashing her parties, and perhaps (Irene believes) having an affair with her husband. In what could be taken as a warning, Clare explains to Irene that they are very different: "It's just that I haven't any proper morals or sense of duty, as you have, that makes me act as I do. . . . Can't you realize that I'm not like you a bit? Why, to get the things I want badly enough, I'd do anything, hurt anybody, throw anything away. Really. 'Rene, I'm not safe" (210).

Nevertheless, although Irene and Clare seem to be quite different, almost opposites, Larsen shows that they have more in common than either of them realizes. Each woman has married the wrong man and is denying some part of herself in order to maintain her marriage. The secretly black Clare has married an unrepentant bigot. Forced to listen without protest to her husband's constant abuse of her own people, she feels lonely and isolated: "I've been so lonely since! You can't know. Not close to a single soul. Never anyone to really talk to" (196). Inevitably, she begins to resent, even hate, the man who calls her "Nig" as a joke and who boasts, "No niggers in my family. Never have been and never will be" (171). Her marriage becomes like a prison with her husband as the jailer. And like many prisoners, Clare contemplates violent rebellion: "Damn Jack! He keeps me out of everything. Everything I want. I could kill him! I expect I shall, some day" (200).

Irene's marriage can also be compared to a prison, but she is the jailer, her husband the prisoner. Brian Redfield is a restless adventurer, trapped in a marriage to a woman who longs for security and stability. Irene struggles to placate her husband and keep him occupied so that he will forget his dream of moving to Brazil. She wants him to be happy, but only on her terms: "It was only that she wanted him to be happy, resenting, however, his inability to be so with things as they were, and never acknowledging that though she did want him to be happy, it was only in her own way and by some plan of hers for him that she truly desired him to be so" (190). Because of their conflicting needs, neither partner is happy in this marriage. Both are frustrated and resentful. And Brian is not the only prisoner; Irene has also imprisoned a part of herself. Although she feels strong emotions--frustration, jealousy, rage--she tries to hide them, clinging to her surface calm and struggling to remain in control. When she hears John Bellew's racist remarks, for example, she fears "that her self-control was about to prove too frail a bridge to support her mounting anger and indignation" (172), but her rage is "held by some dam of caution and allegiance to Clare" (173).

Exposure to such emotionally taxing situations as association with Clare brings is one reason Irene wants to avoid her. But there is another, more significant reason. As Deborah McDowell points out in the introduction to *Quicksand* and *Passing*, Clare disturbs Irene because she "is a reminder of that repressed and disowned part of Irene's self" (xxix). Clare represents the passion that Irene has suppressed in order to maintain her marriage and her place in society.

Apparently, Irene goes even further to save her marriage. There is a strong suggestion that she pushes Clare to her death in the climactic scene:

> She [Irene] ran across the room, her terror tinged with ferocity, and laid a hand on Clare's bare arm. One thought possessed her. She couldn't have Clare Kendry cast aside by Bellew. She couldn't have her free. . . . What happened next, Irene Redfield never afterwards allowed herself to remember.   (239)

If Irene does push Clare, she is not just eliminating a potential rival for Brian. She is also putting an end to the confusion and chaos that Clare has brought into her life. And most important, she is pushing out, destroying that part of herself that Clare represents.

With the death of Clare, Irene can return to directing the lives of her husband and sons. The final scenes of the novel clearly indicate that her marriage will survive. When she goes outside to face the gruesome death scene, Irene takes Brian's coat, leaving hers behind: "Brian! He mustn't take cold. She took up his coat and left her own" (240). But Brian uses the coat to shield his wife: "Brian wrapped his coat about her" (241). They are protecting each other from the coldness of death and of the world. And when Irene faints at the end of the novel, she is "dimly conscious of strong arms lifting her up" (242). The reader understands that those strong arms belong to Brian.

Of course, the price paid to save the marriage is high.   Passion, happiness, and Clare's life are sacrificed. And there is something in Irene's past that she can never allow herself to remember. But it is Clare who pays the ultimate price, just as it is Clare who suffers the most. Because she passes as white, she must endure isolation and humiliation. When she comes to Harlem to be with her own people, she meets death--severe punishment, indeed.

Although she presents a much harsher view of marriage, Larsen's treatment of Helga Crane and Clare Kendry shows that she shares Fauset's belief that the best place for a black woman is beside a black man within black society.   Irene Redfield, the only Larsen heroine who marries within black society, can at least achieve an uneasy peace in her marriage. Helga Crane and Clare Kendry marry men outside black society and suffer the consequences.[10] Deborah McDowell comments on the apparent contradictions implicit in the punishment of Helga and Clare:

> While Larsen criticizes the cover of marriage, as well as other social scripts for women, she is unable in the end to extend that critique to its furthest reaches. In ending the novel with Clare's death, Larsen repeats the narrative choices which *Quicksand*

makes: to punish the very values the novel implicitly affirms, to
honor the very value system the text implicitly satirizes. (xxx-xxxi)

McDowell suggests that Larsen's ambivalence results from her fear of openly
condoning female sexuality.   But I would argue that she is simply following the
novel of manners tradition, the same tradition that Edith Wharton follows in *The
House of Mirth*. Wharton can also be accused of sending conflicting signals in
her novel. While criticizing New York society--and the marriages within it--she
shows that Lily Bart cannot survive outside that society. In the traditional novel
of manners, no lady can survive outside society.

The view of women in society is quite different in *Linden Hills* (1985),
Gloria Naylor's contemporary novel of manners.   In this her second novel,[11]
Naylor depicts a middle-class black society that destroys the people--the women
more relentlessly than the men--who belong to it.

The subjugation of women, particularly wives, is the foundation upon
which this nightmarish society is built.   Founder and patriarch Luther Nedeed
buys his enslaved wife from her white owner but never sets her free. And each
successive Luther Nedeed carefully selects a wife whom he can easily oppress
and ignore.   The early Mrs. Nedeeds are pale, "chosen for the color of their
spirits, not their faces . . . brought to Tupelo Drive to fade against the white-
washed boards of the Nedeed home after conceiving and giving over a son to
the stamp and will of the father" (18).   There is always only one son because
after that child is conceived, the husband never sleeps with the wife again.   Her
only functions are to bear a son, to nurture him until he can walk beside his
father, and then to fade quietly into the background.   These dark-skinned sons
show no signs of their mothers' influence.   They look, walk, think, and act just
like their fathers.

Naylor's fictional society is more conservative and rigidly conformist than
either Fauset's Red Brook or Larsen's Naxos.   Family and marriage are the
cornerstones of the community.   As Luther Nedeed explains, "No one's been
able to make it down to Tupelo Drive without a stable life and a family" (75).[12]
Love is not part of the formula for success in Linden Hills.   Although Winston
Alcott loves his best friend David, he must marry a woman--any well-bred
woman--in order to prosper in Linden Hills.   Uninterested in women, Alcott
selects his wife the way he would choose any other necessary but undesirable
household appliances: "She wanted a husband--I needed a wife. It's straight out
of a soap opera. And they lived happily ever after until the next floor-wax
commercial" (76). So unwanted is this new bride that even the jilted lover pities
her: "David shook his head slowly. 'If that's your attitude, then I feel sorry for
that girl. She's got some life waiting for her'" (76).

Any new wife in Linden Hills has "some life waiting for her." She must be
prepared to give up her rights and her identity. The society is so patriarchal that
a divorced woman is not allowed to live in her husband's ancestral home. When
Laurel Dumont and her husband separate, Nedeed tells her that she must move:
"Whatever is *in* this house and whatever you've added *to* this house is between
you and your husband to divide by whatever laws of whatever century you
choose. But Howard Dumont has decided that there are to be no more Dumonts
at Seven Twenty-Two Tupelo Drive, and according to the original terms of the
lease, that's how things must stand" (244-245). Laurel, who heads a division of

men at IBM, cannot believe that she has no rights in her own home: "There is no way that this conversation is taking place in my living room, with this man looking me straight in the face and telling me that I don't exist. That *I* don't live in this house" (245).

Laurel Dumont is one of three women whose lives Naylor contrasts in the novel. At one point, Laurel reflects on her relationship to the other two women: "In desperation, she thought about the two people who had come the closest to being called friends. The three of them formed a strange triangle where she was in the middle between a woman who admired her and a woman she admired" (240). The woman who admires her is Willa Nedeed, the last of the oppressed Nedeed wives. Willa is a contemporary woman who has accepted the traditional roles of wife and mother: "There was one woman who never went anywhere. She seemed so content nested down there at the end of Tupelo Drive. No, it was more than contentment, a certain smugness as if it were a privilege to wait hand and foot on that prude, Luther. She didn't want a life of her own" (240). Nedeed rewards his wife's devotion by locking her and their son in the basement. Her crime? She gave birth to a pale son who otherwise looked exactly like his father. During her stay in the basement, Willa studies the notes, photo albums, and recipes of the other Nedeed wives. Understanding these records of her foremothers' suffering helps her to find the key to her own existence:

> Willa Nedeed was a good mother and a good wife. For six years, she could claim that identity without any reservation. But now Willa Nedeed sat on a cot in a basement, no longer anyone's mother or anyone's wife. So how did that happen? She stared at the concrete steps leading up to the kitchen door. It happened because she walked down into this basement. . . . She was sitting there now, filthy, cold, and hungry, because she, Willa Prescott Nedeed, had walked down twelve concrete steps. And since that was the truth--the pure irreducible truth--whenever she was good and ready, she could walk back up.   (279-280)

Even though her child is dead and her husband does not want her, Willa is determined to reaffirm her identity as a wife and mother. Having accepted responsibility for her plight, she ascends those twelve concrete steps, carrying her dead child in her arms, moving toward one final tragic union with the father and husband.

While Willa's acceptance of her identity leads, at least indirectly, to her death, Laurel Dumont dies because she has lost her identity. Laurel is an eighties' woman, an overachiever who has risen so swiftly and effortlessly that she has never stopped to think about who she is, where she is going, and why she is going there. She has "lost herself in people's minds" and, like the long-dead Nedeed women, has only faded photographs and newspaper clippings to prove she exists:

> the Phi Beta Kappa pictures in her yearbook, front page of the *New York Times* business section, the bridal pictures in the Dumont family album. All before her twenty-fifth birthday, and in all of them

she had been smiling. No wonder the world pronounced her happy, and like a fool she had believed them. Perhaps, just once, if she had failed a course, missed a plane connection, or glittered less at Howard's parties, she might have had time to think about who she was and what she really wanted, but it never happened. And when she finally took a good look around, she found herself imprisoned within a chain of photographs and a life that had no point. (228)

Like Clare Kendry and Helga Crane, Laurel feels trapped, imprisoned in her high-profile, loveless marriage, in her prestigious but unfulfilling job, and in her impressive but hollow house. And like Helga, she searches in vain for a place to belong, a home:

Georgia wasn't her home, nor Cleveland or California. They had been only way stations that she had passed through. The thought of her dislocation was stifling; the number of places she couldn't claim, dizzying. She had stopped at them all only long enough to get her pictures taken. And just maybe if she could freeze reality around her now, she'd know where she belonged. And with that reference point--with any point at all--she could discover what had gone wrong. (233)

The place where Laurel feels least at home is 722 Tupelo Drive, the house "that defied all their efforts to transform it into that nebulous creation called a home" (227-228). Her house has an emptiness that even her music cannot fill, and she feels utterly alone there. Eventually, she stops trying to find a place for herself; she stops caring. Laurel escapes from her pain in the same way that Helga escaped the pain of childbirth; she retreats from reality. And finally, she chooses the ultimate escape, leaping to her death at the bottom of an empty swimming pool.

Ruth Anderson, the third woman in the triangle, finds a less destructive way to escape the Linden Hills trap. She divorces her respectable husband, moves to an unfashionable neighborhood, and marries a mentally unstable, working-class man. At first, Laurel pities her friend, but she soon learns to admire her:

Strange, she had started calling out of pity for Ruth: a broken marriage and losing that house on Fifth Crescent Drive. And then remarrying a man who was a mental patient and worked in factories--when he could work. But slowly, very slowly, she began to sense that Ruth was actually pitying her--as if Laurel were mired down there on Tupelo Drive and the best thing that could have happened to Ruth was that divorce and moving back to Wayne Avenue. Laurel kept calling because she admired that in the woman: the ability to pretend with such ease. No, she kept calling because she admired *that* woman, *that* ease. And she became the pretender. (240-241)

There is certainly much to admire in Ruth. She stays with Norman Anderson even when he succumbs to the "pinks" (much more frightening than the blues) and smashes everything around him. And although she lives in a seedy apartment with only the few pieces of furniture that Norman has not smashed, she has created a home: "Visitors found themselves thinking, What a nice feeling to be allowed into a home. And it *was* a home with its bare wood floors, dusted and polished, and with the three pieces of furniture that sat in three large rooms: one sofa in the living room, one kitchenette set with plastic-bottomed chairs on uncertain chrome legs, one bed" (33). The Anderson apartment is a home because it is filled with love rather than with material possessions. Ruth and Norman take care of each other, and they care for each other. Their love will survive because it exists outside Linden Hills.

Although Ruth rejects her society husband and the Linden Hills society, she is not punished for her rebellion. On the contrary, she is the only woman in the novel who has found love and even some happiness. And significantly, of the three women contrasted, she is the only survivor.

In *Linden Hills*, the outsiders survive while the society is destroyed, its foundation, the Nedeed home, burning to the ground with the last Nedeed heirs inside. Clearly, Gloria Naylor is taking the novel of manners in a new direction. Her novel rejects the value system of the society depicted and affirms the values of the individual, the nonconformist. Ruth Anderson has chosen love and compassion instead of material possessions and success. She has chosen happiness instead of stability and security. And she has chosen wisely. As Laurel suspects, the best thing that happened to Ruth was moving back to unfashionable Wayne Avenue. It took her away from the living death, the nothingness of life in Linden Hills.[13] In this new novel of manners, the best place for a lady is outside society.

Endnotes

[1] In chapter 6 of *Vanity Fair*, Thackeray's narrator describes how the novel might have been written:
We might have treated this subject in the genteel, or in the romantic, or in the facetious manner. Suppose we had laid the scene in Grosvenor Square, with the very same adventures--would not some people have listened? Suppose we had shown how Lord Joseph Sedley fell in love, and the Marquis of Osborne became attached to Lady Amelia, with the full consent of the Duke, her noble father: or instead of the supremely genteel, suppose we had resorted to the entirely low, and described what was going on in Mr. Sedley's kitchen;--how black Sambo was in love with the cook (as indeed he was), and how he fought a battle with the coachman in her behalf. (54)
[2] See James W. Tuttleton (127) and Richard Chase (157-158).
[3] For a discussion of the Talented Tenth novelists, see Robert Bone (29-50).
[4] Later in the novel, Wharton demonstrates that her heroine has no other vocation. When Lily tries working in a millinery establishment, she is a failure, much too slow and clumsy to compete with the sallow-faced working-class women whom she has pitied. Similarly, in *Vanity Fair*, Amelia Sedley tries in vain to market the skills that she acquired at Miss Pinkerton's "academy for young ladies." When she tries to sell some of her art, the response is scornful: "'Don't want 'em,' says one. 'Be off,' says another fiercely" (476).
[5] In "New Directions for Black Feminist Criticism," Deborah E. McDowell points out that the dominant attitude toward women expressed in the "little" magazines of the Harlem Renaissance period was "strikingly consistent with traditional middle-class expectations of women" (192). Most contributors "emphasized that a woman's place was in the home."
[6] In "Patterns of the Harlem Renaissance," George Kent says of Nella Larsen, "Her work suggests that she had taken more than passing notice of Henry James and Edith Wharton" (43).

And in "Under the Harlem Shadow: A Study of Jessie Fauset and Nella Larsen," Hiroko Sato says, "Jessie Fauset's novels can be regarded as novels of manners of the Negro upper class" (67). See Sato (71) for a discussion of the differences between Fauset and Jane Austen.

[7] One Fauset woman does marry a white man. In *Comedy: American Style*, Teresa Cary yields to the pressures of her mother, who insists upon trying to pass, and marries a Frenchman. Teresa, who gave up a black man too dark to pass, does not have a successful marriage.

[8] In her introduction to *Quicksand* and *Passing*, Deborah E. McDowell says that Larsen is using "clothing as iconography" to capture the conflicts between Helga and Naxos (xviii). See also "New Directions for Black Feminist Criticism," 194. For a discussion of the use of "dress or decoration" in the novel of manners, see Lionel Trilling, "Manners, Morals, and the Novel," included in *The Liberal Imagination*.

[9] In her introduction to *Quicksand* and *Passing*, McDowell says, "Like so many novels by women, *Quicksand* likens marriage to death for women" (xxi).

[10] It is significant that Irene is called by her husband's last name while Clare is always Kendry, never Bellew, and Helga is called Mrs. or "Mis" Green only by other characters, never by the narrator. Clearly, Larsen does not sanction the marriages of Helga and Clare.

[11] Naylor's first novel, *The Women of Brewster Place* (1983), focuses on the lower class.

[12] Naylor plays with "up" and "down" throughout the novel. Because the more exclusive houses in Linden Hills are down the hill, people on the way up move down. But as these people are moving (which is down), they are also going down physically, morally, and spiritually. And so when they reach the bottom of the hill, they have also reached the "bottom" spiritually. "And whenever anyone reached the Tupelo area, they eventually disappeared. Finally, devoured by their own drives, there just wasn't enough humanity left to fill the rooms of a real home, and the property went up for sale" (17-18). Clearly, the move down toward Tupelo Drive is a descent into hell.

[13] The concluding sentence of Frazier's *The Black Bourgeoisie* provides an apt description of Linden Hills: "The black bourgeoisie suffers from 'nothingness' because when Negroes attain middle-class status, their lives generally lose both content and significance" (238).

Works Cited

This Works Cited entry has been constructed by the co-editors from citations noted in the original manuscript; it did not appear as part of the published essay.

Bone, Robert. *The Negro Novel in America*. New Haven: Yale UP, 1958, 1965.

Fauset, Jessie. *The Chinaberry Tree*. 1931. New York: Negro Universities P, 1969.

Frazier, Edward F. *The Black Bourgeoisie*. Glencoe: Free P, 1957.

Larsen, Nella. *Passing*. 1929. New York: Arno P, 1969.

_____. *Quicksand*. 1928. New York: Negro Universities P, 1969.

McDowell, Deborah. "Introduction." *Quicksand* and *Passing*. New Brunswick: Rutgers UP, 1986.

Naylor, Gloria. *Linden Hills*. New York: Penguin, 1985.

Sato, Hiroko. "Under the Harlem Shadow: A Study of Jessie Fauset and Nella Larsen." *The Harlem Renaissance Remembered*. Ed. Arna Bontemps. New York: Dodd, Mead, 1972.

Thackeray, William Makepeace. *Vanity Fair* 1848 Boston. Houghton, 1963.

Wharton, Edith. *The House of Mirth*. 1905. New York Scribners, 1922.

Boyd, Nellie. "Dominion and Proprietorship in Gloria Naylor's *Mama Day* and *Linden Hills*." *MAWA Review* 5.2 (Dec. 1990): 56-58.

In Gloria Naylor's *Mama Day* and *Linden Hills* are two communities, and each has an acknowledged leader who controls its land and inhabitants. The two types of control exercised are dominion and proprietorship.

Dominion denotes having supreme authority, sovereignty, or controlling influence over a land. Mama Day has dominion over Willow Springs, a mystical island between the borders of South Carolina and Georgia. But, it really is in neither state because Sapphira Wade, Mama Day's great grandmother, conjured it away from her slave owner in the early 1800's. Since that time neither South Carolina nor Georgia has been able to decide which state should have the island. It is an isolated island where, like Prospero's island in Shakespeare's *The Tempest*, the natural and the supernatural merge.

Mama Day does not legally own all of Willow Springs, but she is clearly the acknowledged leader and controlling influence of the island. From her modest trailer on the family's property, Mama Day reigns over Willow Springs. From here, she dispenses the necessary wisdom, concern, wit, ethics, and herbal cures to protect her domain and the individuals within it. In essence, she is the island's conscience.

Her leadership and influence and dominion are evident when developers first come to the island attempting to purchase land. The Willow Springs residents immediately send them directly to her. When she refuses their offer, everyone refuses because, in their words, "if Mama Day say no, everybody say no" (6). There is such a finality to her decision that both the developers and the island residents know there is not a chance of anyone even contemplating saying yes to the developers while Mama Day is alive. For she has seen developers come to nearby islands, develop them, and make high profits, but none of the original islanders benefited. In fact they were worse off than before the developers came. She believes that the developers and other outside influences only mean trouble for her and other Willow Springs residents.

Her beliefs and concerns about the negative impact of outside influences are reinforced when Reema's Boy returns to Willow Springs after receiving a college education and the ideas of outsiders from the mainland. Even though he has grown up on the island, he now rejects the islander's traditions, pride, and viewpoints. Now he only wants to see and know through the eyes of those who lived beyond the bridge who had educated him.

The islanders believed if he really wanted to know and understand their traditions, pride, and viewpoints, he would have asked their acknowledged leader and conscience, Mama Day, or her sister Abigail. They also believe that the people who ran the type of schools that could turn their own children into raving lunatics like Reema's Boy--"and then put his picture on the back of the book so [they] couldn't even deny it was him--didn't mean [them] a speck of good" (8).

Naylor uses Sue Henry as a second example to reinforce Mama Day's concern about the negative influence of Willow Springs residents who go off "to fancy schools and settle beyond the bridge--they start forgetting how to talk to folks" (77). Sue Henry works for a physician. When she receives an emergency call from Ambush, whom she has known all of her life, she callously tells

Ambush he must wait until the next day before the doctor can see his wife. This statement is made even before she consults with the doctor.

Since Sue Henry obviously finds it difficult to feel emotion or sympathy for the plight of others, Mama Day becomes her conscience. She intervenes and tells Sue Henry that she will be accountable to her if Dr. Smithfield is not asked immediately to come and help Bernice. Needless to say, Sue Henry immediately calls on Dr. Smithfield, who comes that day to help Ambush's wife.

Because of experiences such as those with the developers, Reema's Boy and Sue Henry, Mama Day has learned to be distrustful of outside recognition and influences. For the developers, Reema's Boy, and Sue Henry are not aware that the modest physical appearance of the island and its inhabitants is not a reflection of the wit, strength, and spiritual wealth of the island. Like Antonio, who saw only barren, parched land when Gonzalo proclaimed the lush green beauty of Prospero's island in *The Tempest*, these three cannot appreciate the true beauty of Willow Springs because they do not possess the spiritual wealth and feeling of community shared by Mama Day and the Willow Springs residents. They cannot see that Mama Day and the residents are concerned about preserving a sense of community, their unique ways and harmony with nature. Mama Day is aware that with material acquisitions, recognition, and real estate development by outsiders will come the destruction of their way of life and the values that have been preserved for more than a century.

True of one who has dominion, Mama Day is not only determined to oversee and protect land usage but she is determined to protect the residents of Willow Springs. Naylor reveals this to us in Mama Day's relationship with Bernice Duvall. She sympathizes with Bernice's plaintive yearning to have a baby. Because she sympathizes, she chastises Bernice's mother-in-law for constantly ridiculing and neglecting Bernice. Mama Day threatens Dr. Buzzard, the island's inefficacious hoodoo doctor when he tells her, "If Bernice comes to me for help, I'm helping her. . . and in all due respect, like you said, it ain't none of your business" (51). Mama Day replies:

> "It ain't, Buzzard, it really ain't. And that's why it would cause me no end of sorrow to make it so. Cause the way I see it, you been walking round on this earth a long time and got just as much right as the next fella to keep walking around, healthy and all--living out your natural life." (51)

After she voices her threat, Dr. Buzzard quickly decides not to use his hoodoo medicines to help Bernice, even if she does come to him for help.

Mama Day knows and cares for the people of Willow Springs and she works in harmony with nature. Thus, when the time is right, she uses her knowledge of nature and herbal cures to enable Bernice to conceive a child.

Also true of one who has dominion, Mama Day recognizes Willow Springs' uniqueness and takes pride in preserving it. She is proud of the annual December 22 celebration of Candle Walk, which is celebrated as a way of receiving help from neighbors without having to compromise one's pride and a way of saying thank you for favors received during the year. Yet, even as she encourages its celebration and preservation in her domain, she recognizes that people and traditions change with time. When some of her neighbors express concern about the unique Candle Walk celebration changing and possibly ceasing in the future, Mama Day recalls how it differed to some extent in each of the three generations prior to this one. She tells them it is logical to expect and accept changes in the subsequent generations' manner of celebrating the holiday.

Because of this mother wit Naylor has ascribed to Mama Day, she has a tolerance for those who do not share her philosophy about life as long as they do not threaten harm to loved ones within her domain. She tolerates Dr. Buzzard's claims to be the most powerful hoodoo person on the island until he says he will offer his questionable services to help Bernice Duvall. She also tolerates Ruby's hoodoo works to gain the affections of Junior, Frances' common-law husband even though she does not condone Ruby's actions. It is not until Ruby harms her niece Cocoa that Ruby feels the wrath and punishment of Mama Day.

However, in Naylor's *Linden Hills*, Luther Nedeed shows no such tolerance for anyone whose lifestyle is different from the way he wants it to be. He also has no empathy or true concern for the individual residents of Linden Hills. He is only concerned about developing a community which preserves the image of prosperity and success to outsiders as they look unto Linden Hills.

Luther Nedeed's role was that of proprietor, one who has the legal right or exclusive title to something: the owner. He owned and leased the land in Linden Hills, a striking affluent community in Wayne County. He is solely concerned with the promotion and preservation of this display of material success to outsiders. Like his father, he believes Linden Hills has "to be a showcase . . . a jewel--an ebony jewel that reflected the soul of Wayne County but reflected it in black" (9). As proprietor, Luther Nedeed believes it is necessary to control who is permitted to become tenants in Linden Hills and to control how these residents live. To gain one of the Linden Hills lots, which Luther Nedeed never sells but leases for 1001 years, each of the residents must give up something: "a part of his soul, ties with his past, ties with his community, his spiritual values, even his sense of who he is" (Ward 70). In essence, Luther Nedeed wants, in his father's words, only "carbon paper dolls" as Linden Hills residents (10).

Because he is only concerned with preserving Linden Hills as he and his forebearers envisioned it, Luther Nedeed does not tolerate the relationship between Winston Alcott and his friend David. Nedeed believes that only heterosexual relationships or unions are good for the community's image. Consequently, he provides Winston Alcott with a choice, either enter into a heterosexual relationship and marry or be exposed at his law firm and be expelled from Linden Hills, thus sacrificing his career and status. Luther feels no concern for Winston, Winston's bride, or David. He feels no remorse even when he predicts that within five years Winston will probably commit suicide like Laurel Dumont, whom he passively watched as she committed suicide. He chose not to stop Laurel because she no longer fit his idea of a desirable Linden Hills resident.

Luther Nedeed believes that even his family functions solely as "carbon paper dolls" or just another working part of his prized property, Linden Hills. His relationship with his wife, Willa, is void of emotion and genuine concern. She is regarded solely as a necessary entity for the reproduction of a son who would inherit and continue to oversee Linden Hills. This is evidenced in the process he uses to choose her as his wife. He always considered choosing his wife as a business venture. First, he methodically and patiently waits until the right moment to pick the perfect woman to reside in Tupelo Drive. He remembers:

> . . . [how] at his tenth college reunion, he'd moved carefully among the . . . [women] who had never managed to marry at all by that time. And he notices those who had lost that hopeful, arrogant strut. . . . And tipping the scale at thirty, the only thing they envisioned for their future was dying alone. Marriage was a sign of relief at that age. . . . [The perfect woman] would quickly forget the foolish dreams that she'd had for a mate ten years ago. She was more than willing to join the life and rhythms of almost any man-- and for a man like himself, she'd bend over backward. (67-68)

Luther actually believes Willa, his chosen bride, was offered a perfectly fair arrangement. In return for Willa's coming into his home and respecting him and the routines of his house, which include producing a son identical to him, he is prepared to permit her to make any purchases without a question. Consequently, when Willa provides him with a son who does not look exactly like him, he feels she has broken the terms of his marital arrangement. He no longer regards her as an appropriate wife for him or an appropriate "first lady" of Linden Hills. He definitely does not regard his son as an acceptable son and heir. Not surprisingly, he no longer permits his wife and child to be seen in Linden Hills. They are evicted from the main living quarters of his home and are locked in the basement, which once served as his mortuary.

In essence, Luther Nedeed regards Linden Hills and its tenants as a business enterprise to be managed and presented as a black showcase of materialistic success and a void of humaneness. According to Henry Louis Gates, Jr.:

> . . . Naylor has conveniently located a historian in the novel to help explain this bivalent situation. Nedeed's organization sponsors not only members of the corporate elite, as it happens, but also historians who analyze these orders. Sententious and decrepit though he is, Braithwaite's analysis of the phenomenon of Linden Hills is considerably more nuanced--and cogent--than most readers allow for: These were to be black homes with black aspirations and histories--for good or evil. (618)

Like Marlowe's Dr. Faustus, who decided to "sell his soul to the devil" in return for knowledge and power, aspiring Linden Hills residents sell their souls to Luther Nedeed in exchange for a place in Linden Hills. In their compromises they all find themselves engulfed in various degrees of sin similar to those individuals in Dante's *Inferno*. "Naylor's Linden Hills, like Dante's Hell, represents not so much a place as a state: the consequences of man's choices" (Ward 68). Consequently, it is not unexpected that following the leadership of this powerful, satanic proprietor, the greater the material success and outside recognition residents experience, the shallower they become. The closer they move in proximity to the Nedeed household, the closer they mirror Nedeed's lack of soul.

In contrast, Mama Day also cares for and wants to preserve her domain, Willow Springs. But she cares for the welfare of its individual residents. She simply wants to preserve the humaneness of its residents. She wants them to remain in harmony with nature and to retain a sense of community, ties with the past, and spiritual values. Mama Day knows that with outside materialistic influences and recognition will come the demise of the soul of Willow Springs.

Naylor uses the concept of dominion and proprietorship in *Mama Day* and *Linden Hills* to underscore the novels' serious moral tone. The ethos of Mama Day and Luther Nedeed as acknowledged community leaders is mirrored in their leadership styles, which are in turn mirrored in the ethos of their communities. The Willow Springs residents, as they reflect the ethos of Mama Day's dominion, retain their soul, conscience, past, and sense of who they are. However, Linden Hills residents sever ties with their past, their sense of community, and their spiritual values. They, like Luther Nedeed, have no soul and no conscience. Naylor is suggesting that the subject of who we are and what we are willing to give up of who we are to get where we want to go is indeed a subject of utmost seriousness.

Works Cited

Gates, Henry Louis, Jr. "Significant Others." *Contemporary Literature* 29.8 (1988): 606-623.
Naylor, Gloria. *Linden Hills*. New York: Ticknor & Fields, 1985.
_____. *Mama Day*. New York: Ticknor & Fields, 1988.
Ward, Catherine C. "Gloria Naylor's *Linden Hills*: A Modern *Inferno*." *Contemporary Literature* 28.1 (1987): 67-81.

Collins, Grace E. "Narrative Structure in *Linden Hills*." *CLA Journal* 34.3 (1991): 290-300.

In her second novel, *Linden Hills*, Gloria Naylor dramatizes the possible negative consequences of achieving the American Dream, an achievement which has eluded most African-Americans for over a century. At a time when education as a means of social mobility is being touted as a savior for African-Americans, Naylor raises serious questions about that means as well as its ends. In the novel, Naylor presents a series of stark vignettes of well-educated, successful, middle-class African-Americans (mostly males) who have achieved the dream at the expense of their racial identities. To emphasize her theme, Naylor employs counterpoint, creating two simultaneous narratives that together explore the loss of racial identity and the need for retrieving that identity. The result is a candid examination of the middle-class black American in the 1980s.

Since its publication in 1985, *Linden Hills* has been analyzed from several perspectives. Critics have examined the novel's indebtedness to Dante's *Inferno*, its treatment of the theme of sisterhood, its portrayal of a perverted Eden, and its relationship to Plato's Cave. What has not been closely examined, however, is the intricate structure of the novel. Naylor juxtaposes the main narrative (Willie's odyssey through hell) with that of Willa, trapped in the vestibule of hell, to draw a damning portrait of misdirected lives.

All critics acknowledge the equal importance of Willie and Willa in Naylor's treatment of the complex issue of racial identity. Larry Andrews has aptly observed that "even their names--Willie and Willa--seem mysteriously connected."[1] In fact, the similarity of names is no accident: "Willie" and "Willa" are diminutives of the name "William," which means "resolute warrior," "protector," or "defender." It is the wills of these two protagonists that unite two seemingly episodic, disparate narratives which coalesce in a frightening dénouement.

Moreover, Willie's literal journal through Linden Hills, set in Roman type, and Willa's psychological journey to self-discovery, printed in sans serif bold, illuminate each other in terms of theme and plot and emphasize the sterility of the other characters. The type also accentuates Willa's isolation, for her narrative resembles a dream sequence. However, once Willa realizes that she has a will, that she can choose to ascend the steps, Naylor abandons sans serif bold, symbolically incorporating Willa's regeneration into the dénouement. Significantly, it is at this point that Willie and Willa meet, for it is Willie's unconscious action, almost an act of grace, that frees Willa from her prison, just as it had been Willa's plaintive cry that had set Willie on his spiritual quest. According to Catherine Ward,

> Willie passes through Linden Hills and, like Dante, analyzes the moral failure of the lost souls he encounters. By the time Willie escapes from the frozen lake at the bottom of Linden Hills and crosses to the safety of a nearby apple orchard, he has experienced a spiritual awakening.[2]

Ward places Willa in the frozen lake, the final circle of hell reserved for traitors, but Willa can more appropriately be placed in the vestibule of hell, in the "miserable condition of the sorry souls who lived without infamy and without praise."[3] In his commentary on *Inferno*, J. Freccero writes of these sorry souls:

> With the abstention from action, they deprived themselves of the one positive element which could win them a place in the cosmos. They are as close to nothing as creatures can be and still exist, for by their double negation, they have all but totally removed themselves from the picture. To be deprived of action is to be deprived of love, and love is the law of Dante's cosmos. . . . There remains nothing for them but the vaguely defined vestibule of hell, and they merit no more than a glance from the pilgrim before he passes on to the realm of love perverted. (qtd. in Dante, trans. Singleton, Part 2, 45).[4]

Willa, at first, denies spiritual kinship with her predecessors, Luwana Packerville and Evelyn Creton, because, she stoutly tells herself, she had "coped and they were crazy. They never changed."[5] Willa wants only what she considers a "normal" life. Naylor, however, makes it clear that all these women will be imprisoned both physically and psychically until they are able to act--to vent true rage at both their plights and their captors.

Willie also has a concept of "normal" life. Even though, allegorically, Willie can be seen as a Dante traveling through hell toward enlightenment (directed by Ruth rather than Beatrice), first and foremost he is the young, disadvantaged black American who has been tantalized by the idea of "progress" for African-Americans. His naive ideas about the way in which the privileged live are tested through what he witnesses in Linden Hills. Willie has assumed that a place like Linden Hills has something to offer him, but his bewilderment increases as he sees both the spiritual decay of the residents and the fences--real and metaphorical--which have been built around the schools, the libraries, the churches. For example, he says to Lester,

> I've seen things done to people down here that are a lot worse than anyone would have the heart to do up in Putney Wayne. 'Cause you see, it takes a lot of honesty. Shit--honest hate or rage or whatever--to pick up a knife and really cut a man's throat. And you're right, it could never happen here in Linden Hills 'cause these people can't seem to find the guts to be honest about anything.   (193)

Willie's example is not an espousal of violence; instead, it is the young poet's metaphor for the degree to which delusion exists in Linden Hills. Willie later realizes that "if anything was the problem in Linden Hills, it was that nothing seemed to be what it really was" (274).

Both Willie and Willa are "outsiders," existential observers of life in Linden Hills. So dark that he has been nicknamed "White," Willie, a high school dropout and poet from nearby Putney Wayne, spends four days in Linden Hills working as a handyman with his light-skinned friend Lester (Baby Shit), a resident of the affluent community. Willa, with her child, has been banished by her husband to the basement, an abandoned morgue, to reflect upon and to "atone" for her alleged sin of infidelity: her son is almost white.

Thus, the "tragic mulatto" theme is introduced early in the novel, reinforcing the importance of racial roots. Although Luther Nedeed V, like the Luthers before him, is dark, he seems to forget that many of his maternal forebears were light. In rejecting his own pale son, Luther destroys the design of Linden Hills. The consequences of his racial astigmatism are skillfully delineated in the contrapuntal narratives, and the irony is underscored in his invitation to Willie and Lester to help trim his Christmas tree so "there would be three pairs of hands to decorate it, two dark and one fair" (287).

The dating is integral to the structure of the novel. Using no chapter numbers, Naylor marks each section of the novel by its date--December 19 to December 24, the time of the winter solstice. It is on December 19 that Willie and Lester are startled by the plaintive cry for "lost time" emanating from lower Linden Hills. The December 20 section opens with the imprisoned woman's plea for the lost seconds: "Just give her one so she could save her child" (66). At that moment, Willa is circling in time, using only her memories to calculate the passage of seasons, days, hours, seconds. Finally, however, her examination of the lives of her predecessors places her within the context of history, bringing her to the present--December 24--and to the will to act.

The parallel journeys of Willa and Willie begin on December 19, when Naylor abruptly shifts scenes from Luther's shutting off the water to the basement to Willa's hearing the water gushing to the rhythm "Iwantyoutolive" (70). Willa drifts off to sleep, cradling her dead child; Lester and Willie wake up in the same cradled position to begin their work in Linden Hills.

The boys' first job is to help at the wedding reception of Winston Alcott, who has repudiated his eight-year homosexual relationship with David to marry for the sake of "respectability." Observing the well-dressed guests, Willie notices that "something was missing from the jeweled sparkle in the air" (83). What is missing, he concludes, is spontaneity. As Willie watches Winston Alcott dancing with his bride, he is appalled to see that "that guy looks like someone had punched him in the stomach and his lips sorta froze up that way" (86). The consequences of Winston's denial of his true feelings are symbolized in Luther's presenting the couple with a "one thousand and one year" mortgage for a house on Tupelo Drive, which is below Winston's former residence at two Crescent Drive and nearer to Nedeed's home. As Catherine Ward has pointed out, "In Linden Hills up is down; the most prestigious lots are those lower down the hill" (70). Winston's future is best summed up early in the novel by the thoughts of Luther Nedeed:

> Unlike his fathers, he welcomed those who thought they had personal convictions and deep ties to their past, because then he had the pleasure of watching their bewilderment as it all melted away the farther down they came. . . . And whenever anyone reached the Tupelo area, they eventually disappeared.   (18)

Like the Nedeed men, Winston has married for convenience, not love; thus his home, a descent into lower hell, will be as spiritually barren as Luther Nedeed's.

The December 20 wedding section then shifts to the abandoned morgue, where Mrs. Nedeed searches for something in which to wrap her dead son. She finds a gauzy, yellowing bridal veil which smells of mildew and dust, a symbolic reminder to the reader of Winston's tenuous relationship with his bride. After drawing this correlation, Naylor introduces the Bible of Luwana Packerville Nedeed, dated 1837, in which Luwana has written, "There is no God" (93).

Thus, obliquely, Naylor sets the stage for the entrance, in the December 21 section, of Maxwell Smyth and Xavier Donnell, two black Ivy League college graduates who have successfully climbed the corporate ladder to become "Super Niggers" (Xavier's term). Viewing himself as a high priest worshipping "a fragile god" (the Super Nigger image), Xavier knows that if the image ever tumbled down, "his own fate wasn't too far behind" (99). He fears that marrying Roxanne (a strong black woman) will topple him from his present position. Essentially, Maxwell is a caricature of what Xavier is eventually to become--a black man who has submerged his blackness in the "Super Nigger" image. After changing the spelling of his name to S-M-Y-T-H, Maxwell has sought other ways to deny his blackness:

> The trick was now to juggle other feats that would continually minimize his handicap to nothing more than a nervous tic. In college he found that his blackness began to disappear behind his straight A average, and his reputation for never sweating or getting cold. . . . Always immaculate and controlled, he kept them all

wondering how it was done, so there was little time to think about
who was doing it.   (103)

Indeed, Maxwell Smyth's "entire life became a race against the natural--and he
was winning" (104). Maxwell's attempt to force emphasis on *what* he is rather
than *who* he is is an attempt to erase his true self as well as his racial heritage.

Maxwell's total alienation from his race becomes more apparent to Willie
when Maxwell shows the boys a picture of a black model in a *Penthouse*
centerfold as an example of progress: "Today, *Penthouse,* my friends, and
tomorrow the world" (116). Naylor vividly describes the sensuous photograph:

> There was an eight-page spread of a lush, tropical forest and a
> very dark-skinned model with a short Afro. Her airbrushed body
> glistened between the thin leopard strips that crisscrossed under
> her high, pointed breasts and fastened behind her back. She wore
> a pair of high, leopard-skin boots that stopped just below her
> knees, and she was posed to pull against an iron chain that was
> wrapped around her clenched fists. Each page offered the reader
> a different view of her perfectly formed pelvis, hips, and hints of her
> manicured pubic hair as she wrestled with the chain held by an
> invisible hand off camera. (115)

Unlike Maxwell, Willie views the picture as social regression: it represents
blacks still in slavery; even worse, the model is a "dead ringer for his baby sister"
(116).

Immediately following Willie's revelation, Willa learns from notes in the
old Bible that Luwana Packerville, bought by her husband, remained a slave,
even though her son had been manumitted when he was two years old.
Luwana's slave status reiterates the message sent by the *Penthouse*
photograph: women are still psychologically and physically enslaved. Therefore,
it is significant that Luwana makes no entries in the Gospel sections of the Bible,
testaments of Christ's redemptive love. In her loveless, powerless state, Luwana
can find nothing in the Gospels to guide her.   Reading Luwana's desperate
letters to herself, Willa finds the meaning of the abrupt ending of the diary "in the
beginning" (125)--There is no God.

In the same section, Willa's examination of the recipe books of Evelyn
Creton (the second Mrs. Nedeed) immediately follows the boys' experience at
the Parker wake, where guests gather, eat voraciously, and leave the table set
for twelve. According to Ward, "[t]he scene is a depraved parody of the Last
Supper as Parker's guests stuff themselves with food, especially with the white
cake that Luther Nedeed brings" (75). The December 22 section opens with
Willie's nightmare:

> Willie, eat it. . . . Eat it. . . . Willie opened another glass door and
> ran down the dark corridor, his knees pulling the bed covers from
> his shoulders and chin as he tried to escape the hands that shot
> out from the long row of erect coffins on his right side. But each
> step materialized another casket, another pale hand with bright red
> fingernails growing and curling like snakes around the cake that

was offered in a shrill echo emerging from those open depths. Willie, eat it. . . . Eat it. (145)

"Will he eat it? Her trembling hands smoothed down the yellowing page" (147). So Willa Nedeed discovers the way in which Evelyn Creton compensated for a life of emotional deprivation: gluttony, purgatives, aphrodisiacs. Whatever the reason for their sexual inadequacy (perhaps the necrophilia at which Naylor hints), the Nedeed men have always used astrology to determine the proper time for conception. Luther V, when he sees his son's complexion, agonizes: "It had been infallible for generations, so what was wrong now?" (19).

The dramatic tension accelerates in the December 22 section with the presentation of the Reverend Michael Hollis, once a profligate young law student who had suddenly felt called to the ministry, drawn by the "raw power that raced" from the preacher's pulpit to the back of the church: "The presence of that type of power connected up with something in his center, where it transformed fear into fascination and mortality into meaning" (159). However, once he sells out to the established church in Linden Hills, his crushing disappointment over his sterility plunges him into licentiousness and drunkenness. On the morning of the Parker funeral, he looks into the mirror and sees a face "that has no reason to live" (164). Willie's aversion to Hollis's degeneration stresses the vastness of the minister's separation from his roots and from his identity as an "agent of God" (177). In Willa's parallel narrative, Willa discovers that the sexually frustrated Evelyn Creton has killed herself with rat poison. Naylor thus links the sexual inadequacy of Hollis to that of Evelyn Nedeed's husband. Simultaneously, Willie and Willa are learning the true extent of perversion in Linden Hills.

Like Hollis, Laurel, in the December 23 section, has abandoned a dream. As Hollis (Michael, the archangel) was to be the agent of God, so Laurel (crown of Olympic victors) was to be the first black Olympic swimmer. Instead, she becomes a resident of Linden Hills, wife of a thousand-and-one-year tenant. Laurel's grandmother Roberta epitomizes the heritage that Linden Hills has destroyed, a loss illustrated by Laurel's inability to appreciate the music of Bessie Smith or Billie Holliday or Muddy Waters. Roberta tells Laurel that blues says "I can" in response to misery; Roberta realizes that Laurel is looking for a spiritual home in her classical music, but she also knows that first Laurel must be at home with herself (236-237). Thus, Naylor draws a further parallel between Hollis and Laurel: Hollis's recognition of his loss is marked by his substitution of "Amazing Grace" for the establishment hymn that Nedeed had chosen. Perhaps Laurel's suicide is a final act of honesty, her recognition that she has traded love for an illusion.

Laurel's tragedy is indeed symbolic of the self-betrayal of the other characters who inhabit Linden Hills. Early in the novel, as Luther Nedeed thinks, when carefully selecting his tenants,

The Tupelo Realty Corporation offered them all this, and a memory was a small price to pay. . . . He'd cultivate no madmen like Nat Turner or Marcus Garvey in Linden Hills--that would only get them crushed back into the dust. . . . Yes, they would invest their past and apprentice their children to the future of Linden Hills, forgetting that a magician's supreme act is not in transformation but in making things disappear. (11, 12)

The theme of invisibility, a constant in African-American literature, provides the clue to the events of the novel. Laurel's suicide and Willie's finding her facedown (and faceless) in the empty pool weave together Willie's nightmare of being called "faceless" and Willa's discovery that Priscilla McGuire Nedeed is becoming faceless in the photographs as Priscilla's husband, Luther, and his growing namesake completely overshadow Priscilla's once vibrant expression until Priscilla finally writes across the blur that was once her face--"Me." Having gained valuable insight from her predecessors, Willa must now grow from her knowledge. In a recorded conversation with Toni Morrison, Naylor comments,

> After she had dug up the remnants of other Nedeed women, I created a way for her to see her own reflection in a pan of water because she had no self up to that moment. And when she realized that she had a face, then maybe she had other things going for her as well, and she could take her destiny in her own hands.[6]

Early on Christmas Eve, the sleepless Willie wrestles with his ideas until he is finally able to compose the first line of a poem which will crystallize his experiences: "There is a man in a house at the bottom of a hill. And his wife has no name" (277). Immediately following Willie's lines come the words which introduce Willa's awakening: "Her name was Willa Prescott Nedeed." Until this point, almost at the end of the novel, the woman has indeed been nameless, but now, at last, Willa is emerging from mourning and despair. As Willie, the poet, is able to provide himself with the missing link to his puzzling thoughts, so Willa is now able to identify herself as a woman. Furthermore, as Willie, alone with his thoughts, is able to declare that there is no such thing as fate or predestination, that people make choices in their lives, so Willa is able to affirm that she, Willa Nedeed, can make choices:

> She was sitting there now, filthy, cold, and hungry, because she, Willa Prescott Nedeed, had walked down twelve concrete steps. And since that was the truth--the pure, irreducible truth--whenever she was good and ready, she could walk back up.   (280)

In the conversation with Morrison, Naylor says that when she realized that Willa, content to be mother and wife, must ascend from the basement, Naylor exclaimed to the character, "Oh, Lord, woman, don't you know what the end of this book has got to be? You've gotta tear that whole house to the ground, or my book won't make any sense" (587).

Weaving together two simultaneous narratives, Gloria Naylor has produced a thought-provoking novel. Willie and Willa are, in effect, alter egos. It is Willie in the main narrative who, through his dreams and dialogue, raises important questions concerning black progress, and it is Willa in the parallel narrative who indirectly answers those questions. The major question is how African-Americans can retain their racial identities while realizing the American Dream. The answer, as Willie and Willa learn, lies in self-examination and rational choice. In a sense, Naylor is the opposite of her character, the historian Braithwaite, who merely records the histories of the residents of Linden Hills but who offers no suggestions for change. In contrast to his limited vision, Naylor, the poet, records, documents, and implies the ways in which African-Americans can progress without the loss of racial identity. By making Willie and Willa travel the path from ignorance to knowledge and regeneration, Naylor provides a key to issues raised in the novel. Even though Willa's journey ends in catastrophe and Willie must still chart his future, together their stories illuminate a direction which other African-Americans may explore.

Endnotes

[1] Larry R. Andrews, "Black Sisterhood in Gloria Naylor's Novels," *CLA Journal* 33 (September 1989): 17.

[2] Catherine C. Ward, "Gloria Naylor's *Linden Hills*: A Modern *Inferno*." *Contemporary Literature* 28 (1987): 69. Hereafter cited in text by page reference only.

[3] Dante Alighieri, *Inferno: Text and Commentary*, trans. Charles S. Singleton (Princeton: Princeton UP, 1980), Canto III, 27. Hereafter cited parenthetically in text.

[4] *Inferno*, trans. Singleton, part 2, p. 45.

[5] Gloria Naylor, *Linden Hills* (New York: Penguin, 1986): 204. Hereafter cited in text by page reference only.

[6] Gloria Naylor and Toni Morrison, "A Conversation," *Southern Review* 21.3 (1985): 589. Hereafter cited in text by page reference only.

Works Cited

This Works Cited entry has been constructed by the co-editors from citations noted in the original manuscript; it did not appear as part of the published essay.

Andrews, Lary R. "Black Sisterhood in Gloria Naylor's Novels." *CLA Journal* 33.1 (1989): 1-25.

Dante. *Inferno: Text and Commentary*. Trans. Charles S. Singleton. Princeton: Princeton UP, 1980.

Freccero, John. "Dante and the Neutral Angels." *The Romanic Review* 51 (1960): 3-14.

Naylor, Gloria, and Toni Morrison. "A Conversation: Gloria Naylor and Toni Morrison." *Southern Review* 21.3 (1985): 567-593.

_____. *Linden Hills*. New York: Penguin, 1986.

Ward, Catherine C. "Gloria Naylor's *Linden Hills*: A Modern *Inferno*." *Contemporary Literature* 28.1 (1987): 67-81.

Toombs, Charles P. "The Confluence of Food and Identity in Gloria Naylor's
    Linden Hills: 'What We Eat is Who We Is,'" CLA Journal 37.1 (1993): 1-18.

> Yet the people went on living and reproducing in spite of the bad food.
> Most of the children had straight bones, strong teeth. But it couldn't
> go on like that. Even the strongest heritage would one day run out.

--Ann Petry, The Street

Gloria Naylor's second novel, Linden Hills (1985), presents a scathing
examination of the precarious struggle for African-American identity in the
nineteenth and twentieth centuries. The novel, concerned with an exploration of
the fictional middle-class black community of Linden Hills, devotes a significant
amount of its attention to detailing the ways in which some African Americans
efface themselves as they try to be both Americans and African Americans. In
this sense, the novel records the specific consequences of W. E. B. Du Bois'
well-known double-consciousness idea.[1]   However, the novel does so by
positioning most of the contemporary inhabitants of Linden Hills as educated
and intelligent people who supposedly are aware of their culture and their black
identity, who have lived through the Civil Rights and the Black Power
Movements, but who nevertheless are unable to effectively create and respond
to healthy ways of seeing self. Naylor insists that the very crumbs of American
life and the corresponding promise of material success will often be the criteria
that many African Americans will use as the yardsticks by which they will
evaluate self and others, no matter that such an adherence to the mythological
American Dream is destructive to self, others, and African-American culture and
identity.[2]   One especially adept way that Naylor captures the struggles for
authentic African-American identity in her novel is by focusing on the food which
the characters consume and the rituals and codes of conduct that surround its
consumption. Put simply, Naylor suggests that food consumption is a viable way
of understanding some of the problematics of African-American identity. For
many of the characters in Linden Hills, certainly its middle-class representatives,
healthy African-American identity is as vaporous as the whiff of scent remaining
after the consumption of expensive caviar.

Linden Hills is set during December 19-24 (Christmas--the season of
giving and material excess) in the fictional middle- and upper-class black
community of Linden Hills in Wayne County, USA, where the further down the
hill one lives, the wealthier one is and, ironically, the more spiritually and
culturally malnourished (bankrupt) one is. Luther Nedeed is the creator of the
Linden Hills experiment.[3] He and his male progeny, all named Luther Nedeed,
had a plan based on the first Nedeed's understanding that the "future of Wayne
County--the future of America . . . was going to be white: white money backing
white wars for white power because the very earth was white."[4] Luther creates
the Tupelo Realty Corporation as his way to have a share of the white-money-
pie, and his only problem "was deciding who [of the blacks] in Linden Hills
should own [the property and build homes]" (10). That is, only those blacks, like
the Nedeeds, who were comfortable with (or consciously unaware of), the idea of
effacing themselves and their culture to achieve material gains would qualify for
admission to the privileged lots of Linden Hills:

> The Tupelo Realty Corporation was terribly selective about the
> types of families who received its mortgages. . . . No, only "certain"
> people got to live in Linden Hills. . . . They had a thousand years
> and a day to sit right there and forget what it meant to be black. . . .
> (15-16)

The current Luther Nedeed invited applications from anywhere in the country
from "any future Baptist ministers, political activists, and Ivy League graduates
. . . since their kind seemed to reach the bottom [Tupelo Drive, the most
exclusive address] faster than the others. . . . Finally, devoured by their own
drives, there just wasn't enough humanity left to fill the rooms of a real home,
and the property went up for sale" (17-18).

In order to explore the madness that lurks underneath these outwardly
successful, upwardly mobile African Americans, Naylor positions much of her
critique of their lives through the visions of two young men, Lester Tilson, whose
family lives at the top of Linden Hills but still in it, and Willie Mason, who lives in
Putney Wayne, the economically poor black community of the city. The two men
have been friends since junior high school and are both poets. That Lester and
Willie are poets is central to Naylor's thematic concerns, for artists throughout
history have pursued goals that are antimaterialistic. Furthermore, as poets,
these young men are able to bring to Linden Hills a wider perspective, one that
is fully predicated on the human and that can recognize and evaluate the lost
souls of Linden Hills. Both poets are out of work. It is by doing odd jobs for the
residents of Linden Hills in the days before Christmas that these two men,
especially the gifted, sensitive, and insightful Willie, are able to peek inside
these people's lives who have "made it" and see the loss of African-American
identity and humanity, which can easily be one of the payments for material
success in America.

One other way that Naylor allows the reader to see inside the vacuity of
these people's lives is through a parallel narrative that focuses on five
generations of Nedeed women. The present Luther Nedeed has imprisoned his
wife, Willa Prescott Nedeed, and his son in the basement of their home
presumably because his five-year old son is too light complexioned and
therefore Willa must have been unfaithful. Luther fails to remember or
acknowledge that all of the Nedeed men had married quadroons or octoroons
and that sooner or later those "white genes" would surface. In her basement-
prison, Willa Prescott survives as best she can on the supply of powdered milk
and cereal that Luther believes will help to teach her his lesson for her
presumed infidelity, subdue her spirit, and cancel any right she thinks she might
have for an independent life.[5]

A major strategy which the Nedeed men use to maintain authority over
their women is to keep them isolated from the community. They accomplish this
mainly by using their class status. That is, because the Nedeed men are the
most wealthy members of the black community, they and their wives are not fully
participating members of the community at large. Indeed, the Nedeed women's
lives are similar to that of Janie in Zora Neale Hurston's *Their Eyes Were
Watching God*; like Janie, they are put on a pedestal because of their social-
economic position and are denied access to the larger black community that
might provide resources that could create alternatives to the effacing process

that is the price one apparently pays for the Nedeeds' kind of American success.[6] Although Janie eventually has a somewhat productive intercourse with the community of Eatonville, the Nedeed women remain isolated, having only their individual selves to rely on and the few avenues of expression available to them: recipes, cookbooks, photographs, ordering (shopping).

It is Willa Prescott Nedeed who, after her child dies in the basement-prison, slowly and painfully begins to explore the boxes and books in the basement and discovers her fellow inmates: the records of the other Nedeed women's existences. She finds the letters of the first Nedeed wife, Luwana Packerville; the recipes and cookbooks of Evelyn Creton, who literally ate tons of food and purged herself to death;[7] and the photographs of Priscilla McGuire, who carefully recorded her own gradual disappearing from life--even from photographs, so that not even her image of herself remained. The life-records of these Nedeed women show their wasting away under the authority of their husbands, even though these particular women had all of the material possessions that mythically should insure their survival. The Nedeed women's life stories, although submerged and separate from the lives of other Linden Hills residents, are actually identical to the fate awaiting all who embrace the Nedeed way to "get over" in America. A part of this way requires, as Barbara Christian puts it, that the Linden Hills residents "must erase essential parts of themselves if they are to stay in this jewel neighborhood. . . . Each of their lives has been damaged by the pursuit of wealth and power that Nedeed embodies. . . . They distort their natural inclinations, introducing death into their lives, even as the Nedeeds, who make their money as funeral parlor directors, have distorted their families in order to create Linden Hills."[8] Past and present reveal a trail of human destruction tied to the Nedeed ambition, passed from generation to generation and from designer house to designer house, to "get over."

Most of the Linden Hills residents have sold their African-American identity, indeed their very souls, for the grand illusion of material and/or professional success.[9] The food these characters eat and the activities and conditions associated with eating underscore their cultural and personal starvation. Interestingly enough, those characters who were never a part of Linden Hills, like Willie "White" Mason and Norman Anderson, or those who mentally or physically leave it, like Lester Tilson, Kiswana Browne, and Ruth Anderson (Norman's wife), are the most psychologically and culturally healthy characters in the novel, and they do not have money, cars, houses, and all of the other material and dominant culture-determined signs of success.

Willie and Lester's visit to the Anderson apartment is a good example of the cultural health in the have-nots' lives. Norman invites Willie and Lester to his and Ruth's apartment because it is cold outside; he says simply and sincerely: "Look, why don't you joy monkeys come on up to the house and have a little something hot?" (32). Norman offers real hospitality even though he is dirt poor, for the Anderson poverty "was a standing joke on Wayne Avenue. People said that if Norman brought home air, Ruth would make gravy, pour it over it, and tell him not to bring so much the next time" (32). Furthermore, the Anderson apartment is threadbare, for every sixteen months Norman went "screaming and tearing at his face and hair with his fingernails, trying to scrape off the pinks. He resorted to his teeth and bare nails only after everything else had failed--jagged sections of plates and glasses, wire hangers, curtain rods, splinters of wood once part of a dresser" (34). Eventually Ruth does not replace the furniture which Norman destroys and she removes glasses and silverware from the apartment, so that finally the Andersons only have three styrofoam cups--cups that cannot be broken or used to scrape off the pinks--and an almost bare apartment. Although the Andersons do not have material possessions, the "dilapidated garden-apartment" is one in which "[v]isitors found themselves thinking, What a nice feeling to be allowed into a home. And it *was* a home with its bare wood floors, dusted and polished, and with three pieces of furniture that sat in three large rooms; one sofa in the living room, one kitchenette set with plastic-bottomed chairs . . . one bed" (33). Norman and Ruth are genuine hosts, the kind who make guests feel welcome: Ruth set the styrofoam cups before Willie and Lester as if they were expensive china, and "Norman poured the coffee and made such a ceremony of unwrapping Willie's cheap blackberry brandy . . . you might have thought it a rare cognac" (33). Into such a scene is projected talking a good-natured laughter, a sense of community.

Willie, Lester, Ruth, and Norman provide the initial commentary on the Linden Hills residents. Ruth says, for example, that she lived in Linden Hills, but she never wants to live there again: "I've had that life . . . and I lasted six months. Those folks just aren't real" (39). Lester says that the Linden Hills residents "are a bunch of the saddest niggers you'll ever wanna meet. They eat, sleep, and breathe for one thing--making it" (39). Lester Tilson, though he lives in Linden Hills--just barely since his family's home is at the top--has taken advantage of the insights which his grandmother, Mamie Tilson, gave to him. She was the only one of her generation of Linden Hills residents to stand up to a Luther Nedeed. She had told Luther Nedeed, "I used to fish with your daddy down in that there pond, Luther, and he gave me this land and I ain't giving it up. So take your frog-eyed self and your frog-eyed son out of here. And I know your evil ways--all of you" (12). Lester remembers his grandmother's legacy and tells Willie, Ruth, and Norman that "[Grandma Tilson] hated those Nedeeds" (40).

Later the same day, Willie's visit to Lester's home is a major contrast to the genuine warmth and community which he had experienced at the Andersons' home. Lester invites Willie to spend the night so that the two young men can have an early start on seeking odd jobs in Linden Hills. Ruth gives them the tip about the possibility of jobs. Lester does not, apparently, follow social protocol in forewarning his mother that Willie would be having dinner and spending the night. Mrs. Tilson's first condescending and hypocritical statement is, "Well, I guess we can always find more, and especially for such a good friend of Lester's" (48). Willie and Lester both know that she has never approved of Willie as a friend for her son. Willie, who "always felt too big and awkward and black" in the presence of Mrs. Tilson, is able to mutter, "Look, I know you didn't plan on me being here. . . . It's sort of short notice and I'm not very hungry anyway" (48). Mrs. Tilson, trying to recover and re-institute her social graces, says, "Nonsense. . . . There's always something for company. *But we're eating like peasants tonight--just fried chicken*" (48, emphasis added).

Rather than the relaxed and unassuming sense of community which Willie had experienced in the Anderson home, here he finds "serialized" smiles, updates on the cost of reupholstering furniture, the obligatory coasters, and a general sense of discomfiture. The dinner itself reveals what Mrs. Tilson and Roxanne, Lester's sister, have given up to live among the privileged:

naturalness.[10] After making sure that her dining table is set with the starched linen napkins, the china, the silverware, and the fragile Norwegian crystal, only then is Mrs. Tilson concerned with how Willie might be perceiving the argument that erupts during dinner between Roxanne and Lester: "Lester, Roxanne, please, not in front of company" or "Now Willie's going to think we're a group of barbarians in this house" (55). Roxanne, on the other hand, is so bent on defending her upwardly mobile boyfriend, Xavier Donnell, and filling the conversation "with the importance of her new promotion," that she only eats "two bites of chicken and [a] teaspoon of potatoes" (54). That Roxanne only nibbles at the "peasant," "common food" rather than "getting down" signals her cultural starvation and deprivation.

Naylor explores additional nuances of this cultural deprivation in her dissection of other residents of Linden Hills, and what they do or do not with food is central to one theme: the absence of positive African-American identity in the lives of characters who are struggling to "make it."

In one scene, Willie and Lester are doing work at a wedding reception in Linden Hills. Ironically, the two are not thought of as good enough to work as waiters, where they will be seen and thus present a reminder to these middle-class folk of what they have given up in their pursuit of American success: their blackness. The families of the bride and groom hire whites as waiters and servers. Willie and Lester are hired to take out the trash and garbage, to help load and unload supplies; but they are able, while doing the dirty work, to occasionally look through the kitchen doors and observe the wedding shenanigans:

> The four-foot wedding cake held miniatures of the bridal party on two sets of golden stairways that ran up each of its sides. . . . This was definitely no fried-chicken-and-potato-salad affair. The [white] waiters were coming into the kitchen and unwrapping trays of marinated shrimp, stuffed artichokes, caviar, and some kind of cheese that Willie didn't recognize, so he knew it must have been expensive. (82)

Surrounding this display of food is the dress of the wedding guests:

> . . . the Halston minks and Saint Laurent fox capes. . . . The impeccable make-up, the manicured hands and custom-made hairdos were only rivaled by the sculptured attire of their male escorts. . . . But even as glass after glass was refilled from the champagne fountain . . . Willie couldn't help feeling that something was missing . . . spontaneity. . . . These niggers would be afraid to sweat. (82-83)[11]

These people are like the airbrushed models and carefully constructed images found in *Ebony* magazine, a lot of fluff, superficiality, and glamour symbolizing nothing. Even the bridegroom is a fake. Winston Alcott is gay, has had a long-term relationship with his best man, David, but refuses to follow his heart and continue his gay relationship because being married to a woman is necessary for his promotion to full partner in his law firm and for continued descent in

Linden Hills to the most prestigious address, Tupelo Drive. As a matter of fact, Luther Nedeed's gift to the bride and groom is "a mortgage on Tupelo Drive" (87). And although Winston should be happy that he has "made it," all he can do, like most of the guests, is present a "frozen grimace" for a smile (87).

Xavier Donnell, boyfriend to Lester's sister Roxanne, is also present at the Alcott wedding, and his date is a white woman, a secretary at his office. He had thought that escorting a white woman would generate the appropriate appearance, and it had, for the wedding guests truly believe in "white for white's sake." During the festivities, Xavier "sat with his arm thrown over the chair of a young, blond woman. He playfully offered her a bit of cheese and she ate it from his fingers" (84). The "bit of cheese" is symbolic of Xavier's own cultural starvation, for after the wedding, he is burdened by the thought that he is falling in love with Roxanne Tilson, and, like Winston Alcott and his rejection of David, Xavier is not convinced that Roxanne is the best match for his professional and pecuniary pursuits. He is unsure whether he should ask Roxanne to marry him because she is not on the same social (or geographical) level as he is; he is unsure what impact such a marriage would have on his position as Vice President of Minority Affairs at General Motors Corporation. He fails to observe, in his so-called dilemma, that Roxanne would be the ideal black woman for him. She has "groomed her life and body with a hawklike determination to marry black, marry well--or not to marry at all. And, at twenty-seven, with a decade's worth of bleaching cremes and hair relaxers, coupled with a Wellesley B.A. and a job in an ad agency, she was still waiting" (53). Moreover, her eating habits, if Xavier knew them, would immediately qualify her for admission to Linden Hills' most exclusive vestibule, for her eating "consisted of nibbles: bits of lettuce and cucumber, dabs of fish and cottage cheese. She never lost weight because periodic depressions would send her nibbling potato chips, French chocolates, and Hostess Twinkies" (53). Xavier need not have lost so much sleep over whether or not he should marry Roxanne, for with Roxanne he would never be burdened by a woman eating greasy pork ribs, collard greens, deep-fried catfish, hog maws, and the like. Roxanne would always present the correct appearance.

However, Xavier had to be positively, absolutely sure that Roxanne would not hinder his prospects at General Motors or his social ascension down Linden Hills. He had worked hard to become the perfect, super nigger, including an Ivy League education-brainwashing, so he consults the epitome of black sophistication, Maxwell Smyth, Assistant to the Executive Director at General Motors, and next in line for the Executive Director position. His life story is a telling one, often humorous, ever sad:

> Maxwell had discovered long ago that he doubled the odds of finishing first if he didn't carry the weight of that milligram of [black] pigment in his skin. . . . In college [Dartmouth] he found that his blackness began to disappear behind his straight A average, and his reputation for never sweating. . . . The pinnacle of his success lay in his French-tiled blue and white bathroom. . . . The only thing his bathroom lacked was toilet paper. . . . Through a careful selection of solids and liquids, he was able to control not only the moment but the exact nature of the matter that had to bring him daily to the [toilet]. His stomach and intestines were purified by

large quantities of spring water and chamomile tea. He found
variety in clear juices--apple, strained cranberry, and, on rare
occasions, small sips of Chardonnay. . . . He learned that the very
tips of broccoli florets, asparagus, and even parsley moved less
noticeably through his system than the stems. Young animal flesh
--baby scallops, calves' liver, and breasts of squab were the purest
to digest. . . . He would have put a forkful of cabbage, a slice of
onion, or a single bean into his mouth with the same enthusiasm as
a tablespoon of cyanide. . . . [He even used a bidet] where he was
sprayed with perfumed and sudsy water.   (102-105)

The above quotation shows most forcibly Naylor's use of food in her scathing
examination of the extremes which some blacks will take to defeat the "natural"
in their pursuit of material success and white acceptance. In fact, at General
Motors, no one could even say Maxwell's butt smelled "because it didn't" (106).
Central to "making it" for the Linden Hills residents is the elimination of anything
overtly connected to positive African-American life and culture, and the food
these characters consume is crucial to Naylor's thematic interest. The ultimate
price which Maxwell pays for his success is his confinement to his bathroom,
where most of the meaning in his life unfolds or drops out.
    It should not, and does not, surprise Xavier that Maxwell's advice to him is
not to marry Roxanne. She is not, in Maxwell's view, perfect enough. He
suggests that Xavier marry a white woman or wait for that special black woman,
exceptional like Maxwell, though he admits that such finds are rare.
    During Maxwell's visit to Xavier, Willie and Lester are cleaning out the
garage for Xavier's mother, and the two young men have an encounter with the
Buppies. The conversation takes an immediate turn to race and the lack of
opportunities available to black people. Maxwell and Xavier contend that
progress is being made and that they are both living proof, in their view, of that
fact. Willie and Lester offer a counter-position that black people are poor
because they are black, that racism and discrimination are still major
determining forces in the lives of everyday black people. Maxwell thinks that
real progress can be measured; one need only look at the most recent issue of
Penthouse magazine to see that racial barriers are no longer operative, for, he
says, "There was a time when you couldn't find a picture of one black woman in
a magazine like *Penthouse*. And see what the centerfold is this month" (115).
That the Maxwell Smyths of the world are completely lost to their people is
captured at the end of the scene when the narrator records Willie's reaction to
the magazine centerfold, for he understands what Maxwell cannot. He
recognizes the exploitation of people, family even, in that photograph--"that
woman was a dead ringer for his baby sister" (116).
    Willie's racial and cultural health and Naylor's use of food to demonstrate
the loss of personal and cultural identity of the Linden Hills residents are
captured in another group scene, much like the Alcott wedding ceremony. Willie
and Lester have come to Mr. Chester Parker's house to do an unspecified job.
Mr. Parker's wife, Lycentia, has died and it is the night before her burial: "[T]he
caterers have set up" (126). Before the guests arrive for the wake, Mr. Parker
tells the young men that he wants them to steam the wallpaper off the master
bedroom so that the next day the paperhangers can put up new wallpaper and

he can bring out the new furniture for his new bride; Mr. Parker plans to remarry as soon as Lycentia is buried. After completing half of the job, the young men return downstairs to peek in on the wake. The narrator captures the coldness and sterility of the guests' lives through their forced and superficial attempts to express their condolences and in their eating behavior:

> People . . . help[ed] themselves to the *cold buffet*. . . . [Willie hadn't really been listening [to the guests' talk] so much as looking down into the faces that were looking up through the clear dinner plates from the glass-topped table. And something was haunting him about the rhythm of the knives and forks that cut into the slices of roast beef. . . . The plates never seemed empty of the brown and bloody meat. . . . Willie knew it was just an illusion. Those plates were actually being emptied. . . . They had to put those forks down (130-134, emphasis added)

Similar to Willie's earlier reaction to the guests at the Alcott wedding, during the Parker wake the monotony and the lack of spontaneity of the people as they eat seize his attention and provide both the description and the criticism of these people's hollow lives. When Luther Nedeed arrives "carrying a cellophane-wrapped cake . . . [h]e was the only guest Willie had seen bringing food that night, and it surprised him," for Willie "knew that his family always fried chicken and baked stuff for a wake and so it was the last thing he expected to see done in Linden Hills" (136). Luther lies and tells the guests that his wife baked the cake. He dominates the conversation, and, although the other guests had already eaten, when he declares that he does not like eating alone, "[o]ne by one, the other knives and forks were lifted and the meal continued with the pathetic motions of children being forced to eat" (138). The guests are like machines, and Willie is surprised that they actually, somehow, manage to consume real food. Naylor's rendering of the black elite of Linden Hills is similar to Nella Larsen's critique of the black middle class of Naxos in *Quicksand*. Larsen's narrator records:

> The great community . . . was no longer a school. It had grown into a machine. It was a show place in the black belt. . . . Life had died out of it. It was . . . now only a big knife with cruelly sharp edges ruthlessly cutting all to a pattern, the white man's pattern. . . . [I]t tolerated no innovations, no individualisms. . . . Enthusiasm, spontaneity, if not actually suppressed, were at least openly regretted as unladylike or ungentlemanly qualities.[12]

Parker gives Willie and Lester the leftover food from the wake; Willie pigs out on it and has wild and crazy dreams with the refrain "Willie, eat it. . . . Eat it . . . . Eat it" (145). The next day Willie tells Lester, "That stuff Parker gave us upset my stomach. . . . There was something strange about that cake. . . . I mean, it didn't taste homemade" (152). Indeed, there is not any "home" in the Linden Hills residents' lives.

Laurel Dumont, for example, realizes, all too late, that there is no home in Linden Hills. She then temporarily leaves hers in search of one. She visits her grandmother, Roberta Johnson, in rural Georgia, for, as a child, it had always been visits to her grandmother that contained the most meaning and warmth in her life. In the section of the novel devoted to Laurel Dumont, Naylor makes the most significant connection between the Nedeed women and the other women who live in Linden Hills. Laurel, like the Nedeed women, lives in a privileged yet empty life, where a house is not a home. In her trip to Georgia, Laurel tries to recapture "home," but her white, liberal, Phi Beta Kappa education at the University of California at Berkeley, her executive position at IBM, her husband, Howard (whose family had lived in Linden Hills for over sixty years and who was "the first black D.A. in Wayne County, hand-picked to be the next state attorney general"), and even her house, a showcase, remind her that her grandmother's house is no longer her home (232).

Roberta Johnson understood this long ago, when Laurel went away to college: "All Roberta knew was that she had cashed in her life insurance to send a child she had named Laurel Johnson to the state of California, and it had sent her back a stranger" (226-227). Roberta Johnson is like the Andersons, Willie, Lester, and Grandma Tilson: down to earth, warm, funky, comfortable, and real. One of Roberta's first gestures upon Laurel's arrival is to offer her some homemade lemonade.

When Laurel explains to Roberta why she has come, Roberta tells her: "But this ain't your home, child" (231). Roberta's intent is to encourage Laurel to make a home for herself on her own territory. It is with this understanding that Laurel returns to Linden Hills. Soon after arriving in Linden Hills, Laurel slips into a depression that overwhelms her. She concludes that her house is sterile, her marriage a charade, and her career meaningless. Although these insights are necessary ones, Laurel's energies spent trying to "get over" mean that she has no resources, especially no cultural or racial ones, that might help her to understand that she can begin again. Instead, she thinks that her life is hopeless (even after Roberta comes to Linden Hills to help her) and plunges into her empty, expensive, specially made diving pool.[13]

All of the characters who live in Linden Hills, or aspire to live there, are presented as individuals who have lost all sense of who they are as African Americans (or as people, period). They are usually highly educated, financially successful, and yet empty shells of human beings. They take no pride in their cultural heritage; most of their efforts are spent in the deliberate removal of most vestiges of black cultural identity. In tracing part of this self-effacing process, Naylor reminds the reader that the first Nedeed even helped the Confederacy during the Civil War and literally owned his wife Luwana. The first Nedeed put the dream of Linden Hills into operation. His sons carried out the dream, and the many willing blacks like Xavier, Maxwell, Laurel, Roxanne, Parker, the Dumonts, ad infinitum, powered the machine that continually perpetuated itself. At novel's end, Luther's wife Willa escapes from her basement prison, burns up Luther's house, Luther, and herself while the other Linden Hills residents "*let it burn*" (304). They do not even protect or value the lives of those like themselves. Only Willie and Lester remain as witnesses to the personal and cultural destruction that is Linden Hills, and only these two young black men and the blacks outside of Linden Hills seem to know that eating barbecue ribs, fried chicken, collard greens, and drinking beer and cheap wine are intrinsically more important than a manicured lawn, an olympic-sized pool, and an empty heart.

Although Naylor does not suggest that the attainment of material success be avoided, she asks, At what price?

Endnotes

[1] See W. E. B. Du Bois, *The Souls of Black Folk*, in *Three Negro Classics* (New York: Avon, 1965): 207-389.

[2] *Linden Hills* carries forward one line of cultural deprivation and cultural ignorance and their impact on individual character that finds expression in a number of African-American narratives. See, for instance, James Weldon Johnson's *The Autobiography of an Ex-Coloured Man*, Jessie Fauset's *Plum Bun* and *Comedy, American Style*, Nella Larsen's *Quicksand* and *Passing*, Richard Wright's *Native Son*, Ann Petry's *The Street*, Ralph Ellison's *Invisible Man*, Toni Morrison's *The Bluest Eye* and *Song of Solomon*, and Alice Walker's stories, "Strong Horse Tea" and "The Diary of an African Nun."

[3] Spelled backwards "Nedeed" sounds like "dead end." Eric Haralson suggests that "Nedeed" spelled backwards is "de-Eden," or hell ("Gloria Naylor," *African-American Writers*, eds. Lea Baechler and A. Walton Litz [New York: Scribners, 1991]: 346).

[4] Gloria Naylor, *Linden Hills* (1985; New York: Penguin, 1986): 8. Hereafter cited parenthetically in the text.

[5] Luther's choices of food provisions for Willa are telling. The powdered milk and cereal are bland, devoid of any of the richness and complexity of African-American food and culture. Furthermore, the food choices are indicative of the sterility and emptiness of the contours of Luther's life.

[6] Compare Zora Neale Hurston, *Their Eyes Were Watching God* (1937; rpt. Urbana: U of Illinois P, 1978).

[7] Two important contemporary eating disorders--anorexia and bulimia--are largely associated with women and issues of identity.

[8] Barbara Christian, "Gloria Naylor's Geography: Community, Class, and Patriarchy in *The Women of Brewster Place* and *Linden Hills*," *Reading Black, Reading Feminist: A Critical Anthology*, ed. Henry Louis Gates, Jr., (New York: Meridian, 1990): 361.

[9] It is impossible to argue that these characters have sold out for personal success, for none of them have achieved anything that might be considered "personal" (intrinsic, subjective, and internal) success or triumph. Catherine C. Ward sees *Linden Hills* as another version of Dante's *Inferno* and thinks that Naylor presents us with a series of characters who indeed sacrifice the personal for the material. Ward writes that "in their single-minded pursuit of upward mobility, the inhabitants of Linden Hills . . . have turned away from their past and from their deepest sense of who they are. Naylor feels that the subject of who-we-are and what we are wiling to give up of who-we-are to get where-we-want-to-go is a question of the highest seriousness--as serious as a Christian's concern over his salvation" (Gloria Naylor's *Linden Hills*: A Modern *Inferno*," *Contemporary Literature* 28 [Spring 1987]: 67). While I do not address the religious or Christian aspects of the novel and how they might relate to cultural-racial-personal identity, I welcome those readings, such as Ward's, that do. This novel is exceedingly complex and engages a variety of perspectives and potentially offers a number of new readings.

[10] Toni Morrison in *The Bluest Eye* (1970) depicts black women who deliberately remove a great deal of their black culture and black identity in their quest to be middle class: "These women go to land-grand colleges . . . and learn how . . . to behave. The careful development of thrift, patience, high morals, and good manners. In short, how to get rid of the funkiness. The dreadful funkiness of passion, the funkiness of nature, the funkiness of the wide range of human emotions" (New York: Pocket, 1972: 68). Helga Crane's friend, Anne Grey, in *Quicksand*, also removes a great deal of her culture as she attempts to "ape" everything white. The irony or sad part of Grey's life is that she thinks she really is a spokesperson for the black masses and racial uplift, while she does not value the culture or the people that she advocates. Interestingly enough, like the Linden Hills residents, underneath the material glitter Anne Grey is an empty shell of a person.

[11] Alfred Pasteur and Ivory Toldson argue that black expressive behavior is the key part of the black experience that explains the black mind. They define black expressive behavior as "the readiness or predisposition to express oneself in a manner characterized by vital emotionalism, spontaneity, and rhythm. Often these traits act in combination with one or more other essential characteristics: naturalistic attitudes, style, creativity with the spoken word, and relaxed physical movement. . . . These interact to produce human behavior that when expressed

or perceived registers images, sounds, aromas, and feelings of beauty to the senses. It is the intensity, duration, frequency, and utilitarian features of the behavior, resembling those traditional African people, which make it unique" (*Roots of Soul: The Psychology of Black Expressiveness* [Garden City: Anchor, 1982]: 4-5).

[12] Nella Larsen, *Quicksand* (1928; rpt. New Brunswick: Rutgers UP, 1986): 4.

[13] Laurel's belief that her life is hopeless and her seeking of freedom in the pool (though empty of water) is similar to Kate Chopin's rendering of Edna Pontellier in *The Awakening* who also came to the realization that her marriage was a fraud, that she had no home in her New Orleans mansion, and who plunged into water (the sea) to find freedom (*The Awakening*, ed. Margaret Culley [New York: Norton, 1967]). With no knowledge of or ability to recognize a tradition of women who had succeeded on their own terms, Edna and Laurel think individual freedom can only be had in death.

Works Cited

This Works Cited entry has been constructed by the co-editors from citations noted in the original manuscript; it did not appear as part of the published essay.

Christian, Barbara.   "Gloria Naylor's Geography: Community, Class, and Patriarchy in *The Women of Brewster Place* and *Linden Hills.*"   *Reading Black, Reading Feminist*. Ed. Henry Louis Gates, Jr. New York: Meridian, 1990. 348-373. Reprinted in Gates and Appiah.
Larsen, Nella. *Quicksand*. 1928. New Brunswick: Rutgers UP, 1986.
Naylor, Gloria. *Linden Hills*. New York: Penguin, 1985.

Berg, Christine G. "'giving sound to the bruised places in their hearts': Gloria Naylor and Walt Whitman." Published with permission of the author.

In Gloria Naylor's *Linden Hills*, multicultural experience and canonical text intersect in the characters of Lester Tilson and Willie K. Mason, the two young male African-American protagonists. These characters admire, honor, and even memorize the poetry of "dead white males" (among others) and are poets themselves. Moreover, their discovery, as adolescents, of their mutual interest in this "sissy stuff" (27) creates a friendship between them that is strengthened by the respect they hold both for each other and for the "lines that helped them to harness the chaos and confusions in their fourteen-year-old worlds" (28). Indeed, poetry performs for them the same function that the act of writing does for Naylor herself: "When I think about the process itself, within the artist, what you are doing is trying to somehow give cohesion to the chaos that is all of you" (Pearlman 99). Lester's preoccupation with poetry defines his world for him. As a teenager, he stuffs his poetry under his mattress; as a young man, he recites it around the neighborhood of Putney Wayne. Likewise, Willie's love of poetry is all-consuming. Because of a lack of privacy at home during his teenage years, he creates stanzas of poetry in his mind and "continued the habit . . . and eventually had a repertoire in the hundreds" (29). By the time Willie is twenty, he can declare with pride: "'You know I have six hundred and sixty-five poems memorized up here--six hundred and sixty-five, and lots of 'em ain't mine. I have all of Baraka, Soyinka, Hughes, and most of Coleridge. And Whitman--that was one together dude'" (45). Not only does poetry instill in these young men a sense of pride and self-worth, but it is a force in their lives so compelling that it alone can form a unique bond of brotherhood between them: "Bloody noses had made them friends, but giving sound to the bruised places in their hearts made them brothers" (28). Poetry provides an outlet for Lester and Willie, especially when they find themselves in need of a way to express their emotions, a way to make sense of their worlds; and as they are drawn into the community of Linden Hills until eventually they confront its dictator, Luther Nedeed, they rely more heavily on poetry--specifically that of Whitman, Stevens, and Eliot--to explain for them the phenomenon of a lost people.

In the same way that lines of poetry steal into the minds of Lester and Willie regardless of the activities in which they are engaged, so, too, poems by canonical writers weave their way into the text of *Linden Hills*. As Naylor crystallizes for her readers the dissolution of the homosexual relationship between Winston Alcott, a successful lawyer and a single man of thirty with a residence on Second Crescent Drive, and David, his lover of eight years, she turns to the most original of all American poets: Walt Whitman. In particular, Naylor chooses one of Whitman's controversial "Calamus" poems, a collection some forty-five poems long (eventually thirty-nine in Whitman's final arrangement) added to the third edition of *Leaves of Grass* published in 1860. The poems in this section are markedly different from those in the first two editions, for they represent love between men--to such an extent that contemporary critics label them Whitman's "coming out" poems. Naylor's decision to incorporate in her novel the third poem in the sequence, "Whoever You are Holding Me Now in Hand," as the speech given by David, the best man at the forced marriage of Winston and another Linden Hills socialite, Cassandra, is fascinating, for the poem operates in several ways. First, it is appropriate that Naylor choose one of the "Calamus" poems because of their homosexual content; indeed, "Whitman was inventing a sexuality through his poetry" (Martin, "The Disseminal Whitman" 79). Despite the changes he makes for his heterosexual audience when reading the poem, then, David can express his true feelings in an inconspicuous manner. Second, from a broader perspective, Naylor is incorporating the words of a poet whose abolitionist views inform many of the poems of *Leaves of Grass*; Whitman is notoriously popular among ethnic Americans as the poet of democracy, as the "harbinger of multiculturalism" (Li 119), and as "that quintessential . . . antiracist poet, whose legacy could be used to break the racist tradition's control over the limits and possibilities of African American literature" (Hutchinson, "The Whitman Legacy and the Harlem Renaissance" 201). Where poetry creates a bond between Lester and Willie, Naylor, in her use of Whitman, underscores the cohesiveness of American literature as a whole, constructing a bridge between the literature of African-Americans and the canon. Furthermore, functioning as a moment in the timeline of American literature, *Linden Hills* teaches us that "black writers open[ing] up the canons of [the English] language . . . and breaking into print in America find themselves already there" (Nielsen 11). The lines of poetry in Whitman's canonical "Whoever You are Holding Me Now in Hand" speak to the experience of African-American characters in Naylor's novel--especially as they are literally spoken by one character to another.

Having already begun their search for extra work around Linden Hills (a search that catapults them into the lives of those in the community), Lester and Willie are thankful to be hired to wash dishes and collect garbage at the site of

Winston's wedding reception. As they survey the "birds of paradise" gathered as guests for the wedding, Willie's first impression of Winston is a troubling one: "Why, that guy looks like someone had punched him in the stomach and his lips sorta froze up that way" (84). Earlier in the sequence of events, at the news of Winston's upcoming nuptials, Lester conveys his surprise and his suspicion that Winston is gay. When Willie suggests that his proof is questionable, Lester declares: "'But you *never* saw him with a woman and then--bam--he's engaged'" (73). Together, Willie's perception of Winston feigning happiness and Lester's appreciation of Winston's hasty engagement set the stage for the superficiality of the affair, for Luther Nedeed's toast in language "'straight out of a gothic novel'" (86), and ultimately, for David's toast as best man to his now-married lover.

     Acting with the utmost self-control and showing his keen ability to perform in his disguise as a heterosexual among heterosexuals, David addresses his speech to Winston's new wife:

> "Cassandra, I've never been very fancy with words. And so when I knew I wanted something very special for this occasion, I went to a man who devoted his life to words and found something that I feel fits this day perfectly. Since this poem will speak about the trials that are ahead of you in marriage--and the joys--I want you to imagine that your new husband is saying these words to you." (88)

That man, of course, is Walt Whitman. And though Whitman certainly "devoted his life to words," he also devoted the "Calamus" section of the third edition of *Leaves of Grass* to exploring the complexity of love between men or comrades, making "Whoever You are Holding Me Now in Hand" especially significant as a piece of communication between its speaker and true intended audience, Winston. The irony of David's introduction to the poem is doubly apparent when he declares that he has "found something that I feel fits this day perfectly"--for the poem owns many subtexts: first for the new wife, then for the heterosexual members of the audience and the grandeur of the event itself, and finally for the lover who has betrayed him. What David instructs Cassandra to accept as a kind of overview about her future marriage is actually a catalogue of David's love for Winston and his last good-bye.

     It is significant, too, and not unexpected, that Willie immediately recognizes the poem as one of Whitman's after hearing just the first four lines: "'Hey . . . that's Whitman. But why would he be reading that one? It's--'" (88). What Willie does not finish saying here, he declares after he hears the next two lines of the poem--the first lines that David deliberately alters to suit his supposed audience, Cassandra, as he imagines Winston speaking to her: "'He's changed the words. . . . Les, Whitman wrote that poem for a man'" (88). If Whitman is able to "diffuse the sexuality" of his poem by making it "not the love of one man for another, but of men for one another," and thus more general, David further obscures both his and Whitman's intentions by reinventing it as a poem about heterosexual love (Simpson 29). Moreover, Willie's discovery that David's speech is a Whitman poem reconfigured for a woman is doubly ironic, since Whitman did recast several of his poems for men to be poems about heterosexual love.[1] On one level, Naylor uses this episode in the novel to further reinforce the literary astuteness of her two protagonists, and we are given proof, indeed, that a number of the six hundred and sixty-five poems that Willie has memorized are by Whitman. Moreover, as one of the two members of the audience aware of the author of the poem and its true meaning, Willie occupies a unique position and can begin to understand the drama that is unfolding. The knowledge of poetry, thus, is an empowering one: it teaches its readers to understand human experience; it gives its readers an advantage. No one, other than Lester (who seems, by comparison, less intrigued, or perhaps more uncomfortable with the matter), will comprehend the many levels of significance the poem carries. Though Willie knows nothing of the relationship between David and Winston, he is able to identify David's toast to the newlyweds as a "charade he had just witnessed" (90).

Given the relationship between David and Winston, the poem is meant to be read in two ways, with two separate messages: first, as David declares he intends it, the lines spoken by Winston to his new wife; and second, as David secretly intends it, the lines spoken by David to Winston as his long-time lover. In addition, the lines of the poem recall the final exchange between David and Winston before the wedding, specifically David's last plea that Winston find happiness: "'The only thing I want you to do is finally to try and start *making yourself.* Make yourself happy with that girl--please, do that . . . . Because she's all you've got now'" (80). With this in mind, David's constructed exchange between Winston and Cassandra is his wish for Winston to truly communicate with Cassandra, to admit to her and to himself that their lives together as husband and wife may not be easy in the very hope of making them easier. The poem begins:

> Whoever you are, holding me now in hand,
> Without one thing, all will be useless,
> I give you fair warning, before you attempt me further,
> I am not what you supposed, but far different. (*TVPP* 368)[2]

On the one hand, David performs the role of Winston speaking these lines to Cassandra, both declaring that Winston is "far different" and modeling for Winston a method of sharing this knowledge with his new wife. On the other hand, however, as lines spoken by David to Winston, the message is such that David is "far different" from what Winston had supposed (perhaps far less tolerant of Winston's betrayal of him--Winston, after all, cannot believe that David can simply end their relationship). "Without one thing," David is, for the last time, declaring, "all will be useless." Though Stephen A. Black finds that "[t]he organization of this poem . . . around a riddle which is never explicitly answered, suggests that the poet may set out to make a poem without knowing exactly . . . what his poem will finally say" (47-48), it seems rather that Whitman's intention is clear (as evidenced by Willie's reaction to the poem): Whitman knows exactly what he wants to say--that he is homosexual and that homosexuality should be accepted--but given the oppressive nature of the period during which he writes, he says it without saying it. And, through Whitman, David does, too. Without Winston's acceptance of himself as a homosexual, neither he nor David can find happiness. The opening line, "Whoever you are, holding me now in hand," illustrates both Winston's acceptance of a stranger--"*whoever* you are"--as his wife and, at the same time, the distance between David and Winston, who have changed, who will no longer "know" each other.

The next two lines of the poem begin to reveal for Willie the "charade" of David's toast as David eliminates the homosexuality that Whitman originally implied. David assigns a female sex to the "follower" and "candidate" where Whitman writes to a "he":

> Who is he that would become my follower?
> Who would sign himself a candidate for my affections?   (*TVPP* 368)

Again, these lines emphasize the lack of knowledge that Winston has about his new wife --and about his new life as a husband. The questions are challenges-- who would be so daring as to love me? In Winston's voice, as questions to Cassandra, they are doubly challenging, for she enters, unsuspecting, not only into a marriage (a serious commitment), but into a relationship that will likely fail. In David's voice, as questions to Winston, the lines seem to further challenge Winston to embrace his true identity and to reflect the necessary boldness of a lover, a "follower" and a "candidate" of affection between men. And in the following six lines, that necessary boldness is tested as Whitman lists the demands of accepting such a love:

> The way is suspicious--the result uncertain, perhaps destructive;
> You would have to give up all else--I alone would expect to be
>   your God, sole and exclusive,
> Your novitiate would even then be long and exhausting,
> The whole past theory of your life, and all conformity to the lives
>   around you, would have to be abandon'd;
> Therefore release me now, before troubling yourself any further --
>   Let go your hand from my shoulders,
> Put me down, and depart on your way.   (*TVPP* 368)

David means for his audience, and for Cassandra in particular, to accept these lines as "'the trials that are ahead of you in marriage'" when two partners join together in matrimony, expect to be the sole focus for each other, and begin to compromise some of their old ways as they create a new life together (88). They hold a deeper meaning, however, and the "trials" are made more critical, as a statement about what David expects--or expected--of Winston for their relationship to mature. For "the way" of homosexual love can only be "suspicious," "uncertain," and "destructive" when it is not welcomed by society-- and by the community of Linden Hills. Whitman "prophetically express[es] . . . the existentialist character of homosexual experience under oppression" as the poem is "direct . . . about the uprooting and jeopardy involved in the homosexual's 'death' to society and the task of self-determination that imposes" (Cady 16). The lines suggest that the lover must be brave, that Winston must be willing "to give up all else," to give up his residence in Linden Hills, his career as a prominent lawyer, his acceptance by such an affluent black community--in short, "[t]he whole past theory of [his] life." Winston would need to be able to accept David "alone" as his "God, sole and exclusive," for he would have to be satisfied with the comfort he would receive in the strength of their relationship and little else. More importantly, Winston would have to be able to withstand his lack of conformity to society's standards and his rejection by Luther Nedeed and Linden Hills--an exclusion from the people in a community who have infected his way of thinking, who have infiltrated his very soul, who have shamed him by their opulence, pride, and materialism to betray his lover, his only hope of achieving a sense of self: "all conformity to" those "lives around [him] would have to be abandon'd." David understands that this would "trouble" Winston, that this, indeed, is what has resulted in Winston marrying Cassandra--and, by extension, everything that Linden Hills represents. Therefore, the last lines of this stanza are especially powerful--"Let go your hand from my shoulders, / Put me down, and depart on your way"--for Winston has made that decision already.

With these lines, we are reminded, once again, of the last confrontation between David and Winston before the wedding. As David tries to tell Winston to accept his choice, to "make [him]self happy with that girl," he reaches out to him: "David sighed and went over to the couch and lifted Winston's face gently" (80). Just before he underscores the fact that Cassandra "is all [Winston's] got now," David takes his hand away from Winston's face, a gesture that signals closure in their relationship and marks the last act of love between them. We see their lover's touch re-enacted in Whitman's ultimatum, "Let go your hand from my shoulder."

Once Whitman has explained the challenges that belie the love he describes, however, he turns his attention to the possibility that such challenges can be met. It is as if Whitman patterns his poem against the fickle nature of human emotions, the "ups and downs" of love between people. Just when it seems that the speaker of the poem is distraught and has lost all hope for a future with his lover, Whitman spends the following stanza in celebration of another alternative: taking heed of the "fair warning" and overcoming the challenges that loving brings. As if to recapture one more time the possibilities of the love between the speaker and his lover, the next fourteen lines of the poem depict the love that exists and the way that it could be:

> Or else, by stealth, in some wood, for trial,
> Or back of a rock, in the open air,
> (For in any roof'd room of a house I emerge not--nor in company,
> And in libraries I lie as one dumb, a gawk, or unborn, or dead,)
> But just possibly with you on a high hill--first watching lest any person,
>   for miles around, approach unawares,
> Or possibly with you sailing at sea, or on the beach of the sea, or some
>   quiet island,
> Here to put your lips upon mine I permit you,
> With the comrade's long-dwelling kiss, or the new husband's kiss,
> For I am the new husband, and I am the comrade.   (*TVPP* 368-369)

The speaker envisions his love as successful, despite the challenges, despite even his own "warning" about the difficulty of meeting the degree of commitment he expects of his lover. In these lines, Whitman glorifies love in nature--"in some wood," "in the open air," "on a high hill," "sailing at sea," "on the beach," or on "some quiet island." This is a wide-ranging and free kind of love; it does not hide--it will not flourish indoors "in any roof'd room" or "in libraries."[3]   The speaker indicates that he will only embrace this love if he can do so outdoors and freely, without shame (though with some caution "lest any person, for miles around, approach unawares").   Such an open declaration of love, however, is problematic, for it can only happen in solitude: "I emerge not . . . in company." Thus, the tender moments shared between lovers are qualified by a necessary privacy and seclusion.

It is significant that David ends his recitation of the poem shortly after this stanza, partly because this qualification is not important for heterosexual lovers; that is, though they certainly should seek seclusion for modesty's sake, society does not shun their love.   As Winston is speaking to Cassandra, then, the lines reflect a healthy and accepted love between groom and blushing bride.   David, as is appropriate for his role of best man, lets the "long-dwelling kiss" resonate, rather than leaving "the result uncertain, perhaps destructive."   When we consider David speaking these lines to Winston, however, the poem becomes at once a reflection on the love that they have shared and a declaration that David cannot view it in society's terms.   David uses Whitman's tender description of love between men to underscore, unbeknownst to his audience, how natural, all-consuming, and liberating the love between David and Winston has been, in spite of the demands for secrecy made upon them by society.

Simpson's analysis of the way in which the poem operated at its first publication illuminates how it works in Naylor's novel as well: for Whitman's heterosexual reader (and David's audience), the "comrade's long-dwelling kiss" would be appreciated as a "gesture of affection only, not desire," but should Whitman's reader be homosexual (as Winston is), "he would see the kiss of the comrade for what it actually was--an expression of homosexual feelings.   So Whitman could have his cake and eat it too--safeguard his reputation and express his hidden, illicit feelings to those who felt as he did" (30-31). Killingsworth also highlights the reception with which the poem was first met: "In many ways 'Calamus' portrays a kind of male-male friendship with which Victorians would have been very much at home" (144).   In the same way, then, and especially because David has changed the sex of the lover in the poem from male to female, the members of the community of Linden Hills will find nothing indecorous about his reading.   David provides his own opportunity to speak in disguise, and as "Whitman accepts the responsibility of speaking for those who cannot speak" (Martin, "Conversion and Identity" 66), so David vocalizes his relationship with Winston--both for himself and on behalf of Winston, who is silenced by the presence of Linden Hills.

Together, David and Winston have explored their love with the same kind of "stealth" expressed in the poem, and they have been able to find, in their solitude, some celebration of love.   The lines further suggest possibilities for their love.   If Winston can accept the challenge of loving David, then this positive alternative might be made real for them.   In reading the poem, David is presenting Winston with a version of how their lives might have been.   When we remember, however, that Winston has not chosen David, we might also see in these lines David's refusal to accept a relationship Winston is ashamed of. David will not compromise; he will not hide his love indoors.   Most importantly, David will not accept an inferior position to Cassandra; if he cannot have Winston as his "sole and exclusive" lover, then he will end the relationship.

Indeed, David's final remark to Winston before the wedding reflects his unwillingness to settle for second best: "'And since I can't be your wife, I won't be your whore'" (80). Finally, there is an interesting duality suggested in the final line of the stanza: "For I am the new husband, and I am the comrade." David is, in effect, calling attention to Winston's now inescapable dual identity; he is Cassandra's "new husband," but he will forever be David's "comrade."

When David chooses to end his version of "Whoever You are Holding Me Now in Hand," he does so with the lines that form the heart of Whitman's poem. If the first three stanzas present "fair warning" to the lover who dares to "sign himself a candidate" for affection, and if the following stanza reflects, instead, the possibility and rewards of a successful love, this last stanza of David's version of Whitman presents yet another alternative for the expression of love. Here, Whitman depicts a deeper and more profound love. For if the lovers cannot proceed with the more physical love described in the previous stanza (marked by the "long-dwelling kiss"), then they may, at least, take comfort in an intimacy unaffected by their separation:

> Or, if you will, thrusting me beneath your clothing,
> Where I may feel the throbs of your heart, or rest upon your hip,
> Carry me when you go forth over land or sea;
> For thus, merely touching you, is enough--is best,
> And thus, touching you, would I silently sleep and be carried eternally.
> (_TVPP_ 369)

As lines from Winston to Cassandra, they express the kind of love that the ceremony of marriage consecrates; David has spoken a poem that is an ode to the joyful wedding of his best friend. It is fitting that Winston, as "the new husband," make such a profession, but in reality, "the room dissolve[s] into a molten vat of air that Winston [is] having trouble breathing" (90). For the lines, as spoken by David to Winston, are unmistakably dynamic. David begins his poem by "telling" Winston that he regrets that he is not strong enough to maintain their relationship, to survive the challenges that confront lovers; he then recreates the possibility of their love existing, as if almost to admonish Winston for betraying it. Finally, then, David offers a last commemoration of their love. He uses Whitman's words to declare what Winston has himself already revealed: " . . . they had known the joys of a communion that far outstripped the flesh--they could hardly just be lovers. No, this man gave him his center. . . . " (79). David is, indeed, a part of Winston; he resides in "the throbs of [his] heart." They are inseparable in this way, regardless of the perceived distance between them and regardless of Winston's decision to marry. David is asking Winston to remember the connection or "communion" they share, to "[c]arry [him] when [he] goes forth." Though Winston will remain in Linden Hills in the new house on Tupelo Drive presented as a gift from Luther Nedeed, David asks him to retain the memory of their love as he journeys forth into marriage and "straight" life. Ultimately, the lines of poetry present a sad and meaningful ending to their relationship, for David knows all too well the adversity they face from society-- and the difficulties, in particular, that Winston faces from the community of Linden Hills. He concedes that this unacknowledged way of loving, after all, is not only their sole option, but is the best one: "For thus, merely touching you, is enough--is best." But he will cherish their love, and he will be satisfied with the experience of their camaraderie long after they are separated: "And thus, touching you, would I silently sleep and be carried eternally." Even Willie is affected by the strength of the sentiment presented in the poem: "Those words spoke of something pretty deep just between two people" (89). Throughout his rendition of Whitman's poem, then, David has been professing his undying love for Winston, as he cleverly uses the poem to verbalize the profound bond that exists between them and to perform what amounts to a eulogy over the death of their relationship in a paean to Winston's marriage.

Left with the last lines of the poem that David speaks, Cassandra can believe that the joys of marriage outweigh the trials, and the members of the community of Linden Hills gathered there can remain ignorant about the real meaning of the poem: they can simply see a best man reciting a perfectly fitting poem on the occasion of his best friend's wedding. However, Whitman's poem continues for another twelve lines: "But Willie knew he hadn't finished reading the entire poem. And he wondered if Winston knew what the rest of it said" (89). The point of David's selection of Whitman's poem and of his omission of the two ending stanzas, of course, is that Winston will recognize both. Though what he speaks out loud to Winston is a final testimony of their enduring love, the message of those last stanzas hangs in the ensuing silence, as Willie perceives: "Did [Winston] know that that guy was standing up there and telling the whole world that he was kissing him off for good?" (89). The last two stanzas of the poem bring the speaker's roller coaster ride of emotions full circle: he is ultimately pessimistic about the relationship succeeding. Willie remembers the lines to himself as he attempts to make sense of the exchange that has just occurred:

> But these leaves conning, you con at peril,
> For these leaves, and me, you will not understand,
> They will elude you at first, and still more afterward--I will certainly elude
>   you,
> Even while you should think you had unquestionably caught me, behold!
> Already you see I have escaped from you.   (*TVPP* 369)

Just as the speaker of the poem relates his disillusionment with love, so David means for Winston to recognize that they must suffer a final parting (one more significant than their being separated) in which Winston will not be able to understand David. Perhaps David refers again to their last conversation; if Winston did understand the principles that guide David, he would not ask him to accept his marriage to a woman. And, indeed, Winston cannot accept that their relationship must end; he cannot understand David's pride. The lovers have been "conned" by the notion that their love could possibly exist, and since Winston has made the difficult decision to cast aside David's love, it is inevitable that such fulfillment elude them both. The reasons for David's insistence that the relationship must end "will elude [Winston] at first," and then later, "still more afterward--[David himself] will certainly elude [Winston]." The lines mark, once again, the distance--not only physical--that will occur between them and that has already begun to occur as David impresses upon Winston, without even speaking Whitman's words, that his wedding to Cassandra results in an inevitable break between them: "Already you see I have escaped from you." Moreover, in the same way that David will lie forever far from his grasp, so Winston's own acceptance of his true homosexual self will elude him, for Winston has clouded his identity with the lie of his marriage. Perhaps most intriguing, however, is a reading of these lines as spoken by Winston for Cassandra, which has been David's intention from the start of the poem. In a way, David wills Winston to express himself again, only this time Winston would be revealing the truth to her: "Even while you should think you had unquestionably caught me, behold!" All in all, the first of these lines that David purposefully omits from his rendition of the poem communicate not only Winston's betrayal of David and the total disintegration of their relationship, but also the falsehood of Winston's marriage to Cassandra.

In the last stanza of the poem, which David also does not read, Whitman turns his attention to the initial riddle that he presents, and he recreates for his reader the meaning of the opening lines of the poem: "Whoever you are, holding me now in hand, / Without one thing, all will be useless." When David speaks these lines as words from Winston to his new wife, we regard the "holding" to be a physical one, an embrace between two people. However, when we consider the closing lines of the poem, we are invited to think of Whitman speaking to a person "holding" the book in which the poem he writes appears:

> For it is not for what I have put into it that I have written this book,
> Nor is it by reading it you will acquire it,
> Nor do those know me best who admire me, and vauntingly praise
> me,
> Nor will the candidates for my love, (unless at most a very few,)
> prove victorious,
> Nor will my poems do good only--they will do just as much evil,
> perhaps more;
> For all is useless without that which you may guess at many times
> and not hit--that which I hinted at;
> Therefore release me, and depart on your way.   (*TVPP* 369)

As Naylor introduces the extra lines as part of Willie's conscious thoughts, she does not print the first four of these--perhaps the reader will fill them in, like Willie has been doing as he listens. The emphasis in these first lines is on Whitman's purpose for writing the poem--or rather on what his purpose has *not* been: "For it is not for what I have put into it that I have written this book." Whitman appears to be deliberately vague here. "[I]t is not for what [he] *has put* into it that [he] has written" this poem and the "Calamus" section of *Leaves of Grass*. Rather, it is for what he *has not put* into it that he is driven to compose: he *has not put* to words a specific love for a man or men. In fact, "[o]n no occasion . . . did Whitman ever sanction a homosexual reading of the 'Calamus' sequence" (Pollack 181). This does not mean that the poem is not about love between men--indeed, Willie's reaction attests to its true meaning. What Whitman is declaring, however, is that he has not been able to express that love completely openly; he has been performing a "charade" in the same way that David does. Simpson explains: "Nowhere does he show the love of a particular man for a particular man. . . . [T]he loving comrade is not described and has nothing to say. . . . Love in Whitman is always general; it is never love for an individual" (32). David's message to Winston in these unspoken lines is twofold. First, David is reinforcing that Winston, as a "candidate for [his] love" has failed to "prove victorious." Second, David is arguing Whitman's riddle for Winston: "all is useless without that which you may guess at many times and not hit--/ that which I hinted at." While Whitman posits his riddle for a heterosexual audience, David asks his homosexual lover to consider its implications: "all is useless" if one does not accept the existence of love between men. Whitman's reader will not understand him or his poem; Winston will not understand David or, more importantly, himself. Although Winston can associate himself with the community of Linden Hills, he will forever be empty inside, "drowning" (90). Ultimately, David articulates for Winston, with the words of Whitman's poem passing silently between them, that Winston must find his own true self. It is not something that he can "acquire"--certainly not from Linden Hills--and David is powerless in the event of their departing on their own ways. Cady understands that departure to signify Whitman's "willingness to follow his new separate vision," one that embraces homosexuality as normal and one that defies "what in 'In Paths Untrodden' Whitman calls 'standards hitherto unpublish'd'" (17). David, speaking words unspoken, makes the decision to follow in Whitman's footsteps and laments the loss of his companion along the way. He takes the challenge that he presents to Winston.

In the larger scheme of the novel, the event of Winston's wedding reception is the beginning of a series of examples meant to illustrate how Luther Nedeed controls the community of Linden Hills. Willie and Lester are just beginning their descent into Naylor's inferno; this episode marks Willie's discovery that "there was definitely something very queer" (90) about its members and confirms for Lester that each of them has "lost all touch with what it is to be *them*" (59). However, the intertextuality that Naylor employs by placing the poetry of Walt Whitman at the very core of the wedding reception merits further consideration. Clearly, Naylor's use of a poem from the "Calamus" collection is motivated by the understanding that those poems "serve as the beginning point for a study of modern homosexual literature, helping to identify a radical imagination implicit in homosexual experience under oppression" (Cady 5). David, Naylor's homosexual character, is given a voice through Whitman, the pioneer of and literary precedent for what Jacob Stockinger terms "homotextuality" in America (qtd. in Martin, "Conversion and Identity" 60). Naylor uses a poem from the canon in constructing a unique communication between two of her African-American characters. Her application of Whitman, however, is even more significant for the examination of race relations that *Leaves of Grass* provides. To be sure, Whitman's anti-slavery views are controversial, particularly in light of the contradictions inherent in his writings as a whole, but his "very attempt to conceive of a poem as a vehicle for conveying a sense of black subjectivity, instead of as a means of promoting general abolitionist sentiment, must be seen as a radical one" (Beach 29).[4] However we view these contradictions, we come to acknowledge that Whitman was forging new territory for the relationship between whites and blacks in America. Naylor furthers this relationship as, in her exploration of black consciousness and "black subjectivity" in *Linden Hills*, she makes space for the voice of Whitman as "Other," marginalized by both his homosexuality and his whiteness in an African-

American novel: the lines of poetry by Whitman, Stevens, and Eliot represent the only white voices.

Overall, Whitman, a self-proclaimed poet of the American people, "One of the Nation of many nations, the smallest the same and the largest the same" (*TVPP* 20), tends to be appreciated as a champion of equality, "one who in *Leaves of Grass* consistently includes blacks and other people of color in his vision of an ideal republic" (Klammer 2). Given the scope and vigor of Whitman's writing and his invitation to readers of all ethnicities to celebrate their own songs of themselves, it is not unusual that he should gain such favor among non-white writers, though we might be surprised by the extent to which they have embraced Whitman. In much of Whitman's poetry is a pattern for self-love that the members of the communities of minority cultures in America, so long oppressed and voiceless, find wholesome and need to emulate. Indeed, "[o]ne of the most fascinating phenomena in American literary history is that Whitman, a white and canonical writer, has been and is still being avidly 'absorbed' by almost all groups of ethnic writers" (Li 109). George B. Hutchinson's study elucidates "the ways in which *Leaves of Grass* affected black poetics and cultural theory," for "Whitman's writing contributed crucially to some of the most fruitful developments in black writing of the twentieth century" ("The Whitman Legacy and the Harlem Renaissance" 201). Although Hutchinson focuses on Alain Locke, James Weldon Johnson, and Jean Toomer, we might extend his list to include Naylor--Whitman's influence still indelible in the latter part of the twentieth century. Elsewhere Hutchinson even declares: "Probably no white American poet has had a greater impact upon black American literature than Walt Whitman" ("Whitman and the Black Poet" 46).

Part of Whitman's appeal, in the end, lies in his early inauguration of the theory of multiculturalism, as he assumes the "voice of a multiethnic, multicultural, multivocal people who can belong and feel at home in America" (Li 110). His writing has become a sourcebook for ethnic writers, and it is, thus, fitting that Naylor draws upon such a voice when writing her novel about the collapse of the African-American community under the influences of white standards of success. As Naylor incorporates Whitman's words into *Linden Hills*, she evokes images of Whitman as a brave homosexual poet, as a proponent of equality among all Americans, and as a filter for "many long dumb voices" (*TVPP* 32). Most importantly, if we perform what Aldon Nielsen asserts should be "insistent readings of the blackness of white writing" (24), we will learn how Naylor finds reflections of African-American experience in Whitman and understand "these leaves" more fully. As David locates himself in "Whoever You are Holding Me Now in Hand," what Naylor reveals, through such intertextuality, is a connection between writers of different races and a continuum of American literature as a whole--a literature that encompasses both Whitman, the original American voice, and Naylor, who simultaneously flavors her novel with a voice from the canon and adds her own original voice to it. Just as Naylor explains that Willie and Lester experience an intense bond caused by their "giving sound to the bruised places in their hearts" (28), so Whitman and Naylor are drawn together in this endeavor as well.

Endnotes

[1] Whitman's "Once I Pass'd Through a Populous City," for example, "was originally homosexual in content but . . . revised to represent a heterosexual encounter" (Cady 6).

[2] This and subsequent quotations of "Whoever You are Holding Me Now in Hand" are taken from volume 2 of *Leaves of Grass: A Textual Variorum of the Printed* Poems, published in 1980 by New York University Press and hereafter abbreviated as *TVPP*. What I have reprinted here is the 1871 version of the poem (as opposed to the final 1881 version that Whitman sanctioned as the text future readers should use) because the poem in Naylor's text is also this 1871 version. Though most of them are insignificant, there are several changes between the 1871 and 1881 versions of this third "Calamus" poem. Apparently, Whitman preferred to omit many of the commas as he revised the poem for the 1881 edition of *Leaves of Grass*. These are not important to this study; however, two significant changes occur. Line 8 in the 1871 version reads, "You would have to give up all else--I alone would expect to be your God, sole and exclusive," while the 1881 version reads: "You would have to give up all else, I alone would expect to be your sole and exclusive standard." The reference to God in the earlier version (the version reprinted in Naylor) reinforces the commitment homosexual lovers require and characterizes such a relationship as a worshipful and sacred one. In addition, line 27 in the 1871 version reads, "But these leaves conning, you con at peril," while in the 1881 version, Whitman omits that crucial comma. The inclusion of the comma, in this case, changes the meaning substantially; the emphasis is on the risk that the reader or lover takes when conning others, when hiding homosexuality. Without the comma, however, we can read the line to mean that the "leaves" of the poem or book "con" the reader.

[3] Whitman may be suggesting that homosexual love does not exist in books since the speaker declares: "And in libraries I lie as one dumb, a gawk, or unborn, or dead." This line reflects some frustration on his part with society's failure to accept homosexuality, for the gay man cannot find, at this time, true solace even in books, in libraries. The gay writer cannot speak what society deems unspeakable, cannot live the life that suits him, and cannot commit his feelings to paper for future members of society. Killingsworth notes: "External evidence suggests that Whitman puzzled over the limits of conventional propriety. He sought literary precedents"--one of the only sources available to him was "a nineteenth-century translation of Plato" where Whitman "found a depiction of male-male love in the language of heterosexual romantic love" (148). Moreover, Cady understands that "the Whitman of *Calamus*" was "in an isolated situation that would be especially difficult for a self-ordained popular poet and gave him no publicly shared tradition and language for the affirmation [of homosexual love] he wanted to make" (7).

[4] As a means of entering the debate over Whitman's position on slavery, see Martin Klammer, *Whitman, Slavery, and the Emergence of Leaves of Grass* and Christopher Beach, "'Now Lucifer was not dead': Slavery, Intertextuality, and Subjectivity in *Leaves of Grass*." See also Betsy Erkkila, "Whitman and American Empire," Sill 54-69; Reginald Martin, "The Self Contradiction Literatus: Walt Whitman and His Two Views of Blacks in America," *Calamus: Walt Whitman Quarterly: International* 27 (1986): 13-22; Ken Peeples, Jr., "The Paradox of the 'Good Gray Poet' [Walt Whitman on Slavery and the Black Man]," *Phylon: The Atlanta University Review of Race and Culture* 25 (1974): 22-32; Mary-Emma Graham, "Politics in Black and White: A View of Walt Whitman's Career as a Political Journalist," *CLA Journal* 17 (1973): 263-270; and Kenneth M. Price, "Whitman's Solutions to 'The Problem of the Blacks,'" *Resources for American Literary Study* 15 (1985): 205-208.

Works Cited

Beach, Christopher. "'Now Lucifer was not dead': Slavery, Intertextuality, and Subjectivity in *Leaves of Grass*." *Canadian Review of American Studies* 25 (1995): 27-48.

Black, Stephen A. "Reading Whitman Psychoanalytically." *Walt Whitman: Here and Now*. Ed. Joann P. Krieg. Westport: Greenwood, 1985. 43-48.

Cady, Joseph. "Not Happy in the Capital: Homosexuality and the *Calamus* Poems." *American Studies* 19 (1978): 5-22.

Hutchinson, George B. "The Whitman Legacy and the Harlem Renaissance." *The Centennial Essays: Walt Whitman.* Ed. Ed Folsom. Iowa City: U of Iowa P, 1994. 201-216.

_____. "Whitman and the Black Poet: Kelly Miller's Speech to the Walt Whitman Fellowship." *American Literature* 61 (1989): 46-58.

Killingsworth, M. Jimmie. "Sentimentality and Homosexuality in Whitman's 'Calamus.'" *ESQ: A Journal of the American Renaissance* 29 (1983): 144-153.

Klammer, Martin. *Whitman, Slavery, and the Emergence of Leaves of Grass.* University Park: Pennsylvania State UP, 1995.

Li, Xilao. "Whitman and Ethnicity." In Sill 109-122.

Martin, Robert K. "Conversion and Identity: The 'Calamus' Poems." *Walt Whitman Review* 25 (1979): 59-66.

_____. "The Disseminal Whitman: A Deconstructive Approach to *Enfans d'Adam* and *Calamus.*" *Approaches to Teaching Whitman's Leaves of Grass.* Ed. Donald D. Kummings. New York: MLA, 1990. 74-80.

Naylor, Gloria. *Linden Hills.* New York: Penguin, 1986.

Nielsen, Aldon L. *Writing Between the Lines: Race and Intertextuality.* Athens: U of Georgia P, 1994.

Pearlman, Mickey. "An Interview with Gloria Naylor." *High Plains Literary Review* 5 (1990): 98-107.

Pollack, Vivian R. "Death as Repression, Repression as Death: A Reading of Whitman's 'Calamus' Poems." Sill 179-193.

Sill, Geoffrey M., ed. *Walt Whitman of Mickle Street: A Centennial Collection.* Knoxville: U of Tennessee P, 1994.

Simpson, Louis. "Strategies of Sex in Whitman's Poetry." In Sill 28-37.

Whitman, Walt. *Leaves of Grass: A Textual Variorum of the Printed Poems.* Eds. Sculley Bradley, Harold W. Blodgett, Arthur Golden, and William White. 3 vols. New York: New York UP, 1980.

Mama Day

Meisenhelder, Susan. "'The Whole Picture' in Gloria Naylor's *Mama Day*." *African American Review* 27.3 (1993): 405-419.

In *Mama Day* Naylor narrates the love story of two black people from strikingly different backgrounds--George, orphaned in the urban North, has grown up in an institution run by whites; and Cocoa, doted on by two black mother figures, has been drenched in the traditions of the rural South. Through the relationship that develops between these two characters, one the product of a white world, the other of an emphatically black one, Naylor deals with the issue of maintaining black cultural identity in the face of attempts by the white world to order, control, and define black people.

In her characterization of Willow Springs, Cocoa's island home situated off the Georgia/South Carolina coast, Naylor presents a world outside white parameters, a place in no state, on no map, connected to the mainland by the flimsiest of bridges periodically destroyed by storms. As the narrator stresses at the beginning of the novel, Willow Springs is not even, in a strict historical sense, American:

> . . . the way we saw it, America ain't entered the question at all when it come to our land: Sapphira was African-born, Bascombe Wade was from Norway, and it was the 18 & 23'ing that went down between them two put deeds in our hands. And we wasn't even Americans when we got it--was slaves. And the laws about slaves not owning nothing in Georgia and South Carolina don't apply, 'cause the land wasn't then--and isn't now--in either of them places.   (5)

Outside white traditions, Willow Springs--with its Candle Walk instead of Christmas, its "standing forth" in lieu of funerals--is culturally independent as well. The vanity of attempts by the white world to assimilate, order, and define this black one is suggested in the anecdote about one Willow Springs resident who returns to do anthropological work. Imbued with the values of the white world in which he has been educated, "determined to put Willow Springs on the map" (7), he misinterprets the island's central myth of 18 and 23, seeing it in relation to the white maps the place transcends:

> . . . you see, he had come to the conclusion after "extensive field work" (ain't never picked a boll of cotton or head of lettuce in his life--Reema spoiled him silly), but he done still made it to the conclusion that 18 & 23 wasn't 18 & 23 at all--was really 81 & 32, which just so happened to be the lines of longitude and latitude marking off where Willow Springs sits on the map. And we were just so damned dumb that we turned the whole thing around. (7-8)

Missing the autonomous cultural identity of Willow Springs, he sees it as a mere reaction to white definitions:

> Not that he called it being dumb, mind you, called it "asserting our cultural identity," "inverting hostile social and political parameters." 'Cause, see, being we was brought here as slaves, we had no choice but to look at everything upside-down. (8)

Throughout the novel, Naylor consistently (and satirically) reveals the futility of the white world's attempts to control either nature or the decidedly black world of Willow Springs. Just as George's "piping system[s]" (52), his engineering feats which "redesign the structures that take care of basic needs" (60), seem trivial in comparison to Mama Day's powers, and his nuclear generator (251) a mere toy beside the force of the storm, the white world's maps, pictures, movies, and myths are depicted as inadequate to express black experience. When one "crosses over" into that autonomous black world, the narrator early on warns the reader, such ways of imaging reality and ordering experience are simply insufficient: "It ain't about right or wrong, truth or lies; it's about a slave woman who brought a whole new meaning to both them words, soon as you cross over here from beyond the bridge" (3).

To underscore the futility of using white artistic forms to express reality across the bridge, Naylor repeatedly emphasizes the inadequacy of photos, charts, and graphs to express the subtle and complex truth of black experience. The inability of a picture to capture George and Cocoa's relationship, for instance, is suggested in the charts and diagrams that constitute his sex education, the "two ugly [headless] blowups of the skinned male and female anatomy" (104) that Mrs. Jackson whacks with her pointer. The "developers" ridiculed at the very beginning of the novel, seeing Willow Springs as a timeless "'pic-ture-ess . . . vacation paradise'" (4), similarly miss the spiritual richness (and awesome powers for good and evil) of the place, its convoluted history still in the making. Even Cocoa senses the inadequacy of pictures to capture Willow Springs. Early in her relationship with George, rather than attempt to explain a spiritual and historical reality he cannot possibly understand, she tries to accommodate it to George's world by "paint[ing] the picture of a small rural community and [her] life with Grandma and Mama Day, so it seemed like any other small southern town and they two old ladies doting over the last grandchild" (126). While "the smoke drifting up over the south woods from Dr. Buzzard's still might as well be painted on a picture, [since] it's always there," and while "the droning from his beehives out by Chevy's Pass, the pounding of the ocean water against the east bluff, the creaking from the wooden slats on the bridge over The Sound" makes the place seem "a still life" (160), such static, "realistic," and two-dimensional images only express the surface of Willow Springs, beneath which flows subtle, but profound change. While "Four pictures *would just about do it*, one for each season" (161; emphasis added), one needs a different kind of vision to understand Willow Springs: ". . . here you'd have to look real close to see a gray hair or so inching around some temples, a little extra roll starting over some belt buckles. But slow, real slow. So slow it's like it's not happening at all. Until it happens. Overnight, some say" (161).

Although to the naive outsider the place seems "a picture postcard" (163), Mama Day, with her more discerning eye, realizes such ways of perceiving reality are foreign and inadequate ones. When, for instance, she watches television pictures of the Phil Donahue show, one episode showing people "all of who got photographs and claim they spotted UFOs," she, with her supernatural ability to communicate across generations, senses how ludicrous Phil Donahue appears, "look[ing] dead serious" (37), asking "'Is there intelligent life in outer space? . . . *And* are they trying to get in touch with us?'" (38). She concludes that such antics "could be summed up in two words: white folks. And when they found a colored somebody to act the fool--like the man from New Jersey, holding up a snapshot of his cousin posing with a family of Martians--she expanded it to three words: honorary white folks" (38).

In contrast to the anthropologist's mistaken view of black culture as an "upside-down" version of a white norm, Naylor suggests that the more complex spiritual reality of Willow Springs subverts white ways of understanding experience. George's sense of "a confrontation with fate" (28) in meeting Cocoa, for instance, destroying the pragmatic, empirical order of his life, seems "like a bizarre photograph . . . developing in front of [his] face" (27). The powder Mama Day inserts in his letter that inexplicably leads him to get a job for Cocoa (ensuring their future meeting) appears "a movie being played in reverse frame to frame" (54). The conjure work and divination so central to Willow Springs also turn simplistic white notions of facts, rules, and reality on their head. Thus, Cocoa's illness is like "a badly dubbed movie" (25) and Mama Day's intuition of the approaching storm like a nickelodeon gone haywire, "the picture mov[ing] backward" until the whole picture "falls into place" (227).

Other white cultural artifacts are depicted as similarly inadequate. A measure of both Cocoa's and George's alienation from their black roots early in the novel is their extensive use of white cultural norms to define themselves and to understand their relationship. George, for instance, sees himself as Shakespeare and Cocoa as "Harold Robbins in general and James Michener when [she] wanted to get deep" (60). He plays the role of white, urbane sophisticate when he asks Cocoa to dinner by sending her roses with a note: "'There are only eleven yellow roses here. The twelfth is waiting on a table at Il Ponte Vecchio if you'd like to retrieve it one evening.'" The absurdity of such posturing is not lost on Cocoa, who thinks, "Now, what kind of fudge stick asked a woman out like this--who's this guy used to dating, Mary Tyler Moore?" (58).

His notions about women come from the white world as well. Never having had a relationship with any black woman, either mother or lover, he knows women only from Mrs. Jackson's "graphic" diagrams of "the rudiments: ovaries, a womb, Fallopian tubes" (141). Sensing that these do not represent the whole picture, he buys books about women in an attempt to understand

Cocoa. In the white world, he finds only "horrif[ying]" images depicting women as "normal only about seventy-two hours out of each month" (141) and "depressing" charts proving women were "shrews through no fault of [their] own" (141-142). A black cultural orphan, trained to be a parody of the stereotypical white male, he can (not surprisingly) only think of his love for Cocoa in terms of white myths. Speaking from a much later time frame with greater insight into his folly, he admits he

> conjured up images of jasmine-scented nights, warm biscuits and honey being brought to me on flowered china plates as you sat at my feet and rubbed your cheek against my knee. Go ahead and laugh, you have a perfect right. I had never been south, and you couldn't count the times I had spent in Miami at the Super Bowl-- that city was a humid and pastel New York. So I had the same myths about southern women that you did about northern men. (33)

As George's final comment suggests, Cocoa too, early in the novel, deals with George according to a white script. Her way of understanding the disconcerting interview she has with him is to see it in the formulaic terms of cinematic melodrama. Aware that they are both play-acting, she thinks with her characteristic sarcasm, "Jesus, all we needed was the organ music and a slow fade to my receding back as the swirling sand of the rocky coastline began to spell out The End" (30). As her sardonic conclusion suggests, both act parts false to their real selves and to their inexplicable attraction to one another: "We had sure become one understanding pair of folks by the time the lights in the theater came up and they pulled the curtain across the screen" (31). What her cynicism misses, however, is the fundamental inadequacy of such dramatic forms to represent their relationship. This interview, of course, is the beginning, rather than "The End," of their love story.

The painful lack of communication they early experience is a function of their attempts to develop their relationship according to a white script. The absurdity of their frequent discussions about the symbolism of Shakespeare is, for instance, not lost on Cocoa. When George asks her out again after what she describes as "one of the most boring evenings in recent memory" (59), she thinks,

> Surely, he jests. I swear, that's the first thing that popped into my head when you asked me out again. I don't know where that phrase came from--had to be something from my high school Shakespeare and you had been going on and on about him earlier in the evening. Just proves that Shakespeare didn't have a bit of soul--I don't care if he did write about Othello, Cleopatra, and some slave on a Caribbean island. If he had been in touch with our culture, he would have written somewhere, "Nigger, are you out of your mind?" (64)

While Cocoa often takes satisfaction in noting George's cultural whiteness, she falls into this trap herself. As confused by George as he is by her, she (no less ludicrously) draws on other white myths to explain his behavior:

I'd read all about your type in *Cosmo*: ambivalent about your mothers, distant and uncaring fathers, should really be gay, but thought other men were too good for you. I kicked myself because I should have known--the yellow roses, the top-drawer restaurant, the open and sensitive attempts at conversation, the gentle manipulation so that I spilled my guts and actually felt good about it. Oh, God, I should have known. Now it was a matter of finding a tactful way to turn you down so you wouldn't start sobbing and pleading in the middle of the street. If I remembered right, *Cosmo* said that your type wasn't given to open violence, but would sink to degrading displays in public.   (64-65)

Having no experience with men like George, unable to dredge up a "file" into which he fits, she cannot believe he "want[s] nothing from [her] but honesty" (63). As she dimly senses when she first meets him, white models of relationships between men and women are inadequate for her to "figure this shit out" (30). Nevertheless, both she and George cling to white romantic myths that threaten their happiness. Cocoa, for instance, obsessed with fears that "it will end," senses the inadequacy of white fairytales for her life in her cynical statement, "Grown women aren't supposed to believe in Prince Charmings and happily ever afters," but merely embraces another more melodramatic one: "Real life isn't about that--so bring on the clouds" (119).

The gravest challenge to their relationship occurs when they return to Willow Springs, where neither George's charts and maps nor either one's white romantic myths operate. To flourish in that milieu, they need to find different ways of understanding reality and their relationship. George, whose only experience of "miracles" and "immortality" comes from football (124), traverses a cultural chasm when he "crosses over" the bridge. The degree of his disorientation is immediately evident: Panicked when he cannot find the place on the map, he (like the white developers) sees it as "paradise" (175) and even fantasizes about schemes for developing the land (albeit in a more ecologically sound way). As these reactions suggest, his failure to enter into the world of Willow Springs or even to understand it (despite his best efforts) results from his inability to abandon his white cultural baggage. As events become more confusing, he clings even more tenaciously to the charts and graphs familiar to him, using his engineering knowledge, for instance, to speed up the building of the bridge, an obsession that symbolizes most graphically his dependence on the white world. Because the bridge remains a technical problem for him, he never sees the real kind of bridge between Cocoa and her history, and between her and himself, which they both need to survive.

Like his charts and graphs, his constant attempts to accommodate Willow Springs to white cultural myths make it impossible for him to understand its more complex reality. Nothing from the white world, neither Mrs. Jackson's anatomical charts nor the tales of female hysteria from his psychology books, can help him explain the female-centered place he enters. Amused, for instance, that all the women in Cocoa's family are called Days, he teases her, "But what, as in your case, if a woman married?" Cocoa's profound response provided a key George needs to understand Willow Springs and Cocoa's relation to it: "You live a Day and you die a Day." Totally missing the deeper significance of this remark, George condescendingly responds, "Early women's lib." As Cocoa's simple comment, "A bit more than that" (218), suggests, George trivializes the history and independence of black women in Willow Springs by trying to understand them in terms of white women. As the novel demonstrates, neither Sapphira Wade's story nor Mama Day's power can be captured with the diminutive label *women's lib*.

A similar tendency makes it impossible for George to understand the central myth of Willow Springs--that of Sapphira Wade, the story of a slave who was not a slave, one who escaped not merely to the North but all the way back to Africa. Faced with a version of slavery and the tale of a female slave that subvert white historical myths, he inaccurately interprets the various versions he hears. Like an anthropologist, he sees the story as another fanciful "legend" characteristic of exotic subcultures and finds Cocoa's way of speaking of Sapphira, "as if you were listing the attributes of a goddess," simply "odd." Missing the significance of Cocoa's reverence and the spiritual truth of his own simile, he reacts "scientifically," seeking the "real" source of what he sees as mere "myth":

> The whole thing was so intriguing, I wondered if that woman had lived at all. Places like this island were ripe for myths, but if she had really existed, there must be some record. Maybe in Bascombe Wade's papers: deeds of sale for his slaves. Where had his home been on this island? Did he have a family? Who erected his tombstone?   (218)

Attempting to understand black women's history in white male terms, he mistakenly hopes for a document to prove the existence of a woman whose story, in fact, reveals the inadequacy of that bill of sale to understand her power and independence. Imitating white histories of slavery, he would erase Sapphira's existence and importance by focusing on her white "master."

George tries several inappropriate white strategies for understanding the relationship between Sapphira and Bascombe Wade. At one point, for instance, he turns it into a version of *Gone with the Wind*, imagining Wade sitting on the verandah of his house in the other place, "watch[ing Sapphira] pruning roses that grew as large as my fist, snipping sprigs of mint for his tea," though even he senses the absurdity of casting Sapphira Wade as a demure Southern belle: "It was a nice image but it didn't feel that way" (225).

These attempts to fit the story of Sapphira Wade into a white mold ultimately prevent George from learning the lesson he needs to glean from her life--namely, the impossibility of possessing the black woman and the tragic folly of such attempts. As he becomes increasingly confused by the women who surround him, he more and more plays the role of "macho" (215) man, yearning, like John Wayne or Huck Finn, for a world without women:

> . . . there was a time when I didn't have any whole world complicated with [women]. A wonderful time. Just dozens of boys. Clean fights. Straight talk. Order. You did what you were supposed to and left it at that. No tantrums. No nonsense. And your hard work was appreciated.   (247)

This fear of black women's powers, and the threat to white male "order" that they pose, leads him immediately to recast Sapphira Wade as an ungrateful, unfaithful "bitch": "Just look at that poor slob buried there--he gave her a whole island, and she still cut out on him" (247). Even when he has his most tangible experience of Sapphira's power during the hurricane, "the workings of Woman [who] has no name" (251), he avoids the full implications of the experience by taming that force, inappropriately recasting events in the shape of a Victorian novel: "I expected the sun to be shining, thought really that we deserved to have it shine after a night like that. Wasn't that the way in those Victorian novels? A wild tempest, flaming passions, and then the calm of a gorgeous sunrise" (255-256). That such insipid, romantic closure is not the shape of stories in Willow Springs is borne out in events following the storm and in George's observation, from a later perspective, that ". . . we were hardly going according to the script" (256).

Just as George rewrites the history of Willow Springs as various white myths, he also sees his relationship with Cocoa as one white love story after another. In no less ludicrous fashion than his dinner invitation, he, at one point while in Willow Springs, "leans over and whisper[s] in [Cocoa's] ear, 'Let's play Adam and Eve.'" While Cocoa's deflating rejoinder, "'. . . just go on and roll around in those woods with your clothes off, and the first red ant that bites your behind will tell you all about paradise'" (222), seems merely amusing, she hints at a much deeper folly in George's fantasy. His vision of two lone lovers who can "defy history" (226) in the garden paradise at the other place is a "picture postcard" version of romance that disregards the complex history of which he and Cocoa are a part.

Perhaps even more ominously, he imagines himself as a particular kind of male lead in the dramas into which he casts himself and Cocoa. While the real story of Sapphira and Bascombe has important affinities with his and Cocoa's, he draws parallels from his own inaccurate white versions; as Cocoa realizes, he (like the Bascombe Wade he imagines) wants "to sit in the rocking chair and play southern gentleman with [Cocoa] in his lap" (224). In fact, George, feeling ever more powerless and out of control in his relationship with Cocoa, fashions a script or them that implicitly casts her as a subservient female in a familiar white drama. In his fantasy of "jasmine-scented nights, warm biscuits and honey being brought to [him] on flowered china plates," for instance, he implicitly casts himself as a plantation owner and Cocoa as an adoring (and decidedly subordinate) wife, "s[itting] at [his] feet . . . rub[bing her] cheek against [his] knee" (33). Later in the novel, when he insists that he and Cocoa stay "forever" in Willow Springs over her strong objections, she articulates the myth he has finally settled upon:

> "Okay, George. This is what you want to hear: anywhere in the world you go and anything you want to do I'm game. I'll freeze myself, starve myself, wear Salvation Army clothes to be by your side. I'll steal for you, lie for you, crawl on my hands and knees beside you. Because a good woman always follows her man." (221)

In subtle ways, George plays out this male role to the end of the novel. The scene in which, after an argument, he carries Cocoa back to his bed "where

[she] belong[s]" (252), comes from a movie familiar to Hollywood but foreign to Willow Springs. His banter with Cocoa about how she got there, "'on [her] hands and knees,'" "'begging [him] over and over'" (253), is another revealing indication of the underlying plot he imagines.

A complicated character, George acts a male role that is, however, more seductive and more complex, for his fantasies of male superiority are overlaid with other more superficially attractive (but equally inappropriate) white ones. Like Prince Charming, convinced that only he can save Cocoa, he kisses her (288) to bring her out of her deathly sleep. Misinterpreting Mama Day's statement that there "'is more than my blood flows in her and more hands that can lay claim to her than these'" as mere "metaphors" (294) like the fanciful ones in the white literary masterpieces he knows, he plays the role of traditional romantic hero, trying to "single-handedly" save "his woman" from evil forces with absurdly futile schemes to swim across the sound--"Quite a feat," he admits, "since I couldn't swim a stroke" (263)--or to row a leaky boat to the mainland.[1] Frustrated by his lack of control, George fashions these scenarios more to prove his manhood than to save Cocoa. While he selflessly and heroically vows, ". . . I knew what I was going to do. It was an issue of priorities. I'm getting up at daybreak I thought, and I'm going to repair that boat. I'm going to put the oars into the oarlocks and begin to row across The Sound. That much I can do for her" (282), he unwittingly reveals that the self-affirmation of the trial (even if it results in his death) is more important than the goal that he claims motivates him: "And at the point in time when I can feel those oars between my hands, whether I make it or not won't be the issue. And if the boat begins to sink--I looked at my hands lit up by the moonlight--I'll place them in the water and start to swim. Yes, I would *begin* to swim. And at that point in time, finishing would not be the issue" (282-283).

While George acts like the chivalrous "real man" admired in the white world, such notions of masculinity are depicted as infantile ones in the novel. Cocoa, for instance, senses that the man she follows in New York, "a really distinguished-looking guy with a tweed jacket and gray sideburns" who "had diaper pins holding his fly front together--you know, the kind they used to have with pink rabbit heads on them" (18), is somehow representative of what she dislikes about urban, Northern men. Mama Day recognizes a similar childishness in George's condescending suggestion that she use her cane and responds with a "little spanking" (205), dragging him on a bone-crushing trek around the island to teach him a lesson. As his "ego . . . take[s] over" and he gallantly "helps" Mama Day and Abigail with their work, he acts not like a man but like a "five-year-old" (217), unaware that his participation, more hindrance than help, is tolerated to keep him out of mischief. When George brushes off Dr. Buzzard's advice to go to Mama Day with the comment that he and Cocoa are "'going to be fine because I believe in myself,'" Buzzard pinpoints the inadequacy of the self-sufficient individualism on which George's notion of manhood rests:

> "That's where folks start, boy--not where they finish up. Yes, I said
> *boy*. 'Cause a man would have grown enough to know that really
> believing in himself means that he ain't gotta be afraid to admit
> there's some things he just can't do alone."   (292)

As Mama Day's comment to Abigail ("'It's gonna take a man to bring [Cocoa] peace'"--and all they had was that boy" [263]) suggests, Cocoa's survival requires not the immature theatrical bravado of a traditional romantic hero, but the actions of a man unafraid to clasp hands with women.[2]

To help him become such a man, Mama Day fashions a ritual for George that is, in every detail, outside the European tradition of heroic quest legends. Sent with Bascombe Wade's receipt for the purchase of Sapphira and John-Paul's walking stick carved with water lilies, both emblems of male failure to be everything for women, symbols of their futile hopes "that the work of their hands could wipe away all that had gone before" (285), George embarks on a quest designed not to acquire a symbol of his individual prowess but to transcend those very values. Significantly, Mama Day sends him to the chicken's nest, associated throughout the novel with the female creative powers (most notably in Bernice's fertility rite [139-140]) that George fears and misunderstands but needs to respect.[3] In bringing back only his hands--evidence for him of his self-sufficiency and "possession" of Cocoa (". . . these were *my* hands and there was no way I was going to let you go" [301])--and clasping them with Mama Day's, leaving behind the symbols of male failure to possess women, George would, Mama Day hopes, undergo a rite of passage into the kind of manhood Dr. Buzzard had described.

Unable to abandon his intense masculine individualism, however, George perverts this ritual by acting another white male role. Refusing to believe his hands are all he is to bring back, frustrated at what he (like the white world) sees as only "mumbo-jumbo" (295), subconsciously afraid of what the chicken represents, he reenacts the archetypal white drama of male oppression, transforming the walking stick, a "thing of wonder" (152) in Mama Day's hands, into a phallic instrument of violence against the Feminine that he can neither understand nor control. Like the hero of his favorite play by Shakespeare, *King Lear*, who cannot accept Cordelia's love, "according to [her] bond, nor more nor less" (i.i.95), George cannot accept shared love from Cocoa. Like his dramatic model, with whom he explicitly identifies, he too becomes a "madman" (301), dying as the fatally flawed hero in a white tragedy.[4]

Naylor's vision of black experience in *Mama Day* is, however, far from tragic. Primarily through the character of Mama Day, she investigates ways of conceiving relationships, history, and reality that make it possible for black people to avoid replaying white dramas. In place of the charts, photographs, and movies of the white world, she posits, through the symbol of the quilt, another way of understanding reality and history that is more complex than George's simplistic reliance on empirical "facts." In contrast to his intense individualism and possessive love, the quilt also symbolizes a relationship between self and others more appropriate for black people, one in which individual identity is not lost but merged into a larger whole.[5] The wedding quilt Mama Day and Abigail make for Cocoa and George is Naylor's most concrete description of the beauty that results:

> The overlapping circles start out as golds on the edge and melt into oranges, reds, blues, greens, and then back to golds for the middle of the quilt. A bit of her daddy's Sunday shirt is matched with Abigail's lace slip, the collar from Hope's graduation dress, the palm of Grace's baptismal gloves. Trunks and boxes from the

other place gave up enough for twenty quilts: corduroy from her uncles, broadcloth from her great-uncles. Her needle fastens the satin trim of Peace's receiving blanket to Cocoa's baby jumper to a pocket from her own gardening apron. Golds into oranges into reds into blues. . . . (137)

Unlike the "community" of New York, in which identity is mutilated and people turned into "gargoyle[s]" (56), the individuality of people in this quilt and in the community of Willow Springs is not lost--the pieces can be readily identified, but stitched together they create something whole, immensely richer and more beautiful than the scrappy rags used to make the quilt. Such a relationship is evident in the sisterhood of Miranda and Abigail: both remain distinct personalities both for their neighbors and for the reader--"two peas in a pod, but . . . two peas still the same" (153), according to Mama Day--but only together do they make "the perfect mother" (58) for Cocoa. Sensitive to the beauty and wholeness that results from such relationships, Mama Day thinks as she stitches, "When it's done right you can't tell where one ring ends and the other begins. It's like they ain't been sewn up at all, they grew up out of nowhere" (138).

The quilt also images the history of Willow Springs, not a timeless "picture postcard" version of "paradise," but one that necessarily includes past and present, joy and pain, triumph and despair. Mama Day thinks, for instance, about leaving her mother out of the quilt because Abigail finds childhood memories of her insanity so painful, but she wisely decides, "I'll just use a sliver, no longer than the joint of my thumb. Put a little piece of her in here somewhere" (137). As she understands, every person, including tormented figures such as Grace and Cocoa's great-grandmother Ophelia, is a necessary piece of the quilt that constitutes the family's history: "Could she take herself out? Could she take out Abigail? Could she take 'em all out and start again? With what?" (138).

This notion of history as a quilt, more than simply a way of chronicling the past, is a complex weaving of past, present, and future. The quilt Mama Day stitches is, for instance, not just a historical "document" of a dead past, but a tangible bridge between herself, Abigail, and the children of Cocoa's that neither will live to see. It is not sewn to become merely Cocoa's sole possession but to be "passed on to [Mama Day's] great-grandnieces and nephews when it's time for them to marry" (136). Significantly, it is Mama Day's understanding of the past as a quilt, her perception of "the whole [historical] picture," that gives her supernatural powers of divination. Working on the quilt, connecting herself with the experience of the past, she is able to get in touch with the future, sensing for instance that George will not soon be coming to Willow Springs (138).

The results of weaving individuals, past and present, pain and joy together is not simply aesthetic beauty but also spiritual strength, psychic health, and social vitality. When Mama Day tries to stitch a piece of her mother's gingham into the quilt and is stymied by the "dry rot" and "fray[ing] threads" that symbolize Ophelia's tragedy, she finally succeeds by using Sapphira's homespun, "still tight and sturdy" (137), as backing. Only by thus quilting together female weakness and strength, a profound recognition of the power in sisterhood, is she able to "shape the curve she needs" (138). In fact, it is Mama Day's perception of life as a quilt, her ability to put suffering in perspective along-side happiness that results in her resilient, life-affirming (but never naive) optimism. With an eye that perceives quilted patterns everywhere, Mama Day senses a spiritual beauty in Nature unframable in a postcard and a joy in life inconsistent with tragedy. Her reaction to one sunset is representative:

> They say every blessing hides a curse, and every curse a blessing. And with all of the aggravation belonging to a slow fall, it'll give you a sunset to stop your breath, no matter how long you been on the island. It seems like God reached way down into his box of paints, found the purest reds, the deepest purples, and a dab of midnight blue, then just kinda trailed His fingers along the curve of the horizon and let 'em all bleed down. And when them streaks of color hit the hush-a-by green of the marsh grass with the blue of The Sound behind 'em, you ain't never had to set foot in a church to know you looking at a living prayer. (78)

The recognition of the connectedness and wholeness of Nature imaged in the sunset--reds next to purples and blues stitched next to greens, all of them "bleed[ing] down" just as the individuals colors "melt" in her quilt--constitutes Mama Day's religion and spiritual sustenance. Mama Day sees similar patterns in her own life. Even though her own history, filled with sadness, is a potential tragedy, she (more than any character in the novel) is able to see life as a quilt, to "look past the pain" (283) and to "live on" (88, 266). In every way, Mama Day (contrary to Cocoa's condescending belief early on) is able to see "the whole picture" (57).

It is this ability to piece together "real" and "supernatural," past and present, individual and other that George lacks. When he looks at Nature's quilt during the storm, for instance, he sees an eerie, "ghostly" sight, "stained" and "smashed" rather than hopeful:

> Standing there for a while, I realized how varied gray could be: the horizon, the sky, the clouds, the water, the foam. It was ghostly off in the distance, smoky overhead, with cinders in the waves spraying up liquid ash, droplets that left salt stains on my shoes. Behind the clouds even the sun had become a smashed pearly gray. I knew it had to be the sun, although it could have been any shape up there. Oval. Square. The whole landscape was blended in gray but each feature was distinct. (248)

Unable to see this scene as an emblem of the ideal relationship between himself and Cocoa ("blended . . . but each feature . . . distinct"), he draws no inspirational sustenance from his vision but instead sees it as a mirror for his own depression over their recent argument: "My breath felt that color too, a heaviness that wanted to push itself out of my chest" (248).

George's misunderstanding of Willow Springs is also the result of his inability to understand it as a quilt. While he mistakenly sees the garden of the other place as an ahistorical, Edenic paradise, it is actually a quilt composed of the flowers of Mama Day's ancestors and tended by her (243). The traditions of Willow Springs, unlike the fanciful legends and ossified customs of the mainland, are also quilts, rituals that bespeak the complex weaving of past and present, individual and community that characterize the place. The consolation that comes from standing forth ceremonies, which even George senses bear no relation to funerals (268-269), results from placing a dead person's past and future side by side to put present pain in perspective. Even the story of Sapphira Wade, which George misinterprets as various white myths, is such a quilt, only understood by stitching together superficially contradictory versions. She is variously seen as

> a true conjure woman: satin black, biscuit cream, red as Georgia clay: depending upon which of us takes a mind to her. She could walk through a lightning storm without being touched; grab a bolt of lightning in the palm of her hand; use the heat of lightning to start the kindling going under her medicine pot: depending upon which of us takes a mind to her. (3)

Just as Sapphira's many-sided image cannot be confined in a two-dimensional photograph, the story of her relationship with Bascombe Wade is a complex narrative, filled with multiple perspectives and subject to diverse interpretations, no one of which constitutes the whole picture. Like Candle Walk, which keeps this history alive and itself changes over time (111), the story of Sapphira and Bascombe Wade cannot be reduced to any of George's white scripts or even to one that focuses only on Sapphira's spiritual triumph. Mama Day's contribution to this quilt is, in fact, her discovery of an empathy for Bascombe Wade's role in this drama. At one point she stitches a scrap from her memory next to the common belief that the light was carried to help Sapphira find her way back to Africa: "Oh, precious Jesus, the light wasn't for her--it was for him. . . . How long did he search for her? Up and down this path" (118). She suddenly understands that Bascombe Wade is neither the male lead in George's drama nor a villain. Just as she stitches together clothing from both her female and male ancestors, Mama Day finally weaves a male perspective into the family quilt, appreciating her relationship to her male ancestors and seeing Bascombe Wade and her own father, John-Paul, in a new way:

> And then she opens her eyes on her own hands. Hands that look like John-Paul's. Hands that would not let the woman in gingham go with Peace. Before him, other hands that would not let the woman in apricot homespun go with Peace. No, *could* not let her go. In all this time, she ain't never really thought about what it musta done to him. Or him either. It had to tear him up inside, knowing he was willing to give her anything in the world but that . . . the losing was Candle Walk, and looking past the losing was to feel for the man who built this house and the one who nailed this well shut. It was to feel the hope in them. . . . (285)

Naylor also uses the quilt to characterize the relationship between George and Cocoa, one so enmeshed in the past that no narrative of simple cause and effect or movie of "beginning" and "end" can capture it. As Cocoa later realizes,

> . . . as we crossed over the bridge, squeezed into the front of Dr. Buzzard's truck, was that the time to turn everything around? I've

asked myself that over and over these years. At what point could
we have avoided that summer? At the beginning of that bridge?
The beginning of so many others? And when I try, George, when I
try to pick a point at which we could have stopped, there is none. I
don't think it would have mattered if we had come a year before or
a year after. You and I would have been basically the same, and
time definitely stands still in Willow Springs. No, any summer we
crossed over that bridge would be the summer we crossed over.
(165)

Unable to understand their relationship as one piece in a historical and
emotional quilt, George further fails to see that his desire for an insular,
exclusive, traditionally "romantic" relationship with Cocoa is as futile as trying to
make a quilt with two rags. His yearning for possession of Cocoa, his failure to
recognize that "all that Baby Girl is is made of people who walked these floors"
(278), that he knows "only part of [her]" while "the whole of [her]" (176) exists in
her connection to Willow Springs, leads to his recapitulating the tragic love
stories of Bascombe Wade and John-Paul.

The rite of passage Mama Day envisions would involve George's
recognition that he must become part of a quilt, connected to the past and to
both the women and men of Willow Springs. As Mama Day realizes, she needs
his hand "so she can connect it up with all the believing that had gone before."
Unwilling to be the "missing piece" she needs, he wants to single-handedly
fashion a bridge for Cocoa rather than be part of a communal one. Failing to
see that "the bridge" that will save Cocoa is actually a quilt, he feels threatened
by Mama Day's belief that "together they could be the bridge for Baby Girl to
walk over" (285). Responding with "blind fury" when the men take his boat and
make it part of the bridge, George misses the art of quilting symbolized in their
act and the wisdom of Mama Day in Buzzard's gentle rebuke: "Your way . . .
woulda been suicide. Our way, that same boat is certain to get you over" (286).

Such failure to see "the whole picture," to see history, community, and
relationships between men and women as quilts, dooms black people to the
madness and suicide characterizing white tragedies. In the history of Willow
Springs, the stories of several characters--including Ophelia, who fails to look
past the pain of losing Peace and to love her two remaining daughters and
Grace, who is unable to stitch Cocoa's vitality next to her husband's betrayal--
reveal the insanity of clinging to one relationship. Similarly, just as George
"los[es] his mind" (290) from his desperate love of Cocoa, Frances and Ruby
both go mad from their desire to possess Junior Lee. Such characters who
cannot weave their relationships, both the joy and pain of their lives, into a
"whole picture" that enables them to look past the pain are doomed to madness
and suicide: instead of quilting, Ophelia thus mindlessly "twist[s] on pieces of"
thread (36, 243) while Ruby turns hair-braiding (and the sisterhood it
symbolizes) into an act of jealous murder. That even Cocoa, tempted "to follow
her man," risks becoming a stock character in a white tragedy, is suggested in
her symbolic illness. Like the foremother for whom she is named and Ophelia in
Hamlet, feeling that all her "motions [are] underwater" (254) and that "everything
[is] swimming" (259), she nearly drowns in her exclusive relationship with
George. "Fighting to remain sane" (290), with "the hollow eyes of a lunatic"
(298), she faces the danger of dying like both of her namesakes.[6] She is only

saved when George, having "gripped [her] shoulder so tightly," lets go in death, "[his] bleeding hand slid[ing] gently down [her] arm" (302).

The person who is part of the quilt, stitched next to but not absorbed by others, independent but not isolated, connected to but not doomed by history, achieves peace and meaningful freedom from the white world. Crossing the bridge to the mainland without fear or danger, Mama Day, more than any character in the novel, aptly interprets and even enjoys connection with the world outside. Enamored with the Radio City "kicking girls" (202) and porno flicks depicting creative uses of sour cream, she is also an avid TV viewer who "reads" the real meaning beneath the white world's superficial images. For instance, when she watches the Phil Donahue show, she responds not to the ludicrous photographs, "proving" the existence of "intelligent life in outer space" (37), but to the "truth" in people's faces:

> Sometimes, she'll keep the volume turned off for the entire hour, knowing well that what's being said by the audience don't matter a whit to how it's being said. Laughter before or after a mouth opens to speak, the number of times a throat swallows, the curve of the lips, the thrust of the neck, the slump of the shoulders. And always, always the eyes. She can pick out which ladies in the audience have secretly given up their babies for adoption, which fathers have daughters making pornographic movies, and which homes been shattered by Vietnam, drugs, or "the alarming rise of divorce."   (38)

Similarly, when she looks at the photograph of Willa's husband, she sees not a two-dimensional image but a three-dimensional one and the spiritual reality buried in it, "the face on Willa's husband--like a bottomless pit" (39). An enthusiastic tourist in New York, although aware of the suffering there (305), she (even more than George) revels in the distinct cultures and personalities that make up midtown Manhattan. Rooted in her own cultural place and connected to her history, she experiences no threat to her identity "across the bridge"; in fact, she brings back to Willow Springs souvenirs of her experience there: "Plastic ashtrays shaped like footprints, Mario Cuomo dolls, drinking cups from the hollowed-out head of the Statue of Liberty, 'Hug Me--I'm Jewish' T-shirts" (304), and a paperweight with snowflakes that fall over the Empire State Building (306).

From these "scraps," which in isolation bespeak the fragmentation of life in New York, she creates a quilt, incorporating George's world into the Candle Walk tradition of Willow Springs by "tak[ing] red ribbon and [tying] little packets of ginger cookies around them souvenirs" (306). Subverting white cultural definitions, looking at the Empire State Building from her own rather than from a white perspective, she sees it not as an awesome engineering feat indicative of triumph over nature, but as an emblem of seeing the whole world as a quilt, all of its scraps connected and the human element put in perspective:

> . . . when you stand on top of that building, you kinda see the world the way God must see it--everything's able to be cupped into the palm of your hand. Them big cities should have big buildings, with

all that plenty around them--it gives folks a chance to keep things
in perspective.   (306)

Just as Willow Springs blurs the white world's photographs and reverses
its movies, and Mama Day turns the meaning of the Empire State Building on its
head, Naylor consistently subverts white literary norms.   Despite George's
tireless efforts, he is never able to rewrite the complex historical drama of Willow
Springs as the romantic movie he imagines: his kiss fails to awaken the princess
(in fact, Mama Day's powers bring Cocoa "out of [her] deep sleep" [273]); the
boat which symbolizes his self-sufficiency and courage is, nevertheless, usurped
by the townspeople and built into their communal bridge; and Cocoa is ultimately
"saved" more by his death than by his heroic actions. Even more complexly, the
"tragedy" that results from George's cultural whiteness is also turned on its head.
The love of George and Cocoa does not "end" as she had expected, and George
does not lose Cocoa in death as he had feared. In fact, George does not really
die but, as his narrative voice from "here in Willow Springs" (61) suggests,
becomes a vital part of the quilt. Having learned something from Mama Day,
after all, he now wisely sees his earlier fascination with control of Nature and
measurement of reality as foolish: "The clocks and calendars we had designed
were incredibly crude attempts to order our reality--nearing the close of the
twentieth century, and we were still slavishly tied to the cycles of the sun and the
moon" (158). No mere memory, documented and reduced to a two-dimensional
photograph (Mama Day has wisely destroyed all pictures of George [311]), he
remains a living presence in Cocoa's life and in Willow Springs.

The quilt motif, so thematically central in *Mama Day*, is also a key to
understanding its form. Developing a vision of history and reality too complex to
be captured in a straightforward linear narrative of beginning and end, cause
and effect, Naylor repeatedly stitches past, present, and future together: the
novel actually begins and ends in 1999 (in such a way that "you can't tell where
one ring ends and the other begins"), and much of the "past" is narrated in
"present" tense. "The whole picture" Naylor presents also requires multiple
narrators: as Mama Day says, "Just like that chicken coop, everything got four
sides: his side, her side, an outside, and an inside. All of it is the truth" (230).
As Cocoa finally understands, the "whole story" of George and Cocoa has "too
many sides" (311) to be captured by a single perspective--even her own. To
express this multi-faceted truth, which needs "a whole new meaning . . . soon as
you cross over" (3) into Willow Springs, *Mama Day* is thus a complex narrative
quilt of distinct voices, including those of a communal narrator, Cocoa, George,
John-Paul, Jonah Day, and Grace (151). As the beginning of the novel
suggests, the reader is not left outside the story as a passive viewer of a movie
or a photograph, but stitched into the quilt of Willow Springs, another "scrap" of
a voice alongside the others:

Think about it: ain't nobody really talking to you. We're sitting here
in Willow Springs, and you're God-knows-where. It's August 1999
--ain't but a slim chance it's the same season where you are. Uh,
huh, listen. Really listen this time: the only voice is your own (10)

No static "document" or traditional, completed historical artifact, the novel
"ain't about chalking up 1985, just jotting it down in a ledger to be tallied with the

times before and the times after" (305); rather, like Candle Walk itself and the family quilt Mama Day (and Cocoa) keep adding pieces to, *Mama Day* is--as Cocoa finally realizes--an unfinished, dynamic story requiring constant revision (". . . when [she] see[s George] again, [their] versions will be different still" [311]) and multiple interpretations (". . . each time [she] go[es] back over what happened, there's some new development, some forgotten corner that puts [George] in a slightly different light" [310]). By thus quilting "the whole picture" in *Mama Day*--his side, her side, the inside, and the outside--Naylor has written no traditional tragedy, history, or romance, but rather "quite a story" (10) of black experience, one as culturally autonomous as Willow Springs itself.

Endnotes

[1] Cocoa's dream highlights how misguided George's plans are: "I was standing over here calling to you--I was in some kind of trouble--but you were swimming in the other direction. The louder I called from here, the faster you tried to reach my voice on the opposite side" (189).

[2] Naylor uses color symbolism in the novel to highlight the choice George faces. His chivalrous act of "whitewashing" Mama Day's chicken coop leaves him as "white as a ghost" (229), while his communal work on the bridge leaves black "streaks of tar on the knees and cuffs" of his "whitewash-speckled overalls" (227). When George finally walks to Mama Day, the choice he faces--to be a white or a black man--is graphically imaged in his clothing.

[3] George's underlying fear of the feminine is alluded to throughout the novel. During his research on women's physical and emotional cycles, for instance, he admits, "It made you squeamish if you dwelt on the fact that you were constantly surrounded by dripping blood, and a little frightened, too" (141). His fear of chickens, referred to several times, is summed up in Mama Day's observation that he prefers them "all wrapped up neat under cellophane" (195).

[4] In their discussions of this play, George acknowledges that he "identifies" with Lear and quotes one line--"None but the fool who labors to outjest his heart-struck injuries" (106)--in particular. As Ward and Homans have pointed out, Naylor also shows in *Linden Hills* how cultural whiteness dooms black people to other white literary norms, Dantesque and other traditional, hellish underworlds.

[5] Wagner-Martin has pointed to the importance of the quilt in *Mama Day* and sees it as an image of "the mystery, the complexity, the interrelations of women's lives and friendships" (7).

[6] Significantly, George is the only character in the novel who calls Cocoa, Ophelia. Mama Day, as if to warn her of the danger she faces, only calls her by that name when she takes her to the other place to tell her of her painful family history (150).

Works Cited

Homans, Margaret. "The Woman in the Cave: Recent Feminist Fictions and the Classical Underworld." *Contemporary Literature* 29 (1988): 369-402.

Naylor, Gloria. *Linden Hills*. New York: Ticknor & Fields, 1985.

_____. *Mama Day*. New York: Ticknor & Fields, 1988.

Wagner-Martin, Linda. "Quilting in Gloria Naylor's *Mama Day*." *Notes on Contemporary Literature* 18.5 (1988): 6-7

Ward, Catherine C. "Gloria Naylor's *Linden Hills*: A Modern *Inferno*." *Contemporary Literature* 28.1 (1987): 67-81.

Juhasz, Suzanne. "The Magic Circle: Fictions of the Good Mother in Gloria Naylor's *Mama Day*." Revised/abridged version of chapter from *Reading from the Heart: Women, Literature, and the Search for True Love*. New York: Viking, 1994.

In most women's romance fiction, the lover acts as a new mother for the heroine, a person who can give her that special brand of nurture that she needs for self-development. Yet there are some novels that offer even more: they incarnate the good mother in the flesh. She is not just an idea, an imaginative transformation: not the hero, who is *like* a mother; she is a person in the story. Indeed, she is the very center of a work from which her power and love emanate as warmth and light spread out from the hearth in the center of a room. She is Marmee in Louisa May Alcott's *Little Women* or Miranda in Gloria Naylor's *Mama Day*. It is easier to believe in her when she is literally present, for these books take as their subject the absolute importance of maternal nurture. "Mothers are the *best* lovers in the world," says Jo March to *her* mother, the beloved Marmee of *Little Women*, and this is a truth that readers of fictions of the good mother know full well. The good mother never goes away, and she loves you always; that is the joy of belonging to the magic circle.

There are some novels, however, that are not simply good mother fictions--they are also romances. Novels that alter the "classic" women's romance pattern by giving to the heroine a good mother, rather than a bad or inadequate or dead mother, inevitably give rise to problems. If in the classic and heterosexual romance the function of the lover is to become a mother to the unmothered heroine and thus provide the opportunity for the development she never had, what is there for the lover to do if she's already had a mother? There's an obvious answer: to marry her, to have sex with her, so that true love is seen as an adult, sexual alliance enabling the daughter to move beyond the family romance into another home, where she in her turn can become the mother.

But what about maturation? Why bring true love into the developmental drama at all, if her own mother can nurture the heroine? That's one issue. Another is whether the hero can compete with the mother as the best lover. "Mothers are the *best* lovers in the world," says Jo March to Marmee, even as she adds, "but, I don't mind whispering to Marmee, that I'd like to try all kinds." The love of the good mother comes first. It can, I've argued, serve as the paradigm for all to follow, so that romantic love replicates its processes and adds adult sexuality into the mix. But what if the romance doesn't measure up? What if the fantasy of the mother-hero turns out to be just that, a fantasy? What does it mean to leave the magic circle?

And what about the mother? Once she becomes a character in her own right, then the mother-daughter bond consists of mother as well as daughter. What needs of the mother get met when the daughter "tries all kinds"? Or to put it another way, what is there for a mother to *do* in romance fiction, the story of the (second) true love?

Bringing sexuality into the picture helps suggest both why women writers might want to combine two needs and how they might have problems doing so. One need is to have a good mother; a second is that romance love, although it is sexual, will be an emotional extension of mother love. The developmental goal of the well-nurtured daughter is to become an adult--that is, a mother, not a daughter. The first home should be left so that a new home can be made. Once this development has been achieved, there is the sense that the rest of the heroine's life will be all right, whatever turns it may take.

And yet, when the romance love story sits alongside the story of a good mother, so that the lover is distinct from the mother, uneasy questions surface regarding the compatibility of the lover's role and the mother's role. In both *Little Women* and *Mama Day* friction occurs exactly where mother love and true love clash. In these novels, true love's happy ending is not guaranteed. Readers of *Little Women* feel painfully betrayed when Jo refuses to marry Laurie and chooses instead the middle-aged German professor. In *Mama Day*, an equally dismaying sticking point is the death of the heroine's loving husband; he is devoted to her, she to him. How can he die? There are other difficult places in these novels related to the power and appeal of the magic circle itself. How do good mothers and good lovers fit into the same book, the same life?

Where, in other words, does the magic circle go? Is it broken, transformed, reestablished? Today I read fictions of the good mother from both sides--looking for answers as well as feelings. True love, after all, is supposed to be forever. Much energy in romance fiction is devoted to trying to satisfy it. Novels that come in series, for example, like the family saga, offer the concept of generation, of daughter becoming mother producing daughter becoming mother, to offset the betrayal of time. But readers pay a certain price for this balm; you have to give up your love for one heroine on behalf of the next. Still, when female identity is understood as fluid rather than rigid, as process rather than stasis, the permutations from daughter into mother into daughter suggest the principle of forever in a way that is both satisfying and exciting, for mothers as well as daughters.

Gloria Naylor's *Mama Day* is a fiction of the good mother that includes the daughter's romance with a man. While it, too, finds this second love story problematic, it renders the magic circle far less equivocally than Alcott does in *Little Women*: as stronger, wider, and more elastic; as deeply powerful. Readers begin to sense how the magic circle might hold despite the changes that growing up brings.

Naylor's story takes place on the contemporary although imaginary island of Willow Springs, somewhere off the coast of North Carolina or Georgia, its people having lived on this spot since pre-Civil War days. Willow Springs is a world of secrets and mysteries: the novel's Introduction makes this clear from the start. It is also a world of insiders and outsiders. Everyone cannot understand; everyone cannot belong. I am a white woman, a white reader: and yet I want to enter. How might my entry be possible? The Introduction sets out some terms. It is emphatic about people like me--people coming from beyond the bridge, people who "gotta be viewed real, real careful" (7)--people who can't listen right and can't understand at all (*Mama Day*, New York): Ticknor & Fields, 1988).

The collective speaker, a "we" who turns out to be the inhabitants, perhaps even the very spirit of Willow Springs, tells the cautionary tale of the son of one of their own people, Reema's boy, who "came hauling himself back from one of those fancy colleges mainside," with notebooks and tape recorders all excited and determined to put Willow Springs on the map. But Willow Springs isn't on the map--because Willow Springs isn't in any state. "Look on any of them old maps . . . and you can see that the only thing connects us to the mainland is a bridge--and even that gotta be rebuilt after every big storm" (5).

Reema's boy brought another world-view to the island; he talked of "asserting our cultural identity" and "inverting hostile social and political perimeters." Consequently, he couldn't listen, he couldn't hear--the right answers to the wrong questions he was asking.

But the Introduction also gives clues for doing it right:

> . . . someone who didn't know how to ask wouldn't know how to listen. And he coulda listened to them the way you been listening to us right now. Think about it: ain't nobody really talking to you. We're sitting here in Willow Springs, and you're God-knows-where. It's August 1999--ain't but a slim chance it's the same season where you are. Uh, huh, listen. Really listen this time: the only voice is your own. But you done just heard about the legend of Sapphira Wade, though nobody here breathes her name. You done heard it the way we know it, sitting on our porches and shelling June peas, quieting the midnight cough of a baby, taking apart the engine of a car--you done heard it without a single living soul really saying a word. Pity, though, Reema's boy couldn't listen, like you, to Cocoa and George down by them oaks--or he woulda left here with quite a story.   (10)

The Introduction offers a lot of information, but it doesn't quite make sense--and that's the point. About Sapphira Wade, who "don't live in the part of our memory we can use to form words"; about 18 & 23--"there's 18 & 23, and there's 18 & 23 --and nobody was gonna trifle with Mama Day's, cause she knows how to use it"; about Cocoa and George, talking about "that summer fourteen years ago, when she left, but he stayed," talking for a good two hours or so--"neither one saying a word." The Introduction, spoken not only in a different season but from another kind of knowing, offers the rudiments of a new way of listening and of reading, an invitation into the world of Willow Springs. If I am willing to "know" by shelling June peas or quieting a baby's cough, if I am willing to use the part of my mind that doesn't form words, if I am willing to accept Cocoa's "talking" to her husband who has been dead for fourteen years, if I am excited by the mysterious allusions to Sapphira Wade and must have more, then, I too can enter what turns out to be a magic circle just as compelling as that of Jo, Meg, Beth, and Amy, with Marmee at the center--the world of Willow Springs (which isn't really there), the legacy that Sapphira Wade left to her great-granddaughter, Miranda Day, that Miranda will leave to her granddaughter, Ophelia. This is a maternal world, after all.

Sapphira Wade is where the novel begins: "She could walk through a lightning storm without being touched; grab a bolt of lightning in the palm of her hand; use the heat of lightning to start the kindling going under her medicine pot . . . She turned the moon into salve, the stars into a swaddling cloth, and healed the wounds of every creature walking up on two or down on four" (3). Sapphira's legend--one that "everybody knows but nobody talks about"--has something to do with her marriage to a white man, Bascombe Wade, seven sons, his freeing of the slaves and deeding of his land to them, his murder, her escape--to Africa, or to death, or into a burst of flames. Sapphira Wade is the mother of this island, and if this novel is about mothers, it is a story that puts its emphasis on maternal *power*. The voice of Willow Springs insists that if I can read outside of the dominant culture--which is white and male, the world beyond the bridge--I, too, can participate in the heritage of Sapphira Wade.

And yet the story proper doesn't open in Willow Springs at all, but up north in New York City; and the narrator is no mother, but a tough slangy young black woman named Cocoa, who notices an attractive man in a coffee shop on Third Avenue, a man whom she encounters again as he interviews her for a job. This territory is familiar: the prelude to romance, a contemporary urban tale of two lonely people destined to fall in love. As the narration switches to his point of view, the moment of recognition we expect appears. As he interviews her, he thinks:

> Yeah, I knew your type well. And you sat there with your mind racing, trying to double-think me, so sure you had me and the game down pat . . . [Yet] all I wanted was for you to be yourself. And I wondered if it was too late, if seven years in New York had been just enough for you to lose that, like you were trying to lose your southern accent. It amused me the way your tongue and lips were determined to clip along and then your accent would find you in the space between two words--"talking about," "graduating at." In spite of yourself, the music would squeeze through at the ending of those verbs to tilt the following vowels up just half a key. That's why I wanted you to call me George. There isn't a southerner alive who could bring that name in under two syllables. And for those brief seconds it allowed me to imagine you as you must have been: softer, slower--open . . . So I had the same myths about southern women that you did about northern men. But it was a fact that when you said my name, you became yourself.   (33)

This latter-day Mr. Darcy is George Andrews, product of the Wallace P. Andrews Shelter for Boys, presently a rising young engineer, another hero who seeks to know the heroine's true self.

Indeed, as the romance blossoms between them, we watch the slowly growing love and trust between them chipping away at the protective armor--the false selves--each one has developed. With Cocoa it is easier to see: her fast talking, hard-ass attitude is so defensive, so self-protective that we delight in watching it slowly crumble. Yet George has his difficulties, too (after all, he suffers from a congenital heart disease). Even after Cocoa finally allows herself to be vulnerable to him, things still aren't right because he won't do the same with her. Although Cocoa has revealed her deepest fears and feelings, George offers, "Only the present has potential" and "deal with the man in front of you."

> I thought you didn't trust me enough to share those feelings. A person is made up of much more than the "now." I had opened up to you about the frightened little girl inside of me because I'd finally come to believe that you would never hurt her. And the more I did that, the more you shut yourself off.   (126-127)

After a bitter quarrel, George leaves. Cocoa spends a night with someone else. George, who has returned to propose to her only to see her leave her apartment building, follows her and waits all night outside the strange building. When she emerges, he slaps her, saying "My mother was a whore. And that's why I don't like being called the son of a bitch." He drags her to Harlem, to the brownstone that used to be a whorehouse where he was born. His fifteen-year-old mother had left him wrapped in newspapers, and the man who found him called the shelter for boys where he grew up. "And how do I *feel* about all of this?" He goes on, bitterly explaining his abiding sense of abandonment. No mother. And Cocoa asks him to marry her. He has finally given her his feelings, and his true past: his mother. But he has also tried to show her why he was right in burying his origins, in going beyond them. His mother has betrayed him utterly; he will not claim her again.

This familiar story of nurturing love is, however, only half of the opening movement of the novel. The narrative of Cocoa and George that autumn exists in counterpoint to events on Willow Springs, narrated by the plural voice of the island. Cocoa--her real name is Ophelia--was raised in Willow Springs by her grandmother, Abigail, and her great-aunt, Miranda, after her father ran off and her mother died. She and George have, in fact, similar origins--the difference being that whereas in New York City there was only the Wallace P. Andrews Shelter for Boys, for Baby Girl, the "crib name" she is called by the two old women, there are many more possible mothers. She belongs to the family of Days, whose original mother was Sapphira Wade herself. She comes from an island where maternal power rules.

To Mama Day, Cocoa is "a little ball of pale fire" who "kicked her right in the eye as she brought her up to her lips to suck the blood and mucous out of her nose" (39). Mama Day not only raised Cocoa, she delivered her, since Miranda is the local midwife and "alternative" doctor, a woman who has a professional relationship of respect and division of labor with the island's white male M.D. Now we see the daughter from the mother's position--of love, empathy, and exasperation. Mama Day doesn't have much to say for those big cities where Cocoa goes to seek her fortune, even though she watches Phil Donahue daily so she can understand what it's like up there--she figures Chicago and New York are pretty much all of a piece. Especially because the cities seem to be keeping Cocoa from her destiny, for, as she has told her grand-niece, "I plan to keep on living till I can rock one of yours on my knee." Cocoa is the only girl left alive in this generation to keep the Days going.

As Mama Day gathers fresh eggs, bakes her welcome home cakes, consults with Bernice, a young wife who wants Mama Day to help her get pregnant, we begin to understand a little of what Mama Day means when she tells Bernice "The only miracle is life itself." Mama Day's maternal work--she is nobody's biological mother, but she is in charge of nurturing all of Willow Springs, and Cocoa in particular--is exactly that, life. In her wisdom, her humor, her frankness, she makes the everyday something deeply and powerfully resonant.

Therefore, when Mama Day first sees Cocoa upon her return to Willow Springs, this daughter is someone very different from that cool New Yorker:

A sunflower . . . the sweat flowing from the reddish gold hair and absorbing every bit of available light to fling it back against those high cheekbones, down the collarbone, on to the line of the pelvis, pressing against the thin summer cotton . . . *the* Baby Girl brings back the great, grand Mother. We ain't seen 18 & 23 black from that time till now. The black that can soak up all the light in the universe, can even swallow the sun . . . it's only an ancient mother of pure black that one day spits out this kinda gold.   (47-48)

Here is connection and heritage: Baby Girl is not only herself, she exists in a line of women. She is like Jo in *Little Women*, belonging to a family, her very identity dependent upon theirs. But there is more, for Cocoa is the one who brings back the great, grand mother. She has a potential and an obligation that contradicts her independent search for fortune in northern cities. Or does it? For Cocoa always knows that Willow Springs is home.

Home. It's being new and old all rolled into one. Measuring your new against old friends, old ways, old places. Knowing that as long as the old survives, you can keep changing as much as you want without the nightmare of waking up to a total stranger . . . Home. You can move away from it, but you never leave it. Not as long as it holds something to be missed.   (49, 50)

As the New York sections of Part I develop Cocoa's love and marriage in the "real world" beyond the bridge, the Willow Springs sections create the life of home, of the magic circle that is always there although the daughter has fled away. The circle is resonant with the ever-present past: "Living in a place like Willow Springs, its sorta easy to forget about time." Mama Day pieces a quilt for Cocoa and George that shows us how the past stays alive. Mama Day's rags come from the other place, the first homestead of the Day family. "A bit of her daddy's Sunday shirt is matched with Abigail's lace slip, the collar from Hope's graduation dress, the palm of Grace's baptismal gloves . . . Her needle fastens the satin trim of Peace's receiving blanket to Cocoa's baby jumper to a pocket from her own gardening apron . . . The front of Mother's gingham shirtwaist . . . Put a little piece of her in somewhere."

But the gingham is almost dry rot and doesn't cut well. Mama Day looks for something to back it with and finds a piece of faded homespun. "Now this is real old. Much older than the gingham. Coulda been part of anything, but only a woman would wear this color." The homespun is wrapped over and basted along the edge of the gingham. And as Mama Day takes careful stitches, she feels a chill.

She tries to put her mind somewhere else, but she has only the homespun, the gingham, and the silver flashing of her needle . . . It doesn't help to listen to the clock, 'cause it's only telling her what she knew about the homespun all along. The woman who wore it broke a man's heart. Candle Walk night. What really happened between her great-grandmother and Bascombe Wade? How many --if any--of them seven sons were his? But the last boy to show up in their family was no mystery; he had cherished another woman who could not find peace. Ophelia. It was too late to take it out of the quilt, and it didn't matter no way. Could she take herself out? Could she take out Abigail? Could she take 'em all out and start again? With what? Miranda finishes the curve and runs her hand along the stitching. When it's done right you can't tell where one ring ends and the other begins. It's like they ain't been sewn at all, they grew up out of nowhere.   (138)

Ophelia's destiny is connected to the first mother, because she belongs to her family, who has formed her as surely as the bits and pieces of all their clothing goes to form the quilt. And Sapphira Wade broke a man's heart. Mama Day's moments of insight, or prophecy, come upon her frequently as she goes through her day, moments when knowledge comes to her through her fingers and through her heart. The mysteries of this family are woven through the narrative of daily life in Willow Springs even as they are woven into Cocoa's quilt.

There is Candle Walk, a ritual that the people of Willow Springs have practiced since the beginning.

> Candle Walk night. Looking over here from beyond the bridge, you might believe some of the more far-fetched stories about Willow Springs: The island got spit out from the mouth of God, and when it fell to the earth it brought along an army of stars. He tried to reach down and scoop them back up, and found Himself shaking hands with the greatest conjure woman on earth. "Leave 'em here, Lord," she said. "I ain't got nothing but these poor black hands to guide my people, but I can lead on with light." Nothing but a story, and if there's an ounce of truth in it, it can't weigh even that much. Over here nobody knows why every December twenty-second folks take to the road--strolling, laughing, and talking--holding some kind of light in their hands. It's been going on since before they were born, and the ones born before them.   (110)

There is the other place where Mama Day goes for nourishment and for magic.

> She tries to listen under the wind. The sound of a long wool skirt passing. Then the tread of heavy leather boots, heading straight for the main road, heading on towards the east bluff over the ocean. It couldn't be Mother, she died in The Sound. Miranda's head feels like it's gonna burst. The candles, food, and slivers of ginger, lining the main road. A long wool skirt passing. Heavy leather boots. And the humming--humming of some lost and ancient song. Quiet tears start rolling down Miranda's face. Oh, precious Jesus, the light wasn't for her--it was for him. The tombstone out by Chevy's Pass. How long did he search for her? Up and down this path . . . Up and down this path, somehow, a man dies from a broken heart.   (118)

What does it mean that someone died of a broken heart so long ago? Why couldn't her own mother "find Peace"? Why is it scary that Cocoa's real name is Ophelia? And what does all this have to do with George, who interests Mama Day greatly? After she and Abigail have talked to him on the phone, she comments: "He said--'She is all I have.' That means sharing. If he got a nickel, she's got a part in it. He got a dream, he's gonna take her along. If he got a life,

Abigail, he's saying that life can open itself up for her. You can't ask no more than that from a man" (136).

Somehow, it's all connected. And there's magic in it, magic that is accepted, understood to be real. Everyone on the island, even the "medical" doctor, Brian Smithfield, knows that Mama Day, her enemy, the evil Miss Ruby, and the comical hoodoo man Dr. Buzzard all use some version of magic. Magic denotes powers and processes that are alternative to what organizes the mainstream, or in the novel, "mainland" culture--which is male dominated, and white. Yet in this novel magic, as well as the "forever" of generations, will come into conflict with true love as it happens in the patriarchal world.

In Part I, the true love romance, which takes place beyond the bridge in the patriarchy, is separate from the magic circle of mother love, which is situated on an island that simply doesn't exist in patriarchy's terms. Cocoa crosses back and forth, finding nurture both at home, in the world of the mother, and from the maternal hero who functions as a surrogate mother in the alien world of the patriarchy. Not until Cocoa and George have been married for four years--not until they have finally decided to have a baby (at George's insistence)--does Cocoa bring George home.

She is asking that the worlds be brought together, and the reason for "crossing over" (Cocoa's phrase) is her decision to become a mother. Mama Day has been thinking about this for years. We might write that off to the old-fashioned dodderings of an old lady (as opposed to Cocoa's modern ambitions for career and independence) except that as the novel progresses it becomes clear that Mama Day's own death hinges upon the birth of Cocoa's children:

> She had it all planned for herself: something nice and simple. A warm flannel gown with ruffles on the sleeves. Propped up in bed with extra pillows at her back. Her windows wide open to let in whatever season of air it was. And Baby Girl's children bringing her in little sips of soup, cups of tea, and heaping dishes of pistachio ice cream. She couldn't with all certainty put Baby Girl in the middle of that picture, but the children she'd get from that boy, having only half his heart, would be there for their old auntie. (203)

Until those children come, she will simply live on, no matter how old she gets.

When they are in Willow Springs, Cocoa's explanation to George of the inheritance patterns of the Day family clarifies Mama Day's desire: "Some kind of crazy clause in our deed. It's always owned two generations down. That's to keep any Day from selling it." Cocoa doesn't own the land--it belongs to her unborn children. These children are necessary for the Days to continue, and Mama Day, the ruling mother, can die only when the deed is accomplished. Cocoa's children belong to Willow Springs, so once George tosses her diaphragm over Brooklyn Bridge, he, too, as the father of these children, must find his way there.

But an overwhelming question now arises: can the maternal hero--that fantasy women create so that true love is possible in a patriarchal culture-- function in the alternative world, the magic circle of the good mother herself? Is he needed? Can he do it? The wrenching conclusion of *Mama Day*, towards which the whole of Part II builds, answers these questions--in a way that many readers find shocking and devastating.

As soon as George and Cocoa arrive on the island, the *difference* between them is underlined. George is an engineer, who tries to prepare for his journey by reading his atlas, to figure out "whether a raincoat would be in order or not, a light pullover for evenings." But "where was Willow Springs? Nowhere. At least not on any map I had found. I had even gone out and bought road maps just for South Carolina and Georgia and it was missing from all those islands dotting the coastline. What country claimed it? Where was the nearest interstate highway, the nearest byroad? (174). Cocoa thinks: "Your maps were no good here . . . but you still came, willing to share this with me" (177). For she knows that "regardless of how well you thought you knew me, it was only one part of me. The rest of me--the whole of me--was here." George's love for Cocoa is what makes this joining a possibility, George whom Mama Day thinks of as "a good-hearted boy with a bad heart," so that Cocoa decides that she need not worry, that she is fortunate, "belonging to you and belonging to them. Ophelia and Cocoa could both live in that house with you. And we'd leave Willow Springs none the worse for the wear" (177).

George is certainly eager and willing to try. He takes exhausting hikes with Mama Day through the East Woods, he plays cards and gets drunk with Dr. Buzzard, and he tries to understand the strange history of the Days when Mama Day and Cocoa explain it to him. Mama Day shows him the solitary grave of Bascombe Wade, keeping his strange vigil for the slave woman to whom he deeded his island: "when the wind is right in the trees, you can hear him calling and calling the name that nobody knows" (206). Cocoa shows him the other graves, tombstones of varying heights with no dates and only one name. "You explained they were all Days, so there was no need for a surname. But what, as in your case, if a woman married? You live a Day and you die a Day." George learns more:

> You showed me how they were grouped by generations: the seven
> brothers and then the seven before them. The sizes of the
> headstones represented the missing dates--but only in relation to
> each other. There was a Peace who died younger than another
> Peace, and so her stone was smaller. There was your mother's
> stone--Grace--and she had obviously died younger than her sister
> Hope. Mama Day, you said, would have the tallest stone. She'd
> already lived longer than any Day before her. The closeness of all
> this awed me--people who could be this self-contained. Who had
> redefined time. No, totally disregarded it. (218)

George grasps the difference of all this from the world beyond Willow Springs. But he can only struggle to comprehend it intellectually. When Cocoa tells him the story of the solitary grave of Bascombe Wade, she adds that the woman was her grandmother's great-grandmother. "But it was odd again the way you said it --she was the great, great, grand, Mother--as if you were listing the attributes of a goddess. The whole thing was so intriguing, I wondered if that woman had lived at all. Places like this island were ripe for myths, but if she had really existed, there must be some record. Maybe in Bascombe Wade's papers: deeds of sale for his slaves" (218). Magic equals "myth"; history can be verified with documents. Is it enough that George wants to belong?

The climax builds irrevocably. First comes a hurricane, bringing devastation to the island. This unleashing of power and fury is the act of the great Mother herself, and "prayers go up in Willow Springs to be spared from what could only be the workings of Woman. And She has no name" (251). Why now, just when vengeance is being wrecked on Cocoa, who has fallen ill with a mysterious fever from which she is not recovering? Vengeance, because the infection has come from Miss Ruby, jealous of Cocoa's flirtation with her young husband Junior Lee. Braiding Cocoa's hair as she used to do when Cocoa was a child, Ruby has poisoned her. And although Mama Day can cause lightning to strike Miss Ruby's house, she alone cannot save Cocoa from the madness and death that Ruby's magic portends. She needs George to help her. "How bad is it gonna be," asks Abigail.

> "How bad is hate, Abigail? How strong is hate? It can destroy more people quicker than anything else."
> "But I believe there's a power greater than hate."
> "Yes, and that's what we gotta depend on--that and George."

But George is from beyond the bridge, points out Abigail. He'll never believe this, and they don't have his kind of words to explain. Miranda says they must wait for him to feel the need to come to them; that she will be waiting at the other place.

> "That boy'll never make it, Miranda."
> "Don't sell him too short too early. He'd do anything in the world for her."
> "I know that. But we ain't talking about this world, are we?"
> "No," Miranda says, "we ain't talking about this world at all."
> (267-268)

Love is the power that can overcome hate, but love is the most complicated force of them all. In the final pages, both mother love and sexual/romantic love are examined and tested, by themselves and in their relationship to one another. If Cocoa's life is to be saved by love, then both her mother and her husband must be able to give her what is needed: each in her or his own right and, more crucially, together: "So together they could be the bridge for Baby Girl to walk over" (285).

Miranda's visit to the other place gives her visions that take her deeper into her own identity and into the meaning of her family, for in order to save Cocoa, she needs to know even more. Miranda is led to the attic, to discover hidden there the very document that testifies to the beginnings of their family: Bascombe Wade's bill of sale for a negress answering to the name of Sa. . . The rest of the name is unreadable due to "water damage." Only a few other words are legible: "*Law . . . knowledge . . . witness . . . inflicted . . . nurse . . . conditions . . . tender . . . kind.*" In seeking the name which she does not know, Miranda calls it "the door to help Baby Girl." In a dream, Miranda opens door upon door, saying, "tell me your name." And what she hears at last is not the great mother's name but a new name for herself: "daughter." For the first time in the book, and in her life, Miranda's identity shifts from mother to daughter. For Miranda has had to be "Mama" since her own mother went mad and drowned herself. Now she learns that need as well as strength is necessary, that the love that will save Cocoa is based in mutual need. To save her daughter, she must at last be mothered as well as mother:

> Daughter. The word comes to cradle what has gone past weariness. She can't really hear it 'cause she's got no ears, or call out 'cause she's got no mouth. There's only the sense of being. Daughter. Flooding through like fine streams of hot, liquid sugar to fill the spaces where there never was no arms to hold her up, no shoulders for her to lay her head down and cry on, no body to ever turn to for answers. Miranda. Sister. Little Mama. Mama Day. Melting, melting away under the sweet flood of waters pouring down to lay bare a place she ain't known existed: Daughter. And she opens the mouth that ain't there to suckle at the full breasts, deep greedy swallows of a thickness like cream, seeping from the corners of her lips, spilling onto her chin. Full. Full and warm to rest between the mounds of softness, to feel the beating of a calm and steady heart. She sleeps within her sleep. (283)

This dream vision is the true center of the novel. The daughter helps to make the mother whole, just as the mother does for her daughter. For the mother never loses the need for nurture--indeed, her maternal strength may depend upon it. Miranda's joy as she is suckled by a ghost mother means both that she has new strength for taking care of Cocoa and also that she needs her daughter as much as her daughter needs her. Cocoa's life, Cocoa's future, are another way to care for Mama Day. Miranda needs Cocoa, and they both need George.

Miranda recalls the will of the men who have loved Day women to keep them in life. This is why Mama Day wants George to keep Cocoa alive--to *connect* the part of Cocoa that belongs to the mother with the part that belongs to the outside world. It is a matter of the work of their hands. Mama Day needs George's hand in hers: "his very hand--so that she can connect it up with all the believing that had gone before. A single moment was all she asked, even a fingertip to touch hers at the other place. So together they could be the bridge for Baby Girl to walk over" (285).

Miranda knows that George believes in himself--"'cause he ain't never had a choice. And he keeps it protected down in his center, but she needs that belief buried in George. Of his own accord he has to *hand* it over to her" (285). And she is afraid, because--and this is the crux of the difference, upon which the entire novel has insisted--although she needs George, George does not need her. "The Days were all rooted to the other place, but that boy had his own place inside him." George, however, the orphan raised at Wallace P. Andrews "to feel responsible for our present actions--and our actions alone" (25), to believe that "only the present has potential" (35), in this way embodies the most basic patriarchal principles for masculinity. Has his love for Cocoa truly affected his training? Has his experience of Willow Springs altered him? Mama Day sees that there's a way George could do it alone, "he has the will deep inside to bring Baby Girl peace all by himself--but no, she won't even think on that." She'll think of a way to get him to trust her: "by holding her hand she could guide him safely through that extra mile where the others had stumbled. But a mile was a lot to travel when even one step becomes too much on a road you ain't ready to take" (285).

George wants to build a bridge all right, but he means it literally. He is spending all his energy in the days after the storm trying to rebuild the bridge to the mainland so that he can take Cocoa across it, to seek medical help. Mama Day knows that a different kind of bridge is in order, a bridge that is based in need and connection. It is Dr. Buzzard, who may be a bit of a charlatan, but who also belongs to the island, who convinces George to go to the other place, who counters George's "We're going to be fine because I believe in myself" with "That's where folks start, boy--not where they finish up. Yes, I said *boy*. 'Cause a man would have grown enough to know that really believing in himself means that he ain't gotta be afraid to admit there's some things he just can't do alone. Ain't nobody asking you to believe in what Ruby done to Cocoa--but can you, at least, believe that you ain't the only one who'd give their life to help her?" (292). To read these scenes is to hope, to pray, to try to give George the same push that Dr. Buzzard does.

The conversation between George and Mama Day at the other place is a desperate ping pong game, with lives at stake. Miranda tells him:

> "I can do more things with these hands than most folks dream of--no less believe--but this time they ain't no good alone. I had to stay in this place and reach back to the beginning for us to find the chains to pull her out of this here trouble. Now, I got all that in this hand but it ain't gonna be complete unless I can reach out with the other hand and take yours . . . "   (294)

To George, all this seems like "a lot of metaphors"; but he'll try to be of use to her. "Metaphors," thinks Mama Day: "Like what they use in poetry and stuff. The stuff folks dreamed up when they was making a fantasy, while what she was talking about was *real*."

Her way (she tells him there is another) is to go back to her chicken coop, find the nest of the old red hen, take the old family ledger, and her own magic cane in there with him: "search good in the back of her nest, and come straight back here with whatever you find" (295).

George finds this "mumbo jumbo" crazy, but he goes. And there in the chicken coop, with the angry hen attacking him, sinking her claws into his wrist, her beak tearing at his hand, he digs violently into the nest: "Nothing. There was nothing there--except for my gouged and bleeding hands. Bring me straight back whatever you find. But there was nothing to bring her. *Bring me straight back whatever you find.* Could it be that she wanted nothing but my hands?"

The idea is intolerable. The hen attacks George, and beside himself, he slashes at her with the walking cane and smashes in her skull. Like a madman, he goes through the coop, slamming the cane into feathery bodies and nest; when the cane breaks, he uses the book. A stitch in his side finally makes him stop his terrible rampage--and laugh.

> There was nothing that old woman could do with a pair of empty hands. I was sitting in a chicken coop, covered with feathers, straw, manure, and blood. And why? . . . I brought both palms up,

the bruised fingers clenched inward. All of this wasted effort when these were *my* hands, and there was no way I was going to let you go.   (301)

George heads for Cocoa's bedside, but on the way he has a heart attack. He reaches her and dies. Miranda knows. "He went and did it his way, so he ain't coming back. . . . In the pantry she rolls up bundles of dried herbs into clean strips of cloth. Now that Baby Girl was going to live, she had to be nursed back to health" (302).

George's death is so shocking because its significance is so brutal. As George wreaks havoc on Mama Day's chickens, he incarnates all the mindless male violence of human history; George--whom we have loved and desired and believed in. Not only has he turned into a savage male, but he has died. I am are both dismayed and grief-stricken.

And yet he has saved Cocoa. He has died so that she might live: died in the way of and on behalf of the patriarchy. His death returns her to the magic circle. Whereas Alcott insists that daughters must enter the patriarchy, offering the tenuous hope that the circle can enlarge to include it, Naylor tells us no, the world beyond the bridge can never be joined with the magic island of mother love without radical change to its very nature, a change that seems impossible. The best the maternal hero can do for the heroine who inherits the great mother's mantle is to die for her. Only in this way does he get to stay a part of her as she becomes in her turn the mother. Thus her own mother power is the result, not of her developmental relationship with a maternal hero, but of her legacy from the other mothers in her original family. The central difference between the two writers is that for Naylor mother love and all that comes with it is understood to be stronger than the culture at large--it is the only power that will give true identity and validity. Alcott cannot downplay the strength of the white patriarchy, but Naylor, black as well as female, can. Because her position is one of such thorough marginalization, I think, her belief in the resources of her alternative identity must be that much more forceful. If a white woman might try to hope for the best in the dominant culture, a black woman may well understand the utter foolishness of this gesture. George must go the way of all who would attempt to enforce masculine dominance upon the world of the mother.

Cocoa regains her health but experiences the loss of her true love. Although George as maternal hero is proven to be a fantasy, he remains the best one we have for trying to live in the patriarchy. Mama Day, watching Cocoa grieve, knows that George is gone but that he hasn't left her, much in the way that Beth March lives on in her sister Jo. Readers listen to Miranda for comfort and hope: "Naw, another one who broke his heart 'cause he couldn't let her go. So she's gotta get past the grieving for what she lost, to go on to the grieving for what was lost, before the child of Grace lives up to her name." From her singular life and identity to the life of the family, in which she comes fully into herself--that is the path she must take. Miranda speaks to the dead George of Cocoa's legacy, and her mission. She speaks of Candle Walk:

My daddy said that his daddy said that when he was young, Candle Walk was different still. It weren't about no candles, was about a light that burned in a man's heart . . . He had freed 'em all but her, 'cause, see, she'd never been a slave. And what she gave of her own will, she took away. I can't tell you her name, 'cause it was never opened to me. That's a door for the child of Grace to walk through . . . And you'll help her, won't you? . . . One day she'll hear you, like you're hearing me. And there'll be another time--that I won't be here for--when she'll learn about the beginning of the Days. But she's gotta go away to come back to that kind of knowledge. And I came to tell you not to worry: whatever roads take her from here, they'll always lead her back to you.   (308)

As a ghost, George has now shed the encumberments of his masculinity: in this way un-gendered--the only way possible--he can stay on in Willow Springs and in the life of its next mother. That is satisfying in its way, for they do get to be together always, in a space that is safe from the evils of the patriarchy (of which George is no longer one). The ghost love story suggests in various ways that mother love and the patriarchy are not compatible. Cocoa leaves New York and marries again--a nice man in Atlanta who is admittedly not the love of her life and consequently no threat to the magic circle. He provides her with affection and two sons. She is thus free to come back, frequently, to Willow Springs, to sit by George's grave and listen, and speak without words, rehearsing their love and its resolution.

The words they speak without sound are the novel we are reading, brought into language by the collective maternal voice of Willow Springs. For Cocoa's story, the story of the daughter who becomes a mother, can only be told and only be heard within the maternal narration. This is how the novel ends, as that voice tells us of Mama Day's final days, in 1999. "When she's tied up the twentieth century, she'll take a little peek into the other side--for pure devilment and curiosity--and then leave for a rest she deserves" (312). She can go now that Cocoa can take her place.

It's Mama Day whom I love best, Mama Day and the world of Willow Springs, which, although it changes, never *really* changes: "Some things stay the same . . . Some things change . . . And some things are yet to be," says the voice of Willow Springs. Because the novel is told not by a daughter but by the very spirit of maternal power, *Mama Day* is especially compelling in its insistence that there is a Willow Springs, that there has to be a Willow Springs, that it isn't on any map but that it won't go away and it won't be corrupted. The priorities of the mother voice are clear, persuasive, and reassuring--and they extend to the place of the maternal hero in the daughter's evolution. Yes, he is, finally, a fantasy. But if there is always a Willow Springs, then maybe it doesn't matter so much.

The authority and the strength of Naylor's insistence upon the centrality of maternal power seems to me to come from a conjunction of the imperatives of blackness and femaleness, because the dominant white male culture would disempower both. But where do I come in, a white woman, mother and daughter? Despite my deeper complicity in the world beyond the bridge, the novel has permitted me the reality of my feelings for Mama Day and Willow Springs. Black maternal power has helped me to confirm my own deep belief in the centrality of mother love. It has taught me that the magic circle does not exist on any map. It has to be inside us. Mutual love and need--one way to define the magic circle--do not go away. The changes that occur over time may not mean the breaking of a connection but the way to continue it.

Tucker, Lindsey. "Recovering the Conjure Woman: Texts and Contexts in Gloria Naylor's *Mama Day*." *African American Review* 28.2 (1994): 173-188.

> Papa Legba has no special day. All of the days are his.
> --Hurston, *Tell My Horse* 129

"There are just too many sides to the whole story," Cocoa tells George near the conclusion of Gloria Naylor's 1988 novel *Mama Day* (311). The truth of this remark is reinforced by the structure of the novel itself--by the fact that Cocoa's words are spoken in a time which has not arrived (1999) and addressed to a person who has been many years dead. Indeed, this very "speakerly" novel has gathered together many voices, past and present, living and dead, individual and collective; and while the oral quality of this work may not trouble readers and critics, certainly the brand of realism that had come to define Naylor's work in *The Women of Brewster Place* and *Linden Hills* had suddenly, it seemed, become contaminated with ingredients of magic and fantasy. One reviewer complained that "the reader is never sure what is imagined and what is authentic, what is to be believed and what is unbelievable" ("'Magical' Powers" C3), and another objected that "what is meant to be mystical too often ends up mystifying" ("*Mama Day* a Victim" G8).

What may be the source of such negative commentary is not so much Naylor's ambivalence about whether she is writing a realistic novel or a fantasy so much as it is subject matter which, because of its reliance on African magico-religious views of the world, asks for a different narrative mode as well as a different kind of response from readers. For example, the collective voice, which introduces the reader to the community of Willow Springs, concludes with a critique of ethnography and its methodologies. The failure of the ethnographer is due to his inability to hear and to ask the right questions, a failing that, the voice seems to warn us, may be our own: ". . . he coulda listened to them," the voice explains, "the way you been listening to us right now. Think about it: ain't nobody really talking to you" (10). The reader, feeling as if she has been caught eavesdropping, may find herself affronted by this kind of trickery, or she may accept the truth of the narrator's words and take the discourses on their own terms, problematic as they may be.

The problem, of course, has to do with the fact that *Mama Day* is a novel chock full of conjurers--Ruby, Dr. Buzzard, the maternal ancestor Sapphira Wade--in addition to Mama Day herself, and the reader may be at a loss about how to treat the subject, since the conjurer, and especially the conjure woman, has existed mostly on the margins of folklore and ethnography and is therefore barely credible. Clearly Naylor is taking some risks with the subject, yet I want to argue that conjure addresses the undervaluation of African medicinal practices and belief systems, even as it comments on the subject of the power--not only in relation to medicine, but also to ancestry, religion, and finally to language and signifying practices.

Not surprisingly perhaps, stories about conjuration have found their most congenial home within the parameters of the folktale, where the conjure woman, whether she is represented as comic or demonic, remains difficult to see. Nowhere is this situation better illustrated than in the 1899 book by Charles W. Chesnutt that bears her name. Chesnutt saw himself and *The Conjure Woman* as marking the beginning of African American fiction, and the fact that he was writing at a time when the post-Reconstruction South was becoming increasingly disenfranchised, suggests that his subject matter may have been, at least in part, dictated by political as well as aesthetic reasons.   Rather like the wily grandfather of Ellison's invisible man, Chesnutt, in a journal entry dated 1880, envisions racism as a "garrison" that 'cannot be stormed and taken by assault," but whose "position must be mined" instead (qtd. in Helen Chesnutt 21).   One way of mining enemy territory was through the writing of a literature that would attempt to teach whites about racism in ways subtle enough to escape notice. Thus it appears that Chesnutt found the female figure of the conjure woman useful for her trickster capacities.   Less a novel than a collection of seven folktales, *The Conjure Woman* contains four conjurers--two men and two women. Their mere number would suggest that conjure is a crucial subject, yet while Chesnutt uses the conjure woman for interesting and effective strategic purposes, I think he does her a disservice.   Chesnutt's own comments, along with recent critical readings, suggest that, while the practice of conjuration operates as a pervasive metaphor within the outside the text, the actual workers of conjure, especially the conjure woman of the title (Aunt Peggy), operate for the most part behind the scenes.   Thus, Chesnutt's conjure woman is denied a textual presence of any serious import.[1]

When we turn to the book itself, we find that both Chesnutt and his critics have seen conjure, as Chesnutt represents it here, as mostly related to the manipulative strategies of Uncle Julius, whose stories are themselves embedded in a frame narrated by a white Northerner, John.   Critics have also seen Chesnutt himself as the real conjurer, "'wu'kin his roots' on an unperceiving audience" (Britt 271).   The book's structure allows the frame narrative--the presumably dominant discourse of the cultivated but insensitive and racist white narrator--to be undercut by the tales of the servile yet wily ex-slave Julius, who uses "goophering" content to change his employer's mind about matters which have an effect on him or his people.   This prompts critic Melvin Dixon to go so far as to argue that the trickster qualities of Julius overcome the black slave's usual emasculation at the hands of his white master, and enable Julius to effect a "symbolic seduction" of the narrator's wife Annie; John's impotency, Dixon continues, is also reflected in "the vocabulary of John's tradition," while Julius's language possesses both vitality and sensuality (193-194).   Although these discussions are interesting and illuminating, they appear to ignore or transcend the conjure woman herself, even as Chesnutt subsumes her in a struggle between two males and transmutes her practices in the name of masculine power.

Possibly as a result of this kind of representation, Naylor seems to see the conjure woman as being in need of textual restitution. Not only does her title render the conjure woman as a concrete presence, but she thereby suggests Miranda Day's connection to the history, legend, and myth that constitute the collective imagination of Willow Springs. Naylor's employment of a communal voice allows her to establish Mama Day's rootedness in the place, since this voice not only gathers up the many voices of the community, past and present, but allows the consciousness of Mama Day to come through when it is important to do so. Thus the communal voice succeeds in demolishing the boundaries between omniscient and limited-omniscient points of view, even as the novel's subject matter demolishes the boundaries between the mimetic and the magical.

But Mama Day is more than vehicle; she appears as a careful representation of a figure often willfully misunderstood and undervalued in historical and ethnographic studies of conjurers, many of whom have been observed not only in the Caribbean and in New Orleans, but in the Carolinas as well. In such texts we often find figures who are sometimes sinister, but almost always baffling as well. Indeed, early discourses on the subject are self-evidently distorted by European ethnocentrism--not to mention Christianity--but even more recent studies betray a white patronization, and it is not until Zora Neale Hurston's work appears on the scene that we get anything close to a positive (or an insider's) view of the conjure woman.[2] For example, several master narratives on Caribbean, especially Jamaican, history[3] maintained that conjurers were crafty, even diabolical, and these studies made the telling observation that practitioners of obeah were usually African, by which the authors appear to mean persons newly arrived to the Americas and still in possession of an African knowledge.

The earliest and most exhaustive study done of folk beliefs in the American South, including long chapters on conjuration and voodoo, was Newbell Niles Puckett's *Folk Beliefs of the Southern Negro* (1926). It was also one of the most biased. Viewing conjuration, indeed all black religion, as fetishistic and therefore primitive, conjurers--root-doctors and hoodoo men--appear to him only as practitioners of witchcraft. Puckett makes little mention of women, although he does say that they are "not entirely excluded" from the practice (311). Another scholar, Norman E. Whitten, describes the conjurer a bit more objectively as a "professional diviner, curer, agent finder, and general controller of the occult arts" (315-316); Whitten adds that they can be "Negro or white, male or female" (317). While the main focus of Whitten's study is the practice of "malign occultism" in North Carolina, he also devotes a lot of space to conjurers from South Carolina, who appear more interesting, perhaps even more authentic to him. He separates practitioners into part-time workers and professionals and goes on to observe, almost admiringly, that "the real professional South Carolina conjurers know not only what to do but also why they do it" (318).

Certainly the most well-known women practitioners were the great voodoo queens of New Orleans--in particular Sanité Dédé, who, as a free quadroon from Santo Domingo, practiced in the 1820s and 1830s, and Marie Saloppé, a native Congolese, who also practiced in the 1820s and whose specialty was the removing of hexes. Perhaps the most famous was Marie Leveau, who was also free-born and believed to have psychic powers, and who remained the reigning head of voodoo for forty years (Mulira 49-51). In his lengthy discussion of voodoo, Puckett pays little attention to Leveau, viewing her mostly as a sham.[4] However, as a genuine voodoo priestess (and superb show woman), she is best remembered through Hurston's recording of her grandson Luke Turner, who recounts ritual practices before her altar in which she dances with a snake and calls for the great trickster Legba to appear (*Mules and Men* 200-204).

Other early studies done by white anthropologists and folklorists also succumb to racist stereotyping. For example, a 1895 study by Leonora Herron and Alice M. Bacon describes conjure doctors as "agents of vengeance," the only recourse to justice possessed by the Negro, who, "brought up in ignorance, and trained in superstition," invoked "secret and supernatural powers to redress his wrongs" (360). Herron and Bacon also report the consensus that conjurers "are usually tall and very dark; and a distinguishing mark seems to be extreme redness of the eyes"; they are also said to be "'singular and queer . . . always looking at some distant object'" (361). A 1930 study of "Mojo" retains much of the same bias, and like Herron and Bacon's work dwells on perceived oddities: one conjurer is described as "tall and dark with grave eyes," while others are catalogued respectively as "undersized," a "dwarfed mulatto," as "almost an albino, with green eyes and a cunning little face" (Bass 381). Yet Bass seems to change her attitude when she speaks about a special conjure woman:

> . . . the most powerful conjurer I know today is a tall, dark[5] woman. Her straight-backed, small-breasted figure seems in some strange way to suggest unusual strength. Her eyes are grave and wise, terribly wise in the ways of ghosts and devils and mojo, as well as in the practice of medicine. (381)

A less sensationalized picture of the conjure woman appears in Leonard Barrett's study of a Jamaican healing center--called a balmyard--which two healers--a mother and a daughter--have operated in an impoverished district of Jamaica since 1871. The mother, herself the daughter of an African slave mother, from whom she learned extensively of herbal medicine, nonetheless received some call to heal and underwent special initiation experiences. When she died in 1929, her daughter, known to the community as Mother Rita and already a medium and skilled in the knowledge of herbal medicine, took her place (Barrett 287-289). In one of the most recent and thorough studies of the Sea Island slave religions, Margaret Washington Creel emphasizes the relationship of conjurers--whom she calls "diviners" or "medicine specialists" (56-58)--to the priests and priestesses of African initiation societies, arguing that on the Sea Islands the Gullah elders are very similar to these ancient religious practitioners in their influence on their communities.[6]

A composite picture of the conjure woman emerges from these somewhat disparate studies. One important feature involves ancestry: conjurers are said to be closer to their African roots than other, more acculturated African slaves. Also, conjure abilities are found to run in families; the conjure man or woman inherits his/her aptitude and the mantle of power, along with an expertise in herbal medicines. Conjure women often carry the name *Mother* and hold considerable power within their communities, and conjurers are, almost without exception, especially gifted with psychic abilities, or are known to have second sight. Often they are spoken of as being "two-headed."

When we look more closely at the practices of conjure, as described in ethnographic studies, we once again encounter some problematic discrepancies that suggest a less than objective examination of a different culture. Even Chesnutt's own studies evidence some discomfiture over the material and an internalization of white attitudes. In his 1901 essay "Superstitions & Folklore of the South," one of the earliest pieces to discuss conjure practices in America, Chesnutt suggests that the practices provided a useful literary ingredient, but he tends to disparage the belief systems on which these practices were based (371). For example, he speaks of education's having "thrown the ban of disrepute upon witchcraft and conjuration," and he alludes to the "stern frown" of the preacher and to the "scornful sneer" of the teacher, both of whom have joined forces to drive "this quaint combination of ancestral traditions to the remote chimney corners of old black aunties" (372).[7] About the value of "these vanishing traditions" he seems tentative, suggesting that they "might furnish valuable data for the sociologist," even though such practices, related to "African fetishism . . . brought here from the dark continent along with the dark people," are not of very great value. However, in this same piece--with a two-headedness that mirrors the conjurer's own--he expresses sadness that beliefs that once had "the sanctions of religion and social custom" in their African homeland have become, "in the shadow of the white man's civilization, a pale reflection of their former selves" (371). Such remarks reveal a persistent ambivalence about his relationship to conjure and help to explain the tendency to relegate this special kind of knowledge to the ignorant aunts and uncles of his past.

Later critics, however, have connected conjure to the dehumanizing practices confronted by the African slave in an alien environment. They argue that the realities of the slaves' life made their inclination toward the supernatural inevitable. John Callahan, for example, in discussing Chesnutt suggests that the crucial role of conjuration rests on its emphasis on transformation, and claims that stories about it are not an "escape from history into myth, but are one of history's unofficial sources," that the strongest "individual levers of power" possessed by the African conjurers still failed to withstand the "strongest *institutional* levers of power in the hands of white masters" (44).

While many students of African religious practices have held views similar to Chesnutt's, the sheer volume of research on the practice of conjuration suggests that it is a subject which cannot easily be dismissed.[8] Before elaborating on attitudes regarding conjure, I think it important to suggest the complexity of these practices and their differences. While conjure appears synonymous with witchcraft, rootwork, and voodoo, it may be useful to begin by noting that these terms are linked to the locales where they are practiced, so that Haitian *voodoo* and Cuban *santeria* differ from the *obeah* practiced in the Caribbean. In Roger D. Abrahams' view, the former are "religious systems with rituals and ceremonies" that include "spiritual healing and exorcising" practices, whereas the latter involves a client and a worker (221).

When faced with the task of defining conjure, scholars often create divisions which, while useful, tend to oversimplify the subject and almost always reflect an ethnocentric bias. To associate conjure with sorcery, witchcraft, or necromancy is to further align it with occult practices which in Western traditions have been perceived to be opposed to Christianity and are, therefore, the work of the devil. One critic prefers to view conjure as being comprised of practices which are natural--using plants to cure--and unnatural--using spells and charms. Yet while many conjurers practiced one or the other of these, a number of them practiced both, and the term *unnatural* seems especially problematic. It may be helpful to consider conjure as treating three types of illnesses: (1) natural illnesses for which a knowledge of roots, herbs, barks, and teas is applied; (2) so-called occult, or spiritually connected, illnesses which require spell casting and charms; and (3) illnesses which include both personal and collective calamities that are not the result of malevolent practices.

Using these categories tentatively, we might find the subject of herbal medicine to be fairly straightforward, and the least controversial--although such practices among slaves and their descendants have always been misunderstood, and hence undervalued. Yet as one scholar points out, healing aptitudes in "people close to the soil who grew up in the cultural milieu of herbal lore," and who also had an acquaintance "with the names of these 'medicines'" and their locations, should not really surprise us (Barrett 295).

If we turn to Naylor's depiction of conjure in *Mama Day* we can see that she is intent on representing Miranda's skills as those of a root doctor, a practitioner of herbal medicine. To remove any ambiguity regarding Miranda's expertise, Naylor sets her practices against those of Dr. Smithfield, the off-island "m.d.," and Dr. Buzzard's hoodoo medicine. When Bernice takes the fertility drug Perganol and becomes seriously ill, it is Miranda who makes the correct diagnosis of ovarian inflammation, although she summons Smithfield anyway because she knows that her knowledge does not extend to chemically constructed drugs. Administering a choke-cherry bark mixture to reduce the pain, Miranda waits for Smithfield's arrival, after which they have the following exchange:

> "You give her anything for the pain?"
> "A smidge of choke-cherry bark."
> "I'm not familiar with that one."
> "The way I gave it to her, it knocked her out. Slows down the pulse." . . .
> "I have a feeling I'm going to find myself a sweet little case of ovarian cysts in there. Just hope there's no liver damage."
> "There ain't--I checked her eyes." (85)

It is clear to both the reader and the doctor that Miranda's competence and knowledge are equal to Smithfield's own. His anecdote about the midwife who, to "cut the pain" of childbirth, puts a kitchen knife under the bed, is the kind of commentary that would only be acceptable between colleagues, and clearly Smithfield expects Miranda to find this medical approach amusing. We are also given further information about Miranda's abilities by way of Smithfield's memories of two instances when Miranda has actually performed surgery, has "picked up a knife":

> . . . once when Parris got bit by a water moccasin, and the time when Reema's oldest boy was about to kill 'em both by coming out hind parts first. Brian Smithfield looked at Miranda a little different after that birth. Them stitches on Reema's stomach was neat as a pin and she never set up a fever. (84)

Her subsequent cure of Carman Rae's baby is just as professional and just as successful.

In contrast to Miranda, Dr. Buzzard represents the world of occult medicine and is clearly the hoodoo doctor described in so many studies. With his outlandish hat with its red feathers, his bone necklace, and the business he does with his charms of "genuine graveyard dust and three penny nails in a red flannel bag," he is almost a caricature. The distance between him and Miranda is highlighted when the newly arrived George repeats to Miranda what Buzzard has said of their "'professional rivalry'" (196).[9] Miranda's anger at the comparison is articulated when, upset to hear that Frances is practicing counter conjure against Ruby, she comments to her sister,

> The mind is everything. She can dig all the holes she wants around Ruby's door. Put in all the bits of glass and black pepper, every silver pin and lodestone she'll find some fool to sell her. Make as many trips to the graveyard she wants with his hair, her hair, his pee, her pee. Walk naked in the moonlight stinking with Van-Van oil--and it won't do a bit of good. 'Cause the mind is everything. (90)

Nevertheless, as we see during Cocoa's illness, Dr. Buzzard is not only fully aware that his work and Miranda's are different, but he also willingly serves as an intermediary between Miranda and the unbelieving George.

Ruby, on the other hand, is not only an herbal specialist but a practitioner of the kind of magic described above. Her knowledge of herbal medicine appears to equal Miranda's, but she is associated more with killing than healing --indeed has been implicated in at least two murders by poisoning. But Ruby's brand of conjure is both medicinal and symbolic. The bag she buries under Miranda's porch, containing salt, verbena, and graveyard dust, is dangerous in terms of content (salt burns and corrodes; graveyard dust is considered to carry disease) but is also a sign that Miranda reads. She knows the verbena included in the bag is also known as the "herb of grace," and that therefore it represents Cocoa--the literal child of Grace and her engulfment in destructive substances.

Ruby's poisoning of Cocoa is straight conjure. The use of nightshade and snakeroot involves nothing mystifying--both are well-known and proven poisons in the hands of the experienced conjurer--nor does the graveyard dust involve magic. Indeed, Hurston has noted that graveyard dirt is poisonous, and that studies have shown it to contain bacteria from yellow fever, scarlatina, typhoid, and other infectious diseases many years after burial. ". . . it appears," Hurston concludes, "that instead of being a harmless superstition of the ignorant, the African men of magic . . . discovered that the earth surrounding a corpse that had sufficient time to thoroughly decay was impregnated with deadly power" (*Tell* 238). Other illnesses--the welts, Cocoa's "hallucinations" which are not quite that, the strange appearances of the worms--are common symptoms of conjure told many times in many places yet never quite believed. Nor are they explained away by Naylor, who allows some of the more mysterious events to coexist with the more "natural" ones in this text of many stories.

While Miranda's own powers go beyond her medicinal practices, she nonetheless views sympathetic magic as "a little dose of nothing but motherwit with a lot of hocus-pocus" (97). For example, Miranda has Bernice plant black and gold seeds to aid and abet her fertility and to drive away the influences of her mother-in-law for psychological reasons, and as ritual actions they are clearly of some benefit to Bernice. But there is nothing magical about her prescription.

While Naylor goes out of her way to de-mystify conjuration, there remains a grouping of phenomena that would seem to involve what we perceive to be magic. In order to discuss these aspects of the novel, it is useful to consider a feature that is of some importance to this topic but which I have yet to comment on--namely, Willow Springs itself. Located on the border between Georgia and South Carolina, it is represented (rather like Faulkner's fictional county) as a place not charted on any map, nor is it actually a part of any state. In every other way, however, Willow Springs has the features of the coastal Sea islands that stretch from Pawleys Island off the South Carolina city of Georgetown, south beyond Savannah to Amelia Island on the border of Florida. Naylor's choice of location has obviously been dictated by the historical relationship of the islands to the perpetuation of African culture, for these Sea islands are, with the exception of New Orleans, the most African of places in America. Always important to the slave trade routes because of their easy access from the ocean as well as their proximity to rivers traveling inland, they also became the place where the least acculturated Africans remained.[10]   The distinctive Gullah heritage, that is both social and cultural, makes of the Sea Islands an actual and symbolic African presence, one rich with magico-religious beliefs that ultimately serve as signifying systems. Born from the previously submerged portions of the continental coast after the retreat of the oceans, the islands suggest a place of myth, as well as a new land, even as they share many of its climactic and topographical characteristics with the coast of western Africa.

Furthermore, the dominant ethnic groups that have comprised what is known as the Gullah language and culture of the Sea island region have been from the Kongo-Angolan area (the term *Gullah* is thought to have derived from this latter group) and from the Windward coast. Such groups are important historically and symbolically because they were considered the most rebellious, a fact that cannot have been lost on Naylor.

Also important to Naylor's novel are Gullah beliefs about the spirit world, beliefs that have their origins in African religion. The island represents a world view in which boundaries between animate and inanimate, secular and sacred--even living and dead--are blurred. For African, and especially BaKongo groups, the afterlife was a reality; death was a journey to the spirit world, which, nonetheless, did not constitute a break with life on earth.[11]   Therefore, although their world was peopled by both bad and good spirits, ancestral spirits were especially important in the New World and served as guardians of the living.[12]

In dealing with the spirit world in *Mama Day*, Naylor is careful to differentiate between ghost fear, characterized by the "haint" stories that are so frequently the subject of folktales, and Miranda's acute listening powers. Miranda's trickery of Dr. Buzzard, which consists in playing on his ghost fears, is one way of suggesting these different beliefs. When Miranda's nighttime search for a narcotic for Bernice brings her close to Dr. Buzzard's still, offering her "just too good a chance to pass up" (81), she throws her voice into the woods, thereby terrifying Buzzard, who takes up his shotgun against the "haints."

On the other hand, Miranda's communication with ancestral voices seems genuine and usually occurs during her solitary walks in the woods or during her clearing of the graves in the family cemetery, activities that reflect with some accuracy African and also Gullah beliefs about the dead. For example, as is customary among BaKongo peoples as well as Sea Islanders, the dead are buried in the woods.[13]   Miranda's family graves are also in the woods, and are arranged in groups of seven, "old graves, and a little ways off seven older again. All circled by them live oaks and hanging moss . . . , " the narrator tells us (10). Oaks are also important features of BaKongo beliefs; trees were planted directly on graves in order to guide the spirits on their journeys into the earth. In any event, the burial site is a place of connections to Miranda. While ghost lore has it that spirits make their presences known by way of warm air, Miranda's connection to the movement of air has more to do with her unusual perception and her ability to listen.

Indeed, this extraordinary ability to see and hear is not always shrouded in mystery. Miranda's lifelong acquaintance with the woods is, to a large extent, responsible for her impressive knowledge since, when "younger, the whole island was her playground: she'd walk through in a dry winter without snapping a single twig, disappear into the shadow of a summer cottonwood . . . "; so comfortable is she in the woods that ". . . folks started believing John-Paul's little girl became a spirit in the woods" (79).

Indeed, Miranda's "reading" ability brings us to the important concept of divination--the ability to read signs--which is not only an important component of African belief systems but is also crucial to the construction of the novel. Naylor suggests that what is often denoted as second sight or precognition is actually an acute awareness of the behavior of plant and animal life. For example, Miranda knows of the coming hurricane, not because of supernatural ability, but because she reads actual signs: the more rapid movement of the waves, the hills the crayfish have made, the nests built further up from the water, the deeper burrows of rabbits, the chickens with their backs to the wind (227). While Miranda appears to have foreknowledge about arrivals, these abilities are set within a larger context of divination, a practice of great importance for African American religion and textuality.

Henry Louis Gates has made us aware of the pervasive influence on these practices of the West African trickster known in Yoruban culture as Esu Elegbara (5-10). Like the many manifestations of the tricksters in the world, Esu is an archaic and still powerful deity known mostly for his double nature (animal and human, male and female). Associated with roads, especially crossroads, he moves between supposedly opposite worlds, upper and lower, sacred and secular. And, as Hurston puts it, "the way of all things is in his hands" (_Tell_ 128). His phallic character also symbolizes his connectedness, his ubiquitous presence as a mediating figure. His survival of the horrors of the Middle Passage guaranteed the survival of African culture in the New World, albeit in a form in which African discourses would be passed on--in ways not obvious to the oppressor culture.

As Gates demonstrates, the Yoruban Esu is, in his mediating capacity, also closely related to the processes of creation, because it is Esu who reads the language of the gods and translates the language for the people. The Yoruban praise poems, and especially the sacred texts known as _Odu Ifa_-- divination poems--carry within them "the myths of origin of the universe," but in a coded form which is "lushly metaphorical, ambiguous, and enigmatic" (Gates 10). Such texts are not written, but have been passed from one generation to the next orally; hence, the divination process is undertaken by means of the configurations of a tray of sixteen palm nuts which are read by Esu and then translated. Gates also makes the interesting point that the Yorubans regard actual written texts as inferior, being derivative and shadowy when compared to the oral textuality of the _Ifa_.

Keeping in mind the notion of Esu as the reader or interpreter of the divine text, I would like to suggest some connections among Esu, tricksterism, conjuration, and the activities of Miranda, who also functions as a trickster figure. Indeed, the relationship of Jonah Day and her father John Paul to Esu is suggested by the fact that like Esu--the original seventh son--both Jonah and John Paul are seventh sons and fated to be conjurers. A number of studies attest to lore regarding the seventh son (Bass 381; Herron and Bacon 360), and

Naylor makes abundant use of number seven in the novel. Willow Springs occupies 49 square miles, for example, but seven is especially related to the activities of the Days. They own 4,900 acres and have a #7 for their post office box; Cocoa has lived in New York for seven years and has written 77 letters home, etc. Clearly, Miranda has inherited the mantle of tricksterism, as we can see by her constant movement along the roads, by her connection to "the other place," and also by her ability to read signs of the elements. She has also served as the mediating figure of the community, the bridge between the everyday world and the sacred world of her African foremother. We see her mediating qualities especially clearly in her relationship with George--who, as an outsider, has temporarily "crossed over."

Although George is immediately responsive to Willow Springs and can see himself "'staying [t]here forever'" (220), he is also distressed when the bridge is destroyed, and, unable to escape the island, he is forced to deal with the consequences of conjure--although there is no evidence he is even aware of the term. When Dr. Buzzard approaches him after the funeral of Bernice's child, telling him ". . . we got us a bridge to build" (269), we understand that there is metaphorical bridge building that is needed, between the scientific and the intuitive, the rational and non-rational, the secular and the sacred.

Miranda's need of George is determined by the past events in the lives of the Days, by losses that have been endured, the suffering of the other Day men with broken hearts, and the problem of the binding and releasing of the women, beginning with the ancestral matriarch Sapphira. Despite George's inability to "read" his environment, which gives to his portions of the narrative great dramatic irony, Miranda depends on George's belief in himself, his ability to work with his hands, his resolve to hold on to what he loves, to never let Cocoa go. But George also desires to "hold on to what was real" (291) and craves to feel "those oars between [his] hands" as he fantasizes about rowing Cocoa across the Sound (282-283). Miranda knows that to help Cocoa George must hand over his belief to her ("Of his own accord he had to *hand* it over to her. She needs his hand in hers--his very hand--so she can connect it up with all the believing that had gone before. . . . So together they could be the bridge for Baby Girl to walk over" [285]).

By placing his hand in Miranda's, by joining the secular with the sacred, the real with the magical, they can save Cocoa. Like many another initiate, he is asked to perform certain tasks which appear to him as the irrational demands of an old woman. Armed only with Miranda's walking stick (a symbol of power) and the ancient ledger which contains within it the partially erased bill of sale (history and knowledge), he is to go to the nest of the brooding hen--the object he most fears--and bring back to Miranda "'whatever [he] find[s]'" (295). George fails Miranda's riddling test because his fear and disbelief get the better of him, although, as he battles the enraged hen, he glimpses something of Miranda's meaning: "Could it be that she wanted nothing but my hands?" (300). While he does save Cocoa because he intuits something about the connection between speech and act, asserting that ". . . these were *my* hands, and there was no way I was going to let you go" (301), he is unable to make a genuine surrender of belief to Miranda, and hence loses his life.

To understand Miranda's enigmatic request better, we should perhaps consider the relationship of language to conjure. The *Oxford English Dictionary* defines *conjure* in part as follows:

I. to swear together, to conspire . . . . II. to constrain by oath. . . .
III. to invoke by supernatural power, to effect by magic or jugglery,
. . . to call up, constrain (a devil or spirit) to appear or do one's
bidding by the invocation of some sacred name or the use of some
spell.

As the above definitions suggest, conjure is never far from oaths, entreaties, invocations--from calling up and spell casting. Nor is language, especially the language of the gods, as the myths of Esu Elegbara show, ever far from "making," from creation. Thus, the intertextuality that so characterizes not only Naylor's novel but African American discourse in general is crucially involved in *making*--difficult enough in and of itself, but in an alien world not to be accomplished without special "signifyin(g)" power.[14]

The stories needed for survival were dependent on a knowledge not only of African traditions but also of New World discourses, against which the African American, through the metaphor of Esu the trickster, could acquire knowledge and power. For the violently displaced African who arrived in the New World without family, kinship system, or cultural group, survival depended on the trickster who had accompanied them on the Middle Passage and could supply the stories that could re-create their world.

Thus, within *Mama Day* are a number of texts that are incomplete, like the bill of sale, or other texts which depend on signifyin(g) practices to subvert the discourses of the oppressor. For example, we as readers are offered more textual information than Miranda herself is privy to regarding Sapphira's bill of sale. We know her name. We know that she was sold at age 20 to Bascombe Wade in 1819. We are told that she was "inflicted with sullenness," that she "resisted under reasonable chastisement the performance of field or domestic labor," and that she delved "in[to] witchcraft." We can also infer that she was sold because, like other powerful Africans, she had successfully resisted enslavement. The citizens of Willow Springs lack this bill of sale and her name, but what they do have is the date on which Bascombe Wade ceded the land to Sapphira, the land which in turn became their own. That year--1823--replaces her name but circulates within the signifying practices of the island as a power-making word. Thus when the islanders speak of girls with their "18 and 23's coming down," or boys breathing "18 & 23" or the ability of some to "18 and 23" outsiders, they are speaking conjure power.[15]

Besides the incomplete bill of sale and the dated deeds belonging to the residents of Willow Springs, we are offered yet another text--the genealogy of the Days. This tracing of the generations is particularly suggestive because of the other texts it signifies again, appropriating and transforming the Old and New Testaments of the Bible and Shakespeare as well.

Especially notable in terms of conjure power are the names of the Days. The first generation is named after figures in the Old Testament.[16] It is interesting to note that, historically, once slaves became familiar with Bible narratives they preferred only certain names--names of leaders such as Moses, or names of kings such as David. Clearly the slaves saw a relationship between the name and the destiny of their offspring, for they never named a son Samson or a daughter Bathsheba (Cody 588-589). However, the names of the first generation of Day men are neither leaders nor kings, but prophets: Elisha, Elijah, Amos, Joel, Joshua, and Jonah, suggesting instead of kingship their connection to conjure. The second generation of Days were given the names of the New Testament apostles.[17]

"Reading" the significance of the daughters if more problematic, but Miranda's name (which means "worker of wonders") suggests Shakespeare's *Tempest* with a radical rewriting of the father-daughter relationship. Ophelia's name also has Shakespearean associations, especially in view of the fact that the grandmother, also named Ophelia, has gone mad and committed suicide by drowning.[18] On the other hand, Cocoa--named Ophelia--is the child of Grace and claims another etymological heritage, since *Ophelia* has as its root word "snake," emblem of the conjure power of Aaron and Moses and an image central to the religion of *voudun* as practiced in New Orleans and Haiti.[19] Abigail's name seems fitting for her more orthodox Protestantism, as do the names of her children--Peace, Grace, and Hope. Yet even these serve to designate conditions, destinies either lost or found--although for the generation after Abigail all have been lost, and "peace" has not yet been regained in the present generation. Loss occasioned by the death of Abigail's sister Peace in infancy is not to be recovered by the offer of Abigail's own child (in terms of name) to the spirit of her deceased mother, for the second Peace also perishes, as do Hope and Grace. While Grace also dies young, the child of Grace--Ophelia--becomes the hope of the Days and the bringer of peace.

But Naylor seems to have more in mind in her textual rendering of this universe with its echoes of the Bible, for besides the stories of prophets--those many men of conjure--there are other Biblical narratives important to the Days -- namely, the Genesis creation myth and the story of Moses. There is little obvious evidence in the novel of this kind of mythic material; however, the enigmatic inscription found at the bottom of the genealogy chart, asterisked (to explain Jonah's being given a last name) and placed within quotation marks reads, "'God rested on the seventh day and so would she.'" This explanation of the family's name doesn't really clarify much. Certainly there is an echo of Genesis and a word play where "resting on the seventh day" comes to have a second meaning. Sapphira is likened, through this text, to the god who is a maker of creation in six days, but whereas the god of Genesis doesn't use the seventh day for creation, Sapphira does, making out of the words *seventh day* another creative event--a special son, wrought of body and word. The "hoodoo" version of creation--"six days of magic spells and mighty words and the world with its elements above and below was made"--suggests the important role of conjure to the African version of the creation myth, especially since, according to Hurston, "the way we tell it, hoodoo started way back before everything" (*Mules* 193).

However, the hoodoo version doesn't end with God's making the world in six days, but includes stories of Moses, because, as Hurston puts it, "many a man thinks he is making something when he's only changing things around. But God let Moses make" (*Mules* 194). While it is common knowledge that Moses, as liberator of the Israelites from Egypt, is an especially important figure for African Americans, what is perhaps less known is the connection of Moses to hoodoo. Again, Hurston's version of the story is important. While man was anxious "to catch God working with His hands" in order to find out his secrets, only Moses "learned God's power-compelling words."[20] However, although Moses "could carry power" and was given "His rod for a present," he needed the knowledge of Jethro, his father-in-law and a true hoodoo man (*Mules* 194). Important to these myths is the activity of making and the metonym of hands.

As previously mentioned, Miranda remarks frequently about hands and their power, not only in relation to the instructions that she gives to George, but in relation to her own gifts and those of all the Day men. However, the subject of hands also appears in the single fragment of myth we are given, the story of the origins of Willow Springs, which goes as follows:

> The island got spit out from the mouth of God, and when it fell to the earth it brought along an army of stars. He tried to reach down and scoop them back up, and found Himself shaking hands with the greatest conjure woman on earth. "Leave 'em here, Lord," she said. "I ain't got nothing but these poor black hands to guide my people, but I can lead on with light."   (110)

What is rendered as fanciful story here is acted out in the ritual of Candle Walk which, although half-forgotten and misunderstood, still carries on the Willow Springs text of creation. Observed on the 22nd of December, the time of the midwinter solstice, Candle Walk suggests a recognition of the fact that this longest night of the year also marks the beginning of the return of the sun from its lowest zenith, a rebirth that correlates with the rebirth of the terrestrial world. Thus, the ritual gestures that make up Candle Walk suggest a conjoining of cosmic and terrestrial: the candles carried by each islander in a night procession across the island configure a winding stream of light which, in its serpentine movement, becomes a signature of the power of all the elements--air, earth, fire, and water. The exchange of gifts "from the earth" that are "the work of your own hands" points to the importance of making and of the need for each individual to imitate the creative act which created the island itself (110). To that end the candles--used to welcome and accompany the spirit[21]--represent the spirit of the Great Mother who has returned in a ball of fire to Africa, and also stand for "the light that burned in a man's heart"--the spirit of the white man Bascombe Wade who loved Sapphira and who surrendered all his land to her and her offspring. Both are parents of this island and part of its story of origins.

Such stories of origins--cosmogonic myths--introduce another form of narrative. Unlike folktales, myths, in general, have a serious purpose and often embody ritual and theological ingredients that are meaningful to the culture that has produced them. Within myth is found the ideological content that determines a sacred form of behavior for a particular culture. However, cosmogonic myths appear to have an especially important function in many cultures worldwide. Mircea Eliade has argued that, for cultures in which the sacred plays a dominant role, the cosmogonic myth enables the escape from linear time to sacred time, the time of beginnings. This "paradigmatic model for all other times" (76) is important because it is recoverable--in Eliade's words, "*a primordial mythical time made present*" (68)--and because it is the means by which the community is restored. Indeed, as Eliade has also pointed out, in many societies the medicine man or community healer cannot effect a cure for the ills of the community until the creation story has been recalled and retold. Thus, when Miranda wonders if Cocoa will have a child to "keep the Days going," she seems to suggest that this "child of Grace" not only represents the line of the Days, but the very cosmos that is Willow Springs as it exists in both sacred and secular time (39).

For the African or African American story of origins, Esu performs an important mediating function. Although many trickster figures are only mediators *within* the secular world, Esu operates as a mediator *between* the secular and the sacred (Badejo 4). This trickster presence is a necessary one for Naylor's restitution of the text of conjure, not only because he adds another side to the story, but because he also adds another world, and hence a different kind of narrative. Thus Naylor's text, the story of the conjure woman, is also the story of "the beginning of the Days," a story that includes a goddess who must be recovered--as Sapphira will be recovered by Cocoa. It is also the story of the spirit of Africa that has traveled to the New World on wind and water. It affirms the staying power of the oral tradition, and although it is written down, it still must be "heard"; although listened to in the way the communal voice has demanded (". . . listen. Really listen this time" [10]), it must also be "read" in Esu's way, must be accompanied by a knowledge that includes the ongoing processes of seeing, hearing, and making.

Endnotes

[1]   This point is debatable. In his recent discussion of women and conjure, Houston Baker argues that, while Chesnutt uses Aunt Peggy "to influence the economy of [Uncle Julius's] situation," the stories actually "project the veritable control of a plantation by the conjure woman's ministrations" (78).

[2]   See especially Zora Neale Hurston's 1935 work *Mules and Men*, which recounts her anthropological study of hoodoo, including her own initiations into its mysteries, undertaken with the grandson of Marie Leveau, Luke Turner.

[3]   Of these, the *Report of the Lords of the Committee of the Council appointed for the consideration of all matters relating to Trade and Foreign Plantation* (1789), authored by Edward Long; *The History, Civil and Commercial, of the British Colonies in the West Indies* (1801), by the well-known historian of Jamaica Bryan Edwards; and John Stewart's *A View of Jamaica* (1832), all see the conjurer as pagan, evil, and often linked to slave rebellions.

[4]   Puckett mentions hearing that Leveau's funeral was attended by a "large number of superstitious Negroes," and recounts another source as saying she was afraid of snakes. He concludes that "so great has been the web of fancy woven around this unique character that an original painting of her, which an antique dealer could not sell for $2 just after death, is now worth over $250" (180).

[5]   The numerous references to the darkness of skin suggests, at least to me, that these conjurers may have been more recently arrived Africans or perhaps the least acculturated.

[6]   Creel mentions one early account in which the observer speaks of such an elder, "Maum Katie, an old African woman who remembers worshipping her own gods in Africa. . . . She is bright and talkative, a great 'spiritual mother,' a fortune-teller, or rather prophetess, and a woman of tremendous influence over her spiritual children" (291).

[7]   This and other remarks like his disparagement of Wheatley's accomplishments as a writer suggest Chesnutt's tendency to link inferiority not only to what is African, but also to what is female.

[8]   The most notable of these is Harry Middleton Hyatt's *Hoodoo--Conjuration--Witchcraft --Rootwork*, a five-volume compendium of field work on conjurers, spells, and cures.

[9]   It has been argued that, in the case of New Orleans voodoo practitioners, the great voodoo queens of the nineteenth century who practiced a religion were replaced by male voodoo doctors, suggesting that the loss of the religion resulted in the loss of power for women, while "male dominance of the world of hoodoo" was secured by the 1940s (Mulira 56).

[10]   Although in 1798 the Georgia Constitution prohibited slave importation (the United States followed in 1808), slaves from Africa continued to arrive on the Sea Islands well into the 1850s. Since the mainland had less use for slaves at this point, and preferred the more

acculturated blacks anyway, many of these late arrivals remained on the islands (Jones-Jackson 9).

[11]   BaKongo cosmology was complex and represented existence in terms of "four moments of the sun" which, in turn, correlated with the life cycles of beings on Earth. These were, according to Creel, birth, ascendancy, setting (death and transformation), and fourth, "Midnight, indicating existence in the other world and eventual rebirth" (Creel 52-53).

[12]   Jones-Jackson observes that, even when islanders die away from the islands, their relatives make every effort to have them returned for burial, reflecting a view that is held among the Igbo, Yoruba, and other Nigerians, who "believe without question that the dead are dependent on their ancestors for spiritual nourishment and thus must be buried among them to find peace" (26).

[13]   Deeply wooded areas are thought by the Gullahs to be sacred because the spirits of the ancestors reside there (Jones-Jackson 27).

[14]   Gates argues that signifyin(g) is the "black trope of tropes," suggesting a double-voiced speech act in which black signification is forced to operate within the signifying practices of white discourse acts, in Bakhtin's words, by "inserting a new semantic orientation into a word which already has--and retains--its own orientation." Signifyin(g) is then, "repetition with a . . . difference," and the (g) represents the trace of black difference (50-51).

[15]   Naylor's choice of year is interesting. The number 23 is magical, but perhaps an historical event, namely the Denmark Vesey slave revolt which occurred in the Carolinas in 1822, had some bearing on her choice of year. Vesey, a free and literate black, was influenced, like other leaders of revolts (Turner and Gabriel, for example), by the telling analogues of the Bible, but unlike other leaders, Vesey did not disparage the usefulness of black folk beliefs and had, as his second-in-command, a man named Gullah Jack, an Angola-born Sea Islander and conjure man (Levine 75-77). Although the revolt was suppressed and Vesey killed, we could infer that Sapphira's own 1823 victory over Bascombe Wade was influenced by these events. In any case, 1823 may mark, for some Sea Islanders, a new beginning.

[16]   Cody notes that slave names did not reflect Biblical influences until the 1830s, when efforts to convert slaves were initiated (589).

[17]   John-Paul's name is the only doubled one. He has taken on the name of a brother who died. However, Hurston notes an association of John the Baptist with Esu (*Tell* 129).

[18]   Erickson argues that, instead of a "newly empowered Caliban, . . . Naylor's subversive strategy is to create a black female equivalent to Prospero" (141), thereby breaking the literary linkage to Shakespeare and his creation of subservient daughters.

[19]   Hurston, in an attempt to demystify Haitian serpent worship, argues that the serpent is a "signature" of the deity Damballah (another name for Moses) whose rod was serpent-like and symbolized conjure power.

[20]   Hurston says that hoodoo lore has it that it was the snake living "in a hole right under God's foot-rest" that told Moses "God's fire-making words" (*Mules* 194).

[21]   Hurston records a similar candle ceremony in Jamaica associated the Pocomania rituals. Essentially lighted candles are "to attract the spirits" (*Tell* 4). Hyatt also mentions that the white candles stand for peace (2: 799).

Works Cited

Abrahams, Roger D. ed. *Afro-American Folktales: Stories from Black Traditions in the New World.* New York: Pantheon, 1985.

Badejo, Deidre. "The Yorubs and Afro-American Trickster: A Contextual Comparison." *Présence Africaine* 147 (1988): 3-17.

Baker, Houston A., Jr. *Workings of the Spirit: The Poetics of Afro-American Women's Writing.* Chicago: U of Chicago P, 1991.

Barrett, Leonard E. "Healing in a Balmyard: The Practice of Folk Healing in Jamaica, W.I." *American Folk Medicine: A Symposium.* Ed. Wayland D. Hand. Berkeley: U of California P, 1973. 285-300.

Bass, Ruth. "Mojo." Rpt. in Dundes 380-387.

Britt, David D. "Chesnutt's Conjure Tales: What You See is What You Get." *CLA Journal* 15.3 (1972): 269-283.

Callahan, John F. *In the African American Grain: The Pursuit of Voice in Twentieth-Century Black Fiction.* Urbana: U of Illinois P, 1988.

Chesnutt, Charles W. "Superstitions & Folklore of the South." 1901. Rpt. in Dundes 369-375.

Chesnutt, Helen. *Charles Waddell Chesnutt: Pioneer of the Color Line.* Chapel Hill: U of North Carolina P, 1952.

Cody, Cheryl Ann. "There Was No 'Absalom' on the Ball Plantations: Slave-Naming Practices in the South Carolina Low Country, 1720-1865." *American Historical Review* 92.3 (1987): 563-596.

Creel, Margaret Washington. *"A Peculiar People": Slave Religion and Community-Culture Among the Gullahs.* New York: New York UP, 1988.

Dixon, Melvin. "The Teller as Folk Trickster in Chesnutt's *The Conjure Woman.*" *CLA Journal* 18.2 (1974): 186-197.

Dundes, Alan, ed. *Mother Wit from the Laughing Barrel.* New York: Garland, 1981.

Eliade, Mircea. *The Sacred and the Profane: The Nature of Religion.* Trans. Willard R. Trask. New York: Harcourt, 1959.

Erickson, Peter. *Rewriting Shakespeare, Rewriting Ourselves.* Berkeley: U of California P, 1991.

Gates, Henry Louis, Jr. *The Signifying Monkey: A Theory of African American Literary Criticism.* New York: Oxford UP, 1988.

Herron, Lenora, and Alice M. Bacon. "Conjuring and Conjure Doctors." 1985. Rpt. in Dundes 359-368.

Hurston, Zora Neale. *Mules and Men.* 1935. Bloomington: Indiana UP, 1978.

_____. *Tell My Horse: Voodoo and Life in Haiti and Jamaica.* 1938. New York: Harper, 1990.

Hyatt, Henry Middleton. *Hoodoo--Conjuration--Witchcraft--Rootwork.* 5 vols. Washington: American U Bookstore, 1970.

Jackson, Bruce. "The Other Kind of Doctor: Conjure and Magic in Black American Folk Medicine." *American Folk Medicine: A Symposium.* Ed. Wayland D. Hand. Berkeley: U of California P, 1976. 258-272.

Jones-Jackson, Patricia. *When Roots Die.* Athens: U of Georgia P, 1987.

Levine, Lawrence W. *Black Culture and Black Consciousness.* New York: Oxford UP, 1977.

"*Mama Day* a Victim of its Own Conjuring." *Orlando Sentinel* 14 Feb. 1988: G8.

"'Magical' Powers Lost Inside *Mama Day.*" *Pittsburgh Press* 3 Apr. 1988: C3.

Mulira, Jessie Gaston. "The Case of Voodoo in New Orleans." *Africanisms in American Culture.* Ed. Joseph E. Holloway. Bloomington: Indiana UP, 1991. 34-68.

Naylor, Gloria. *Mama Day.* New York: Ticknor & Fields, 1988.

Puckett, Newbell Niles. *Folk Beliefs of the Southern Negro.* Chapel Hill: U of North Carolina P, 1926.

Whitten, Norman E. "Contemporary Patterns of Malign Occultism among Negroes in North Carolina." *Journal of American Folklore* 75 (Oct.-Dec. 1962): 311-325.

Christol, Hélène. "Reconstructing American History: Land and Genealogy in Gloria Naylor's *Mama Day*." *The Black Columbiad*. Eds. Werner Sollors and Maria Diedrich. Cambridge: Harvard UP, 1994. 347-356.

Discussing the visions and revisions as well as the attempts at redefinition of the New World developed by African American writers implies discussing their reassessment of American history and their multioriented search for new forms, traditions, myths, legends, stories, and interpretations which, if they do not necessarily run counter to white experience, exist on its edges, sometimes uncovering an unknown continent. Such destructuring of white, traditional history remains the uniquely useful act that can reveal the meaning and the specificity of black experience. Trapped in white definitions, deprived of their culture, expropriated of their land, bound by what Ralph Ellison called "the familial past," alienated from self, black authors can recapture their language and their power by rejecting the India that Columbus thought he had found and by replacing white "official history" with their own stories. In his essay "The Topos of (Un)naming in Afro-American Literature," Kimberly W. Benston defines black literature as one vast genealogical revisionist poem "that attempts to restore continuity and meaning to the ruptures or discontinuities imposed by the history of black presence in America" (152).

Such attempts are even more necessary if the author is a black woman: doubly invisible in the eyes of history, she alone can reread her own story within a field of gender and ethnicity that implies both conflict and the search for consensus and communality, transcribe or recreate her group's own "social dialect," thus resurrecting the distant silenced names that give shape to her experience and, more largely, to that of her community. "Under the recorded names," writes Toni Morrison, "were other names . . . recorded for all time in some dusty file, [hiding] from view the real name of people, places, and things. Names that had meaning . . . When you know your name, you should hang on to it, for unless it is noted and remembered, it will die when you do" (329). Such a "recorder of names" is Gloria Naylor in her two novels *Linden Hills* and *Mama Day*. Whether these names are found in old recipe books or discarded letters and papers forgotten in a cellar but finally brought to light by the last epiphany of *Linden Hills*, or in an old ledger kept in an attic and resurrected by the "genealogical revisionism" of *Mama Day*, they form the core of the narration. In *Mama Day*, especially, topography and genealogy are the two essential elements that determine the stance of the narrative voice and allow Naylor to reconstruct a parallel black history, to reinvent America by subverting its historical and mythical elements.

Topography

> Our latitudes and longitudes have other names
> Fiction/Nonfiction.
> --Ntozake Shange, *A Daughter's Geography*

From the very start Naylor establishes the necessary relation that links people, history, and land. Blacks were originally taken from the land, and the journey back to origins has to start with the reappropriation of the land, in *Mama*

Day the definition of a free territory, Willow Springs, an island that belongs to the blacks who live on it.

Ownership of the land is the first sign of independence. It has to be established legally by contract ("[deeded] all his slaves every inch of land") (*Mama Day* 3). *Linden Hills* starts with a long description of the dispute over the exact location of the place and with the history of the various deeds establishing the property rights of Luther Nedeed. In the same way, *Mama Day* emphasizes the importance of the piece of paper, the "deed," that confirms the territory as "black territory," as if for a people defined as a piece of property the legal, material deed making them masters of the land was the palimpsest of their freedom and autonomy. Moreover, the land is owned two generations down so that no one can sell it. It belongs to the blacks eternally ("Belongs to no one except the black people on it"; "It belongs to us, clean and simple" [5]). The reiteration of this motif throughout the novel stresses the stability gained by ownership of the piece of land where the Day family has built a house, a garden, and, more important, a graveyard. Each Day has his or her own grave with his or her own name engraved on it. Set in opposition to the disruptions of black family life, Willow Springs is the very symbol of continuity and permanence. When George, the black "outsider," visits the island, he marvels at the fact that Ophelia, his wife, knows all her ancestors, and he envies these "people who could be this self-contained. Who had redefined time. No, totally disregarded it" (218).

Willow Springs's geographic situation also emphasizes its difference. Linked with the American continent by a bridge which is regularly destroyed by hurricanes, it cannot be inscribed in the American geography. It "ain't in no State," neither in Georgia nor in South Carolina; it appears on no official maps. Naylor even calls it "un-American ground" (5). In fact, the population reject any kind of American filiation by tracing their ancestors back to Wade, the first and last white master, who was Norwegian, and to Sapphira Day, his slave, who was African. If they still maintain political and commercial relations with the American continent, they do so on their own terms and do not depend on the American system of law and justice. Reminiscent of the Gullahs, the freed slaves who fled to the Sea Islands when the Civil War ended and kept their distinctive dialect and culture, the people of Willow Springs have in fact colonized and invested their own territory. Thus, Naylor creates a land on the edge of things, out of official charters, totally autonomous, a kind of nation in its own right whose existence cannot be negated since the first page of the novel offers a map, the iconographic evidence of this "new World" revisited.

The remote island of *Mama Day* inscribes itself on a piece of paper (like the deed that ensures its ownership), the visible charter establishing its existence. Yet, as in *Linden Hills*, whose circular structure reminds the reader of Dante's *Inferno*, Willow Springs also seems to spring from Shakespeare's "American fable" *The Tempest*, the topography of which, to quote Leo Marx, prefigured "the moral geography of the American imagination" (72). Naylor plays with the founding myths of America as a garden, but also as a howling desert, placing at the center of her imaginative construction the conflicting images of the pastoral Eden and the forces of death. The main character Miranda, the hurricane that echoes Prospero's tempest, allusions to magic and the Book of Spells all impart a mythical dimension to the story, as if the tale were reenacted with Miranda as the new Prospero of the island. Initially the New World was a utopia, and Willow Springs shares some of the characteristics of the primeval Paradise. The island seems to be outside of time: "nothing changes here but the seasons" (160). It is compared to a still life, to a "picture postcard." George, taking a walk in the morning, notices that "it smelled like forever" (175); he is attracted by the "primal air," and admires the trees "which had to have been there for almost two hundred years" (175). The luxuriant, beautiful, untouched vegetation reminds the reader of other unspoiled worlds such as those seen by Captain John Smith or by Columbus himself. The small, preserved community with its quaint characters such as Dr. Buzzard, and its witches such as Ruby and Miranda, leads a simple rural life, protected from the "modern life of the cities," where blacks have become "honorary white folks" (38), to use Miranda's derogatory words. Such an isolated pastoral environment seems favorable to George's Adamic dream: "Let's play Adam and Eve" (222), he tells Ophelia, who wisely brings him back to earth by alluding to the hard work attached to rural existence.

Naylor clearly balances the mythical elements of this Paradise rediscovered with darker elements. Though it stands on the edges of the American continent, Willow Springs has been "infected" by some original sin and has not been spared suffering, losses, suicide. When George optimistically exclaims; "We could defy history!" (222), Miranda's next chapter opens with the word "Death." The roots of such pain have to be found in the familial past which reflects the racial past. Owning the territory is not enough; reappropriation of land has to go with the reappropriation of time and thus of history.

Genealogy

He had barely had a chance to live. He was just learning to write his name.

--Linden Hills

The history of the race and familial history are inextricably linked in *Mama Day*. The map of the island of the first page is followed by a genealogical tree. A woman named Sapphira Wade figures as the only founder of a family of seven sons (fathers unknown), who fathered seven sons, the seventh one siring three generations of women. As in the Bible, from which this genealogy is obviously drawn, Sapphira has "rested" after her seventh son and given the name Day to her family. This genealogy is immediately followed by the certificate of sale of a slave woman named Sapphira, age twenty, of pure African stock, to Bascombe Wade, on August 3, 1819. Thus the arresting, unusual first three pages of the novel offer a clue to the inner structure of the book, introducing what Barbara Christian has called a "creative dialogue" between public and private life, history and biography, the past and the present (209). Genealogy, a search for filiation and lineage, finds itself at the intersection of these patterns as it concerns the individual private and family sphere, but also largely serves to remedy the failures of memory through its minute literal reconstitution of human history.

Any genesis of "black" history has to go back to the original trauma of slavery (here the sale of Sapphira in 1819) and to the sexual exploitation of black women. Any kind of filiation starts with a white master. *Mama Day* alludes to the different miscegenations that made one of Miranda's ancestors say, for instance, "Some of my brothers looked like me and some didn't . . . In them times it was common to have a blue-eyed child playing next to his dark sister" (151). Ophelia herself constantly insists on the fact that she is black in spite of her "golden" skin: "you hated to think about the fact that you might also be carrying a bit of him [Wade]," says George. "Even your shame was a privilege few of us had. We could only look at our skin tones and guess. At least you knew" (219). Thus, establishing one's filiation, or one's genealogy, even if it implies uncovering a story of violence and rape, is a structuring and ethical process which is emphasized by the very structure of the novel.

In fact, slavery and its history are "revisited" by Naylor: Sapphira is presented as an independent, active agent who was owned in body but not in mind, who may have killed her master or driven him to "deed his land" and to despair, who "took" her freedom--a genuine femme fatale. With her independence she freed her sons: Her seven sons "lived as free men 'cause their mama willed it so" (151). Indeed, she was not herself a slave: "He [Wade] had freed 'em all but her, 'cause, see, she'd never been a slave" (308). The real victim seems, finally, to have been Wade himself, who lost everything--his land, his love, and his life. Such an inversion of perspectives, a true rewriting of history, sheds a much more positive light on the woman who was sold in the original document, and who becomes the founding mother of a dynasty, for which she invents a symbolic name, the Days.

Uncovering the genealogy of the Day family involves the process of uncovering the names of its members. *Mama Day* could be viewed as an attempt to reconstruct of Book of Names of a black family who is the family of blacks. Bearing in mind the importance of naming and its specific symbolism in black history and literature, the reader immediately sees that the Days *own* their names, as they own their land. Every time their personal story is told--at least seven different times in the novel--it takes the form of a litany of names, Miranda, Ophelia, Abigail, Peace, which *are* the story. Moreover, the discovery of family names goes with the discovery of the self: the main character, first nicknamed Baby Girl, then Cocoa, recovers her real name, Ophelia, only after her aunt Miranda tells her the story of her grandmother Ophelia, who committed suicide in despair over losing one of her children: "it's her [Cocoa's] family and her history. And she'll have children one day . . . She ain't a baby. She's a grown woman and her *real* name is Ophelia" (116), a name that saved her life and "helped to hold her here" (267). Meaning grows from such genealogical archaeology; only this work of patient reconstitution (like the quilt sewn by Miranda which serves as a metaphor for the link between generations) can lead to knowledge and self-knowledge. In one of Miranda's dreams she "opens door upon door . . . She asks each door the same thing: 'Tell me your name'" (283). What she discovers is a string of women's names: Savannah, Samarinda, Sage, who are Sapphira's sisters, thus creating the large family of women slaves who had escaped, if not in body at least in mind, from slavery.

The Book of Names of *Mama Day* is essentially composed of women. In spite of two earlier generations of men, the word and the power have been given first to Miranda, then to Ophelia, following their original ancestor, Sapphira. In *Linden Hills* the voice and power of women has been hushed up until one of the Day women rose from the cellar and destroyed the Nedeed house. In *Mama Day* women are the source of power: born to the seventh son of a seventh son, Miranda is the central character of the story, the "little mother," the woman with a gift who understands the voices of history and can interpret them. As for

Sapphira, various legends, all reported in one place or another in the book, show her as a "namer" ("a woman who brought a whole new meaning to words" [3]), the liberator of slaves, an African who "left by wind," the "great, great, grand, Mother" (218), which she is literally and figuratively, carrying the attributes of the goddess. She is also referred to as the one whose name nobody knows: she lives beyond words and, as the "unnamed," is close to the sublime, the stance of unchallenged authority. As the "greatest conjure woman on earth" (110), she even signed pacts with God, who has abandoned the island to her rule.

Woman's power, however, is viewed as both positive and negative. It can give life, as in the amazing scene of Little Caesar's conception by Miranda; it is also destructive, as embodied in the hurricane which "could only be the workings of Woman. And She has no name" (251), a statement that can be compared to George's: "That was power. But the winds coming around the corners of that house was God" (251). The other motif of the novel of "the man with the broken heart" (151; 308) is also indicative of the formidable power of women to inspire such passions that even the white master Wade perished, burned by the fire of Sapphira.

Yet the fire which ends *Linden Hills* and destroys the tainted kingdom of the Nedeeds is not the ultimate word of *Mama Day*. Unlike *Linden Hills*, *Mama Day*, though it speaks at times in dialogically racial and gendered voices, seems to enter what Mae Gwendolyn Henderson calls "a dialectic of identity," articulating "a relation of mutuality and reciprocity with the 'Thou'--or intimate other(s)" (19). The revival of the familial past and the reiteration of motifs which gradually uncover the story of the Days by questioning their genealogy develop a parallel, alternative history in which black experience is remodeled and transfigured, in which ruptures and tensions, pain, suffering, and death can be transcended and eventually stilled like the waters of the novel's last sentence. Language itself may be the ultimate medium of effecting this metamorphosis, language as the "archive" of history, a language forgotten but reinvented by the legends and tales, preserved in the conversations and dialogues between the dead and the living. One ritual of the island asks the living to put some moss in their shoes before they enter the graveyard so they may hear the voices of their ancestors. *Mama Day* resurrects these voices and, stressing the importance of the oral tradition in black culture, underlines the necessity of listening to all the voices, including the voices of the past.

Voices

> So has the book been written
> So has your heart become perfect.
> --Jay Wright, "Son"

Mama Day uses a great number of narrators, including the reader, to develop its central themes. "Think about it: ain't nobody really talking to you. We're sitting here in Willow Springs and you're God knows where. It's August 1999 . . . the only voice is your own" (10), says the first introductory narrator. First-person sections are written--or uttered--by George, Cocoa, Miranda, John Paul, and even Jonah Day, every narrator bringing a new clue to the story and adding meaning to it. Yet in spite (or because) of this polyphony of voices, this multivocality, the narrative "I" seems to fulfill the function ascribed by Benston to the primal name as central source, "a force which drives into history . . . as a poetic intelligence, a receptacle into which history flows in order to be carried by the vector of the poem into the present" (167).

Thus, a transcultural genealogical myth is created. Sapphira's legend does not live in "the part of our memory we can use to form words" (4). She belongs to some prelinguistic age, not yet in history but close to its edges. Miranda, as seer, *griot*, nurse, and doctor, with her prescience of things to come and knowledge of things past, has a voice that can be described as shamanistic. Considered together, the lineage of women going from Sapphira to Cocoa encompasses fire, air, land, and water, all elements unified in the vital logos, Jay Wright's Nommo, which they embody. "Speaking in tongues," these women are one with the forces of nature that surround them (Henderson 22). The three essential elements are also found on their island; air (wind, hurricane), water (the Sound, waves, drowning or crossing the Sound in dream), and fire (lightning or the Candle Walk). Thus, the concrete objectification of the island's topography and the imaginative vision of the narrators combine to create a highly metaphorical space in which what is discovered is not only Columbus's island or some New World revisited but a no-man's-land poised between chaos and form, the place where the original Word was uttered. The paradigmatic family of the Days becomes the paradigm of the human family, its genealogy the genealogy of the human race beyond color and history.

It is a primitive ritual, the Candle Walk, whose meaning had been lost, but has been rediscovered through the resurrection of the Days' history, which brings its epiphany to the novel: "It weren't about no candles, was about a light that burned in a man's heart" (308). Because of George, and because of the other voices, including male and even white voices, the story of hatred and sorrow has become a story of love. The motif of the man with a broken heart, which implied violence, revenge, enslavement, suffering, and death, has been replaced by the motif of the man with light in his heart. When Ophelia tries to describe George to her young son, she can describe only him as "a man who looked just like love" (310). In the same way, the words of the legal document selling Sapphira to Wade have been erased by age, and the only words left are "*Law. Knowledge. Witness. Inflicted. Nurse. Conditions. Tender. Kind*" (280) --terms that define the inheritance passed on to Ophelia. This inheritance sees the reconciliation of master and slave, and the reconciliation of black men and black women. The words of the message emphasize the new code (law reinforced by knowledge) whose key words are "tender" and "kind." Even though George does not understand Miranda's message ("Could it be that she wanted nothing but my hands?" [300]) and literally dies from a broken heart, meaning has been handed over to Ophelia, who has heard Miranda's voice: "She needs his hand in hers--his very hand--so she can connect it up with all the believing that had gone before . . . So together they could be the bridge for Baby Girl to walk over. Yes, in his very hands, he already held the missing piece she'd come looking for" (285). The terms used--"connect," "bridge"--underline the fact that knowledge and wisdom have been acquired and handed over to future generations, here embodied by Baby Girl/Ophelia, the first adventurer who crossed the bridge to go to the continent. In her next novel, *Bailey's Cafe*, Gloria Naylor takes us back to the mainland, for as one of the characters contends, "even though this planet is round, there are just too many spots where you can find yourself hanging onto the edge . . . and unless there's some space, some place, to take a breather for a while, the edge of the world--frightening as it is--could be the end of the world, which would be quite a pity" (*Bailey's Cafe* 28). The journey back to the island of origins, this kind of Middle Passage revisited, the exploration of the interface between life and death have thus opened, "bridged," the way to some kind of reconciliation between the self, society, and history.

In *Linden Hills* Naylor uses sexual domination and the oppression of women by both white and black men as a model for all other exploitive systems. The original sin of Linden Hills is Luther's buying his land with the money he got from selling his octoroon wife and children into slavery. The Nedeed wives are granted neither value nor life. They have no recorded history: they do not exist in the twelve-volume history of the area written by Dr. Braithwaite, the professor from Fisk. Naylor calls attention to the fact that any kind of history that does not take into account black women's existence and voices is irresponsible and as sterile as Dr. Braithwaite's dead willows and bonsai trees. The awakening of the "last woman," a Day woman, finally gives a "face" to the thousands of black women who have been (literally in the novel, and figuratively in American history) kept in the netherworld, erased, blotted out of the Book of Names. Unlike *Linden Hills*, which stresses ruptures, crises, discontinuities, *Mama Day* tries to restore the lost unity of man and nature, of men and women. Owing to the special topography of Willow Springs and to genealogical archaeology, peace which had been lost (as expressed in the metaphorical story of the little girl, Peace, drowned in the well, whose suffering is finally freed by Miranda) has been regained. Thus, the book offers perfect proof of the centrality of African American women's shaping of a vision that overthrows the old white, male, elitist-centered view of the universe and becomes "an expressive site for a dialectics/dialogics of identity and difference" (Henderson 37). Rejecting Columbus as founder of America and great father figure, it opens alternative, generous views of new communities, reinventing language and thus utopia, to connect the natural world and the possibilities of a more harmonious social order.

Works Cited

Benston, Kimberly W. "I Yam What I Am: The Topos of (Un)naming in Afro-American Literature." *Black Literature and Literary Theory*. Ed. Henry Louis Gates, Jr. New York: Routledge, 1990.

Christian, Barbara. *Black Feminist Criticism: Perspectives in Black Women Writers*. New York: Pergamon, 1985.

Henderson, Mae Gwendolyn. "Speaking in Tongues: Dialogics, Dialectics, and the Black Woman Writer's Literary Tradition." *Changing Our Own Words*. Ed. Cheryl A. Wall. London: Routledge, 1990.

Marx, Leo. *The Machine in the Garden: Technology and the Pastoral Ideal in America*. Oxford: Oxford UP, 1964.

Morrison, Toni. *Song of Solomon*. New York: Knopf, 1977.

Naylor, Gloria. *Bailey's Cafe*. New York: Vintage, 1993.

_____. *Mama Day*. New York: Vintage, 1989.

Storhoff, Gary. "'The Only Voice Is Your Own': Gloria Naylor's Revision of *The Tempest*." *African American Review* 29.1 (1995): 35-45.

In Gloria Naylor's novel *Mama Day*, Reema's boy comes from the university to conduct anthropological studies in Willow Springs, the novel's mysterious setting. Attempting to preserve "cultural identities" against "hostile social and political parameters," he frustrates Willow Springs' residents, for he does not "listen" to the stories they have to tell him. With this character, Naylor introduces the text's central theme, the necessity of establishing narrative authority:

> Think about it: ain't nobody really talking to you. We're sitting here in Willow Springs, and you're God-knows-where. It's August 1999 --ain't but a slim chance it's the same season where you are. Uh, huh, listen. Really listen this time: the only voice is your own. (10)

This passage foregrounds Naylor's persistent concern throughout her literary career--establishing her individual voice. In her famous interview with Toni Morrison, Naylor candidly discloses her anxiety about writing outside established traditions:

> I wrote because I had no choice, but that was a long road from gathering the authority within myself to believe that I could actually be a writer. The writers I had been taught to love were either male or white. And who was I to argue that Ellison, Austen, Dickens, the Brontës, Baldwin and Faulkner weren't masters? They were and are. But inside there was still the faintest whisper: Was there no one telling my story? And since it appeared there was not, how could I presume to? Those were frustrating years.   (574)

That her own voice be heard, it is necessary for Naylor to clear a space for "her own story," a text among texts. Her ambitious narrative project is in essence a declaration of independence--an acknowledgment of the academic canon's value, but also an assertion of her racial and gender difference. Without repudiation of texts that she obviously loves, she can tell *her* story, but never at the expense of her own unique narrative voice.

Naylor's quest for her own "voice" is, of course, a central concern for most African American writers, discovered in "the tension between the oral and the written modes of narration that is represented as finding a voice in writing" (Gates 21). Her experimentation with voice in *Mama Day* represents a dramatic advance in her artistic talent over her two previous works. Unlike both *The Women of Brewster Place* and *Linden Hills*, where the narrator's voice is distinct from the voices of her characters, and where there is occasionally a tone of condescension, Naylor achieves in *Mama Day* what Gates calls a "speakerly text"--one that "would seem primarily to be oriented toward imitating one of the numerous forms of oral narration to be found in classical Afro-American vernacular literature" (181). Mama Day's voice serves as a spiritual ballast in the narrative, a guide to elemental (religious) truths that the other characters must discover to set themselves free. But Naylor's employment of free indirect discourse throughout the novel metaphorically unites her with Miranda; the distinction between the writer's authority and the speaker's set of communal values in Willow Springs is mitigated, if not erased. The free indirect discourse, then, acts as Naylor's thematic commentary, a sign not only of the strength of the black oral voice but also of the transcendent solidity of Mama Day's thoughts and feelings.[1]

Naylor thus situates herself at the center of contemporary critical discussions of texts. Criticism has in the past twenty years reformulated the notion of literary history as a dynamic interplay of texts: We are now led to see a single work not simply as an autonomous, free-standing edifice but intertextually, as a text that "talks" with and to other texts. J. Hillis Miller characterizes the literary work as "inhabited . . . by a long chain of parasitical presences, echoes, allusions, guests, ghosts of previous texts" (446). Similarly, Roland Barthes describes the text as a "multi-dimensional space in which a variety of writings, none of them original, blend and clash . . . a tissue of quotations drawn from the innumerable centres of culture" (146). Several African American critics, including Robert B. Stepto and Henry Louis Gates, Jr., have discussed textual affinities between works and their African American precursorial models; Susan Willis and Michael Awkward have focused on intertextuality of black women writers specifically. In delineating a specific type of intertextuality termed "signifyin(g)," Gates explains the revisionary impulse of black writers: "It is clear that black writers read and critique other black texts as an act of rhetorical self-definition. Our literary tradition exists because of these precisely chartable formal literary relationships, relationships of signifying" (290).

In this debate, Naylor occupies a complex position, for she not only rewrites black texts but white canonical texts as well. Awkward has already shown how *The Women of Brewster Place* is revisionary of earlier black texts, especially those by Morrison, and demonstrates that Naylor's "revisionary gestures with respect to elements of Morrison's novel" clarifies her literary relationship to Jean Toomer's *Cane* (101). Certainly *Mama Day* reads like a virtual encyclopedia of African American expressive culture. In a multitude of literary allusions and narrative echoes, Naylor pays homage to (among others) Charles Chesnutt, Toni Morrison, Alice Walker, Ralph Ellison, Jean Toomer, Ernest J. Gaines, Ishmael Reed, and (of course) Zora Neale Hurston. But while she is occasionally critical of earlier black texts, she more often supplements the insights expressed in their works. Earlier black texts incarnated in *Mama Day* tend toward celebration rather than revision.[2]

But Naylor's strategy is tricky when she handles classic white texts. In her handling of Shakespeare's *Midsummer Night's Dream* in *The Women of Brewster Place* and of Dante in *Linden Hills*, Naylor pays homage to these canonical works, but also revises and reshapes them. While Shakespeare celebrates Puckish irrationality because it creates romantic love and the renewal of a comic society, Naylor tempers his celebration: "Puckish irrationality," given society's injustices of race and gender, may lead poor black women into tragic domestic situations where they act against their own best interests, and those of their children.[3] In *Linden Hills*, Naylor undertakes a wholesale revision of Dante's *Inferno*, but rather than reaffirming Christian morality, Naylor indicts middle-class materialism, positioning at the center of her Dantesque hell Luther Nedeed.

Mama Day is an imaginative interrogation of Shakespeare's *The Tempest*. Notably, Naylor's revisionary impulse undermines a New Critical understanding of the play, which posits *The Tempest* as a covert ideological argument in favor of the European colonizing project of the seventeenth century. In discussing the play, New Critics habitually tended to reduce the drama to an allegorical tract about the benefits of colonialism--often with racially insensitive and politically obtuse consequences. As such, Prospero allegorically figures as the Empire's vested authority; the mysterious island, a distant colony of the empire; and Caliban, the legitimately dispossessed native. G. Wilson Knight succinctly summarizes many years of Shakespearean criticism. Apparently unaware of the irony of his own words (and the tragic history belied by them), he writes that Prospero is representative of England's "colonizing, especially her will to raise *savage* peoples from superstition and blood-sacrifice, taboos and witchcraft and the attendant fears and *slaveries*, to a more enlightened existence" (255, emphasis mine). But in her own reconstruction of Shakespeare's play, Naylor dramatically deconstructs embedded New Critical ideological assumptions--many embarrassingly exposed in Knight's discussion--regarding patriarchal bias, an exclusively Protestant view of nature, the ahistoricism of political assertions, and the Eurocentric construction of "Otherness" as justification for exploitation and enslavement. Naylor's narrative denies the complacent sureties of much New Critical analysis. In short, she rescues the Shakespearean text for a gender-conscious, multicultural, multiracial audience.[4]

As the first hint of her revisionary project, Naylor names her main character Miranda. This naming displaces the reader from an accustomed position; no longer depending on Prospero's focal point of view, the reader must now listen to an unfamiliar voice--not the father's but the daughter's, surely among those least empowered in Shakespeare's play. In *The Tempest*, Prospero is a teacher who instructs his daughter and will have no backtalk. But in *Mama Day*, the matriarch (who has no children) is the guide, not only over her household but over the island generally: "Mama Day say no, everybody say no" (6) to the encroachment of corporate real estate developers (the contemporary colonialists) who would steal Willow Springs from its indigenous people.

Moreover, Naylor's Miranda, like Charles Chesnutt's reconfigured Conjure Woman, is endowed with powers that are in congruence with the Life Force on Willow Springs. She cooperates with Nature, helping all living things come to life. Shakespeare's Prospero wields his magic to control and subdue the forces of nature, thereby epitomizing his "dominion over the fish of the sea, and over the fowl of the air, and over every living thing that moveth upon the earth" (Genesis 1:28). Naylor's Miranda, however, consistently cooperates with natural forces. To illustrate Miranda's connection with the Life Force, Naylor continuously associates her with eggs, as a symbol of fertility. For example, she candles eggs to check for fertilization: "Her fingers curl gently around a warm egg that shows a deepening spot with tiny veins running out from it . . . Candlelight makes the shadowy life within her wrinkled hand seem to breathe as she rotates it real careful" (41). It is as if life emanates from her--as in fact it does later in the novel when she assists Bernice in conceiving.

While Prospero's books demarcate his identity as the apotheosis of rationalized order, Miranda is associated with eggs. This association, of course, is not to be understood in a depreciative or condescending way. Rather than an adversarial relationship with nature, she enjoys a reciprocating renewal in an animistic universe; Naylor continually challenges Prospero's separation between the spiritual and material worlds in the candling scene by having Miranda communicate with her chickens, a practice consistent throughout the novel. As we shall soon see, her elemental connection to eggs--and all eggs symbolize-- becomes a crucial code in the novel's psychological dynamics. Nature, in turn, responds to her, as if moved simply by her presence: "The scent of pine and grass burst out as the sun moves for a minute from behind a group of clouds" (41). Miranda does not require magical arts to coerce a response from nature; instead, her sensitivities align with natural forces because she honors all life. In Naylor's Willow Springs, the sacral dimension of experience conflates with the purely phenomenal whenever Miranda speaks.

The novel's two settings sustain Naylor's revisionary enterprise. A truism of the New Critical school of criticism is that *The Tempest* devises a contrast between two islands: the "uncharted isle" that manifests Nature, and the presumptive world of England that figures for "civility." But Naylor's division is not so secure, for she transforms Manhattan into a "wondrous isle," thereby deconstructing the facile binary of "Civilization vs. Primitivism." For Naylor (herself a New York City inhabitant), Manhattan is not the antithesis of Willow Springs but its complement. Seen in the proper perspective, Manhattan is as wondrous as Willow Springs, and one place cannot be entirely appreciated--or loved--without a full understanding of the other. Each is incomplete without the other (thus, George must visit Willow Springs, and Miranda at the novel's end must make a hilarious visit to New York). Indeed, given a willingness to discover magic in everyday life, Manhattan itself is wondrously mysterious. The novel begins in a dirty Manhattan coffee shop, and while everything seems plastic, artificial, and anonymous, it is here where George and Cocoa meet, eventually brought together with the assistance of Miranda's puckish dust. Although Cocoa at first sees only the surface of New York, symbolized by her categorizing people solely in terms of race and ethnicity, George shows her that the categories she creates are arbitrary, condescending, and divisive--and that the island is much more like Willow Springs than she thinks: The "city was a network of small towns, some even smaller than . . . Willow Springs" (61). In New York City, as in Willow Springs, people play out dramas of love and happiness, grief and loss.

George is alert to the human drama played out beneath the surface Cocoa only notices. It is he who understands the great significance people impute to the smallest details--the meaning of a yellow rose to a florist on Jamaica Avenue, or the significance of a certain candy store in Harlem. George's sensitivity to Manhattan's mysteries testifies to Naylor's own fairness in creating her male protagonist. Speaking to Morrison, Naylor says that she is concerned primarily with fairness in characterizing males: "I bent over backwards not to have a negative message come through about the men" (579). Her "positive message" is subtly conveyed--in fact, in danger of being misread. A civil engineer, George at first glance seems the stereotyped male chauvinist: he loves football; he sees women mechanically, coordinated (he thinks) with a twenty-eight-day menstrual cycle; he plays simple card games according to mathematics, assuming that winning is "the only thing"; he seemingly reduces human "basic needs" to "water supply, heating, air conditioning, transportation" (60). He is usually dogmatic, particularly with women. George is only half-kidding when he says, ". . . you keep 'em laid and you keep 'em happy" (221).

Yet George nevertheless possesses a deeply literary imagination, a potentiality of responding to the spiritual and emotional dimensions of life. He much prefers to conceal or disguise his own sensitivity, however. George likes to think of himself as coldly logical and empirical; he declares that he has "a very rational mind" (124). But George is also deeply moved by art and the aesthetic planes of experience (especially Shakespeare); despite his assertion that the "mechanics" of football interest him the most, he rhapsodizes over ballet-like wide receivers (such as Lynn Swann) catching the ball. His interest in mythology and life's hidden patterns is made clear in his fascination with the folklore on Willow Springs. He defeats the rural cardplayers with probability statistics, but he is so touched by their ovation that he gets drunk with Dr. Buzzard and his friends--an amusing reinscription of Shakespeare's drunken "lower characters" in The Tempest.

Despite his intuitive connection to the mysterious and wondrous, George nevertheless resists the encroachment of the unpredictable and uncontrollable in his life: ". . . everything I was," he says, "was owed to my living, fully in the now." For him, his past is an antagonist. George's success owes chiefly to his ability to repress his painful past; because of the tragic losses he suffered as a child, he considers it important to relate more cognitively than emotionally to his world. The orphaned son of a prostitute, he has learned to shield himself from any emotional pain by concentrating only on the tangible limits of what he could accomplish through concentrated effort: "No rabbit's foot, no crucifixes--not even a lottery ticket" (27). At Wallace P. Andrews (the orphanage where he grew to maturity), George learns Ben Franklin's meaning of industry, self-application, economy--and of limited horizons:[5] ". . . it wasn't the kind of place that turned out many poets or artists--those who could draw became draftsmen, and the musicians were taught to tune pianos" (26-27). The loss of his mother predisposes him to construct rationally explicable patterns to protect his psyche, especially when he perceives wholly emotional, nonpredictive experience. For example, he monitors the calendar to anticipate Cocoa's PMS, rather than attempt to understand that her frustration with him may arise from other sources, including his reluctance to face her frustration honestly. He refuses to sympathize with Cocoa's very understandable anxiety in returning to Willow Springs with her new husband, though she explains her feelings about her marriage several times to him.

Much as Shakespeare's plots emphasize the importance of transformative experiences, Naylor's narrative impels George to revise entirely his world picture. Because of his tortured childhood, George is only half a person. A good man who has the potential to become whole, he must undergo a fundamental change in character. George must value his own feelings, and those of others, much more than he does. Both Shakespeare and Naylor, then, shape their dramas to underscore the necessity of appreciating a wider range of experience, one that embraces the joy of life, but also the irrational and the terrible. In The Tempest, Prospero must undergo change to be whole--as must Miranda, Ferdinand, and Antonio. But Caliban refuses to acknowledge even rudimentary structures of rationality; in The Tempest, Caliban resists change and refuses to undergo transformation. He cannot accept a different interpretation of the world, one that acknowledges order, reason, and a cosmic structure that is (perhaps) identifiably European.

George is Naylor's revised Caliban, but George's condition is the inverse of Caliban's. While Caliban resists reason and a patriarchal order, George resists emotionality and Miranda's womanist vision of life. Caliban and George share several narratological features: Both lose their mothers; both are dispossessed because of their losses; both enjoy ardent sexual desire; both become drunk, then give their allegiance to false leaders (Caliban to Stephano and Trinculo, George to Dr. Buzzard). But their most significant similarity is that George, like Caliban, refuses the possibility of his transformation. Despite his past as an abandoned child, George has risen highly in the world, but at great cost. Clearly the highly competitive, egocentric, racist, and male-dominated world of Manhattan requires a certain ruthlessness and focused determination for an African American male to succeed. And George has become a wealthy entrepreneur. But his one-sided emphasis on achievement has gained him status and riches, yet led him away from wholeness of self, as his lack of empathy for and understanding of women demonstrates. In gaining the world, George has risked his soul.

What must George do to be saved? Naylor positions him in the narrative to undergo a test. Cocoa, the unwitting victim of Ruby's jealousy over Junior Lee, has been hexed with an herbal poison. In her illness, Cocoa must depend on George to save her, but because of a hurricane, George cannot bring her doctors and traditional medicine; instead, he is asked to save Cocoa Miranda's "way," but she gives him bizarre and inexplicable instructions. Like a lost child in a fairy tale, George must rely on an elderly woman whose advice seems to him irrational and irrelevant. But Miranda's words are patently symbolic and are essential for him to achieve his maturity.[6] At this point in the novel, Naylor abandons realist conventions and adopts a mythic or parabolic mode, similar to the nonrealistic style of _The Tempest_. It is a mistake to read this section of the novel--George's quest to the henhouse--literally. Naylor instead shifts the novel's diegesis to another level, moving from a provisional realism to a mythic plane--what is often described in contemporary criticism as "magic realism."

The reader must make a correspondent shift in interpretive strategies. Carl Jung's theories of archetypes provides one means of negotiating the tension between the mimetic and the mythic at this point in Naylor's narrative. Jung held that beyond the individual unconscious there exists a "collective unconscious," shared by all people, which is the repository of "archetypes." Archetypes are the inherited patterns of psychological experience--the basic images and shapes of myth and of culture as a whole. Seeing Miranda and George's relationship within a Jungian context clarifies the plot's mysterious resolution. George sets out on an archetypal quest to recover an aspect of his own psyche that he has disavowed and discounted throughout much of his life: Miranda symbolically challenges George to go to the henhouse to recover his complete Self.

Authentic selfhood in the novel depends upon a discovery of one of the most important Jungian archetypes, the anima/animus: the unconscious image representing the "contrasexual" side of the individual's psyche (Jung, "Aion" 147). Jung believed that human beings have within them the repressed features of the opposite sex, that the individual is necessarily a "contrasexual figure."[7] The male, though he may identify himself as "masculine" (according to the predominant social construction of masculinity), possesses also a "feminine" dimension in his psyche that he has been taught to deny in a patriarchal society through the socialization process. In this way he cuts off an essential aspect of his own humanity. Jungian theory must be seen within the context of Jung's own time: Men, Jung writes, have traditionally had much more opportunity than women to experience fields like "commerce, politics, technology, and science"

("Ego" 206). For Jung, the qualities that lead to success in these public fields--aggression, leadership, logic, rationality, forcefulness--are distinctively masculine, given a sexist coding, and are so identified by Western culture. The male's conscious self is thereby described as typically "masculine," as defined by cultural constructs of masculinity. As the male is socialized into a male-dominated culture, he is usually taught to accentuate those qualities his culture deems "masculine," and to disown and distance himself from those attributes his culture stipulates as "feminine."

Yet this distancing, Jung argues, leads to a psychic disharmony. In a man, the anima is the repressed "woman within," and embodies powerful traits culturally defined as 'feminine': intuition, sensitivity to nature and beauty, and emotionality. The anima personifies symbolically all that is expressed for a man's psyche as the "feminine" image: a nurturing, nature-connected, poetic earth goddess, linked to images of fertility, growth, and the powers of instinct and intuition. The anima, then, represents the archetype of what for a man is the "totally other," yet this construction is, ironically, the feminine principle within him. In order to become a whole person, for Jung, the man must acknowledge and accept his own anima, must celebrate the feminine within him. Not to do so, to repress that aspect of his self completely, results in an essential loss of identity, for it means a severance from a vital part of his unconscious.

In *Mama Day*, this psychological transaction is framed in symbolic terms. Miranda tells George to take her father's cane and Bascombe Wade's ledger, and to leave these items in the chicken coop. As in many fairy tales, Miranda's instructions entail sexual directives. The phallic cane and the ledgers (associated with the Bascombe business acumen) represent George's predilection to affirm his masculinity, not simply in action but in perspective; in leaving behind the symbolism of masculinity and corporate self-assertiveness, George would relinquish an insistence on a social construction of Self that denies him anima. Miranda thus asks him symbolically to set aside his own masculine will, which has guided his consciousness until this time, and choose another totem that expresses a different aspect of his repressed character. She asks him to "search good in the back of [the hen's] nest, and come straight back here with whatever you find" (295). Significantly, she does not explicitly tell him precisely *what* to retrieve from the chicken coop. George, however, finally refuses Miranda's way: He goes to the coop, fights the terrifying hen, discovers --he supposes--nothing in the nest, returns to Cocoa, and dies sacrificially at her side of a heart attack.

What George misses in the coop is central to the novel's archetypal meaning. Naylor tests the reader also: She never reveals what he was supposed to find. Miranda's "way," however, is consistent with her character. She has sent George to gather *eggs*, the text's dominant symbol of the anima. Throughout the novel, Miranda has identified herself with eggs, while George has rigorously avoided them. Since childhood he has been terrified of hens, which he perceives as preternaturally fierce,[8] and his special diet proscribes eggs to reduce cholesterol. In "Miranda's way," George is asked to acknowledge the symbolic potency of eggs, but given his own psychological development, he cannot: "I turned the whole nest over, *eggs bursting and splattering into the straw*" (300, emphasis mine). Not only does he smash the eggs, but he ruins the nests and kills the hens: "I went through that coop like a madman, slamming the cane into feathery bodies, wooden posts, straw nests--*it was all the same*" (301, emphasis mine). George cannot even perceive the eggs. In this test of selfhood, George fails because he lacks faith to "let Cocoa go" in favor of Miranda's wisdom, seeing his test only as "wasted effort" (301). His masculine will, essential to his survival as abandoned child and later as successful CEO, proves to be tragically inappropriate in the mysterious chicken coop. More was required of him--to gather the eggs, to trust Miranda, to celebrate his anima image.

The symbolic egg is, of course, a trope for Miranda's entire way of life. It implies her commitment to Willow Springs, her love of nature, and her work as midwife--helping women conceive. If contextualized within Jungian theoretics, the egg becomes even more significant as an objective representation of George's anima. Because of his childhood, George cannot honor a spirit beyond his own will: "When things were under control--and I lived my life so that was usually the case--there was no need to think about having to deal with some presence that might be governing what was beyond my own abilities" (231). By suppressing the "Eternal Feminine" within him (the intuitive, emotional, and imaginative dimension of his personality that continuously resurfaces in the novel despite his rationalizations and resistances), George fails to complete his quest and dies. To this extent, the novel becomes his tragedy.

Miranda's grief over George's death expresses the great Shakespearean theme of reconciliation that pervades *The Tempest*. For Shakespeare as for Naylor, tragic loss, inevitable for all human beings, is world-wrenching; it is never possible to restore that which is lost. But it is possible to reconcile oneself to the loss. Knowing intuitively that George must do "it his way," Miranda "goes inside the coop to look around at the bloody straw, the smashed eggs, and scattered bodies. Now, she has the time to cry" (302).

Miranda is prepared to accept loss because earlier she, too, has undergone a test of character and, like the happy child in fairy tales, survived and matured. Miranda's successful test represents the converse of George's failed one. For Jung, women too possess a psychic "masculine" dimension, an aggregate of qualities defined by a sexist culture as "masculine" but repressed in the socialization process of a patriarchal culture: "Just as the man is compensated by a feminine element, so woman is compensated by a masculine one" ("Aion" 151). In this sense, a woman's psyche, like a man's, is "contra-sexual." Yet in being pressured to distance herself from her animus by a sexist culture, the female may also undergo a division of selfhood--a splitting off from the rational or argumentative side of her being ("Ego" 206ff). As Jung writes, "In the same way that the anima gives relationship and relatedness to a man's consciousness, the animus gives to woman's consciousness a capacity for reflection, deliberation, and self-knowledge" ("Aion" 154). Miranda is set the test of affirming and celebrating her own animus image.

In a sense, Miranda's condition is a mirror image of George's. Her pain, like George's, may be discovered in her repressed childhood memories of pain and loss. Miranda also has shielded herself from her past; like George, her mother died when Miranda was a child, committing suicide by throwing herself into The Sound off Willow Springs when her youngest daughter Peace accidentally fell into a well and was killed. George's mother also drowned, apparently a suicide, in Long Island Sound. Thus, both Miranda and George understandably resist confronting their tortured childhoods. Throughout her life Miranda has evaded the symbolic truth of the well where Peace died, saying she "just ain't ready to face" the loss of her mother and baby sister (174). She fears the well at least partly because she fears becoming engulfed by the unbearable grief of her mother's pain over the death of Miranda's sister Peace. Miranda fears, in a phrase, her own self-destructive irrationality and emotionality, the legacy of her family's self-torture and excruciating loss.

But Miranda is eventually able to confront her loss, and in doing so she expiates her family's legacy. In a deeply moving scene, charged with psychological symbolism, Miranda uncovers the well and gazes into its terrible depths. Gathering her courage with her eyes closed, she finally looks into the pit and experiences the agony of her mother as she died. But she is rescued from her own possible suicide by another vision:

> . . . she opens her eyes on her own hands. Hands that look like John-Pauls's [her fathers]. . . . In all this time, she ain't never really thought about what it musta done to him. Or him either. . . . and looking past the losing was to feel for the man who built this house and the one who nailed this well shut. It was to feel the hope in them. . . .   (285)

At last, Miranda can "look past the losing," accepting her painful losses completely but with self-possession; she can, through an imaginative identification with her father, realize the full meaning of his words "just live on" (88). John-Paul counseled stoic resignation and acceptance of what cannot be changed, and this truth Miranda fully embraces. The operative symbol, her animus image, is the (re)visioned hands of her father. She is finally her *father's* daughter.[9]

Recognizing her father's "gifted hands" (89) as her own, Miranda undergoes a symbolic identification with her father. She does not resist or deny the masculine element within herself--in Jungian terminology, the animus-- symbolized by the affirmation of her father's hands as hers. Identification with the animus frees her to sympathize with her father, with all the other men in the Day family line--and with George, who she knows will repudiate "her way" of acceptance and self-affirmation. In accepting the animus--the psychic principle Jung associates with judgment, reason, and rational discernment--Miranda saves herself but not George, who must make his own separate psychic journey into the depths of the Self. But such journeys are never guaranteed, and unlike the fairy tale versions of life, where all characters return and live happily ever after, some choose death rather than face the full complexity of the Self.

Miranda does, however, save her niece Ophelia/Cocoa by reason, judgment, and emotional perspective. Ophelia, grieving over George's death, temporarily considers following the direction of her Shakespearean namesake (and of her grandmother) by committing suicide. But Miranda rebukes her severely ("I had never seen Mama Day so furious--never," Ophelia/Cocoa says [302]). Her suicide would be the height of irrationality and self-denial, of elevating momentary feeling and emotion over reflection, deliberation, and judgment--for Jung, a disastrous repression of the animus. So Cocoa too lives on and reconciles herself to her loss, which over time "becomes endurable" (308). Cocoa learns John-Paul's difficult but life-affirming lesson: "just live on."

Jung once wrote that the power of literature inheres in its sometimes unconscious expressions of primordial images of humanity. The study of literature has immense value because in the recognition of these images, these archetypes, human beings are brought together:

> The moment when this mythological situation reappears in always characterized by a peculiar emotional intensity; it is as though chords in us were struck that had never sounded before, or as though forces whose existence we never suspected were unloosed. . . . At such moments we are no longer individuals, but the race; the voice of all mankind resounds in us. ("Relation" 320)

This concern to find the imagery that sounds "the chords" animates the work of both Shakespeare and Naylor; for these two authors--different in race, gender, time, and space--the fundamental struggle of life is to connect with the mysterious voices within ourselves--voices too often muffled by the roar of social conventions, regionalism, racism, and sexism. Early in Miranda's life, she learns that ". . . *there is more to be known behind what the eyes can see*" (36). For Naylor, coming in touch with that unknown means relinquishing ourselves, that which we supposedly know for sure--the tangible and empirical divisions of race, gender, and regionality. By trusting our own voice and by telling our own story, which at its best incorporates and affirms the Other (especially the Other that is within us), we become truly ourselves.

Endnotes

[1] One especially beautiful example of Naylor's free indirect discourse is the following: "Miranda kinda blooms when the evening air hits her skin. She stands for a moment watching what the last of the sunlight does to the sky down by The Sound. . . . It seems like God reached way down into his box of paints, found the purest reds, the deepest purples, and a dab of midnight blue, then just kinda trailed His fingers along the curve of the horizon and let 'em all bleed down. And when them streaks of color hit the hush-a-by green of the marsh grass with the blue of The Sound behind 'em, you ain't never had to set foot in a church to know you looking at a living prayer" (78).

[2] An analysis that considers the great variety of African American precursorial models that Naylor signifies upon would be the subject for yet another paper. Perhaps only one example will suffice to demonstrate Naylor's revisionary powers: at *Mama Day*'s conclusion, Cocoa/Ophelia decides, at the behest of Miranda but also because of her own good sense, not to commit suicide over her husband George's death. I suggest that, at this point, Naylor is revising Zora Neale Hurston's *Their Eyes Were Watching God*. Both women suffer through a terrible, life-changing storm, and both lose their men, each dying in at least a partly self-sacrificial way. Janie's shooting Tea Cake is the inevitable consequence of her own vitality, her own profound commitment to life that must transcend her romantic love. Her endurance is in a sense a foregone conclusion. So, too, is Cocoa's grieving survival of George's death. As I attempt to demonstrate, however, Naylor is interested in the psychological basis of Cocoa's vitality and of her psychic wholeness at the novel's end.

[3] Barbara Christian has demonstrated that, in these two earlier novels, Naylor reveals the "effect of place on character"--and how economics and issues of class complicate a black woman's life choices--a point not made clear in Shakespeare's canonical texts.

[4] In her revision, Naylor develops themes similar to contemporary New Historicist readings of *The Tempest* (see, e.g., Brown, Greenblatt, and Leininger). Obviously, Caliban is a central figure in New Historicist analysis; for a thoughtful discussion of Caliban's legacy for African American studies, see Baker.

[5] George's character is the site of conflict in African American culture, perhaps going back to the debate between Booker T. Washington and W. E. B. Du Bois, between the "practical" benefits of technical training and the rewards of a humanistic liberal arts education

[6] For the classic discussion of psychological meanings expressed in fairy tales, see Bettelheim.

⁷ Jung's theory of the anima/animus has been modified by, among others, Dr. Jean Baker Miller (75-80). As Miller points out, "The notions of Jung and others deny the basic inequality and asymmetry that exists" (79). Thus, to understand the anima/animus as "a reflection of the whole dichotomization of the essentials of human experience" is necessarily fallacious--as both Cocoa and the reader discover in Naylor's narrative.

⁸ If seen within a Jungian context, the ferocious red hen is a negative, insidious, but unrecognized mother image, the introjected model that "helps the [son] betray life" (Jung, "Aion" 149). His mother's abandonment of him--understood only from George's perspective as a small child, and never entirely recuperated within a more realistic, adult context--casts him in the role of a person without worth. His entire career as a business magnate may thus be seen as a resistance to her "rejection" of him. Yet the ferocity of his ambition might be seen as a tacit admission that there may be some truth to his (wrongly) interpreted narrative of her tragic life.

⁹ *Mama Day* is also a revision of William Faulkner's *Go Down, Moses*. Miranda's reading the Bascombe ledgers recalls Ike McCaslin's discovering in the family's records the terrible truths of "the distaff" line of the family (see "The Bear"). However, Naylor revises Faulkner also, like discovering to his horror that his grandfather raped a black slave, and later the daughter born of this rape, decides his only course can be of a futile "relinquishment" of history, deciding to live in relative seclusion and denial. He therefore "relinquishes" the McCaslin patrimony. Miranda's response is much more positive: She *literally* rewrites history to emphasize acceptance, peace, and forgiveness: "It's all she can pick out until she gets to the bottom for the final words: *Conditions . . . tender. . . kind*" (280).

Works Cited

Awkward, Michael. *Inspiriting Influences: Tradition, Revision, and Afro-American Women's Novels*. New York: Columbia UP, 1989.

Baker, Houston A., Jr. "Caliban's Triple Play." *"Race," Writing, and Difference*. Ed. Henry Louis Gates, Jr. Chicago: U of Chicago P, 1986. 381-395.

Barthes, Roland. *Image Music Text*. Trans. Stephen Heath. New York: Hill, 1977.

Bettelheim, Bruno. *The Uses of Enchantment*. New York: Knopf, 1976.

Brown, Paul. "'This thing of darkness I acknowledge mine': *The Tempest* and the Discourse of Colonialism." *Political Shakespeare: New Essays in Cultural Materialism*. Ed. Jonathan Dollimore and Alan Sinfield. Ithaca: Cornell UP, 1985. 48-71.

Christian, Barbara. "Gloria Naylor's Geography: Community, Class, and Patriarchy in *The Women of Brewster Place* and *Linden Hills*." *Reading Black, Reading Feminist*. Ed. Henry Louis Gates, Jr. New York: Meridian, 1990. 348-373.

Gates, Henry Louis, Jr. *The Signifying Monkey: A Theory of African American Criticism*. New York: Oxford UP, 1988.

Greenblatt, Stephen. "Learning to Curse: Aspects of Linguistic Colonialism in the Sixteenth Century." *First Images of America: The Impact of the New World on the Old*. Ed. Fredi Chiappelli, et. al. Berkeley: U of California P, 1976. 2: 561-580.

Henderson, Joseph. "Ancient Myths and Modern Man." *Man and His Symbols*. Ed. C. G. Jung. New York: Doubleday, 1964. 104-158.

Jung, C. G. "Aion: Phenomenology of the Self." *Portable* 139-142.

_____. "On the Relation of Analytical Psychology to Poetry." *Portable* 301-323.

_____. *The Portable Jung*. Ed. Joseph Campbell. Trans. R. F. C. Hull. New York: Penguin, 1971.

_____. "The Relations Between the Ego and the Unconscious." *Portable* 70-139.

Knight, G. Wilson. *The Crown of Life*. New York: Barnes & Noble, 1966.

Leininger, Lorie. "Cracking the Code of *The Tempest*." *Bucknell Review* 25 (1980): 121-131.

Miller, Jean Baker, M. D. *Toward a New Psychology of Women*. 1976. Boston: Beacon, 1986.

Miller, J. Hillis. "The Limits of Pluralism III: The Critic as Host." *Critical Inquiry* 3.3 (1977): 128-142.

Naylor, Gloria. *Mama Day*. New York: Ticknor & Fields, 1988.

_____, and Toni Morrison. "A Conversation: Gloria Naylor and Toni Morrison." *Southern Review* 21.3 (1985): 567-593.

Stepto, Robert B. *From Behind the Veil: A Study of Afro-American Narrative*. Urbana: U of Illinois P, 1979.

Willis, Susan. *Specifying: Black Women Writing the American Experience*. Madison: U of Wisconsin P, 1987.

Hayes, Elizabeth T. "Gloria Naylor's *Mama Day* as Magic Realism." Published with permission of author.

Three days before the hurricane of the century has even been predicted by the National Weather Service, Miranda ("Mama") Day is in her kitchen peeling peaches for a pie when suddenly she "feels death all around her" (226). Looking out the back door of her trailer to find "wind steady from the southeast and not a cloud in the sky," she nevertheless unequivocally knows that not only will a hurricane hit Willow Springs, but it will "be a big, big storm," a hurricane "born in hell" (227), "an 18 & 23er" (228). No one in the world except Miranda knows that this hurricane is coming to devastate the southeastern United States, and only after she has intuited the future arrival and magnitude of the as-yet-unformed hurricane does she recall empirical evidence from nature that could support her intuition. Her foreknowledge is presented as magical--that is, rationally unexplainable according to the laws of nature as we know them--and at the same time absolutely real, as the hurricane later proves by arriving as she had predicted, with devastating force.

The magical is as quotidian in *Mama Day* as peach pie. This matter-of-fact juxtaposition of the supernatural with the everyday is the salient characteristic of the literary mode *magic realism*. As the oxymoron of the name aptly demonstrates, magic coexists with a seeming antithesis, realism. As the double-noun phrase "magic realism" further indicates, magic is not subordinate to realism but is an organic part of the whole, no more heavily or less heavily weighted than the real. (For this reason, I prefer the double-noun phrase to the more grammatically orthodox adjective-noun phrase "magical realism" now coming into use).

Wendy Faris's view of the magic in magic realism as "exist[ing] symbiotically in a foreign textual culture--a disturbing element, a grain of sand in the oyster of . . . realism" (168) calls attention to the underlying epistemological conflict inherent in the mode, for realism is grounded in rationalism/empiricism, while the supernatural is grounded in nonrationalism. The surface of the magic realist *text*, however, is not disturbed by the interpenetration of the magical and the realistic. Instead, *readers* are unsettled as they hesitate between contradictory interpretations of the antinomy the text presents, an antinomy that can best be resolved through a radical attenuation of the rationalist definition of the real to include magic. To insist upon a traditional rationalist definition of the real is to reject magic realism out of hand.

In the hands of Naylor and other African American writers, magic realism is postmodern subversiveness at its best. Explorations of the ontological, "the dominant of postmodernist fiction" (McHale 10), occupy a prominent place in African American magic realist texts, challenging the rationalist metanarrative of realism. When Brian McHale in *Postmodernist Fiction* singles out the following as typical postmodernist questions: "What happens when different kinds of world are placed in confrontation, or when boundaries between worlds are violated?" (10), he foregrounds questions quintessential to African American magic realism. The boundaries traditionally drawn in Cartesian epistemology between the rationally knowable world and the supernatural world are violated, blurred, or ignored so regularly in African American magic realist texts that both the boundaries and the rationalist ideology producing them are interrogated and subverted. Magic realism thus becomes a voice for long-marginalized nonrationalists, allowing them, in Theo D'haen's view, to become "subjects of their own story and not . . . objects of a . . . colonial [text]" (199). Further, the magic realist mode allows African American authors to write, to the greatest extent possible, from within the alternative nonrationalist paradigm they are presenting rather than from within the prevailing Cartesian paradigm they are decentering. Faris perceptively calls magic realism a "revitalizing force" for literature arising from "the 'peripheral' regions of Western culture" (165). Indeed, African American magic realism is at the cutting edge of postmodernist literature in North America.

Gloria Naylor's 1989 novel *Mama Day* is a striking illustration of African American magic realism. Although the opening paragraphs of the text recount the extraordinary magic of Sapphira Wade, archetypal mother of the African American island community of Willow Springs and conjure woman *par excellence*, Naylor intertwines the magical with the real primarily through her eponymous heroine, Miranda ("Mama") Day. The communal narrator, the collective voice of the community, presents Miranda as occupying the position of matriarch and leader of Willow Springs largely, although not exclusively, through her extraordinary intuitive connection to the supernatural. That Miranda is the community spokesperson is made clear in the prologue: greedy mainland real estate developers eager to buy waterfront property on Willow Springs are sent straight to Miranda for an answer, "'cause if Mama Day say no, everybody say no" (6). Miranda's word is law in Willow Springs because she is shrewd, sensible, devoted to and protective of the community--and a powerful conjure woman. A direct descendant of Sapphira Wade, as well as the firstborn of the seventh son of a seventh son, Mama Day's magical heritage is prestigious, but her actual conjuring achievements are what earn her the position of community leader. As the communal narrator says admiringly, "There's 18 & 23 [a combination of extraordinary magic and extraordinary chutzpah], and there's 18 & 23--and nobody was gonna trifle with Mama Day's, 'cause she knows how to use it" (6), on anyone who threatens the community, whether from within or without. For the citizens of Willow Springs, Mama Day's nonrational ability is a reality, presented as fact by the communal narrator in the prologue.

Magic realism, like other types of realism, must always have one foot in the world defined as "real" by rationalists, the world governed by natural law.

For *Mama Day* to function as magic realism, then, Miranda's magic must be shown through empirical verification to be "real" rather than imaginary or illusory. Miranda's first live appearance in the text does just this, fleshing out the interpenetration of the natural and the supernatural established in the prologue. Naylor's choice of limited omniscient narration in this scene (and in others centering on Miranda) is shrewd, for readers can share in the intimate workings of an extraordinary intuitive mind while still remaining situated outside that mind, in the "real world" of a third-person narrator.

When we first meet Miranda in person in the text, she is disarmingly unimposing, a small, toothless, arthritic octogenarian standing in the kitchen of her silver house trailer, removing an ancient tea kettle with no whistle from the stove burner. Suddenly she stops what she is doing, "concentrates awful hard" (34) on the column of steam coming from the kettle, and smiles. "My, what a pleasant surprise," she thinks, "Baby Girl [her great-niece Cocoa] is coming in today, a little earlier than expected--and on the airplane to boot" (34). There is no rational explanation for Miranda's knowledge. Cocoa has written that she will arrive the next day, by train, and she has asked to be met at the station; moreover, she has never before come home by plane. Yet when Miranda calls her sister Abigail, Cocoa's grandmother, she offers no explanation for her knowledge of Cocoa's change in plans, simply stating flatly, "Baby Girl is coming in today" (36). Nor does Abigail question Miranda's intuition. Instead, amusingly, she questions *Cocoa's* self-knowledge: "And she [Cocoa] thought she was catching the train up there [in New York] tomorrow night" (36). Accepting Miranda's foreknowledge as fact, Abigail immediately flies into action to prepare for Cocoa's unexpected early arrival.

Even when Cocoa is not in the cab of Dr. Buzzard's truck (Buzzard having been sent to the tiny nearby mainland airport to pick her up), the sisters still do not question the validity of Miranda's intuition; instead, they berate Dr. Buzzard for not waiting longer for Cocoa's plane. Only when Buzzard tells them that he watched Cocoa's plane land does Abigail for the first time question Miranda's foreknowledge: "Maybe, you were wrong--she wasn't on that plane" (47). "Yes, she was," Miranda snaps; she has no doubts whatsoever. And of course she is correct; Cocoa is hiding under a tarp in the back of the truck, determined to surprise her family "one way or the other" (47). The letter about the train arrival was part of Cocoa's plan to surprise her foster-mothers by arriving early, but as soon as Cocoa saw Buzzard's truck at the airport, she knew that Mama Day had somehow--as usual--intuited her plans. All three women, and Buzzard, too, accept unconditionally Miranda's supernormal abilities, which have been verified so often over the years that Miranda's magic has achieved the status of empirical fact. In this way, Naylor establishes a nonrationalist epistemology as completely valid--indeed, as normative--for Mama Day and those close to her.

The distinguishing characteristic of African American magic realism is the dominant presence of what Faris terms "ancient systems of belief and local lore" (182) and Toni Morrison terms "information discredited by the West" (388). Intuitive thinking, or "connected knowing," the ancient system of nonrationalist thought long denigrated by post-Enlightenment rationalists, is practiced with consummate skill by Miranda, as her foreknowledge of Cocoa's early arrival and of the approaching hurricane demonstrate. Other examples of Miranda's intuition occur throughout the text: she knows that "a cloud of dust and gravel" on the distant road is Ambush coming for help; that Bernice won't conceive a child for many months; that Cocoa won't marry for three years or more; that Little Caesar is dead and that Bernice is on her way to the other place with him; that lightning will strike the bridge; that George will die during his visit to Willow Springs, although she resolutely refuses to acknowledge this intuition for fear it will come true; that George has died, even though Miranda is at that very moment expecting his return to the other place.

These examples of foreknowledge, all verified in the text, are presented so matter-of-factly that they underscore the normalcy of Miranda's intuitive, supernatural knowledge of the future. (Indeed, Miranda comments on the *diminishment* of her intuitive powers; whereas once foreknowledge came to her continually and without effort, she must, as an octo- and nonagenarian, "really concentrate" [173] and wait longer before intuitive knowledge comes to her). On the textual level, Naylor is building Miranda's credibility so that, in the crucial ontological and epistemological battle between George and Miranda at the novel's climax, readers will believe that Miranda can indeed save both Cocoa and George through nontraditional means. On the subtextual level, Miranda's magical foreknowledge of the future valorizes intuitive "connected knowing" as a successful alternative to rational "separate knowing."

Animism, an ancient system of belief, everywhere informs *Mama Day*, as it does many African American magic realist texts. The Africans enslaved in America brought with them and disseminated their animistic beliefs, which, in isolated African American communities like Willow Springs, remained relatively pure for generations. Animists perceive a much more fluid boundary between the natural and the supernatural than do rationalists, a perception presupposing a close connection between the material world and the spirit world. Indeed, animists assume continuous interaction between worlds--between, for example, human beings and the spirits of natural forces, natural objects, or animals. In *Mama Day*, it is entirely appropriate that the people of Willow Springs, recognizing the child Miranda's extraordinary unity with nature in her ability to walk through the woods "without snapping a single twig" or to "disappear into the shadow of a summer cottonwood," begin to believe that she literally "became a spirit in the woods" (79). Continuous interaction is also assumed between the world of the living and the world of the dead. Animists believe that a person who dies does not cease to exist but merely "crosses over" to "the other side," the spirit world; he or she can cross back to "this side" or communicate with the living from the other side. In particular, dead ancestors and family members are thought to hover nearby for a long time before crossing over, ready to offer warnings or helpful advice. For animists, as Lawrence Levine notes in *Black Culture and Black Consciousness*, "the universe was not silent; it spoke to those who knew how to listen" (66).

For African American magic realist writers, the interface between the world of the living and the world of the dead is a site of particular interest. In *Mama Day*, Naylor does some self-reflexive, postmodernist playing with this interface in her choice of narrators. The two first-person-singular narrators, George and Cocoa, speak to each other directly and with great immediacy throughout the text, yet at the end of the novel, we discover that George has been dead for fourteen years before their dialogue even begins. Despite foreshadowing throughout the text, George's death nevertheless surprises chiefly because his narrative voice is so compellingly alive. Though already dead and speaking in the past tense (as does Cocoa in her narrative sections),

George never indicates in any way during his narration that he is dead. Moreover, George's narration ceases after he recounts his actions and feelings just before the moment of his death in the text; although there are fourteen more years of the story to cover, George "dies" as a narrator at the point in the text where he dies as a character. The dead George's liveliness as a narrator effectively erases the line of demarcation between "this side," the locus of Cocoa's narration, and "the other side," the locus of George's.

Although *Mama Day*, unlike other African American magic realist texts, is singularly lacking in tangible, corporeal ghosts, the dead are nevertheless living presences in the novel. For example, at the "standing forth," the funeral service for Little Caesar, the people who speak address the dead child directly, as if he were present, and all conclude with, "When I see you again, you'll be . . . " (268). Bernice clearly expresses the community's belief in the interpenetration of the natural world and the spirit world when she apologizes to her dead child during the standing forth because she "didn't remember for a moment that you were still here" (269). Miranda demonstrates the same belief when, after Abigail's death, she gives her traditional "You there, Sister?" greeting to "the warm air" and listens for Abigail's reply in "the rustling of the trees" (312). Miranda also speaks to George shortly after his death, asking him to help Cocoa find the answers she will be seeking. "One day she'll hear you, like you're hearing me" (308), Miranda tells George--and she is right. Cocoa communicates at length with the dead George in later years whenever she visits Willow Springs; in fact, one such "conversation" between Cocoa and George comprises at least half of the narrative text of the novel.

Cocoa and Miranda are the only two characters in *Mama Day* who hear the dead, but others could, the text implies, if they learned to listen. What the two women hear as they weed the family graveyard is dead Day ancestors recounting their own personal histories. Similarly, as Cocoa and George walk through the graveyard and sit on the porch at the "other place," Cocoa hears "silent whispers" (223) and "voices" (224) repeating over and over, *"you'll break his heart"* (224). She is upset by the words and by their increasing volume, but George hears nothing. Interestingly, George does apparently hear the words "*Waste. Waste*" (248) as he looks at Bascombe Wade's tombstone after his fight with Cocoa, but he quickly frames the experience as metaphor: "*Waste. Waste* . . . . Yes, those leaves could easily be crying that" (248). Rationalist George is not willing to entertain even the possibility that he is hearing voices from "the other side."

For Miranda, the boundary between the worlds of the living and the dead is a permeable membrane, so attuned is she to the nonrational. She hears the "sound of [Sapphira's] long wool skirt passing," the "tread of [Bascombe Wade's] heavy leather boots," and the first-generation Willow Springsians "humming . . . some lost and ancient song" (118). She speaks to George and to Abigail after their deaths, as mentioned above. When Miranda is searching for a way to break Ruby's deadly fix on Cocoa, it is to the dead she turns for help. She goes to the other place to seek out Sapphira, her great-grandmother, "the great, grand Mother" (48) of Willow Springs, searching deep in her unconscious and finally meeting Sapphira in a dream in which Miranda is an infant nursing at the Mother's breast and sleeping in the Mother's arms. When Miranda awakens, she knows that she must "look past the pain" (283) in the boarded-up well in the garden of the other place for the answer she seeks.

It is important that the scene at the well be grounded in the narrative conventions of realism, for the magic that occurs functions effectively as magic realism only if it is anchored in conventional empirical reality. Naylor relies on mimetic scene representation with particular attention to sensory detail: "A few scattered runners of wild ginger done taken root among the holly, them double pairs of heart-shaped leaves twining themselves up along the hewn stones toward the mouth of the well. . . . A tearing, scraping sound as the metal threads [of the spikes] give way, splintering the wood and dusting her arms with dry flecks of cement" (284).

When the well is uncovered at last, Miranda looks in for a long time but sees nothing. Finally, she closes her eyes and listens. Suddenly, "circles and circles of screaming . . . piercing her ears" come "with a force that almost knocks her on her knees" (284). These are the screams of her dead great grandmother, mother, and baby sister, and in looking past their pain and the pain of the men who loved them, she intuits a way to save Cocoa. No rational explanation of the screams is possible; none is required, and none is given. The screams of the long dead women are every bit as real as the wild ginger leaves, crumbling mortar, and rusted spikes at the old well. The supernatural is presented as an organic part of the phenomenal world and is described using the same realistic narrative conventions, effectively erasing the boundaries between the two worlds.

Lore, as Morrison notes, is among the "information" typically discredited by the West. In the finest tradition of magic realism, Naylor erases the discreditation by pointedly valorizing African American lore in *Mama Day*. Such valorization occurs throughout the text as we watch Miranda, an exceptionally capable root doctor, healer, and midwife, practice medicine. Though she has augmented her expertise during years of healing the sick and delivering babies, the source of her extensive knowledge of medicine, particularly natural pharmacology, is African and African American lore passed down to her. Her encyclopedic lore-based knowledge of the medicinal properties of plants rivals if not surpasses Dr. Smithfield's medical-school knowledge of synthetic pharmacology, and she is by all measure just as competent an obstetrician, gynecologist, and general practitioner as he.

Indeed, it is Dr. Smithfield who verifies Miranda's ability as a physician, thus validating the lore that serves as her medical textbook and the connected knowing that guides her. His respect may be a bit grudging--she is, after all, his rival, an "untrained" (according to AMA standards), unlicensed root doctor--but it is genuine. Dr. Smithfield's appreciation of Miranda's ability dates from a successful Caesarean section that she performed shortly after he began practicing medicine. With no operating room, no surgical tools, and no surgical training, Miranda performed the C-section guided solely by her general, lore-based medical knowledge and her intuition, saving both mother and child--and the mother never even ran a fever afterwards, as Dr. Smithfield admiringly recounts.

When Smithfield and Miranda consult about Bernice's illness, theirs is a professional discussion between equals as they exchange pharmacological knowledge and review the data Miranda has gathered through the physical exam she has given Bernice. The limited omniscient narrator tells us directly that Smithfield is a good doctor, implying that we should trust his medical judgment of Mama Day as "another good doctor" (84). Because Smithfield is both an outsider to Willow Springs and an "expert in the field" who has been reluctantly won over by Miranda's skill, his validation of Miranda's lore-based training and intuitive approach to medical practice holds great weight. Providing rationalist validation for Miranda's medical "magic" is Dr. Smithfield's function in the novel --an important function in this magic realist text.

Other lore is validated by events in the text. The yellow powder Miranda slips into the note Cocoa sends to George after her job interview inspires George--as intended--to pursue a romantic relationship with Cocoa, whom he says he had succeeded in forgetting and wanted to forget. Even more magical is the silvery powder that Miranda sprinkles around Ruby's house, making lightning strike Ruby's house not once but twice. Miranda no doubt learned about these powders through lore. As partial confirmation, there is no evidence in the text that Miranda has herself discovered and perfected the science of causing lightning to strike, but there *is* evidence, through legend, that Sapphira knew a thing or two about lightning ("She could walk through a lightning storm without being touched; grab a bolt of lightning in the palm of her hand; use the heat of lightning to start the kindling going under her medicine pot" [3]). Because most of Miranda's medical and pharmacological lore has been passed down to her from or through Sapphira, Miranda's knowledge of aphrodisiac and lightning-attracting powders most likely has come from the same source, though the skill with which she puts this knowledge to use is her own.

Just as Dr. Smithfield validates Miranda's medical lore, George validates her "magic powder" lore, but quite unintentionally. It is George who reports the surprising, memory-jogging effect of the yellow powder that sticks to his hands when he reads Cocoa's letter, yet he does not recognize the yellow powder as "magical" in any way or as having any but the most coincidental influence on his behavior. It is also George who explains the scientific validity of Miranda's silver "lightning" powder: if "someone purposely electrifies the ground with materials that hold both negative and positive charges," George states, then he or she will "increase the potential of having a target hit" by lightning "twice in exactly the same place" (274). His categorical conclusion that "no one was running around Willow Springs with that kind of knowledge" (274) ironically validates Miranda's lore, for someone clearly *is* running around Willow Springs with that kind of knowledge. George, of course, has no idea that Miranda has waited until the proper kind of storm cloud is on the horizon before scaring Ruby into her house and sprinkling silver powder all around the building. (After encircling Ruby's house with powder, Miranda walks all the way to the bridge to warn the repair crew that lightning is likely to hit there. Does she sprinkle powder on the bridge? We are not told so, but lightning does indeed destroy the newly-repaired section of the bridge, thus keeping George and Cocoa on the island so that Miranda has a chance to save Cocoa).

From lore to foreknowledge to communication with the dead to supernatural connected knowing and intuitive thinking, the nonrational is consistently valorized in *Mama Day*. To validate the nonrational, however, is to undermine the hegemony of rationalist epistemology. An African American magic realist text can be viewed as a "cognitive map that discloses the antagonism between two views of culture, two views of history, . . . two ideologies" (Wilson 222-223)--and two epistemologies. The epistemological antimony between rationalism and nonrationalism evidences itself in *Mama Day* as an ontological battle between Miranda and George over finding a cure for

Cocoa's grave illness. The question of what is "real" becomes not merely a semantic or philosophical debate but a life-and-death issue for the characters. George is convinced that only "real" medicine--hospitals, specialists, FDA-approved medications, tests using the latest technological tools--can diagnose, treat, and save Cocoa, while Mama Day is equally convinced that only a nonrational, "connected knowing" approach to Cocoa's illness will result in a cure, as the cause of the illness is the very "real" fix Ruby has put on Cocoa. The ontological, the exploration of reality and being, is crucial to all magic realist texts--indeed, to all postmodernist texts--but nowhere is it more important than in *Mama Day*, whose action is subtly but unmistakably structured to explore ontological questions.

When Cocoa becomes deathly ill, George is frantic to get her to a hospital on the mainland as quickly as possible, but the hurricane has blown down the bridge and damaged all the boats. Though George knows why everyone in Willow Springs wants him to work *with* Mama Day, under her guidance and using her methods, in saving Cocoa--Dr. Buzzard has explained to him both Ruby's fix on Cocoa and Ruby's power--he rejects out of hand the native lore and ancient beliefs implicit in such a view of Cocoa's illness. He considers belief in hoodoo, magic, the supernatural, or any manifestation of the nonrational to be not simply misguided but "pathetic" (286), not merely silly but "beyond ridiculous" (227). After hearing Buzzard's explanation of Cocoa's illness, the frustrated George concludes angrily, "Snakeroot. Powdered ashes. Loose hair. Chicken blood. I would work [rebuilding the bridge] till I dropped to get you [Cocoa] out of there" (287). He "just cannot believe" (286) in the nonrational, though clearly he is the only one on the island who does not, and the only one who believes that Mama Day is a "crazy old woman" (296) rather than an extraordinarily powerful intuitive thinker able to perform miracles through connected knowing.   In George Andrews, Naylor has created the quintessential rationalist.

Nurture rather than nature has made George a rationalist. In the Wallace P. Andrews Shelter for Boys where the orphaned George was raised, pragmatic rationalism reigned.   Mrs. Jackson, director of the shelter, dealt strictly with "facts," never with emotions, intuitions, or imagination. "Our rage didn't matter to her, our hurts or disappointments," George recalls, ". . . only rules and facts" (24). When a boy broke a rule, Mrs. Jackson would "list . . . simple facts . . . without emotion" (24) before meting out a harsh but standard punishment. "Only the present has potential, *sir*" (23) was the lesson she inculcated, by the strap, if necessary--no big dreams, no wishful thinking, no uncontrolled emotions, no bewailing one's fate. George's heart murmur is treated as a fact--nothing more, nothing less. He takes his heart medicine, manages the high school football team rather than playing on it, and learns to lead a controlled life--as does every boy at Wallace P. Andrews Shelter, which, as George observes without irony, "was not the kind of place that turned out many poets or artists" (26). When George left the shelter at eighteen, he recognized himself as having only "what I could see: my head and my two hands, and I had each day to do something with them" (27).

George, like the other confirmed rationalists, sticks to what he considers --*knows*--to be "the facts," a word that he uses repeatedly: "the *fact* of seeing you [Cocoa] the second time that day" (27); "a *fact* that there was no way I was going to give you that job" (33); "a *fact* that when you said my name, you become yourself." (33); (this he says about a woman he has never met before). George's experiences in life until the day he meets Cocoa have, in his words, "proved beyond a shadow of a doubt that you got nothing from believing in crossed fingers, broken mirrors, spilled salt--[or] a twist in your gut in the middle of a Third Avenue coffee shop" (33). His intuitive foreknowledge when he first sees Cocoa that he will see her again, an intuition "so strong, it almost physically stops [him]" (27), is a unique experience for George. When Cocoa appears in his office later that day for a job interview, George is completely unnerved; he feels "as if someone had stuck a knife into my gut" (28). Throughout the interview he keeps "searching for some . . . *rational* explanation" (31, emphasis added) for his nonrational intuition in an effort to couch it in familiar, non-threatening terms. Cocoa notices that George "seemed downright scared of me and anxious to get me out of that office" (29), and she is correct. Though he consciously belittles "superstition," as he dismissively labels all forms of the nonrational, he finds it "terrifying" (28). He warns himself, "Don't get near a woman who has the power to turn your existence upside-down by simply running a hand up the back of her neck" (33). The nonrational frightens him by upsetting his knowable, controlled, rational world.

In Willow Springs, faced with the crisis of Cocoa's imminent death, balked in every rational attempt to get his wife to a hospital, George desperately tries to "hold on to what was real . . . [:] ten more feet added on to the bridge--that was real. And the sun coming up to bring in the outlines of the other shore--that was also real" (291). If anything other than empirically observable, quantifiable data is considered "real," if the rationalist order is upset, changed, or replaced by a nonrationalist order, then the foundations of George's world collapse and he is adrift in a world over which he has no control. Nonrationalism is equivalent to insanity for George, who hopes "for deliverance from the acute madness of [Willow Springs]" (286), exemplified by the matriarch he accuses of being a "crazy old woman." He concludes that "if this [the nonrational] was reality, it meant I was insane" (258).

As a rationalist, George is a "separate knower" using a binary epistemological system. Hierarchical, either/or thinking characterizes this system, which lends itself to imperialist notions of the ignorant, childlike native and the enlightened, superior colonial power. When George is in Willow Springs, literally the only person there who does not accept the ontological validity of the nonrational, he demonstrates the imperialist patriarchalism of the rationalist by persistently perceiving his own views as central and those of the Willow Springs community as "other," misguided, and inferior.

In contrast, Miranda, a true postmodernist, sees nonhierarchical multiplicity rather than hierarchical certitude in the world around her. As she explains to George, "There are two ways anybody can go when they come to certain roads in life--ain't about a right way or a wrong way--just two ways" (295). Miranda's is the "connected knowing" nonrationalist way. She needs only George's "hand in hers--his very hand--so she can connect it up with all the believing [by Day men] that had gone before. . . . So together [she and George] could be the bridge for [Cocoa] to walk over" (285). Miranda's amazing nonrational abilities have been verified so consistently in the text that the reader has faith that she can pull off another miracle here, if only George will trust her.

But George is suspicious of anything that smacks of magic. He is outraged and scornful when Miranda tells him to search the henhouse and bring her back whatever he finds. He thinks that her way of saving Cocoa is completely invalid and therefore is the "wrong" way, and he is so angry at "this mumbo jumbo" (295) of Miranda's that he almost strikes her. Although in desperation he later follows Miranda's instructions to search the henhouse, and though he even realizes that all she wants is his willing cooperation, he does not, cannot, will not believe in the validity of the nonrational or participate in any kind of connected knowing. Losing control, he rampages through the henhouse "like a madman" (301), killing hens and destroying the coop with Miranda's cane until he suffers a fatal heart attack. That George's violent rejection of nonrationalism results in his death points up the dangerous limitations inherent in an exclusionary, hierarchical epistemology like rationalism. Ironically, George dies to maintain rationalist boundaries between worlds, while Cocoa lives because Mama Day erases those boundaries.

Like other African American magic realist texts, *Mama Day* foregrounds the ontological, expanding the boundaries of the real by inscribing supernormal events as empirical fact. Concomitantly, *Mama Day* interrogates rationalist ideology by dramatically illustrating its limitation through George's needless death. For George, the term "magic realism" could never be other than an unresolvable paradox, an oxymoronic phrase with emphasis on "moronic." For Miranda, Cocoa, and the people of Willow Springs, on the other hand, the magical is the real. Though George persists in discrediting the nonrational (and the feminine with which he clearly but unconsciously associates it) by labeling it "other," ridiculous, even insane, the ending of the novel subverts this rationalist view and valorizes Miranda's nonrationalist ideology. There is no question that Mama Day, though female, old, African American, and a nonrationalist--and likely to be discredited for any or all of these qualities--becomes, through this magic realist text, the subject of her own story and not the object of George's or anyone else's colonial text.

Through the conflict between George and Miranda, *Mama Day* brilliantly contests "the comforting security--ethical, ontological, epistemological--that 'reason' offer[s]" (Natoli and Hutcheon ix). Naylor responds to McHale's postmodernist question, "What happens when different kinds of world are placed in confrontation?" by animating just such a confrontation, one that ultimately affirms the validity and power of the nonrational. Isabel Allende might have been speaking of *Mama Day* when she defined magic realism as "a way of seeing in which there is space for the invisible forces that move the world . . . . [Magic realism] is the capacity to see . . . all the dimensions of reality" (187-188), even those--especially those--unrecognized or discredited by the West.

Works Cited

D'haen, Theo L. "Magic Realism and Postmodernism: Decentering Privileged Centers." In Faris, Wendy B. and Lois Zamora, *Magical Realism: Theory, History, Community.* Durham: Duke UP, 1995. 191-208.

Faris, Wendy B. and Lois Parkinson Zamora, eds. *Magical Realism: Theory, History, Community.* Durham: Duke UP, 1995.

McHale, Brian. *Postmodern Fiction.* New York: Methuen, 1987.

Morrison, Toni. "Memory, Creation, and Writing." *Thought* 59 (1984): 385-390.

Natoli, Joseph and Linda Hutcheon, eds. "Introduction." *A Postmodern Reader.* Albany: State U of New York P, 1993.

Naylor, Gloria. *Mama Day.* New York: Vintage, 1989.

Bailey's Cafe

Montgomery, Maxine Lavon. "Authority, Multivocality, and the New World Order in Gloria Naylor's *Bailey's Cafe*." *African American Review* 29.1 (1995): 27-33.

Bailey's Cafe, Gloria Naylor's latest and most ambitious novel to date, is a hauntingly lyrical text steeped in biblical allusion. With this fourth novel, which completes a series including *The Women of Brewster Place*, *Linden Hills*, and *Mama Day*, Naylor acquired the self-confidence necessary to define herself as a writer. *Bailey's Cafe* "took me through the final step," Naylor remarked during a recent book tour stop. "I had envisioned four novels that would lay the foundation for a career. This one finished that up" (qtd. in Due F2).

In what is part of her ongoing search for an authorial voice with which to tell--or, rather, retell--the experiences of women of color, Naylor chooses to locate her fourth novel within a specifically cultured and gendered context where voice and all of its associations are directed toward subverting the myriad forms of authority patriarchy legitimizes and constructing a new world order among partially dispossessed women world-wide. The novel itself is comprised of a series of loosely connected stories--each one from a different woman's point of view--and it culminates with a magically real, communal celebration of the birth of Mariam's son George during the Christmas season. For the first time not only is there oneness among a culturally diverse group whose traditions and customs span the globe, but the voices of women also unify in the ritualization of George's arrival. George's long-awaited birth, like that of the Messiah, could signal either an end or, hopefully, new beginnings for the pluralistic group present. But in this climactic scene, after conjuring an image of global harmony, Naylor denies the reader/audience the privilege of knowing the fate of the young mother and son: Does Mariam find acceptance among an American Jewish community? What is to become of George, now en route to Wallace P. Andrews Boys' Home?

The novel's unresolved closure serves to encourage a participatory involvement from the reader/audience and is a strategy present in much of African American writing.[1] Bailey, the fatherly World War II veteran and proprietor of the cafe, is unable to offer a satisfactory ending to the moving stories that unfold. Instead, he merely invites the reader/audience to empathize with the women whose tragic tales comprise the written text: "If this was like that sappy violin music on Make-Believe Ballroom, we could wrap it all up with a lot of happy endings to leave you feeling real good that you took the time to listen," Bailey informs us in "The Wrap." "But I don't believe that life is supposed to make you feel good, or to make you feel miserable either. Life is just supposed to make you feel" (219).

Naylor uses Bailey's voice in establishing the time, place, mood, and character for each woman's story, except that of Mariam, a curiously virginal unwed mother whose touching account of anti-Semitism and sexism recreates a vital sisterhood among women of color across the Diaspora who often find themselves at odds with notions of female sexuality prescribed by patriarchy. Ultimately, Naylor's goal as creator and sovereign of the decidedly new fictive cosmology which emerges in the novel's ambiguous climactic scene is to effect some sort of unity among the widely disparate voices of women, not just within but outside the text. Karla Holloway, in her discussion of the responsive strategy of black women's narratives, refers to the technique as "a collective 'speaking out' by all the voices gathered within the text, authorial, narrative, and even the implicated reader" (11). Thus, in retelling Mariam's tale, Eve and Bailey's otherwise reticent helpmeet Nadine forms a duet, for the male voice is severely limited in its ability to decode the very private experiences the women relate. Bailey can offer empathy but not immediacy between Mariam, the speaking subject, and the reader/audience.

Naylor's particular triumph as a contemporary African American women writer has much to do with her success at moving beyond the one-dimensional portraits of male figures that brought her criticism with the publication of *The Women of Brewster Place*. Bailey, unlike his fictional predecessors residing at the decaying Brewster, is no mere shadow of a man. He is endowed with a certain psychological depth and complexity of character, despite the ambiguities associated with his assumed name. It is Bailey whose veiled comments offer insight into the close relationship between the written text and the distinctly black oral forms of expression from which it evolves. "Anything really worth hearing in this greasy spoon happens under the surface. You need to know that if you plan to stick around here and listen while we play it all out" (35).

Unfortunately, the other men who people the novel's fictional landscape do not fare as well as Bailey does. They are largely responsible for perpetuating the oppression that the women face. Nowhere is this more evident than in Eve's song. One in a long line of larger-than-life central mother figures in Naylor's canon, Eve is the first customer to arrive at Bailey's. Sexual escapades with Godfather, the stern, dictatorial preacher who rears her, and with the childish prankster Billy Boy, result in her ostracism from her small Louisiana delta home. But it is in her highly symbolic trek from Pilottown to Arabi to Bailey's Cafe that Eve, who emerges as a strong yet sensitive woman with an acute business sense and a love for well-kept gardens, manages somehow to escape the tragic fate toward which she seems destined.

Godfather, a figure for male authority, is ubiquitous in his influence within the delta community. Perhaps the most definitive change in Eve's evolving consciousness occurs when she comes to recognize his church as a social construct reflecting the hierarchies of a society which relegates women to the undesirable position of subservient "other": "To be thrown out his church was to be thrown out of the world" (85). Eve's leave-taking occurs as Godfather strips her of the clothes and purges her of the food he has provided. Naked and hungry, she is forced to provide for herself amidst dire economic circumstances. Eve successfully recreates herself, however, in preparation for her role among a community of outcast women. That she has no clear-cut parental ties suggests that she is at once natural and supernatural--more than a mere woman--and her song is replete with references to organic matter, especially the rich delta soil. Godfather claims to have found her "in a patch of ragweed, so new I was still tied to the birth sac" (83). As she grows into womanhood, her burgeoning sexuality, given fullest expression during her earth-stomping with Billy Boy, rekindles her awareness of a vital oneness with the rich earth. One of her many rendezvous with Billy Boy takes place under a juniper bush while Eve is "low to the ground, trying to blend in, with my brown hair, brown skin, and brown sack dress" (86). At one point, Eve recalls the essence of the Louisiana delta:

> The delta dust exists to be wet. And the delta dust exists to grow things, anything, in soil so fertile its tomatoes, beans, and cotton are obscene in their richness. And since that was one of the driest winters in living memory, the dust sought out what wetness it could and clung to the tiny drops of perspiration in my pores. It used that thin film of moisture to creep its way up toward the saliva in my mouth, the mucus in my nose. Mud forming and caking around the tear ducts in my eyes, gluing my lashes together. There was even enough moisture deep within my earwax to draw it; my head becoming stuffed up and all sounds a deep hum. It found the hidden dampness under my fingernails, between my toes. The moist space between my hips was easy, but then even into the crevices around the anus, drawing itself up into the slick walls of my intestines. Up my thighs and deep into my vagina, so much mud that it finally stilled my menstrual blood. Layers and layers of it were forming, forming, doing what it existed to do, growing the only thing it could find in one of the driest winters in living memory. Godfather always said that he made me, but I was born of the delta. (90)

Eve, whose name means 'mother of all living,' is essentially self-generated. She is what Karla Holloway describes as the ancestor, and it is her narrative in particular whose discrete patterns signal the recursive structure present in black women's writing--a structure repeated in the other narratives which comprise the text.[2] Not only does Eve's song, with its references to the Louisiana delta soil, suggest a dissolving of traditional historiography, it reveals a freedom from imposed gender-specific labels. "I had no choice but to walk into New Orleans neither male nor female--mud," she informs the reader/audience. "But I could right then and there choose what I was going to be when I walked back out" (91).

One cannot help but to associate Naylor's fictionalized Eve with her biblical predecessor, who uses her feminine charms to entice a gullible Adam to eat of the forbidden fruit and thus defy divine law. In a similar sense, Naylor's Eve encourages a creative revisioning of the spaces that traditionally have defined women's lives. That Eve walks, she tells us, a thousand years before reaching Bailey's, is an important allusion linking her role among a community of women to the millennial reign of Christ. On one level, she is a redemptive figure for women such as the feisty Jesse Bell, who turns to heroin and female lovers when her marriage into the wealthy Sugar Hill King Family ends in a bitter divorce. The newspaper misrepresents Jesse in its sensationalized account of her divorce. Her lament that she "didn't have no friends putting out the *Herald Tribune*" suggests the exclusion of the experiences of women of color from the written word and the printed text (118). Yet in the retelling of her story Jesse "reads" her own life-story in such a manner as to subvert the voice of Bailey, who sets up her narrative. According to Jesse, Eve's role in Jesse's recovery is questionable at best. Eve relies upon magic or the power of conjure in curing Jesse's addiction to heroin by engineering a series of well-crafted illusions which allow Jesse to have unlimited access to the enslaving drug. During Eve's unconventional treatment of Jesse, in a moment of exasperation, Jesse tells Eve to go to hell. Eve's rather pointed response directs attention to the ambivalent fictional world that informs the novel: "I think you've forgotten that's where we are" (141).

Naylor's Eve is thus a character that can be placed within the antithetic poles Daryl Dance uses to define the mother-figure in African American writing (123). Neither an Eve, in the biblical sense, nor strictly a Madonna, she resides somewhere between two extremes. Her ability to manipulate reality and her close affinity with the supernatural are qualities that invite a comparison with folk figures such as the shape-shifting trickster or the revered conjure woman. Despite the many ambiguities surrounding Eve's character, her role in the narrative action is to be considered in terms of her effect on her female wards. Jesse, the omniscient narrator points out, is cured in less than a month.

Naylor sets out to reclaim the stories of women by giving voice to those individuals whose experiences are often excluded from written history. By dedicating her novel to "the two Luecelias: *1898-1977, 1951-1987*," for instance, she reveals the novel's blurring of traditional conceptions of time, space, and identity. Her heavy reliance upon Scripture, particularly that from the Old Testament canon relevant to female sexuality, as an intertext sheds light on her attempts to redeem her female characters from the places assigned to them by a male-authored text and to restore their status and dignity.[3] Notions of morality which the Bible sanctions are held up for scrutiny. When Sister Carrie of the Temple of Perpetual Redemption quotes the Bible in condemning Jesse Bell because of her succession of female lovers, Eve, who was reared by a preacher, quotes the book as well: "Thou also, which hast judged thy sisters, bear thine own shame for thy sins that thou hast committed more abominable than they: they are more righteous than thou: yea, be thou confounded also and bear thy shame, in that thou hast justified thy sisters" (135). In her citation of this Old Testament passage from Ezekiel, Naylor thematizes the importance of global harmony among al women regardless of race, religion, ethnicity, or even sexual preference. Eve turns Sister Carrie's narrow, legalistic, and homophobic perspective on its ear by stressing the essential oneness between Jews and Gentiles and encouraging a non-judgmental stance toward issues of morality set forth in divine law. In her revisionist use of Scripture, Naylor thus ushers in a new era for women whose lives were once circumscribed by a discourse that is male-authored, and therefore paves the way for a more sensitive reading of the texts of African American women.

A creative juxtaposition of chapter titles drawn from the realms of music and drama with individual narratives reminds the reader/audience of the close relationship between the written text and the performance mode likely serving as inspiration for the novel. The title of Sadie's touching narrative, "Mood: Indigo," for instance, is taken from Duke Ellington's popular 1931 jazz composition, and Naylor admits that Sadie and suitor Iceman Jones floated into her consciousness on the strains of that tune (Due F2). More than any other musical form, it is the blues, with its characteristic repeti-tion-with-a-varia-tion scheme, that anticipates the discrete linguistic patterns of the text. An enigmatic epigraph serves to introduce the novel:

> hush now can you hear it can't be far away.
> needing the blues to get there
> look and you can hear it
> look and you can hear
> the blues open
> a place never
> closing:
> Bailey's
> Cafe

The stories which comprise the novel echo and reecho each other, but resist closure. In an interview with Toni Morrison, Naylor mentions that she feared the sense of finality suggested by her first novel, *The Women of Brewster Place* (582). Already she had begun the emotional trek to Linden Hills, whose environs are visible from Brewster. Within the tradition of African American women's fiction, Naylor's texts are unique in that they are symbiotically related: Brewster's community activist Kiswana Browne is from the middle-class Linden Hills; Cocoa, in *Mama Day*, is a cousin to Willa Prescott Nedeed, who perishes along with her husband and son in the apocalyptic flames which destroy the Nedeed home in *Linden Hills*; Cocoa's husband George sees Bailey's Cafe from Harlem. That Mariam's son, also named George, is to attend Wallace P. Andrews Boys' Home echoes the storyline in *Mama Day*, for Cocoa's husband is a product of that academy.

What the narrative moves toward is the creation of a reality deeply rooted in the black vernacular that more closely reflects the particular experiences of marginalized women across the globe. The unusual location of Bailey's Cafe, which exists everywhere and nowhere, points to its symbolic significance. The cafe is situated "between the edge of the world and infinite possibility" and represents the unexplored boundaries of a creative consciousness that is at once both black and female (76). Echoed throughout the stories the women relate is female subjectivity to male desire. Such is the case with Sweet Esther, whose pervasive hatred for men stems from the commodification of black women within the context of a rural economic system. Esther suffers exploitation as her elder brother barters her to an older, propertied farmer in exchange for higher sharecropping wages. Passively, Esther surrenders to the farmer's whims while he chooses to be intimate with her only in the cellar of his home. The pink and lace-trimmed bed where she must sleep alone reveals her confinement to a socially prescribed gender role. Her monologues point to a profound self-hatred in a world that evolves no terms for her existence:

> I like the white roses because they show up in the dark.

I don't.
The black gal.   Monkey face.   Tar.   Coal.   Ugly.   Soot.
Unspeakable. Pitch. Coal. Ugly. Soot. Unspeakable.   (95)

By demanding white Christmas roses from her male callers at Eve's, who are
allowed to visit her only in a dark, secluded basement, Esther, whose name
means "I will be hidden," relives her painful past.[4] She also adds her solitary
voice to those of the other women whose stories are included in "The Jam," and
therefore breaks the troubling discursive silence surrounding her tragic life.

In what is an original revision of the classic Christmas story, the text
culminates with a portrait of a radically transformed society where all externally
imposed limitations and labels are blurred.[5] Prefigured in *The Women of
Brewster Place* by Mattie Michael's dream/nightmare of the women's communal
efforts to dismantle the restrictive brick wall at the novel's ambiguous end, the
utopian postwar new world order that emerges in *Bailey's Cafe* is one
constructed around Mariam, a type of Madonna who gives birth to the future,
figured by young George. Mariam, the outcast mother, is a bridge between the
past and future in terms similar to those critic Daryl Dance sets forth. "She is
unquestionably a Madonna," Dance writes regarding the African American
mother, "both in the context of being a savior and in terms of giving birth and
sustenance to positive growth and advancement among her people" (131). Eve,
whose act of scoring the plum is a conscious ritual reversal of the genital
mutilation that Mariam has endured, assumes the role of midwife at George's
birth.[6] Consistent with the woman-centered cosmology that Naylor is bent on
recreating, a new social order appears with a family of choice replacing the
traditional nuclear family. Moreover, there is harmony between opposing rituals
and traditions drawn from a multicultural community. Gabriel, a Russian Jew,
presides at the naming ceremony. Like the messenger angel who visits the
biblical Mary and announces the birth of Christ, his role in the text is that of
guide or foreteller, for it is he who offers Mariam directions to Bailey's Cafe.
Naylor elevates the dispossessed women in the text to a position of honor with
what is a womanist reconceptualization of the once-burdensome domestic
sphere. It is Peaches who, at first, intones the gospel song inscribing the
identities of Mariam and George:

Anybody ask you who you are?
Who you are?
Who you are?
Anybody ask you who you are?
Tell him--you're the child of God. (225)

As the other members of the group join in with the singing of this popular
Christmas carol, now a cultural code among an international community of
outcasts, their voices unite in a call-and-response pattern that expresses the
hope for world peace:

Peace on earth, Mary rocked the cradle.
Mary rocked the cradle and Mary rocked the cradle.
Peace on earth, Mary rocked the cradle.
Tell him--was with the child of God.   (226)

The systems privileged at the novel's end--oral, female, and collective--not only bear a recursive relation to those present in the unwritten modes serving as the text's beginnings, they also suggest an end to the old dispensation of a male dialectic. In this regard, *Bailey's Cafe*, a culmination of the concerns Naylor explores in her earlier novels, represents a maturity of voice and vision for the talented writer, even as it reveals her attempts to revise codes of power, dominance, and assertion present in a male text. Rather than being an end, the novel heralds what is an auspicious new beginning. In her efforts to define herself as a writer on a contemporary literary landscape, Naylor dares to engage important issues affecting women of color world-wide and thus rescues the stories of women from silence and oblivion. At a time when women across the globe are experiencing unprecedented oppression, Naylor's voice is a clarion that demands to be heard.

Endnotes

[1] Jill Matus (49-68) discusses at length the rather problematic ending of Naylor's first novel, and her insights are relevant in an examination of *Bailey's Cafe*.

[2] Holloway offers a thoroughgoing analysis of the ancestral figure in black women's narratives in *Moorings and Metaphors*. Within the larger context of her discussion of the characteristic features of African American writing, Toni Morrison presents a definition of the ancestor that sheds light on Naylor's characterization of Eve in "Rootedness" (343).

[3] I am indebted to Mae G. Henderson's discussion of Toni Morrison's *Beloved* for insight into Naylor's womanist appropriation of Scripture.

[4] The biblical Esther is a Jewish maiden who, as queen of Persia, was used by God to deliver ancient Israel from massacre. Her supreme act of bravery entails defying secular law forbidding uninvited entry into the king's court. Despite her willful self-assertion, Esther obtains the king's favor and engineers the deliverance of the Jews. She is a heroine--a redemptive figure among colonized Israelites--and Naylor's naming her character after this Old Testament figure suggests the attempt to create a fictionalized world peopled by women of epic stature who resist the limitations patriarchy imposes.

[5] Naylor employs here a rhetorical strategy reminiscent of that used by Reverend Jesse Jackson in pointing out the hypocrisy of the Republican presidential administration, whose social policies revealed an insensitivity to the particular needs of historically disenfranchised groups. In Reverend Jackson's carefully aimed broadsides, the Biblical Mary becomes a symbol for the economically disadvantaged single mother, and King Herod is a figure for an indifferent and at times hostile political system.

[6] Naylor's treatment of genital mutilation or female circumcision recalls that involving Tashi in Alice Walker's *Possessing the Secret of Joy*.

Works Cited

Dance, Daryl C. "Black Eve or Madonna? A Study of the Antithetical Views of the Mother in Black American Literature." *Sturdy Black Bridges: Visions of Black Women in Literature.* Ed. Roseann P. Bell, Bettye J. Parker, and Beverly Guy-Sheftall. New York: Anchor, 1979. 123-131.

Due, Tananarive. "Naylor's Specialty: Bruised Characters in Soul-Searching Tales." *Miami Herald* 8 Nov. 1992: F2.

Henderson, Mae G. "Toni Morrison's *Beloved*: Re-membering the Body as Historical Text." *Comparative American Identities: Race, Sex and Nationality in the Modern Text.* Ed. Hortense Spillers. London: Routledge, 1991. 62-83.

Holloway, Karla F. C. *Moorings and Metaphors: Figures of Culture and Gender in Black Women's Literature.* New Brunswick: Rutgers UP, 1992.

Matus, Jill L. "Dream, Deferral, and Closure in *The Women of Brewster Place.*"
    Black American Literature Forum 24 (1990): 49-63.
Morrison, Toni. "Rootedness: The Ancestor as Foundation." *Black Women
    Writers (1950-1980): A Critical Evaluation.* Ed. Mari Evans. New York:
    Anchor, 1984. 339-345.
Naylor, Gloria. *Bailey's Cafe.* New York: Harcourt, 1992.
_____, and Toni Morrison. "A Conversation: Gloria Naylor and Toni
    Morrison." *Southern Review* 21.3 (1985): 567-593.
Walker, Alice. *Possessing the Secret of Joy.* New York: Harcourt, 1992.

diPace, Angela. "Gloria Naylor's *Bailey's Cafe*: A Panic Reading of Bailey's
Narrative." Published with permission of author.

This reading of Gloria Naylor's *Bailey's Cafe* (1992) focuses on the
aftermath of the catastrophe of slavery in America as it continues to be played
out at the end of the twentieth century. By foregrounding the catastrophes of the
atomic bombings of Hiroshima and Nagasaki in Bailey's narrative and
juxtaposing them to the subsequent narratives of Sadie, Eve, Esther, Peaches,
Jesse Bell, and Stanley, Naylor puts under erasure habitualized and
automatized responses to the catastrophe of slavery and its aftermath.

Nested, as they are, between the atomic bombings (Bailey's narrative), at
the beginning of the novel, and the aftermath of the Jewish Holocaust and
Diaspora (Gabe's and Mariam's narratives), at the end of the novel, the
narratives function as *mise en abyme*. In this sense, the narratives are situated
between two large sign systems (the atomic bombings and the
Holocaust/Diaspora), and what, at first, might have seemed to be a lesser sign
(the narratives) becomes a large sign that opens to the "void" (76 and passim)
that abuts the cafe.

As such, the narratives, as embedded representation of two larger signs,
may seem less catastrophic; yet they resemble the larger signs in their shared
brutality and devastatingly far-reaching consequences. This re-semblance,
moreover, enlarges the narratives as a sign of enormity equal to that of the
others. Such a configuration--a figural structure of the text--renders the
narratives as a large sign system of the catastrophe of institutionalized racism--
the aftermath of slavery. Thus, Naylor explodes to smithereens any black/white
delusional desire not to view racism in the latter part of the twentieth century as
a catastrophe comparable to the atomic bombings and the Jewish
Holocaust/Diaspora.

Viewed from this perspective, the wounds and screams that underscore
the characters' narratives of "broken dreams" (144) and "brokenheartedness"
(The Bible and Culture Collective 300) emerge from the catastrophic damage of
racism in post-slavery America. Reflecting on Sadie's tragic narrative, Bailey is
moved to state: "My father used to tell me that a star dies in heaven every time
you snatch away someone's dream. Dreams had been dying around Sadie all of
her life" (64).

Dreams have been *snatched* and *dying* for all the characters who, except
for Gabe who is a "white Falasha" (159) and Mariam who is an "Ethiopian Jew"
(143 and passim), are African American and who find Bailey's cafe/void, stay at

Eve's boardinghouse, or stop in front of Gabe's pawnshop. Like "a flock of wounded doves screaming" (90), they temporarily alight in one of these three places, shifting signifiers of recuperative space. One needs only to point to Eve's reverberating refrain, her response to Daddy Jim about Peaches: "--Leave your daughter here, Eve says, and I'll return her to you whole" (113 and passim); or to Naylor's conceptualization/spatialization of the cafe/void to localize her intertextual project of a hermeneutics of recuperation.

Early on, Bailey informs the reader that the previous owner "knew that this place had to be real mobile" (28) because

> Even though this planet is round, there are just too many spots
> where you can find yourself hanging on to the edge just like I was;
> and unless there's some space, some place, to take a breather for
> a while, the edge of the world--frightening as it is--could be the end
> of the world . . .   (28)

Bailey is behind the grill "for the same reason that they keep coming" (4). For some, the cafe may be "the last place before the end of the world" (68); whereas, for others, it may be the place/space of "infinite possibility" (76)--"the back door [that] opens out to a void" (76). For Mariam, the only one who plunges into the void, it is "a wall of water . . . [,] a running stream to bathe in. And the void out back produced exactly what her childlike mind called up: endless water" (228).

The other characters, however, are "poised on the edge of aggression and terror, unable to dismount, caught in the imploding vortex . . . the black hole of paranoid politics" (Kroker and Cook iii) that advocates institutionalized racism, actualized in the dominant will to power and oppression, and perceptible in such dead-end signs as patriarchy, misogyny, and abuse--all needed to subjugate African Americans, women, and others on the margin. Except for the pioneering "Yuma squaw" (167) and her black husband (Stanley's paternal grandparents)-- she who managed to survive the "genocide" (173) of her people and he who escaped enslavement in 1849, many of the black/white minor characters replicate racist behavior institutionalized by the dominant, as evident in the "pathetic" (183) whites and "Ku Klux Klan" (176) members--the Gatlins and Peters; patriarchy (Godfather and Daddy Jim); misogyny (Eli King, the "nag" [96], and the pervert/abuser of Esther); homophobia (Sugar Man and Eli King); servitude (the Van Morrisons, the pimps, etc.); hypocrisy/repression (Sister Carrie); and other signs of systematic vilification as suffered by Stanley and inflicted upon him by all whom he encounters at the university, the prison, and the corporate world.

The other characters suffer, not only from "broken dreams" and broken hearts, but also from broken spirit. Their bodies become a "spatialized field whose boundaries are freely pierced by subatomic particles in the microphysics of power" (v). Theirs are *fractual bodies* and *fractual entities*," "recycled signs" of racism (v). Given a "breather" (28), they may decreate themselves from the onslaught of a racist society and, therefore, create "infinite possibility" (76), or they may step "at the edge of the world" (68) into the nihilating *simulacrum* that has been created for them.

Even though this reading focuses on Bailey's narrative, the text's polysemy and its polyphonic texture do not privilege his narrative. In fact, all the narratives are equally significant and are interconnected: one does not colonize nor marginalize the other. By its very nature, "a polyphonic text cannot be reducible to a single voice/unity, single concept . . . [or] a univocity of meaning" (The Bible and Culture Collective 129; 132). "But nobody comes" in this cafe, cautions Bailey, "with a simple story. Every one-liner's got a life underneath it. Every point's got a counterpoint" (34). Bailey adds that "anything really worth hearing in this greasy spoon happens under the surface" (35).

It is the "under the surface" of Bailey's Pacific experience that frames the other narratives as *mise en abyme* and that elicits a "*panic reading*" (Kroker and Cook ii). Bailey's Pacific experience is replete with "sign-crimes" (37 and passim) that haunt the entire text, as well as the last decades of the twentieth century. The "A-bomb" (23) dropped on "Hiroshima" (26) and the second atomic bomb dropped on "Nagasaki" (26) situate the novel within the nihilistic condition that, in part, characterizes the postmodern and, thus, post-slavery American culture. Bailey's Pacific narrative produces a kind of reading that is "a way of participating directly in the ruins within and without of late twentieth-century experience" (Kroker and Cook ii).

Fewer than ten pages, mostly italicized to convey subjectivity and embedded in the first section of the novel--"MAESTRO, IF YOU PLEASE . . . " -- pertain to Bailey's story of his three-year stint in the navy, where he learned to cook and kill. Yet, Naylor's writing in these pages (as if black marks that bleed on white pages) is extremely powerful and memorable because it is disturbing and unsettling for the reader, thus calling for a "*panic reading*" which thrusts the reader into the "void."

Bailey's Pacific experience locates repeatable scenes/signs of cruelty and brutality that having occurred during World War II portend a grim future that is actualized in the oppressive present of the narratives but symbolically extends to the second half of the twentieth century. The catastrophes of slavery and World War II have occurred, but what Bailey--a metonymy for militarists, warmongers, and racists--did not take into account is how each catastrophe would affect the "*unborn children*" (26), in addition to the millions nihilated, maimed, and transfigured. It takes hundreds of killings before Bailey is cognizant of his complicity in the catastrophe and the aftermath of the atomic bombings of Hiroshima and Nagasaki. Similarly, it has taken more than a hundred years for some individuals to recognize their complicity in the catastrophes of slavery and racism, while many remain willfully ignorant. Bailey's trajectory in the Pacific, then, is emblematic of this process of recognition/misrecognition.

In the second paragraph of the novel, Bailey lets the reader know that the cafe may be the site of his Ph.D.-in-progress, "majoring in Life" (3), but that the "Pacific" was the site of his "first diploma" (3). Not until drafted in 1942 did World War II register as more than newspaper headlines. Once he realized that he was to be shipped to the Pacific, however, he was able to say that "nobody missed the meaning of Pearl Harbor" (20).

Hoodwinked to think that World War II would be a window of opportunity for African Americans, Bailey quickly learns that navy life replicates pre-World War II American society: segregation is alive and well, as are Jim Crow and the reductive attitude toward African American accomplishment, exemplified in the case of Dorrie Miller, who was "the Satchel Paige of the war in the Pacific" (20). Two other allusions to the Pacific War actually predate Bailey's marriage to Nadine. The first refers to "*winning* the war against the Japanese," to his impending nervous breakdown, and to Nadine's threatening letter/proposal, the "one-line letter: If you don't make it home, I'm marrying the butcher. Love, Nadine" (13). The second explicitly points to the fear of marriage ("a man palsied with fear" [18]) which plunges Bailey into his war experience. In a long sentence that reflects his fear of entrapment, there is a parenthetical disjuncture: ". . . but these next few minutes are going to be the worst of my life (*I had yet to meet the Japanese*) . . . , (18, emphasis added).

The Pacific experience, then, unfolds, not as flashback nor retrospection, but as *analepsis* (a term coined by Gérard Genette). The *analepsis* ensures that these events are to be read as purposive parallelism to the subsequent narratives to remove automatism and, thus, to effect a deautomatized response to the crime-sign of racism. Bailey's Pacific experience and the traces of World War II throughout the novel are instances of internal *analepsis*, pointing to "a time within that of the whole narrative" (The Bible and Culture Collective 74 and passim). Since the events in Bailey's story might have been introduced at a later point in the timeline of the novel, which spans from 1849 (167) to 1949 (216), their placement at the beginning functions to foreground racism in the subsequent narratives.   .

Basic training indoctrinates Bailey into the credo of killing the other:

--Who you gonna kill?
--We're gonna kill Japs!
--Louder
--Japs! Japs!
--Louder
--Japs! Japs!
--Who you gonna fuck?
--We're gonna fuck Japs!
--Louder   (21)

It is not surprising that this seduction of war and death spills into many books written about war. In *Pacific Destiny* (1981) by Edwin P. Hoyt, for example, the epigraph of one of the chapters reads:

Kill Japs,
Kill Japs,
Kill more Japs.   (167)

"THAT SIGN HUNG," writes Hoyt, "above the fleet landing at Tulagi and was painted on the buildings at the . . . headquarters in Noumea and Admiral Halsey closed every letter with the slogan" (167). In this book and others similar to it, the ideological indoctrination that takes place during basic training camouflages a systemic military science of oppression, destruction, and death.

In Guadalcanal, Bailey does his own killing, but it is also at this juncture that he states: "I stopped calling those people Japs" (22). Why? First, because as the Americans and allied forces had pushed back the Japanese "inch by inch, island by island" (23), Bailey learns they had been "on the winning side, long before the A-bomb was dropped" (23). Knowing this, Bailey, nonetheless, continues to participate in a prolonged massacre prior to reaching "--the enemy's land" (23), as reinforced by the iteration of "*We weren't getting into Tokyo*" (21), repeated five times. Secondly, Bailey begins to perceive that "the concept of difference has nothing ontological about it. It is only the way that the masters interpret a historical situation of domination. The function of difference is to mask at every level the conflicts of interest, including ideological ones" (Wittig 408).

Internalizing the militaristic slogans of following orders and fighting like a man, Bailey contributes to the horror of war. As the troops get closer to Tokyo, the killing and destruction escalate and are concretized in Bailey's catalog of atrocities equal in horror to the atrocities that took place during the Jewish Holocaust: he blasts every island; he burns the enemy alive, and witnesses *"the explosion of a hundred entrails"* (25). Nothing can eradicate the scene at Saipan: "*A family picnic. All bathed. New clothes . . ."* (25).

At "Okinawa" (25), *"one last island before Japan"* (25), Bailey becomes shellshocked (*"I chewed up the palm of my hand and spat out the blood to keep from dozing at night. I could stop myself from sleeping, so there would be no dreams"* [25]). Having decimated hundreds of Japanese (22-28), Bailey realizes that he could not face *"the very young, the deformed, and the old"* (25) who were waiting in Toyko. Doomed to know that he was to survive catastrophes that could have been prevented, Bailey confronts his own private hell. His anguish is augmented by the bargain he has made to *"come out alive"* (26): *"Take. This. Cross. From. Me. And yes, I offered any god who would answer even the rights to my unborn children. And the only god to answer claimed them"* (26). Bailey's will to survive destroys the lives of others. He gains nothing but loses all in his bargain to live: *"Hiroshima in exchange for my soul"* and *"then Nagasaki"* (26).

Bailey, fearing for his *"immortal soul"* (23), could not march into Tokyo to confront the evil he had helped to set loose upon the world. On August 6, 1945 when the bomb was dropped on Hiroshima, "a hundred thousand people were killed" (Hersey 2). In his heart-rendering account *Hiroshima*, published first in 1946 and updated in 1989, John Hersey chronicles the lives of six survivors and revisits them forty years later. Many of the survivors, the *hibakusha*, literally meaning "explosion-affected persons" (92), were not only maimed physically, psychologically, and spiritually, but they also were ostracized, forgotten, and neglected.

The Japanese militarists also helped to bring out this catastrophe (93). In "Toward the Unknowable Future," the introduction to *The Crazy Iris* (1985), a collection of short stories about the atomic bombings and their aftermath and written by survivors and second generation writers, Kenzaburō Ōe writes that although the "massive wreckage of life, limb, and livelihood caused by the atomic bombings of Hiroshima and Nagasaki was, for single-bomb attacks, unprecedented in human history, many of the 'second-generation survivors' (children of those directly affected) were the first to acknowledge clearly that Japan and the Japanese were aggressors in the Pacific War that brought on the atomic bombings" (9). Ultimately, the short stories in *The Crazy Iris* and *Bailey's Cafe* "question both the American and Japanese governments' responsibilities for the atomic bombings" (10).

Additionally, however, Naylor questions the American government's responsibility for slavery and racism. Although political initiatives to abolish all nuclear arms have been put into effect internationally, no such claim can be made for the eradication of racism. In *Bailey's Cafe*, Naylor advances the project by clearly exposing the markers of the marginalized, devalued, discounted, and discredited who are affected by the catastrophe of racism, as the *hibakusha* were affected by the atomic bombings.

Can love exist among the ruins? Can life exist? Can flowers bloom? Despite the horrific narratives of broken lives and global devastation, Naylor is a proponent of affirmation and hope. There is love between Bailey and Nadine (even marriage). Mariam gives birth to George. And, then, there is Eve's garden, blooming profusely in all seasons. Eve's garden is as recuperative as "Bailey's cafe." Her flowers even grow out of season, as the Christmas rose for Esther. Eve's flowers, similar to the iris in Masuji Ibuse's short story "The Crazy Iris" are "crazy" and belong "to a crazy age!" (35).

They do belong to a "crazy age," but Eve is aware of the past, the ruins, and the wasteland. Unlike Bailey, who contributes to the devastation of Hiroshima ("*my seed rained on that city from black clouds, withering the camellias, curling the leaves of oaks, scalding the feathers of songbirds. My seed flowed with the inland tides, sweeping heaps of trout and salmon into piles among the rotting sea turtles*" [26]), and, therefore, perpetuates the waste by disseminating "*les fleurs du mal*," Eve's seeds provide succor. Not only does Eve have "a love of well-kept gardens," where "even the stone wall blooms," but also "she's got some kind of plan to all of this" (91-92). Certainly, it is the best garden around since paradise was lost, and it is the first one created by Eve/Naylor.

Works Cited

The Bible and Culture Collective. *The Postmodern Bible*. New Haven: Yale UP, 1995.

Hersey, John. *Hiroshima*. New York: Vintage, 1989.

Hoyt, Edwin. *Pacific Destiny*. New York: Norton, 1981.

Ibuse, Masuji. "The Crazy Iris" in *The Crazy Iris*. Ed. Kenzaburō Ōe. New York: Grove, 1985. 17-35.

Kroker, Arthur, and Cook, David. *The Postmodern Scene*. New York: St. Martin's, 1991.

Naylor, Gloria. *Bailey's Cafe*. New York: Vintage, 1993.

Ōe, Kenzaburō, ed. and intro. "Toward the Unknowable Future." In *The Crazy Iris*. New York: Grove, 1985. 9-16.

Wittig, Monique. "The Straight Mind: Feminist Issues." In *Feminist Literary Theory*, 2nd. ed. Ed. Mary Eagleton. Cambridge: Blackwell, 1996. 408-411.

Stokes, Karah. "Ripe Plums and Pine Trees: Using Metaphor to Tell Stories of Violence in the Works of Gloria Naylor and Charles Chesnutt." Published with permission of author.

In *Bailey's Cafe* (1992), Gloria Naylor uses the image of a plum to describe the violence of female genital mutilation. To tell the story of Mariam, one of the narrators in the chapter titled "Mary (Take Two)" demonstrates on a plum with a sharp knife what has been done to Mariam's body. By using the figurative mode rather than telling the story literally, Naylor circumvents the conscious defenses of an audience who might resist a literal description of such violence and avoids objectifying its victim. Naylor's use of metaphor to tell the story of violence is inherited from her literary ancestor Charles Chesnutt, whose "Po' Sandy" (1899) uses a similar shift into the figurative to reveal the violence of the slave system. Naylor and Chesnutt use metaphor as a narrative sleight of hand to beguile the reader into listening to stories of violence and into identifying with its victims.

What both authors are doing in shifting from literal to figurative and back again is, of course, a type of signifying.[1] The shifting conceals the message from inappropriate listeners and reveals it to receptive ones, and sometimes these auditors are the same person at different times: the message becomes clear when the listener is ready to receive it. For a listener to be able to "hold a conversation" (Gates 84) is to be able to follow shifts from literal to figurative as the speaker crosses boundaries, a conscious move. It is also to be aware that communication can happen both through words and through the body's gestures, a "speaking with the hands and eyes" (Gates 74-75). I would like to point out that one way this signifying delivers messages is by using metaphor to engage our physical selves in a way that precedes consciousness.

By displacing violence onto a ripe plum and a pine tree, both writers connect with the reader's unconscious processes in the same way as a great poem or a good therapist. The metaphor is like a Trojan horse: the narrator produces it and the reader's unconscious process carries it into the city heavily guarded by conscious defenses. The reader's unconscious then engages with the metaphor according to his own remembered sensory experience, bringing it close to his own body, whether or not the conscious mind is aware this is happening.

Part of the project of many African American writers has been to testify to what people have suffered under racist oppression, yet telling and listening to the story of violence is difficult for both writer and reader. How does one convey in words an act that has the power to unmake language? As Elaine Scarry has explained, the "tact and immediacy" of language necessary to convey the story of pain work at cross purposes, one negating the other (9). For the reader, the experience of reading about someone's pain can call up defenses that block its perception. As individuals and social groups, we resist listening to stories of violence (Herman 8-9). We may numb ourselves or simply avoid reading depictions of terrible pain. Alternately, to avoid feeling the pain represented in a text, we may identify with the perpetrator, not the victim, becoming voyeurs or participants.

Naylor has invented many strategies for telling the story of violence without dehumanizing its victims. *The Women of Brewster Place* (1982) testifies to Lorraine's experience of gang rape, yet prevents the reader from positioning him- or herself as violator or observer, as Laura E. Tanner explains. In her analysis of this scene, Tanner shows that Naylor keeps the reader in the point of view of Lorraine rather than her attackers by reporting what Lorraine--not an attacker or observer--sees, hears, and feels (83-84). Even after Lorraine can no longer feel, Naylor does not allow the reader the same numbness, instead conjuring feeling through naming what the victim did not feel: "She couldn't feel the skin rubbing off her arms against the cement. . . . She didn't feel her split rectum" (171). In this way, Naylor draws on the unconscious, which does not process negatives (O'Connor and Seymour 120). In order to imagine not feeling a particular sensation, the reader must imagine it before she can negate it. Tanner shows how Naylor engages the reader in the story of the victim, not the violator, thus enabling the victim's story of violence to be told (86).

In *Bailey's Cafe*, Naylor follows a different strategy, using extended metaphor to involve the reader and to connect with the reader's unconscious processes. Sensory images, it seems, can engage the unconscious. According to Freud, the unconscious operates in images, while conscious thinking works by means of images along with words (Wyatt 42-43). Wyatt posits that, because unconscious processes function in images, that these processes take charge when one reads "descriptions of concrete images of actions described in physical detail," often delivering a message counter to the manifest one a text delivers in abstract terms (43).[2]

Although in novels there are no actual images but only verbal descriptions of them, reading the words produces images in the reader or listener, a phenomenon that therapists following Milton Erickson have been exploiting with their patients for years. Therapists routinely use such word-evoked images to gain access to resources unavailable to the conscious mind. In fact, images evoked by words and constructed by the reader/listener are closely connected to the listener because he must construct them by drawing on memories of his own sensory experience. The strength of the connection is in leaving spaces for details that the listener fills in from his own experience (O'Connor and Seymour 27-29).

The stories of violence in *Bailey's Cafe* and "Po' Sandy" are told in metaphor; the violent act is not wrought on a human body, but on an inanimate object, and therefore is once removed from the reader. Paradoxically, this distance encourages the reader in two ways to identify with the victims. First, by distancing the violence from the reader, working in metaphor relaxes the vigilance of the reader's conscious defenses. Second, metaphor also evokes sensory images--visual, auditory, kinetic, olfactory, gustatory, and rhythmic--that encourage the reader's unconscious processes to engage with the story. These details, extrapolated from his or her own experience, engage the reader physically with the metaphoric object. Reading a description of a sensory image encourages the reader to remember, consciously or not, corresponding details from a previous sensory experience; what we have not experienced we construct from similar or analogous experiences. This type of reading engages us physically with the material, as it produces measurable physical changes such as salivation (O'Connor and Seymour 26-27). A certain type of writing, then, sensory description, we read with our bodies. Once our bodies are engaged with the text in this way, it may be easier to transform that engagement into identification.

Further, Naylor uses kinesthetic, olfactory, and gustatory images in a way that encourages the reader to read with her own body. A visual image can be far removed from the reader: one can picture seeing something from a distance. One is far more likely to be emotionally dissociated from a visual image than from one that draws on another of the senses (O'Connor and Seymour 171). A word, that coin of conscious thought, is also a visual image. However, an image that appeals to touch, taste, or olfaction, especially if it evokes a memory from the reader's experience, is felt on or even within the reader's body. Once thus intimately connected with the material, she cannot instantaneously remove herself. Naylor therefore begins her description in the less-threatening realm of visual images and then synesthetically links them to these more-immediate senses.

To tell the story of Mariam's mutilation, Naylor draws on all these properties of metaphor and imagery. Mariam, an Ethiopian Jew, has been infibulated. Because she does not have the linguistic facility to do so--she is retarded--she does not narrate her own story in words. Instead, it is told by Eve, Nadine, and an omniscient third-person narrator who mostly speaks from the viewpoint of Mariam's mother, with brief passages from the point of view of a high priest's wife and that of Mariam herself. But Mariam begins the story by handing Eve a ripe plum, thus linking her with the fruit (145).

Naylor describes the plum at length with sensory details that encourage reader engagement. "The fruit looked tender and soft. The reddish black skin was so thin you could already smell that the flesh would be sweet" (145). The details appeal to several senses: sight ("reddish black"), touch ("tender and soft"), smell ("smell"), and taste ("sweet"). Naylor also links senses in synesthesia, which strengthens their impact. The fruit *looks* tender and soft, combining sight and touch; you could *smell* the flesh would be sweet, linking smell and taste. By appealing to many senses rather than focusing only on one, this mixture also engages the greatest number of readers, because each person is most comfortable functioning within one of the senses (O'Connor and Seymour 32-33). A reader first engages through whichever sensory representational system is most comfortable for her, and then connects with those secondary to her habits of thought.

While she ensures that we can smell, feel, and taste the plum, Naylor also links it to the human body, transforming our sensory engagement into identification. She first makes certain that we connect the plum with the body through linguistic ambiguity, referring to its "flesh" and its "skin." In the second passage describing the plum, she more closely links it to the human body, saying that it bruises easily (engaging us again in a kinesthetic image, inviting us to remember the feeling of bruising) and comparing the stem end to a "belly button" (147). The "two plump mounds" linguistically suggest the mound of Venus and visually represent the large labia; the "fleshy walls" and "hard little nub" move the focus visually and kinesthetically to the inner labia and clitoris. The "clear juices already beading up" set the whole image in motion and demonstrate the potential for sexuality--a female sexuality that the metaphor suggests is pleasurable and nourishing.

Naylor furthers her transformation of plum into human body by interweaving description of the plum with Mariam's story. The plum is introduced by having Mariam hand it to Eve. Eve describes the fruit in sensory detail, as noted above, and commands Nadine to bring her a knife. Eve explains that although Mariam is pregnant, her statement that no man has touched her must be true: "There was no way for the girl to be lying, or the whole village would have heard her screams" (146). These screams segue into the screams of Mariam's mother in childbirth. Naylor begins the account of Mariam's life, related from the view point of Mariam's mother, shifting back and forth from the plum to Mariam's story leading up to and including her infibulation at age six, and the analogous process performed on the plum.

For the reader, linked sensorily with the description of plum as fruit, and subconsciously with the plum as human body, the mutilation of the plum is shocking. We see, smell, taste, and feel the fruit; we feel superimposed on our bodies the tenderness and potential for bruising. The rhythm of Naylor's jump-cuts from Mariam's story to description of plum and knife becomes quicker as the segments become briefer through this section, in which Eve and Nadine begin to talk about the plum as if it were a body, not a fruit. The motions of the knife are interwoven with discussion of the ritual mutilation, which they never explicitly name.

> [Nadine]: I know my Bible well, I said, and this *isn't* in the Law of Moses. [Eve] was positioning the fruit, lining up the exposed head of the pit with the tip of the blade. No, she said, it's not. It's older than that. It's the law of the Blue Nile.   (150)

Naylor cuts back to Mariam's story. We hear the women of the tribe planning to be there to "squat the naked girl over the hole dug into the hut of blood" (150). After a brief two-sentence quote from the Song of Songs (8:8-9), which could be interpreted to refer to female circumcision, Eve cuts out the plum pit (151).

The plum slicing is connected with Mariam's story as before. When the pit falls to the counter, it "carried ragged pieces of dark amber flesh with it" (151). Immediately we shift to the description of the wounding from Mariam's point of view, one of the few brief passages narrated from her viewpoint. "It is a white-hot world of pain. A world filled with high-pitched screams, with the singing of women, with the gentle moans of her mother and grandmothers, with the press of soft breasts and soft arms against her heaving body" (151). This shift makes it clear that the dark amber flesh belonging to the fruit also belongs to Mariam. Working in metaphor here allows Naylor to supply some graphic details of violence. We see "juice" dripping from the knife and small chunks of fruit spattering Eve as she intently scrapes the "meaty sections" from inside the halves of the plum. Eve then scrapes out the flesh of the plum until there is nothing left but a shell of "delicate outer skin" (151). Immediately switching to Mariam's story in the next sentence, the narrator informs us that "the child's hanging skin is held together with acacia thorns" (151).[3]

In this chapter, Naylor also comments on the relation of violence to language--how violence silences its victims. Unlike the other stories that make up the novel, this character's story is not narrated in first-person by the character herself, but in third person, by Mariam's mother. Mariam's inability to speak may itself be a result of her birth being complicated and slowed by her mother's scar tissue, as Walker, in *Possessing the Secret of Joy*, mentions sometimes happens.[4]

Because Naylor shows us how Mariam's voice has been silenced by the pain she has been made to suffer, and replaced with the voice of the patriarchal system that represses her, she suggests that this tradition is a form of torture like that of any other repressive regime (Scarry). Mariam's only words are "No man has ever touched me." Even though Mariam cannot speak well enough to tell her own story, amputating her sex organs and sewing up her orifices has ensured that her body speaks for her, and this is what it says: that she is untouched sexually. Her health and potential for sexuality are sacrificed to form her body into a message to her future husband that no man has been there before him. Anything a circumcised woman has to say verbally is subordinate to this message, No man has ever touched me.

Naylor repeats Mariam's statement six times in this chapter, communicating a range of meanings to the reader before finally allowing it to deconstruct itself by demonstrating its self-contradictory nature. No man has touched her--no *man*, but a woman, aided by Mariam's female relatives, wielded the knife that mutilated Mariam's body. Another reverberation presents itself in the space Naylor allows it: no man has touched her, yet, compared with the damage that women have done to her body in order to ensure she is sexually untouched at marriage, could anything a man might do, with or without her consent, be more traumatic? Finally, Naylor allows the statement to dissolve into meaninglessness. No man has sexually touched Mariam, yet she is pregnant, like other girls who had thought they were protected from pregnancy because they were circumcised (Walker and Parmar 342). A reader from a culture that does not practice this amputation might see a different contradiction inherent in her statement: no man has touched her sexually because there are very few sexual parts left to touch. In deconstructing the binary opposition of the pair of terms touched/untouched, Naylor follows Chesnutt (Werner 20-21) in her critique of the way linguistic systems enforce patriarchal power.

If she could speak, who knows what Mariam might have had to say? Alice Walker compares mutilation to sexual blinding, and to her own blinding at eight by her brother's BB gun (Walker and Parmar 267). Naylor represents it as a silencing.

Naylor's literary ancestor Charles Chesnutt also tells a story of violence and silencing by using metaphor in "Po' Sandy." Chesnutt uses metaphor differently than Naylor, yet its effect, like that of "Mary (Take Two)" is to make us listen to the story of violence and identify with its victims. Chesnutt delivers two messages to us in "Po' Sandy": he not only conveys the extent of the slave system's barbarity, but also makes us aware of the language that, drawing on our tendency to deny the truly horrible, renders this barbarity invisible. His metaphor is more deeply camouflaged than Naylor's, so it may only be after much thought that we become conscious of his messages. Most readers are probably conscious that Naylor's plum represents a woman's body, while Chesnutt's readers are at first probably not consciously aware that the pine tree is vehicle for an elaborate metaphorical rendering of human torture.

Rather than offending with a literal story the audience who would rather not hear about slavery, Chesnutt distracts us with what appears to be a shift in genre to fairy tale, but is actually a shift to speaking in metaphor, a type of signifying (Gates 84). Sandy wishes to be turned into a tree, and he is turned into a tree. His wish and its fulfillment, corresponding to the folktale theme of the wish overheard and granted, tricks the reader into expecting a fairytale instead of a comment on the slave system. Fearing to lose Tenie the same way he lost his first wife, who was sold while he was being worked on another plantation, he laments, "I wisht I wuz a tree, er a stump, er a rock, er sump'n w'at could stay on de plantation fer a w'ile" (45). Any social commentary is trebly masked by the conventions of the plantation tradition, the fairy tale, and the figurative. At the end of the story, after our expectations of a magical escape have been thwarted and our emotions curiously engaged in the fantastical account of Sandy-the-tree's being sawed into lumber, we might become aware that Chesnutt has delivered a message about the very subject we expected him to avoid, the violence of the slave system. Even if we do not understand his message consciously, we might receive it subconsciously, because the scene of Sandy's death, though obviously fabulous, is peculiarly harrowing.

Why so disturbing? Although not *realistic*, the story is quite *accurate* in its portrayal of the slave system. In "Mars Jeems' Nightmare," the white narrator, John, opines that because he grew up there as a slave, Julius, the storyteller, regards himself as "an appurtenance" of "the old plantation": as a thing, almost an inanimate object (65). Although John notes it as a picturesque detail, to treat human beings as if they were inanimate objects is exactly what the slave system does. In "Po' Sandy," Chesnutt makes us see the grotesque consequences of treating human beings as inanimate objects by transforming Sandy into a literal thing, a tree.[5]

Chesnutt uses the metaphor of the tree to ensure that the reader will perceive what happens when a human being is treated as an inanimate object for the slaveholders' use. The mind of the free reader of "Po' Sandy" is probably incapable of imagining the dehumanization of being enslaved. We most likely unthinkingly assume that Sandy, under the slave system, still retains a degree of control over his actions and his own body. We resist fully understanding the extent of slaveholders' power, assuming the enslaved had some command over their movements, their family lives, or their own bodies. We forget that if the enslaved did have any influence over what happened, it was not granted them under the slave system, but obtained in spite of it.

This reluctance to perceive the full extent of dehumanization allows conventions of speech that make the system's violence invisible.[6] In the polite discourse of slaveholders, the enslaved were referred to as "servants," implying both that they were paid for their labor and that they were free to seek employment elsewhere. In contrast, Mars Marrabo assuages his discomfort at selling Sandy's previous wife by returning him one dollar of the profit--as if Sandy were a willing partner to the deal, and as if his relationship to his wife were translatable into dollars and cents. Mars Marrabo tells Sandy he has sold his first wife as if the plantation owner had no choice in the matter: "[D]e spekilater had gin him big boot [profit], en so he was bleedst [obliged] ter make de trade" (42). This language leads the reader to ask, What exactly forces him to trade Sandy's first wife?

In "Po' Sandy" Chesnutt makes visible these polite euphemisms by having the enslaved use them while talking between themselves. In the complaint about the slave system that inspires Tenie to conjure him, Sandy himself speaks as if he were merely annoyed at being worked on one plantation, and then another, as if he were complaining of sheer ennui at a course of action taken of his free will. "I'm gittin' monst'us ti'ed er dish yer gwine roun' so much" (44). Broadening the humor, his list of his deprivations places the loss of his first wife and his potential separation from his beloved second wife at the list's end, seemingly as an afterthought. "[I]t 'pears to me I ain' got no home, ner no marster, ner no mistiss, ner no nuffin. I can't eben keep a wife: my yuther ole 'oman wuz sol' away widout my gitten a chance fer ter tell her good-bye" (44-45). The irony of having the enslaved tell their side of the story using the enslaver's conventions of speech emphasizes the distance between polite convention and brutal reality, making it clear to the reader how language allows the slave system's brutality while at the same time obscuring it (Werner 21-22).

Literalizing the metaphor--transforming Sandy from a human being who is treated as a thing into a literal thing--allows us to approach understanding the peculiar horrors of the slave system. After Chesnutt has made visible the disparity between the conventions of speech and the reality of slavery, he makes enslavement visible to us by making it literal. The tree metaphorically represents the man; yet it makes literal the fact that he is treated not as a man, but as a thing. Both irony and metaphor combine to make Sandy's death scene particularly horrifying.

What makes the scene so barbarous is that it exactly mirrors in metaphor the "system . . . under which such things were possible": husbands were tortured and killed in front of their wives. Tenie returns from nursing a sick slaveholder and finds the tree that was her husband chopped down. Even though she knows he is doomed to die, she runs to the sawmill to explain and to beg his forgiveness. Her accepting responsibility for an act committed by slaveholders again makes visible the disparity between the conventions of polite speech and the gruesome terms of enslavement. The mill hands, thinking her insane, tie her to a post to keep her from jumping in front of the saw, essentially forcing her to watch as Sandy is cut into boards before her eyes (55), and replicating a scene like the one in Frederick Douglass' *Narrative* in which his Aunt Hester is whipped bloody while the young Douglass watches (26) or any number of other scenes during slavery, recorded and unrecorded.

Chesnutt uses the same techniques to engage the reader with the pine tree that Naylor uses in her scene with the plum. He has already connected the tree with Sandy's body when we see that Sandy's arm has a hole where a woodpecker began to build a nest and his leg is scarred when the tree is slashed for turpentine (49). The scene of Sandy's death appeals to many senses, drawing heavily on kinesthetic imagery. Bloodlike sap runs out of the logged stump. The tree creaks, shakes, and wobbles; it causes the axe to glance off the wood (52). Once loaded, the tree gets stuck in the swamp. It temporarily throws off its chains (53). In short, it struggles heroically like a captured human being about to be lynched. Chesnutt also engages us kinesthetically with Tenie's struggle, having Julius use active dramatic verbs. He reports that she runs up the hill to the sawmill, panting and crying, and "th'ow[s] herse'f on de log, right in front er de saw," weeping (54-55). Finally, the mill hands "kotch holt er her" and "tie her arms wid a rope," where she watches her husband slowly killed, hearing his screams of agony (55).

Because unlike Naylor's "Mary (Take Two)," the piece's relation to real physical violence is masked by its tone, Chesnutt's reader may at first be unaware of the social commentary. Therefore, instead of the reader connecting metaphorical with literal violence, this connection is revealed to the reader by one of the characters. Annie understands the tale and "translates" it, mirroring the shift from literal to figurative with her own shift, when she says "What a system it was . . . under which such things were possible!" (60). Her husband John thinks that *things* refers to the man's literally being turned into a tree, and exclaims in surprise, "What things? . . . a man's being turned into a tree?" (60). But Annie's use of the word refers instead to the sawmill's analogue: men being separated from the wives who love them, tortured and killed.[7]

Chesnutt here also communicates with unconscious processes through the reader's senses. He provides sensory information about Annie's physiological state that can evoke a similar response from the reader. The "dim look in her fine eyes" suggests the eyes are filled with tears, and further, that the fine eyes are unfocused. This indicates she is not seeing the scene around her, but the story image that Julius has created. Her lament, "Poor Tenie," signals her identification with the enslaved woman. Readers may find themselves unconsciously mirroring Annie's physiology, as people do when speaking with each other.

In telling stories that cross the boundary from literal to figurative and back again, both Chesnutt and Naylor are putting into action a type of signifying. Naylor's four novels to date have in fact insisted that signifying, this African-American, boundary-crossing, mode of speech, is necessary to effectively tell and to listen to stories of violence. Two of her novels in particular feature a prominent scene of teaching, or attempting to teach, a character how to listen to a story that signifies. In the dream scene at the end of *The Women of Brewster Place*, for example, Naylor describes educating Kiswana Browne, so that she may hear and participate in telling the story of how violence affects the lives of Brewster's women.[8]

Throughout the novel thus far, Kiswana, who has grown up removed from black folk traditions in Linden Hills, is not fully a member of Brewster's community and this is figured by her relation to their speech. For example, complaining about his refusal to heat the building in winter, the tenants retaliate verbally at their landlord by signifying on him, but Kiswana is ignorant of this nonliteral mode:

> "Guess he figure niggers don't need no heat."
> "Yeah, we supposed to be from Africa, anyway. And it's so hot over there them folks don't know what [heating] oil is."
> Everybody laughed but Kiswana. "You know, that's not really true. It snows in some parts of Africa, and Nigeria is one of the most important exporters of oil in the world."
> The women stopped laughing and looked at her as you would at someone who had totally missed the point of a joke that should need no explanation. (182)

Here Kiswana is unaware that the point has nothing to do with the literal African continent and everything to do with figurative verbal invention.

However, later in the scene, when the women dismantle the wall where Lorraine was raped and Ben killed, Naylor shows that Kiswana has begun to understand the community's use of the figurative. First denying their references to blood, which is no longer literally on the wall, then crossing the literal - figurative boundary by using the term herself in the narrator's free indirect discourse, Kiswana enters into Brewster's speech community.

> "There's no blood on those bricks!" Kiswana grabbed Ciel by the arm.
> "You know there's no blood--it's raining. It's just raining!"
> Ciel pressed the brick into Kiswana's hand and forced her fingers to curl around it. "Does it matter? Does it really matter?"
> [Kiswana] wept and ran to throw the brick spotted with her blood out into the avenue. (187)

Her participation in dismantling the wall signals that Kiswana has understood the figurative message about violence: that it affects all of them. Together they tear down the wall that makes Brewster into a dead end. The women's response to the figurative bloodstains implies that they are now united in their response to violence.

Highlighting more emphatically the importance of knowing when to shift from literal to metaphorical, *Mama Day* begins rather than ends with "schooling" not a character, but the reader. In order to educate us, the narrator tells the story of Reema's boy, who returns from college as an anthropologist to investigate what "18 & 23" means. On the first page of text, the narrator uses the expression as a noun that refers to the birth of a child to another child--"early 18 & 23." In the same paragraph, the phrase is used as a transitive verb, meaning to take advantage of someone in a business deal--"he tried to 18 & 23 me"--and as an adjective describing the summer recounted in the novel, a summer with a severe hurricane. The term has no literal denotation (that is, none known to the present community), only an infinite number of figurative applications dependent on context.

Because he cannot make this particular kind of switch from literal to figurative, Reema's boy cannot ask the proper question--he apparently asks for literal information--or apply metaphorically the stories he receives in answer to his questions. Consequently, he does not understand residents' attempts to translate the meaning of 18 & 23 as it is inscribed in plain sight on their bodies:

> He coulda asked Cloris about the curve in her spine that came from the planting season when their mule broke its leg, and she took up the reins and kept pulling the plow with her own back. Winky woulda told him about the hot tar that took out the corner of his right eye the summer we had only seven days to rebuild the bridge so the few crops we had left after the storm could be gotten over before rot sat in.   (8)

Unable to follow the narrator's shift from literal to figurative, he is unable to hear the story the reader is about to hear, the novel itself (10).

Critics have agreed on the importance of this small but salient episode and proposed all sorts of interpretations for it: that it underscores the point that being part of a community requires knowing how to negotiate that community's storytelling customs (Donlon); that it introduces the novel's central theme of claiming narrative authority (Storhoff); that it shows that white standards are inadequate for portraying black reality (Meisenhelder). I would suggest that, in addition to these, the story of Reema's boy teaches us how to read the novel by following the narrator's shifts from literal to figurative and back.

Although he has been to "one of them fancy colleges mainside," Reema's boy has not been properly "schooled" to be able to "hold a conversation" in the folk sense: he is unable to understand when the speaker has shifted from speaking literally to speaking figuratively, or signifyin(g) (Gates 84). He has heard "18 & 23" all his life, yet he is unable to process the community's explanation that "it was just our way of saying something"--a figurative way of conveying information (7). Instead, he insists that this phrase represents the literal numerals 81 and 32, the longitude and latitude of Willow Springs, and that the natives reverse these numbers to "[invert] hostile social and political parameters." However, in a bit of signifying on the young man himself later in the novel, the narrative voice offers a humorous explanation for his backwards understanding: it reveals that he nearly killed himself and his mother at birth by "coming out hind parts first" (84).

Therefore, the much-discussed introduction is a bit of "schooling" in how to read the rest of the novel: metaphorically, like a folk tale rather than a factual report. In this way, the tale of Reema's boy links *Mama Day* with the African American trope of "the talking book." Inverting the figure of the talking book, a European text that "refuses" to speak to the African listener until he rejects his African heritage for white culture and literacy (Gates 127), Naylor creates a text dependent on the forms of African narrative. The reader cognizant of these modes is able to "overhear" and participate in the dialogue between Cocoa, George, and the voice of Willow Springs, just as the necessary audience overhears a performance of signifying. Unless listeners are properly schooled in African American culture and aural understanding, Naylor's book will not speak to them.

How does one convey in words a violent act that has the power to unmake language? Both Naylor and Chesnutt use metaphor to tell the story of violence in such a way that it is heard and identified with. Evoking sensory images that gain access to preverbal parts of the understanding, they encode a message that the reader understands a little at a time, as we become able. Most generous of all, through Annie's example in "Po' Sandy," that of Kiswana in *The Women of Brewster Place*, and Reema's boy in *Mama Day*, they educate us to be able to hear the stories they tell. We merely have to begin to listen, with our intellects and with our bodies.

Endnotes

[1] See Gates' *The Signifying Monkey*, especially chapter 3, "Figures of Signification."

[2] Wyatt uses this theory to explain the long-term popularity with girls of novels like *Little Women*: in her view, the non-sensory-based speeches that preach patriarchal muting of girls' selfhood are undercut through repeated sensory images of physical movement, expressiveness, and nurturance (43).

[3] Mariam has been infibulated, which is amputation of the clitoris, hood, small labia, and much of the large labia. What is left is sewn up: a small opening is preserved, by inserting matchsticks, slivers of wood, or a straw, for urine and blood to pass through (Naylor 151; Walker and Parmar 366-367). When a woman is given to her husband, in order for him to penetrate her, the woman's scar tissue must be recut open by the midwife; often the husband must cut an opening in the new wife in order to sexually penetrate her (Walker 139). It can take months for a husband to be able to penetrate a new wife. Sometimes she bleeds excessively and must be taken to the hospital. Childbirth, of course, brings with it an analogous set of complications and pain for the woman (Walker and Parmar 192). Many of the most vocal proponents for abolition of this ritual amputation are the doctors who must deal with the myriad health problems it causes.

[4] Clues that suggest this possibility are the fact that Mariam is her mother's firstborn, and that there was much blood at her birth (148).

[5] Sundquist notes that "the white economic conjure of slavery" turns Sandy "into a material part of the plantation" (376).

[6] Werner notes that Julius "parodies the way in which white folks, especially when they want to evade their own position in an unjust system, employ different signifiers to obscure what from the Afro-American perspective appear to be identical signifieds" (22).

[7] Here I concur with Callahan, who remarks that Annie understands the story "instantly and completely" while John takes it literally (49).

[8] For a discussion of the function of dreams in *The Women of Brewster Place*, see especially Matus.

Works Cited

Callahan, John. *In the African-American Grain: The Pursuit of Voice in Twentieth-Century Black Fiction*. Urbana: U of Illinois P, 1988.

Chesnutt, Charles. *The Conjure Woman*. 1899. Ann Arbor: U of Michigan P, 1969.

Douglass, Frederick. *Narrative of the Life of an American Slave Written by Himself*. 1845. New York: Penguin-Signet, 1968.

Freud, Sigmund. "The Unconscious." *General Psychological Theory*. Ed. Philip Rieff. New York: Collier-MacMillan, 1963. 116-150.

Gates, Henry Louis, Jr. *The Signifying Monkey: A Theory of African-American Literary Criticism*. New York: Oxford UP, 1988.

Gates, Henry Louis, Jr., and K. A. Appiah, eds. *Gloria Naylor: Critical Perspectives Past and Present*. New York: Amistad, 1993.

Gregory, Robert. Unpublished paper on Chesnutt.

Herman, Judith Lewis, M.D. *Trauma and Recovery*. New York: Basic Books, 1992.

Hudson, Mark. *Our Grandmothers' Drums*. New York: Grove Weidenfield, 1990.

Matus, Jill L. "Dream, Deferral, and Closure in *The Women of Brewster Place*." Gates and Appiah 126-139.

Meisenhelder, Susan. "'The Whole Picture' in *Mama Day*." *African American Review* 27.3 (Fall 1993): 405-420.

Montgomery, Maxine Lavon. "Authority, Multivocality, and the New World Order in Gloria Naylor's *Bailey's Cafe*." *African American Review* 29.1 (Spring 1995): 27-33.

Naylor, Gloria. *Bailey's Cafe*. New York: Harcourt Brace, 1992.

_____. *Linden Hills*. New York: Penguin, 1986.

_____. *Mama Day*. New York: Vintage, 1989.

_____. *The Women of Brewster Place*. New York: Penguin, 1983.

O'Connor, Joseph, and John Seymour. *Introducing Neuro-Linguistic Programming: Psychological Skills for Understanding and Influencing People*. New York: Aquarian/Thorsons-HarperCollins, 1993.

Scarry, Elaine. *The Body in Pain: The Making and Unmaking of the World*. New York: Oxford UP, 1985.

Storhoff, Gary. "'The Only Voice is Your Own': Gloria Naylor's Revision of *The Tempest*." *African-American Review* 29.1 (Spring 1995): 35-46.

Sundquist, Eric J. *To Wake the Nations: Race in the Making of American Literature*. Cambridge: Belknap/Harvard UP, 1993.

Tanner, Laura E. "Reading Rape: Sanctuary and *The Women of Brewster Place*." Gates and Appiah 71-89.

Walker, Alice, and Pratibha Parmar. *Warrior Marks: Female Genital Mutilation and the Sexual Blinding of Women*. New York: HB&C, 1993.

Werner, Craig. *Playing the Changes: From Afro-Modernism to the Jazz Impulse*. Urbana: U of Illinois P, 1994.

Wyatt, Jean. *Reconstructing Desire: The Role of the Unconscious in Women's Reading and Writing*. Chapel Hill: U of North Carolina P, 1990.

Nash, William R. "The Dream Defined: *Bailey's Cafe* and the Reconstruction of American Cultural Identities." Published with permission of author.

From the invocation of Langston Hughes' "Harlem" in *The Women of Brewster Place* (1982) through the chronicle of African American folklife in *Mama Day* (1988), the presence and power of the dream motif in Gloria Naylor's work is undeniable; significantly, however, it is also mutable, changing in every work to indicate another facet of Naylor's complexly crafted presentation of African American experiences. In *The Women of Brewster Place*, Naylor gives the reader seven stories of dream deferral, a cycle of disappointment, frustration, and qualified triumph that leads the inhabitants of the dead-end street to form a new community. In Naylor's second novel, *Linden Hills* (1985), she inverts that imagery, showing the terrible price that members of the "rising" African American middle class (ironic because their economic ascent moves them lower and lower in the Dantean landscape of Linden Hills) pay for cashing in their cultural heritage in favor of the dominant cultural version of the American Dream. Naylor takes that lesson--the need for the preservation of African American heritage--a step farther in her next novel, *Mama Day*, which profoundly illustrates the importance of dreams within the African American folk community. In her most recent novel, *Bailey's Cafe* (1992), Naylor again takes up the dream metaphor, calling the cafe part of a "relay for broken dreams" (144); however, she turns it to a somewhat different purpose than in her earlier works. Where conflict exists between black and white dreams in her first three novels, in *Bailey's Cafe* Naylor subsumes white-defined dreams within the structure of a Black Cultural Nationalist presentation of African Americans, thereby undercutting their general culturally accepted meanings and articulating a series of different perceptions of success, gender roles, and American history.[1]

Novelist and critic Charles Johnson, who treats *The Women of Brewster Place* in his *Being & Race: Black Writing Since 1970* (1988), defines cultural nationalism in the following terms:

> Cultural Nationalism [presents] an apparently new American hunger for spirituality, moral values, breadth of vision, and a retreat from materialism in its more vulgar forms. . . . The political ground from which it springs is a sickened reaction against racism, individualism seen as selfishness and opportunism, American imperialist adventures after World War II, corruption in government and business, and the denial of black racial identity uncritically accepted by a few early proponents of integration. As such, the primary thrust of Cultural Nationalism is the reaffirmation of the hope of black men and women. . . . that they can lead lives of deeper creativity and spirituality.   (120)

Johnson's descriptions of the sources of Cultural Nationalism might well read as an interpretive handbook for the characters populating Naylor's fiction. In *Bailey's Cafe*, as in her earlier novels, one sees numerous characters struggling with forces such as governmental manipulation, financial exploitation and exclusion, and systematic denial of racial identity; however, through the major characters, *Bailey's Cafe* offers new perspectives on the struggle. Bailey and Eve, whose positions in this new world suggest parallels with Adam and Eve,[2] and their figurative "offspring" Miss Maple all find ways to subvert various white dreams, redefining traditional expectations and illustrating how both the other patrons of the cafe and the reader can transcend the systematic oversight and oppression that Cultural Nationalism seeks to undermine. Given the presence and power of the forces arrayed against the characters, the successes in the individual stories that the text comprises are at best bittersweet. Although the novel can present only a qualified positive resolution, Naylor nevertheless suggests the possibility for some growth that might lead to real changes in social and cultural definitions of African American identity from both inside and outside the community.

Bailey, Eve, and Miss Maple, like all the regulars at the cafe, come to their "edge of the world" as a result of formative experiences within the dominant culture (28). In each case, they have suffered rejection and failure that might have crushed a lesser person; however, each of them has found a means of subverting the assigned significance of their shortcomings and elevating themselves to a position of power that directly challenges those limitations. For Eve and Miss Maple, the challenges are deep and potentially devastating, and in presenting them Naylor opens the reader to entirely new definitions of sexuality and gender roles. In order to prepare the reader for those strong statements, Naylor begins with Bailey[3] who, although complex in his own right, presents a reasonably clear starting point for the identity reconstruction process.

Bailey begins with the warning that one cannot get the entire story of the cafe and its inhabitants "in a few notes. . . . [t]he answer is in who [he is] and who [his] customers are" (4). Although potentially a bit off-putting, the warning serves to introduce one of the novel's main points: it is a book about *being*, not about definition. In preparation for the series of stories we will hear in the text, Bailey establishes some of the parameters that will facilitate our understanding of them.

He begins by showing the dangers inherent in relying on limiting definitions of selfhood and reality. The child of servants in a wealthy black home, Bailey "grew up in Flatbush believing that Brooklyn was the capital of the world and that all colored people except for [his] family were rich" (4). Although he offers a perfectly rational explanation for his interpretation, one sees how expectations and empirical observation can limit one's perceptions. As he grows and hears his parents' conflicting definitions of various aspects of their life, Bailey begins to learn the value of multiple definitions and perspectives--his understanding of the Van Morrisons, who employ his parents, gains depth only when he hears (and communicates) his father's approval and his mother's disgust for them. Both his parents form opinions about the Van Morrisons that evolve from their particular preconceived notions of the world; as Bailey learns that he can and must balance these perceptions in order to grasp the meaning of his and his parents' experience more fully, he suggests to the reader the dangers inherent in judging too quickly or too harshly--only if we suspend or balance judgment, as Bailey does, can we benefit from the text.

Having provided the reader with that brief object lesson, Bailey then takes up his major point: the subversion and redefinition of the "American dream." We quickly learn that Bailey is obsessed with baseball, and the history of the sport's integration provides us with a subject for his point. Like many others, Naylor records an image of the African American experience in baseball that suggests the injustice and oppression superior athletes such as Josh Gibson, Satchel

Paige, Smokey Joe Williams, and Oscar Charleston faced because of institutionalized racism. Rather than merely crying foul or complaining about missed opportunities, however, Naylor uses this historical incident as a means by which to assert a version of reality that undercuts dominant attitudes and provides the model for the "blackening" of white dreams that recurs throughout the text.

In the course of his descriptions of the black leagues, Bailey rather pointedly explains the "need" for the Negro Leagues.

> I didn't question why Negroes had separate teams; watching their games and then the white games, it was pretty clear to me. The Negroes were better players. And just like us at school, who wanted to team up with the pee-pants who had snot running out their noses? No, winners stay with winners. But they could have been a little more fair-minded and let the likes of Honus Wagner or Ty Cobb on their teams.   (9)

Bailey's statement, which is striking for both its insight and its acerbity, suggests something important about the limitations of conventional definitions and the possibilities inherent in the flexion of those definitions. The most common understanding of the Negro Leagues is that they limited some of the greatest players of the game from having the kind of success that they rightly deserved. That characterization presupposes a heritage of victimization and oppression that has lasting, painful ramifications. By inverting the terms of segregation's significance, Bailey turns pain to celebration and affirms the power of the Negro League (and, by extension, the black race) to stand apart and be strong. In his description of the greatness of the black teams, Bailey articulates the first of the series of nationalist dreams that we will see in the novel. The *white* American Dream might be the major leagues, but Bailey clearly and pointedly shows how that is a pale imitation of his black dreams.

The re-establishment of particular players' reputations and the articulation of individual identities also has a significant place in this process. If Bailey merely complains in general, then he runs the risk of appearing a loudmouth with no reason other than racial pride for his proclamations. However, by naming names he avoids this pitfall and provides ample proof for his argument. Specifically, Bailey undercuts the common practice of comparing Negro League players to white Hall of Famers who might be better known, saying that "it leaves [him] confused, why these newspapermen look back at Pop [Lloyd]'s career and call him the Black Honus Wagner; all things being equal--or in this case unequal--the highest compliment to pay the Flying Dutchman is to call him the White Pop Lloyd" (10). This radical statement explodes an entire pattern of cultural definitions and suggests that the "rehabilitation" process by which sportswriters (and sports historians) have tried to "recover" the game is corrupt because of the influence of racist preconceptions about primacy and significance. Since no Negro Leaguer could possibly be as important as a Major Leaguer, then it "makes sense" to overlook records and make patronizing comparisons based on the established order. Using statistics, anecdotes, and pointed comparisons, Bailey deliberately undercuts this approach and thereby undermines the entire definition system of the established order.

In a final stunning blow, Bailey topples the established perceptions of race and sports by exploding the mythic stature of Jackie Robinson, who has just broken the color barrier as the novel begins. Admitting that he brought a great deal to the Brooklyn Dodgers, Bailey also notes that Robinson "*barely* made it into the Kansas City Monarchs" and "is a dime a dozen in a long-established *league*" (11). He then goes on to complain about African Americans who overlook the Negro Leagues in favor of Robinson's success in the white leagues, thereby illustrating the inviability of assimilation, a premise that Naylor has strongly avowed (*In Black and White* 1992). Because Robinson has bought into the white dream and taken a cadre of loyal African American fans with him, then, as Bailey explains it at least, the possibility for real integration no longer exists. With the Negro Leagues permanently and immutably relegated to second place in the cultural consciousness, there will be no room for black team ownership and acquisition of real power. Knowing that his position is unpopular, Bailey nonetheless clings to it, suggesting that "there are other cafes" for people who disagree (12). Although Bailey's position might appear excessively confrontational, it reveals a deep concern for the African American community. Aware of the difficulties that he and other African Americans face within the framework of the dominant white power structure, Bailey nevertheless resists the temptation to settle for the easy fix or the partial response to the issue. A lover of the game, he cannot settle for its corruption by the false promises of an integration that weakens its fiber. Instead, he suggests a different way of looking at the situation that calls for a more honest response to the issues at hand and that decries the acceptance of a set of dominantly-defined inferior answers.

In Bailey's monologue on baseball, Naylor provides a number of touchstones for the reader that both illustrate what is to come and suggest responses to the cultural forces at work in the historical moment of the novel's publication. The change in perception and the redefinition of the sports-American dream that baseball typically represents establishes a pattern that will persist throughout the novel; just as Naylor puts a Cultural Nationalist interpretation on African American sports history and on integration and segregation in particular through Bailey, she will take up other issues through the "nationalization" of other characters' dreams. In terms of the extra-textual applications, Naylor takes up the metaphor of the Negro Leagues at a moment when they have a particularly strong cultural significance[4] and redefines it, showing how what has been more typically a symbol for the failure of the African American community to achieve the American Dream can in fact be the engine for the reconfiguration of the dream itself--and thereby a source for the revision of African American identity in more positive terms.

Although baseball is the major point of Bailey's first conversation and a convenient means by which to get a sense of how the Cultural Nationalist agenda works in the text, it is not all that he thinks of or discusses. Significantly in his first speech, he notes that his marriage to Nadine, a strong, quiet woman who laughs internally without ever smiling, has given him "a whole different way of looking at her--and women" (19) that will stand him in good stead as he serves and helps narrate the stories of the various patrons in the cafe. It is this "new way of looking at women [and men]" that the reader must also internalize as s/he reads the various narratives in the main section of the text. Just as Bailey illustrates the dangers inherent in rigid acceptance of cultural definitions and patterns of judgment through his explanation of the reality of black baseball, he occasionally steps in to introduce situations that remind the reader of the ground rules of the novel's fictional world. In Jesse Bell's story, for instance, Bailey interrupts a tale including elements of adultery, lesbianism, and drug abuse to show Sister Carrie, the cafe's resident fundamentalist, and Eve, the proprietor of the unique boardinghouse down the block from Bailey's Cafe, battling over who has the right to pass judgment on the patrons of the cafe. As Eve reveals her upbringing in a minister's house and outstrips Carrie's knowledge of her beloved Bible, Bailey reminds the reader that judgment must be reserved if one is to learn from the stories the patrons tell.

Bailey also offers the reader an illustration of the risks accompanying excessive devotion to the dominant social order by telling Sadie's story. Born into the world of oppression and exploitation that fits the conventional definition of "whore," Sadie internalizes dominant cultural standards of behavior and values that lead to her ultimate self-destruction. Coming to rest in the bonds of a materialistic dream of the white picket fence, Sadie stumbles into prostitution in an effort to keep her house; when she fails in that effort, she turns to alcohol to preserve her dream house and again to prostitution to buy the alcohol she depends upon. Literally homeless, Sadie lives within a dream of whiteness and domesticity that sustains her; unfortunately, that sustenance becomes a substitute for reality. When Iceman Jones offers to marry her and give her a home, she rejects him in favor of her dream. Although she believes herself happy because she still has her "stars"--those of her dream and those on the label of the wine she is addicted to--the reader sees in her illusion a tragic example of a life destroyed by adherence to dominant cultural dreams. Naylor places Sadie's narrative at the beginning of the text, thereby offering a cautionary tale for the reader to which s/he can refer as a means of better grasping the significance of most of the stories in the text. After Bailey has charted the rough outlines of the fictional territory and has shown the reader the dangers of complacency, the other characters present dreams that need revision. The main interpreters of these dreams are the other two principal narrators, Eve and Miss Maple.

In many ways, Eve is the most familiar of the narrators in *Bailey's Cafe*. Scarred by her Godfather's rejection of her after discovering her sexual desires, Eve has made a place for herself down the block from Bailey's Cafe where she can nurture women like herself who have been burned and branded by societal definitions of what morality and proper behavior "should" be. In many ways she clearly resonates with other nurturing figures in Naylor's canon, particularly Mattie Michael of *The Women of Brewster Place* and Mama Day. Like each of her predecessors, Eve commits herself to empowering women rendered powerless by circumstance and experience. However, unlike both Mattie Michael and Mama Day, she does so in terms that recognize oppressive social conditions and teach survival rather than pure transcendence. Rather than dreaming of tearing down walls, Eve shows the women within her walls how to articulate their individual positions of power and to claim their right to selfhood by inverting the dreams that once bound them. As a part of this process, she challenges a series of cultural definitions about womanhood that severely limit her boarders' dreams.

Naylor has said that "the core of [*Bailey's Cafe*] is indeed the way in which the word *whore* has been used against women or to manipulate female sexual identity" (Fowler 150). The term, and all of the shame associated with it, is an integral part of Eve's experience. Like Mattie Michael before her, Eve wears the label as punishment for the "crime" of allowing her natural sexual desires to manifest themselves. Literally and figuratively purged from her old life by Godfather, Eve begins the long journey away from this nadir and becomes in the process the "delta dust" that infiltrates every orifice of her body. On the surface, "delta dust" might seem to be a metaphor for the suffering of her journey, the thousand-year walk away from her first home in Pilottown. However, Eve points out, there are a great many women who come to her door bearing the marks of their suffering who do not "know about delta dust" (81). What the women who gain admission to Eve's house seem to share is some awareness of the extent to which outside forces have circumscribed their feminine identities; delta dust is, after all, the substance that stopped Eve's menstrual flow. Delta dust is also a force larger than the particular male, Godfather, who set her on the road toward her present reality. This is what Eve seeks--a consciousness of suffering that extends beyond individual injustice. Only with some willingness to acknowledge the magnitude of the forces arrayed against them can the women benefit from Eve's nurturance and rehabilitation.

"Rehabilitation" might be a problematic term in relation to Eve's house, since one does not typically associate that concept with a bordello, even when the currency of the house is fresh flowers from Eve's garden (a link to the emphasis on growth and nature in *Mama Day*) and not cash. Nevertheless, Eve's main business is a sort of re-education of her boarders. Beginning with the nurturance of self-esteem that comes with each bouquet of flowers, Eve helps her boarders learn their own worth and, in the process, escape from the bondage of dominant-cultural dreams that have limited their development (Fowler 125). Like Bailey, she helps her boarders redefine the dreams and take control of their situations in terms more congenial to their experiences. For boarders like Peaches, the subject of "Mary (Take One)," who has scarred her hauntingly beautiful face as a means of freeing herself from the male dreams of possession that plague her, Eve's restoration of selfhood holds much promise. By setting the price of Peaches' daffodils high and demanding that she accept only the "freshest" of flowers, Eve weeds out the men who still wish to objectify her and works towards the discovery of a single man who will understand her value.

This subversion of larger societal dreams is direct and powerful and offers some hope for the future; Eve's promise to Peaches' father, who is in some ways responsible for her suffering because of his obsession with her beauty, is "Go home, my friend. I'll return your daughter to you whole" (114). Although Eve is no plastic surgeon and cannot repair the physical damage Peaches has done to herself, she does indeed help the still-beautiful woman heal, a successful attempt clearly figured in Peaches' articulation of her identity in the spiritual she raises at George Andrews' birth late in the novel.[5] Eve's success in helping Peaches is perhaps the strongest and most clearly positive of her actions. Although she has much to offer to her other boarders as well, many of them labor under the burden of heavier dreams, situations that demand more of her and them than the regulation of flower prices and the restriction of visitors.

In "Jesse Bell," the story that follows Peaches' tale, Naylor takes up themes she treated in *Linden Hills*, namely the dangers African American women must face when they marry into class-conscious families; however, through her experiences with Eve, Jesse Bell finds ways to redefine the suffering and make it the foundation of new dreams. Of lower-class but extremely proud origins, Jesse Bell marries into the King family, a powerful, class-conscious clan like the Nedeeds. Unlike the Nedeeds, however, the King men do not always choose women willing to cast off their former identities in service of the family dream. Jesse Bell is a prime example; despite the resistance she encounters from King patriarch Uncle Eli, she struggles valiantly, and for a time successfully, to assert herself and to preserve her identity. The positive aspects of her Bell family identity are numerous, and one sees in it a system of defense that the other King women lack. Early on in her marriage she gains control of her own household, mastering her husband with her strong sexuality and her culinary skills, and for a time she even manages to bridge a gap between the Bells and Kings that suggests new hope for inter-class relations within the black community.

That hope is, unfortunately, short-lived and withers with the birth of her son; as Jesse Bell stands hopelessly by, he and her husband gradually grow away from her until she is left with nothing of herself or that life to call her own. Part of the blame for this rests with her, as she gives into a dominant dream of her familial role and sacrifices herself to her new family, saying of her husband and son "they were all I lived for" (118). The larger portion of the blame, however, belongs to Uncle Eli, who tries to erase her family identity as he simultaneously promulgates a vision founded on a view of blackness and black heritage that spells doom for Jesse Bell's family and her sense of self.

Although Jesse Bell "didn't see a damn thing wrong with being colored" (125), in marrying into the King family she has joined a society rules by dreams of assimilation. Uncle Eli's main goal is the elevation of the race in general, and his family in particular, to the level of whites; he sees Jesse Bell as a threat to his plan and deliberately sets out to undermine her influence. In her account of the events at her house, one sees how Uncle Eli has spread lies about her that play into the white preconception of blacks; the myths about orgies, card parties, drunkenness, and knife fighting all originate in a white-defined conception of blackness that assigns the African American community a place of shame. Uncle Eli's ready use of this mythology, as well as his aspirations of assimilation, illustrate his implication in the oppression of blacks through the power of white dreams. Naylor has spoken at length about the impossibility of assimilation as a response to the question of race relations in America (*In Black and White* 1992); the fact that white folks are Uncle Eli's "god" indicates the completeness of his corruption (125). Like the Luther Nedeeds, Eli wants what the dominant culture values, and his service to this dream leads to the destruction of Jesse Bell and her family just as the Nedeed women have suffered gradual obliteration.[6]

Unlike the Nedeed women, however, Jesse Bell does not take her erasure passively; she fights it as she sees it creeping into her home throughout her son's adolescence, and when she finally breaks with the King family for good, she seeks alternative means of self-affirmation. When alcohol and lesbianism no longer give her the respective release and the sense of self she requires, she turns to heroin for solace. Ironically, of course, Jesse Bell's attempts at gaining release ultimately leave her feeling increasingly bound; however, on her arrival at Eve's she undergoes a process of purging and self-restoration that allows her the chance to finally achieve a form of freedom and the chance to control her own dreams.

When Jesse Bell finally finds Eve's after several failed attempts, one of Eve's first actions is to take her to the back door of Bailey's cafe, which looks out into oblivion, and to ask her what she sees. Jesse Bell's initial reply that she sees "nothing" convinces Eve that she is not yet ready to quit taking heroin; since visions appear in the void only when one dreams them, Jesse Bell's blankness indicates that she is still mired in the nihilism that led her to her addiction in the first place. Only when they look again and see the common vision of the private bathroom they both dreamed of as little girls does Eve believe that Jesse Bell has enough hope left to quit. When she knows that this woman can still dream, then Eve is willing to help her. In the process of delivering her help, however, Eve turns Jesse Bell's dream of freedom from addiction into a repeating nightmare as she takes her new boarder through withdrawal, back into addiction, and through withdrawal yet again. Only when Jesse Bell has repeated the process a sufficient number of times can she change her dream from freedom to survival--a grimmer, but nevertheless more realistic, aspiration.[7]

The pattern of Jesse Bell's story also emphasizes Naylor's Cultural Nationalist ideas. All of the killing forces that have shaped Jesse Bell's dream are characterized by figurative or literal whiteness. The white power that holds sway over Uncle Eli and the white powder that Jesse Bell craves are not fundamentally different on a symbolic level, as both lead to the gradual obliteration of Jesse Bell's familial and individual identities. Jesse Bell has merely changed white masters in her struggle for release; it is only when Eve gives her the power to triumph over whiteness through her successful struggle with her addiction that Jesse Bell can truly control her dreams and begin to reclaim her identity despite all the forces marshaled against her. Her control extends even to her insistence that dandelions, which Eve would normally weed out of her garden, be *her* flower. Jesse Bell knows that her "gentlemen callers" come because "of those lies in the paper" that Uncle Eli has spread, and those "who try to visit her get their flowers smashed right in their faces at the door" (116). Her refusal to entertain anyone is part of the means by which she can reject others' definitions of her--Uncle Eli has even given her name particular significance as "Jesse Bell came to mean that no-good slut from the docks" (131)--and begin to reclaim a life of her own and with it the right to dream.

Eve's treatment of Jesse Bell emphasizes both her connections to and differences from earlier Naylor heroines. Like Mattie Michael and Mama Day before her, Eve gives Jesse Bell a ritualized bath as part of her nurturance; however, unlike her predecessors, Eve has a role in Jesse Bell's suffering that indicates deeper layers to this image. Eve's method of curing Jesse Bell by repeatedly re-addicting her and then forcing her into withdrawal is as nightmarish as it is effective. Rather than offering a respite from suffering, Eve forces Jesse Bell to suffer relentlessly until she knows beyond doubt that she can survive and resist the temptation to submit once again to the whiteness that has held her so hard for so long. In the portrayal of this process and the promise that there are countless materials out of which to make the needles Jesse Bell depends on as an addict, Naylor illustrates the magnitude of the threat white culture presents to black dreams and identities. The process of self-purification is damaging and painful, but, as Jesse Bell learns, it is the only way to get to the point where the whiteness is no longer in control, the location one must reach in order to build anything of value.

Eve's guidance in Jesse Bell's dream revision and her illustration of the hard edges of her love partially prepare us for "Mary (Take Two)," the section of the novel that recounts the travails of Mariam, the African adolescent who appears on the block pregnant and insisting that she is a virgin. Because she has been subjected to the process of infibulation, her claim that "*no man has ever touched me*" is provable, and she does appear to be the bearer of a miracle (143). That her baby will be George Andrews, whose sacrificial action to preserve Cocoa's life in *Mama Day* makes him something of a Christ figure, further emphasizes the extraordinariness of her situation. Equally, if perhaps not more, important, however, is the ritualized mutilation she has undergone. A practice enacted to ensure chastity, infibulation represents the fruition of a series of dreams designed to control women's identities and selfhood. Because she wants her daughter to be valuable within their culture, Mariam's mother buys into the dream and has the "midwives close her up . . . tightly" (152), thereby ultimately heightening her suffering.

Mariam comes to the block and Bailey's Cafe, therefore, bearing a legacy of pain and gender oppression that extends well back into the heritage of many African cultures. In showing the reader this image, Naylor offers a version of one of her principal tenets: the belief that African Americans need to "build self-esteem from the cradle" (*In Black and White* 1992). As an adolescent within a culture that institutionalizes mutilation as a means of controlling female sexuality, Mariam as individual reflects the tragic result of not instilling self-esteem; furthermore, as a representative of the "cradle" of civilization and particularly of African American civilization, Mariam's infibulation stands as a warning to readers of the damage consistently inflicted on women, and particularly women of color, throughout history.

Mariam cannot ultimately break free of the rigidity of dreams that shape her experience; when she wishes to cleanse herself after George's birth, in the manner of her heritage, she calls up "endless water" for purification and perishes in the void behind the cafe (228). Nevertheless, her story, and the birth of her son, offers the other patrons of the cafe a chance to see the need for the subversion of dominant dreams; although she does not live to hear the song Peaches raises, Mariam is, in many ways, the inspiration for the articulation of selfhood it represents. As the African link in the chain of empowerment the patrons are forging through their dream revisions, Mariam is central to the success of Naylor's Cultural Nationalist project; she represents the reclamation of a heritage that includes both pain and celebration and the possibilities inherent in a life touched by a full awareness of that heritage. All of the patrons of the cafe are changed by Mariam's presence and George's birth--Eve cries for the first time, Esther smiles, and Peaches sings; in bringing Mariam into this world Naylor pointedly illuminates the cultural sources of much of the rehabilitation process she chronicles.

With her limited understanding of Western culture and her alternative experiences of women's roles, Mariam proves something of a challenge to the readers' preconceived attitudes. More difficult, however, is Miss Maple, the cleaning "lady" at Eve's who, in many ways, presents the clearest articulation in the novel of Naylor's dream agenda. Miss Maple challenges almost all of our society's established notions about gender, race, and success. Through his methodical, dispassionate account of his heritage, his struggle, and his eventual success, Miss Maple brings the Nationalist subtext of *Bailey's Cafe* into focus.

Naylor has commented that Miss Maple and Bailey are "bookends" for the stories in *Bailey's Cafe* and explained the ways in which the two men are diametrically opposed--Bailey as the most conventional of males, Miss Maple as the least bound by gender definitions (Fowler 150). She also notes that one cannot have the story of these women's suffering without accounts of men's suffering, "*the same way we could not have white people without black people here in America*" (Fowler 150, emphasis added). In her deliberate equation of the racial makeup of America with this figure who so strongly challenges myriad social definitions, Naylor articulates the importance of this portrait to the framework of her text. She also indicates her sense of the limitless possibilities inherent in the redefinition of racial roles as well; as Miss Maple learns that manhood can take many forms, he simultaneously grasps the breadth of his father's understanding of blackness. This understanding enables him to take control of his own dreams and thereby to assert a strong personal and cultural identity and to claim a position of prominence in the textual world indicated by his *employment*, not just residence, at Eve's and his intentions of leaving the limbo in the near future.

The richness of Miss Maple's story as cultural commentary manifests itself early on in the details of his personal heritage. The son of wealthy landowners in California, Miss Maple bears living witness to the historical role African Americans played in the settlement of the American West. With the inclusion of details such as the 1855 California state convention of African Americans (169) and the intermarriage of African- and Native Americans, Naylor uses Miss Maple to explore a side of American history that remains unknown to most people--even people of color, as Naylor illustrates when Miss Maple pointedly notes that Sugar Man has no sense of the importance of his string of middle names: Beckwourth Booker Taliaferro Washington Carver, all of which represent African Americans whose accomplishments merit broad societal recognition. By introducing this extended list of prominent African American historical figures and emphasizing that many black people do not recognize them, Naylor reminds the reader of the damage that received versions of the American past have done to many African Americans' sense of self and calls for readers to challenge also such established definitions and opinions.

In the example of Miss Maple's father, a seemingly ineffectual, passive intellectual who rejects conventional definitions of manhood and racial expectations in order to teach his son "how to be [his] own man" (173), the reader sees what one who internalizes this textual lesson can become: a truly free person, who literally and figuratively beats the forces of oppression into submission with superior strength, intelligence, and sense of identity. In the cathartic battle with the Gatlins, who have assaulted Miss Maple and his father and defiled the set of Shakespeare volumes the father purchased for his son, Miss Maple finally sees the strength and grace in his father; up until that point, the son has been blinded by his internalization of societal ideas about manhood and appropriate responses to racism. Literally and figuratively stripped naked by the devastating encounter with the Gatlins, Miss Maple must set aside a number of his preconceptions in order to survive. He and his father must dress in women's clothing in order to protect themselves as they assert the manhood that the racist white society would deny them; similarly, the son finally comes to see how the father's unconventional world view affords him a measure of freedom and power unlike anything he has ever seen before. As Miss Maple struggles to make his way in the world, he will adopt both his father's attitude and, in times of necessity, the manner of dress that went with that moment of enlightenment as a means of defining himself and defending himself in the face of onslaughts from the white world.[8]

The idea of being surrounded by whiteness takes on even more significance when one considers that Miss Maple's father has developed his unique sense of self in the middle of a vast and very successful cotton plantation. Usually the image of an African American surrounded by whiteness indicates a sense of powerlessness and frustration; however, Miss Maple's father represents an inversion of that pattern. His isolation within the whiteness of the cotton enables him to develop the strong but flexible awareness of identity, born of his inversion of the American dream of financial success, that he passes on to his son. And ultimately Miss Maple shows his own power and Naylor illustrates his symbolic importance when he calls down his own version of this white sea in the snowfall that greets his look into the void behind the cafe.[9]

Before he dreams the snowfall, however, Miss Maple must undergo a series of trials that strengthen his resolve and his ability to resist white oppression. As he suffers through imprisonment, racism at Stanford, and institutionalized discrimination in his job search, Miss Maple becomes in many ways more and more like his father. Like him, Miss Maple resists destruction and refuses to believe that success in his search for work is impossible; also like him, he adopts women's clothing as a means of self-defense when more conventional methods of dress are either useless or detrimental to his purpose.[10] Throughout this search, the reader sees Miss Maple dreaming of personal success while resolutely resisting the boundaries of the society that would limit him. Regardless of how often he is rejected, Miss Maple persists in his pursuit of employment, stopping his visits to particular companies only when they make their racist hiring policies explicit. Although this process does not yield him a job, it does illustrate the extent to which his power grows, as he makes it impossible for racism to exist tacitly in these situations--by forcing companies into the position of articulating their discrimination, Miss Maple changes the dynamics of control in the situations, if only slightly. And one has the sense that in the long run these slight changes are worth much more than the deceptive tokenism that threatens him at Waco Glass and Tile, the ninety-ninth place he applies for a position as a marketing analyst.

In the ninety-ninth interview, Miss Maple very nearly lands a job. Because the way has been paved with the hiring of the "second in command at layout and design" (207), Miss Maple would not be the radical addition to the company that he would have been in the first ninety-eight places he applied. Although that seems to be promising at first and the position appears to be a "dream job," as it were, one soon sees that the hiring of Miss Maple's black predecessor, like Jackie Robinson's breaking of the color barrier in baseball, has closed the door on opportunities for real integration and progress. The second in command lives a life bound by extremely tight limits, a restrictedness figured in the cleanness of his bib over the lobster thermidore and the ritualized catharsis of his rage through the shredding of that same bib. Miss Maple narrowly escapes a similar fate by asserting himself at the lunch table--when he gets comfortable, he violates the tight parameters of experience that the job would require him to live in, and he must again take to the streets.

The events at Waco Glass and Tile force Miss Maple to temporarily abandon his conventional dreams of success and independence and lead him to Bailey's Cafe and a position as Eve's housekeeper and bouncer. In that role, he completes the explosion of conventional boundaries that began with his father's lessons and finds his way to a new sense of self beyond the reaches of the power structure against which he has struggled so valiantly for so long. Comfortable in a space between conventional definitions, Miss Maple can both clean the rooms literally and "clean house" when the "gentlemen callers" become unruly.

From that position, Miss Maple also becomes the clearest example of success on the block. In his spare time between cleaning and keeping order and at Eve's urging, Miss Maple writes jingles for marketing contests; his superior knowledge of the marketplace and his experience with the products combines to make him incredibly successful at this game, and at the end of the novel he stands almost ready to leave the block with the capital necessary to start his own business. The beautiful irony of his position is that in his jingles, most of which play upon dominant societal constructions and racial attitudes, he has found a way to exploit the companies that would not hire him and to achieve his original goal of financial independence without having to give in as the second in command before him did. One might argue that the companies exploit him as well by getting slogans from him; however, it seems most significant to note that he is getting paid for this work by companies that would not knowingly hire him. He has realized his personal dream and simultaneously redefined the American dream of corporate success. In this portrait, and particularly in the final image of white snow flakes melting in the "amber world" of the champagne Miss Maple has bought with his contest winnings, Naylor suggests the potential inherent in a world view grounded in a refusal to submit to dominant ideals and an insistence on both the value of the self and the right to dream despite repeated threats to those dreams and that identity. In this way, she does indeed fill the agenda of "reaffirm[ing] the hope of black men and women" that Charles Johnson identifies as central to the Cultural Nationalist approach.

Although Miss Maple appears to be headed back to the world armed with the tools he will need to realize his dreams and therefore stands as a representative of the positive potential for black dreams, one should not make the mistake of assuming that Naylor intends a happy ending for *Bailey's Cafe*. As Bailey himself says,

> If this was like that sappy violin music on Make-Believe Ballroom, we could wrap it all up with a lot of happy endings to leave you feeling real good that you took the time to listen. But I don't believe that life is supposed to make you feel good, or to make you feel miserable either. Life is just supposed to make you feel. (219)

Miss Maple's story, which does make one feel good, is balanced immediately by the tale of George Andrews' birth and Mariam's dream of "endless water" (228) which causes her death. Mariam still does not have control of her dreams, a tragedy that leads her to self-destruction; similarly, her son, George, will also have to die to advance the process of dream reclamation, a circumstance the reader already knows of from *Mama Day* that undeniably qualifies the promise in his birth. The message in this double tragedy is both important and painful: the success Miss Maple achieves in controlling dominant dreams is rare and hard-won. Although it is not impossible to succeed as he has, Naylor does not hesitate to remind the reader on the heels of his victory that failure is equally probable and more common.

The emphasis on the possibility for failure, while it undercuts the hope of the success story, is a necessary balancing comment within the larger structure of the novel. Throughout *Bailey's Cafe*, the process of dream-redefinition has been equal parts pleasure and pain, equal instances of success and failure. Since the power structure the characters have been challenging still exists, then the best that one can hope for is qualified success in the struggle against it, as one sees in the series of stories the cafe patrons tell. Nevertheless, that is not to say that all is hopeless at novel's end; rather, it is indefinite, a situation perfectly reflected in Bailey's statement that one must face life with "more questions than answers." Such a situation can make life "a crying shame" (228); however, it can also lead to the kind of success that Miss Maple has had with his contests. The central determining factor is how one approaches life--the idea of having "more questions than answers" means, in addition to not knowing enough, that one is willing and able to resist definitions. Taking this path, Naylor suggests, leads to the balance of pleasure and pain that her characters are achieving and that is infinitely preferable to the life of just pain that comes with the pressure of too many definitions. In this final statement, Naylor suggests once again that the key to success of any sort is the rejection of dominant definitions and the aggressive pursuit of self through the process of asking more questions than the received answers provide. By avoiding that bondage to definite and defining ideas, one can gain the strength and the sense of self necessary to take control of one's own dreams.

Endnotes

[1] In a 1993 interview, Naylor strongly disavowed her previous devotion to Cultural Nationalist ideas (Fowler 143); however, in a videotaped interview that appeared in the same year as *Bailey's Cafe* (*In Black and White* 1992), Naylor's focus is almost exclusively on the importance of her Cultural Nationalist ideas in her work. Although one might speculate that her work on the forthcoming *Sapphira Wade* will take her away from her earlier intellectual positions, *Bailey's Cafe* is clearly influenced by her nationalism.

[2] For a full discussion of Eve as Biblical figure, see Fowler 124.

[3] By his own admission, "Bailey" is not the cafe owner's "real" name; he adopted it in response to customers' assumptions that it must be his identity since it is the name on the cafe window and he is the proprietor of the cafe. This denial illustrates the process of un-naming by which members of a society, particularly minority members, suffer the loss of identity in the face of cultural and/or social assumptions. It seems reasonable that the owner of Bailey's Cafe would be Bailey. While this is a relatively benign example, it points to one of the serious problems that Naylor addresses through the systematic un-naming that is part of this text: identity consistently stands at risk from outside influences, and one must learn to control those forces if he or she is to either preserve or recreate a personal identity.

[4] Although one might consider a number of sources in the course of discussing the prominence of the Negro Leagues as metaphor in recent years, perhaps the most pertinent example for the issues at hand is August Wilson's Pulitzer Prize-winning play, *Fences* (1986), in which an aging ex-ballplayer, Troy Maxson, uses his inability to break into the major leagues as a sort of shorthand for all of his racial frustrations. Although Maxson and Bailey would undoubtedly agree about the greater skills and achievements of players in the Negro Leagues, Maxson cannot see beyond the limitations--hence the title of the play--that Bailey takes up and turns into strengths.

[5] For an interesting reading of the particular significance of the song, see Fowler 138-139. Fowler also delineates the Biblical metaphor Naylor implements in her stories of Eve's

boarders and treats the whole issue of rehabilitating feminine identity through the exploration of the term "whore."

[6] Naylor has commented on the "Nedeed" name as an inversion of "de Eden," an indicator of the Hell that Linden Hills represents; however, the name is also a corruption of "Needed," and it is that variation that resonates more strongly in Jesse Bell's case. Like the Nedeed women who are cast aside after bearing the one son they are required to produce, Jesse Bell is gradually no longer *needed* by the King family. The irony of her increasing uselessness to the King clan resonates powerfully in the name of the earlier group of women with whom she shares so many similar experiences.

[7] See also Fowler, 126, for a consideration of Jesse Bell's repeated addictions and a commentary on the Biblical quotation Naylor integrates in the passage.

[8] Given the Cultural Nationalist tone of this section of the novel, one might well wonder what to make of the fact that a set of Shakespeare volumes is so profoundly important in the first moment of Miss Maple's development. Although one could view Shakespeare as a sort of shorthand for the dominant European culture that a Nationalist agenda would seek to subvert, one must not overlook that Miss Maple and his father are having Shakespeare *on their own terms*; they do not rewrite the plays, but in asserting their rights to claim the volumes from ignorant whites who have no sense of their value, they revise their cultural meaning. In a sense, Miss Maple and his father have laid a claim on a symbol of whiteness, thereby taking power away from the surrounding culture that would deny them. The motif also continues a process in *Bailey's Cafe* that several critics have noted throughout Naylor's canon: her invocation and revision of Shakespearean motifs in her work. See, for example, Peter Erickson's essay, "'Shakespeare's Black?': The Role of Shakespeare in Naylor's Novels," reprinted in Gates and Appiah, 231-248, and his review of the novel, Gates and Appiah 32-34.

[9] The presence of snow in the void resonates in many ways with Richard Wright's use of snow imagery in *Native Son*; however, where Bigger Thomas is controlled by the whiteness and ultimately trapped in it, Miss Maple demonstrates his total control of it through his dream of snow as a sign of celebration instead of despair.

[10] Interestingly, Miss Maple notes that he would not have to resort to wearing women's clothing if he chose instead to pass as a member of a culture in which business clothing was more informal (201). However, he cannot retain his American identity and dress in those clothes, and to reject his cultural identity is unthinkable if Miss Maple is to preserve his sense of self. In presenting this detail Naylor makes clear the foundation of her nationalistic position; the African roots she presents in the story of Mariam's suffering must be balanced with the Americanness that Miss Maple clings to if one is to assume the position of strength required to manage one's dreams and assert identity in the terms she advocates.

Works Cited

Andrews, Larry R. "Black Sisterhood in Naylor's Novels." In *Gloria Naylor: Critical Perspectives Past and Present*. Eds. Henry Louis Gates, Jr. and K. A. Appiah. New York: Amistad, 1993. 285-302.

Christian, Barbara. "Gloria Naylor's Geography: Community, Class, and Patriarchy in *The Women of Brewster Place* and *Linden Hills*." In *Reading Black, Reading Feminist: A Critical Anthology*. Ed. Henry Louis Gates, Jr. New York: Meridian, 1990. 348-373.

Christol, Héléne. "Reconstructing American History: Land and Genealogy in Gloria Naylor's *Mama Day*." In *The Black Columbiad: Defining Moments in African American Literature and Culture*. Eds. Werner Sollors and Maria Diedrich. Cambridge: Harvard UP, 1994. 347-356.

Erickson, Peter. "Review." In *Gloria Naylor: Critical Perspectives Past and Present*. Eds. Henry Louis Gates, Jr. and K. A. Appiah. New York: Amistad, 1993. 32-34.

_____. "'Shakespeare's Black?': The Role of Shakespeare in Naylor's Novels." In *Gloria Naylor: Critical Perspectives Past and Present*. Eds.

Henry Louis Gates, Jr. and K. A. Appiah. New York: Amistad, 1993. 231-248.

Fowler, Karen Joy. "Review." In *Gloria Naylor: Critical Perspectives Past and Present*. Eds. Henry Louis Gates, Jr. and K. A. Appiah. New York: Amistad, 1993. 26-28.

Fowler, Virginia C. *Gloria Naylor: In Search of Sanctuary*. Twayne United States Authors Series, #660. New York: Simon & Schuster Macmillan, 1996.

In Black and White: Gloria Naylor. Matteo Bellinelli, dir. San Francisco: California Newsreel, 1992.

Johnson, Charles. *Being and Race: Black Writing Since 1970*. Bloomington: Indiana UP, 1988.

Levy, Helen Fiddyment. "Lead on with Light." In *Gloria Naylor: Critical Perspectives Past and Present*. Eds. Henry Louis Gates, Jr. and K. A. Appiah. New York: Amistad, 1993. 263-284.

Naylor, Gloria. *Bailey's Cafe*. New York: Harcourt Brace, 1992.

_____. *Linden Hills*. New York: Penguin, 1986.

_____. *Mama Day*. New York: Vintage, 1989.

_____. *The Women of Brewster Place*. New York: Penguin, 1983.

Rifkind, Donna. "Review." In *Gloria Naylor: Critical Perspectives Past and Present*. Eds. Henry Louis Gates, Jr. and K. A. Appiah. New York: Amistad, 1993. 28-29.

Saunders, James Robert. "The Ornamentation of Old Ideas: Gloria Naylor's First Three Novels." In *Gloria Naylor: Critical Perspectives Past and Present*. Eds. Henry Louis Gates, Jr. and K. A. Appiah. New York: Amistad, 1993. 249-262.

Showalter, Elaine. *Sister's Choice: Tradition and Change in American Women's Writing*. Oxford: Clarendon, 1991.

Wakefield, Dan. "Review." In *Gloria Naylor: Critical Perspectives Past and Present*. Eds. Henry Louis Gates, Jr. and K. A. Appiah. New York: Amistad, 1993. 30-31.

Page, Philip. "Living with the Abyss in Gloria Naylor's *Bailey's Cafe*." Published with permission from *CLA Journal* and the author.

In Toni Morrison's *Jazz*, the imagery of wells is significant. Because Violet Trace's mother committed suicide by jumping into a well, Violet's severe depression and near suicide are centered on her fears of wells: "the well sucked her sleep" (102), she is "scare[d] by deep holes" (223), and she is lured by the "limitless beckoning from the well" (101) and by "the pull of a narrow well" (104). The well is an image of death--enclosed, dark, and final, much like a grave or a coffin. It is a fixed point, a closed circle, where variation, alternatives, movement, play, indeed life, all cease. Yet Violet's extreme withdrawal is erroneously based on her attempts to repress her mother's suicide, her own suicidal tendencies, and therefore the well. Her recovery is couched in terms of her acceptance of the well as a necessary and even salutary fact of life: when she and her husband Joe are spiritually reunited at the end of the novel, "she rests her hand on his chest as though it were the sunlit rim of a well" (225).

The narrator of Morrison's novel, a curious mixture of first-person gossip and third-person omniscience, provides an extended gloss on this image. When she "dream[s] a nice dream" for Golden Grey, she places him "next to a well," "standing there in shapely light," "not aware of its mossy, unpleasant odor, or the little life that hovers at its rim, but to stand there next to it and from down in it, where the light does not reach, a collection of leftover smiles stirs, some brief benevolent love rises from the darkness" (161). The narrator reaches the same position as Violet: the choice is not whether to plunge into the death-hole or to try to avoid it; instead, mental health is found *next* to the well, where the play between light and dark, life and death, self and other can be welcomed. For the narrator and Violet, as well as for Joe, Golden Grey, and Morrison, only after the well is acknowledged can one attain psychological wholeness.

Jacques Derrida, meditating on the ontology of books, describes "the unnameable bottomless well" (*Writing* 297) as "the abyss" (296), an image of the center that is "the absence of play and difference, another name for death" (297). Any book, as a completed, enclosed entity, "was to have insinuated itself into the dangerous hole, was to have furtively penetrated into the menacing dwelling place" (297-298). For Derrida, only by repetition, only by embracing the play, does one escape from this well/trap. If we return to the book, to the hole, we attain a "strange serenity" (298) and we are "fulfilled . . . by remaining open, by pronouncing nonclosure." As for Morrison, the well is a potentially dangerous opening, abyss, or "labyrinth," but at the same time an opportunity for discovery, peace, and self-development. The well is destructive if taken as a fixed, monologic entity; but it is beneficial if taken as an unavoidable part of a fluid, multivalent, and complex orientation toward the open-endedness of being.

Such a link between Derrida and African American novelists such as Toni Morrison and Gloria Naylor is not as surprising as it may appear. Derrida and others urge a shift from a monologic, either/or perspective to an open, both/and stance in which attention is focused not only on fixed entities but on the *différance*, the endless flux within and between them. Presence *and* absence, self *and* other, ordinary space *and* the well are equally acknowledged. Such thinking thus shifts from the traditional Western emphasis on fixed entities and the irreconcilable separations between opposites to a blurring of boundaries and an embrace of inclusiveness.[1]

A similar shift is often advocated by those who have been historically excluded from mainstream Western culture. Feminist theorists, for example, have welcomed the doubled perspective afforded by women's insider/outsider status.[2] Similarly, the ambiguous status of African Americans within but outside mainstream American culture has necessitated a "double-consciousness," to use W. E. B. Du Bois' famous term. The doubleness is not only a curse but also a blessing, for it leads to "second-sight" (Du Bois 5) and a "special perspective" (Ellison 131), which allows for openness, the embrace of contradiction and paradox, and a broad inclusiveness, even of one's deepest fears.[3] Black feminist theorists have emphasized the unique perspective of black women as the other Other in American culture, a perspective that especially enables them to see all other perspectives.[4]

Like Morrison's fiction, Gloria Naylor's novels are empowered by her ability to carry readers into the bittersweet conditions of contemporary life. By depicting the complex and paradoxical mixtures of tragedy and joy in African American characters' lives, Naylor leads her characters and readers into the ambiguous but strangely satisfying realm of the *différance*, into life not in avoidance of the abyss but at its edge.

In Naylor's fiction, the only literal image of a well is the crucial scene in *Mama Day* in which Miranda overcomes her fears and opens the well where her sister Peace killed herself. As Gary Storhoff asserts, Miranda "ha[d] evaded the symbolic truth of the well" (42), fearing to face her family's tragedy. She had only sensed the loss felt by Peace's mother, ignoring the loss and grief also borne by her father. As for Violet Trace, opening the well enables Miranda to re-connect with the past, in her case to identify with her father's pain: "looking past the losing was to feel for the man who built this house and the one who nailed this well shut" (285). This opening at the edge of the well gives Miranda access to her paternal ancestry, which heretofore had been overshadowed by her reliance on her female ancestors, especially the Days' legendary foremother, Sapphira Wade. Opening herself to her father's grief not only contributes to the community's ongoing re-interpretations of its history and its identity, but it leads her to an understanding of George's strength of will and to her discovery of the means of saving her niece Cocoa.[5]

For Miranda, as for Violet, the well symbolizes the tragic familial past and the grief that cannot be borne or even admitted. To prevent future family tragedy, she must accept the past tragedy. She must "look past the pain" (283) --hers as well as her father's. To do so constitutes a reawakening: "She sleeps within her sleep. To wake from one is to be given back ears as the steady heart tells her--look past the pain; to wake from the other is to stare up at the ceiling from the mahogany bed and to know that she must go out and uncover the well where Peace died." The well itself is an image of death and decay: "a bottomless pit," full of "foul air," the surface of the water "slimy and covered with floating pools of fungus" (284). At first Miranda feels nothing, but, "refusing to let go of the edge," she closes her eyes and then viscerally feels the repressed pain: "And when it comes, it comes with a force that almost knocks her on her knees. She wants to run from all that screaming" (284). As in *Jazz*, the position at the side of the well is essential, for there one comes into significant relationship with the unimaginable. In such proximity, that other is no longer a fixed or originary entity inflated out of proportion because of its inaccessibility; instead, one can learn to know it by returning to it, consumed neither by its presence nor by a futile attempt to decree its absence. Instead of a deadend, the well becomes a vehicle for growth, play, serenity, insight, love.

Through a variety of metaphorical wells and well-like images, Naylor's fiction probes the issues associated with wells. Both Brewster Place and Linden Hills, the communities in which her first two novels are set, are like wells: the former is an urban block, closed from the bustling city by a high brick wall; the latter is a V-shaped hill whose circular drives wend downward to the Nedeed house. As Barbara Christian argues, both communities are "self-enclosed," cut off from the rest of American society, much like African Americans throughout American history ("Gloria" 352). Life in these well/traps is hellish, in Brewster Place primarily because of the impositions of white power, and in Linden Hills primarily because of the greed, envy, and social ambitions of the residents. In *The Women of Brewster Place*, there is no outside perspective, but *Linden Hills* includes the more humane attitudes of Willie and the Andersons, who live not in Linden Hills but just outside it. For them, generosity, empathy, and love far outweigh status and economic success; their perspectives, symbolically on the rim of the well, allow them to nurture their own and others' souls rather than to lose their souls like the residents of Linden Hills.[6]

In both novels, other well-like images reinforce the negativity. In The Women of Brewster Place the alley is a deadend within the deadend of Brewster Place. The domain of C. C. Baker's macho gang, it stands in opposition to the female-dominated street. In this novel there is no fusing of the two genders, no accommodations, only deadends. Hence, when the fragile Lorraine, who had futilely sought accommodation between her lesbian lifestyle and the community of heterosexual women, mistakenly enters the alley, it literally becomes her tomb. In Linden Hills, each house becomes a well/tomb for the African American inmates, each of whom has given up his or her soul in order to gain supposed status.[7] Laurel Dumont's empty swimming pool is literally her death/trap when she dives into it. But the house as tomb is most graphic for the generations of Nedeed women. Each is trapped, and/or allows herself to be trapped, in the house and obsessions of her husband. The series comes to its macabre conclusion with the last woman, Willa Prescott Nedeed, who, having failed to produce the proper replica of her husband, is locked in the basement with the corpse of her son, too white-skinned to satisfy her husband. In that well, a former morgue, she is "entombed in 'otherness'" like all black women (Werner 51) and like all African Americans. And in that well, Willa discovers traces of the myriad sufferings of the former Mrs. Nedeeds--in their journals, their recipes, their photograph albums. What she finds are not full representations but fragments, suggestive of the fragmented lives to which the women were reduced. According to Margaret Homans, Willa finds "a record simply of effacement and silencing" (159), not presence but presence of absence, a pattern repeated once again in Willa's own life (160). Forced in her captivity to confront herself, her history, and the histories of her predecessors, Willa awakens to her responsibilities for her own life (Ward 192). Having descended into the well, she can return to life only momentarily, only long enough to reorder her life, symbolized by her cleaning the kitchen, and to settle accounts with her husband. Despite the brevity of her return, the self-awareness she achieves in her agony indicates the power of such confrontation with the past and the hidden self, power that Miranda Day is able to marshall after she opens the well her father had sealed shut.

Mama Day is replete with examples of characters' harmful fixations on narrow objectives, obsessions that limit them to the closed unity of the well. The Day family history is marked by former suicides; Frances and Ruby exhaust themselves in their single-minded pursuit of Junior Lee; and George kills himself in his determination to be Cocoa's sole savior. As Susan Meisenhelder argues, characters who try to achieve their purposes in isolation (in a well) always fail, but success comes to those who perceive the quilt-like pattern of life in which everything and everyone is independent--a distinct piece of the fabric--but joined in harmony with all the other pieces.

In this novel, unlike Naylor's first two, the emphasis shifts from narrow failures to integrated successes. In The Women of Brewster Place Mattie mothers other women in her dimly realized sense of compassion but is powerless to prevent Lorraine's death, and the women's ritual attempt to tear down the wall is similarly futile. In Linden Hills, the community's failure is even worse, especially since it is self-imposed, although the momentary awakening of Willa and the potential of Willie suggest promising alternatives. But in Mama

Day, Miranda opens the well, thereby augmenting her already prodigious spiritual power. In *Mama Day* and *Bailey's Cafe*, the settings are again isolated communities, but in both the isolation is more positive than negative. Willow Springs, a place outside real history and geography, allows for a new perspective, not limited to the racial stereotypes and cultural restrictions of ordinary places.[8] Through Miranda, Abigail, Dr. Buzzard, and the whole island, Naylor delineates the therapeutic values of a position outside but adjacent to mainstream America, a position at the rim of the well that enables the characters and the reader to gain insight into the well and to live in harmony with their acceptance of it.

In *Bailey's Cafe* Naylor sets up a complex dynamic between the crushing stories of the characters who have drifted into the mystical neighborhood and the neighborhood itself, presided over by "Bailey" and his wife Nadine who run the cafe, Eve who manages the boarding house/bordello, and Gabriel who owns the pawn shop. The lives of these visitors to the neighborhood of Bailey's Cafe have been marred by their horrific encounters with racial and gender discrimination. That monologic power has been inflicted implacably, brutally, without question or hesitation. It has driven underground--into the well--the sensibilities and the dreams of each visitor. Each visitor tells a life story about his or her encounter with the symbolic well.

Sadie, never desired or loved, "f[e]ll through the cracks of the upswings and downswings" (41). Innately possessing a sense of beauty, "*class*" (68), and elegance, she is driven deeper and deeper into her private sorrow by inexorably harsh conditions. She tries to make a home with Daniel, but his drinking and the "trains thundering by" (64) their shack drive her further inward. When all her dreams fail,[9] liquor bottles become her personal well, as she finds solace only in the "stars" printed on them (65). The result of her years of psychological deprivation is that she internalizes the well, "the endless space of the black hole waiting to open in her heart" (64). The pathos of Sadie's story is that the brutality of her life has pushed her so deeply into the well that her dreams of a house, a picket fence, geraniums, laughter, Waterford crystal, and a good meal are so disconnected from reality that she cannot accept Iceman Jones' offer of a shared life (72-77).

Esther, another victim of male subjugation, is driven even farther into the psychological well. Directed at age twelve by her older brother to have sex in the dark basement with a man he calls her husband, she develops a psychosis that allows her to exist only in the dark basement of Eve's boarding house. Aside from the johns who must bring her white roses and call her "little sister," her only companions are the spiders and a radio hero called The Shadow. Because her brother cautioned her that "*We won't speak about this, Esther*," silence becomes her mode, as she never has "a word for what happens between us in the cellar" (97). She is at the bottom of the well, isolated in the dark, lacking Willa Nedeed's contacts with any predecessors, and therefore unable, like Willa, to reclaim her life.

For other lost souls, the well takes other forms. For Mary/Peaches it starts as the wall her father builds around their house to keep boys out and becomes the internal wall she builds between her repressed self and her whore self that she sees reflected in every man's lustful eyes. She disfigures her face in a futile attempt to eliminate that lust and thereby to integrate her two selves. For Jesse Bell the well is the alcohol and the heroin that she uses to blot out her history of mistreatment and loss. Her only sustaining hope is to return to her childhood bedroom, which becomes the image she dreams of.

Between these unfortunate visitors to the neighborhood and the four proprietors (Bailey, Nadine, Eve, and Gabe), is Miss Maple. He has experienced the well of prejudice he encountered at Stanford, during his three years in prison for evading the draft and then in the humiliation of his unsuccessful job search. But he is spared the extreme brutality that the women experienced and, perhaps as a result, he develops a more integrated response characterized by his female persona, his job as Eve's bouncer and janitor, his plans for his own company, and his success in jingle contests. He is the beneficiary of a radically diverse genealogy that includes African American, Native American, and Mexican ancestors, and a very wise father. That mixed ethnicity translates into his successful mixing of genders, when he sensibly yields to sexual aggression in prison and later chooses comfortable female clothing. These accommodations allow Miss Maple to find his own identity (to "be my own man" [173]), to be secure in his gender ("I am a man" [212]), and to be free ("And Eve has allowed Miss Maple to be one of the freest men I know" [216]).

Miss Maple thus shares many of the characteristics of the four proprietors of the neighborhood's businesses. They offer acceptance and solace based on a hard-nosed acknowledgment of life's brutalities, on a relativistic incorporation of multiplicity, on a gritty compromise at the rim of the well.

The neighborhood, in particular the cafe, is a metaphysical crossroads. It exists nowhere and everywhere, "right on the margin between the edge of the world and infinite possibility" (76). Like Willow Springs, it is not on any map, and yet "you can find [it] in any town" (112). It is a spiritual "way station" (221), a place "to take a breather for a while" (28), a place you have to already know about in your soul before you can find it: "If they can't figure out that we're only here when they need us, they don't need to figure it out" (28). As the epigraph[10] and the musical terminology in the chapter titles suggest ("The Jam," "Mary (Take One)," "Miss Maple's Blues," "The Wrap"), it is an incarnation of the blues (Montgomery 30). Here one is "damned-if-you-do-and-damned-if-you-don't" (229), and from here "the choices have always been clear: you eventually go back out and resume your life--hopefully better off than when you found us--or you head to the back of the cafe and end it" (221). The philosophy is tough love--you are neither hassled nor coddled; you follow the "routine" at the cafe or you don't eat; you play by Eve's "house rules" or you don't play (92).

Behind the cafe is the well. It is a "void" (76), an "endless plunge" (76), "black empty space" (137), where many visitors come to commit suicide (162). But, once the well is accepted--that is, once the implacable harshness of life, including death, is accepted--out back is also where dreams come true. Sadie and Jones "dance under the stars" out back (40), and Sadie "smile[s]" and "ha[s] her first real kiss" (76). There, Jesse Bell at first sees nothing but upon Eve's insistence looks again and sees her dream of "the simple bedroom she'd had as a girl" (137). There, Eve arranges the dream setting for Mariam: "the void out back produced exactly what [Mariam's] childlike mind called up: endless water" (228). There, Miss Maple, liberated from the confining impossibilities of real life,

steps off boldly into the midst of nothing and is suspended midair
by a gentle wind that starts to swirl his cape around his knees. It's

a hot, dry wind that could easily have been born in a desert, but it's bringing, of all things, snow. Soft and silent it falls, coating his shoulders, his upturned face. Snow. He holds his glass up and turns to me as a single flake catches on the rim before melting down the side into an amber world where bubbles burst and are born, burst and are born. (216)

The abyss is not threatening to Miss Maple or the four proprietors because they are accustomed to it, because they have accepted it and all it represents. They live at the edge of the well, so it is absorbed into their stoic acceptance of anything that life can dish out to them. Collectively, Bailey, Nadine, Eve, and Gabriel provide this perspective, which Naylor strongly privileges. They are clear-sighted, straightforward, and direct: Bailey claims "I call 'em the way I see 'em" (32) and praises Nadine for the same quality: "like me, she calls 'em as she sees 'em" (116). Like Miranda and Abigail in *Mama Day*, they are all realists, not trying to be nice but honest. Despite their sometimes rough exteriors, they are compassionate and tolerant, as their lives exist to help others endure or pass beyond the pain. They have no illusions about life, expecting little from it: Gabe knows that "the world, it still waits to commit suicide" and that "we do nothing here but freeze time" (219), and Bailey accepts that "the brotherhood of man . . . is a crock of bull" (220), that "people are people" (222), and that "life is [not] supposed to make you feel good, or to make you feel miserable either. Life is just supposed to make you feel" (219).

Also like Miranda and Abigail, these four proprietors all have extraordinary strength of character, which has prevented them from becoming victims. Nadine confines her letters to Bailey to "short short" ones, but with "perfect timing" (13), and unlike most people "doesn't bother" to "translate [her] feelings for the general population" (19). Eve, when confronted with her tyrannical father, escapes, treks through the delta, and eventually establishes her rigidly-run boarding house and her beloved garden (92). These characters are larger than life, possessing almost superhuman powers. Gabe is able to rescue Mariam; Bailey "can get inside a lot of heads around here" (165); and Nadine "look[s] like an African goddess" (13). Eve is the most mythical, becoming one with the delta dust (86) and walking across the delta for "a thousand years" (82). She knows the cafe routine before she arrives (80), "already knew" Esther's story (99), and "sets up" Mariam's dreamscape (224). She is a dreammaker, a transcendent heroine, a tough *griot*, reminiscent of Eva Peace in Toni Morrison's *Sula*. Like the other three, she is also an exile from ordinary reality: "it seemed there was nowhere on earth for a woman like me" (91). She and Nadine are the kind of women Naylor admires, women who have "turned their backs on the world" and who have "been selfish to some degree" (Naylor, "Gloria" 572). They, like Miranda, Abigail, Bailey, Gabriel, and Naylor, have said, "*I am here.* That *I* contains myriad realities--not all of them pretty, but not all of them ugly, either" (Naylor, "Love" 31).

Through her four presiding figures, and often through Bailey as their principal spokesperson, Naylor creates a world view that privileges tolerance, open-endedness, and complexity, all of which become possible when one has acknowledged and accepted the abyss, when, like Miranda, one has had the courage to open the well. The neighborhood accepts all comers, all who have suffered and who need relief. Customs from all over the world are welcomed:

Miss Maple admires the loose-fitting business clothes of nonwesterners (201), and Bailey enjoys the music of many cultures. At the end of the novel, the ritual performance of George's circumcision brings the community together in a celebration of cross-cultural harmony. This valuing of tolerance contrasts sharply with the refrain of intolerance and bigotry recited by the visitors to the neighborhood. As Karen Joy Fowler comments, the book's "abundance plays against the particular pains contained in the various characters' stories" (27).

The neighborhood's ethos of tolerance is reinforced by the belief that everything always remains open. Bailey expresses the apparently shared views that life has "more questions than answers" (229) and that "no life is perfect" (228). Instead of having answers or perfection, human beings are caught in endless flux: "If life is truly a song, then what we've got here is just snatches of a few melodies. All these folks are in transition; they come midway in their stories and go on" (219). Everything remains open partly because everything is more complex than it may appear. Iceman Jones knows "that most things aren't what they seem" (70), and Bailey warns readers "if you're expecting to get the answer in a few notes, you're mistaken" (4). This insistence on complexity is expressed in the metaphor of going under the surface. Bailey, listening closely to the stereotyped opinions of Sister Carrie and Sugar Man, warns readers not to oversimplify: "If you don't listen below the surface, they're both one-note players" (33). Hearing only that one note is insufficient, for everyone in this novel--and, Naylor implies, every human being--has a complex story: "But nobody comes in here with a simple story. Every one-liner's got a life underneath it. Every point's got a counterpoint" (34). Bailey's advice for readers is that "Anything really worth hearing in this greasy spoon happens under the surface. You need to know that if you plan to stick around here and listen while we play it all out" (35). Readers must learn what the four proprietors have learned and what the victimized visitors are struggling to learn--how to go below the surface, to "take 'em one key down" (34). All must learn not only tolerance for others but tolerance and understanding of the multiple layers of meanings.

In several respects the form of this novel exhibits these values of openness and depth. The musical metaphors around which the narrative is structured push the written medium toward a nondiscursive, nonprescriptive mode, a mode that suggests rather than defines, that opens rather than narrows. Similarly, the point of view is not restricted to one voice or one perspective. Although Bailey is the principal narrator, usually introducing and concluding each character's story, his voice is not sufficient. Maxine Lavon Montgomery argues that this multiplicity is necessary because "the male voice is severely limited in its ability to decode the very private experiences the women relate" (28). But the larger point that Naylor implies is that *no* single voice is adequate to convey the characters' experiences. A single voice would metaphorically place the text in the well, in a confining monologism; therefore, a multiplicity of voices is necessary to convey the multiplicity of life, to ensure that life and the novel keep their play. For this reason, Bailey's voice is insufficient to narrate Mariam's story, and both Nadine's and Eve's are required.

To avoid the constrictions of a single perspective, Naylor includes the voices of nearly every character: direct transcription of Sadie's thoughts alternates with Bailey's narration (72-78); Eve (81-91), Mary/Peaches (102-112), Esther (95-99), and Miss Maple (165-213) take over the telling of their stories; Jesse Bell's first-person narration is interpolated into Bailey's narration (137-

141); and Nadine and Eve narrate Mariam's lifestory (143-160). To emphasize the plural narration, Naylor even includes the direct words of minor characters, such as the anonymous soldiers and their officer who shout their determination to "kill Japs" (21), the unnamed customers with whom Bailey argues (31), the stereotyped religious zealot Sister Carrie and the equally stereotyped hipster Sugar Man (32-34 passim), the miscellaneous customers who visit Esther in the basement (95), Esther's brother who makes his repeated admonition ("*We won't speak about this, Esther*" [95 passim]), and Miss Maple's father who declares his principles (185). Naylor also underscores and extends the plural narration by unexpectedly shifting one character's indirect discourse to another character's point of view; for example Miss Maple's narration is interrupted by a straightforward transcription of the Gatlin boys' direct thought: "What they couldn't tear apart, they stomped--*My God, look, it ain't got a tail after all*" (180, emphasis added) and Bailey's narration is similarly interrupted by Gabe's thought: "And banging down old radios and flinging used overcoats into boxes and sweeping up a dust storm. *Puppy, cover your ears, a goy shouldn't be hearing these things*" (221, emphasis added).

In addition to creating a communal narration that implies the need for all perspectives to be heard, Naylor's narrative technique tends to transform the written text into oral performance. On one level, the entire text carries the sense of being spoken directly to the reader. From beginning to end, Bailey's language sounds more spoken than written, with its contractions, its informality, its casualness: the novel starts with "I can't say I've had much education. Book education" (3) and ends with "And that's how we wrap it, folks" (229). As in the latter sentence, Bailey frequently addresses readers directly: we are customers at his cafe ("And if you've got a problem with how I feel, well, there are other cafes" [12]); we are recipients of his lessons ("If you don't listen below the surface, they're both one-note players" [33]); we are taken under his wing ("But I think you've got the drift" [35]); we hear his complaints ("I want you to know right off that Nadine lied on me" [161]); and we receive his hints ("And what I heard is too ignorant to believe. And just guess who I heard it from? [Sister Carrie and Sugar Man, in case you need a hint]" ([223]). The sense that readers are listening directly to the novel is sustained when both Nadine and Miss Maple also address us. Nadine begins her narration with "You already know that my name is Nadine" (143), and Miss Maple interjects a "dialogue" with readers in which the latter's presumed questions are posed and then answered: "And now I'm going to hold a conversation with what I assume are some of your more troubling thoughts about this whole endeavor" (203).

On another level, the language of the text is addressed to and heard by the other characters. Several times Bailey directs asides to Nadine, implying that she is listening to his narration: "(Nadine, nobody asked you)" (4), "(Just let me make this one last point, Nadine)" (11), and "(I told you I'd be getting to you, darling)" (12-13). Nadine acknowledges that she has heard Bailey's long address to the reader: "You already know that my name is Nadine, and my husband's told you that I don't like to talk" (143). This mutual participation in the narrative peaks during the community's involvement in the circumcision of the new infant, George. Everyone is there, even Esther: "and, wonder of wonders, Esther smiled" (225). Peaches begins to sing a spiritual and soon everyone is singing: "One voice joined in. Another voice joined. And another" (225). They sing of the harmony of human beings and God, that each one is "a child of God," and that there is "Peace on earth" (226). The joyful singing makes them forget about the baby: "You see, folks, that's why almost a whole hour passed without it dawning on us that we hadn't found out if it was a boy or a girl" (226). The three males share the male roles appropriate for the ritual: Gabriel is the father and rabbi, Bailey is the godfather, and Miss Maple "took the role of the other male guests to help [Bailey] respond to the blessing" (226). The text then includes the call of the rabbi and the response of the other males (227). As Bailey comments, "it was really touching."

Just as Bailey is impressed with the Jewish communal ritual ("And that's what I like most about Gabe's faith; nothing important can happen unless they're all in it together as a community"), Naylor structures her novel so that this most important event--the first birth on the block--brings this community together. Individuals may--and will--be trapped in their well-like tragedies, but communities, as in the brick-throwing celebration in *The Women of Brewster Place* and in the annual candle walk in *Mama Day*, can gain at least momentary relief by singing, by performing time-honored rituals, by telling and hearing each other's stories and by embracing each other and each other's cultures. Multiple voices create communities and thereby help characters avoid the isolation of the well.

As the novel's multiple narrations and its orality increase the connections among the characters and readers, the shifts in point of view often enact the principle of going beneath the surface. Bailey uses the metaphor of going "one key down" (34) to indicate the deeper layer(s) of meaning beneath the surface meaning. Bailey illustrates this strategy in his transcriptions of Sister Carrie's and Sugar Man's actual words and then in his translations of what the two really mean (33-35). First he presents their actual words, but then, in italics, tells us what they are really saying "one key down" and on "even a lower key" (34). Through Bailey, Naylor thus creates an explicit model for the reader: the stories of Naylor's characters must be read as Bailey reads the words of Sister Carrie and Sugar Man, not merely for their surface meaning but for the layers of deeper meanings. Naylor structures her stories of the novel's characters to encourage such a reading strategy. In "Mood: Indigo," the narration of Sadie's story goes one key down when it shifts from Bailey's point of view to the italicized paragraphs that directly depict Sadie's dream of middle-class comfort with Jones (72-77). Similarly, the narration goes beneath the surface when it shifts from Bailey's voice to the voices of Eve (81-91), Esther (95-99), Mary/Peaches (102-112), Jesse Bell (117-132), and Miss Maple (165-213).

In "Jesse Bell" the narration descends even lower when Sister Carrie and Eve duel with contrasting Biblical passages (134-136) as commentaries on Jesse. During this exchange Eve sarcastically signifies on Carrie when she calls out "somebody in here likes Ezekiel. Somebody even likes the *sixteenth chapter of Ezekiel*" (135). Eve subdues Carrie with this and similar counter-passages that emphasize divine love for the fallen. Naylor invites the reader to play the Biblical game by quoting Ezekiel 16:6 without identifying it, letting it stand as a concluding, and tolerating, comment on Jesse: "*And when I passed by thee, and saw thee polluted in thine own blood, I said unto thee when thou wast in thy blood, Live; yea, I said unto thee when thou wast in thy blood, Live*" (136).

The narration continues to push the usual limits when Jesse's indirect discourse is frequently interpolated, without warnings or transitions, into Bailey's narration. For example, when Bailey narrates "Jesse didn't quite know what it meant, but this weird mama-jama was beginning to really scare her" (137), "weird mama-jama" is Jesse's term for Eve, not Bailey's. The technique is most obvious in the following paragraph, in which the first person shifts abruptly from Bailey to Jesse: "Jesse has never tried to describe for me what it was like that second time around. She says there are no words for the experience. I can only tell you this, Bailey, I sincerely prayed to die" (141).

Besides drawing characters and readers closer together, the multiple, shifting narration of this novel reinforces the connections among the participants, and, by extension, among all human beings. Since the point of view can flow back and forth among the characters, and since the characters can overhear each other's narrations to the reader, the physical and psychological distances among them are metaphorically eliminated. All can join in each other's dream fantasies; all can participate in the celebration of George's birth. One passage in particular, a "one key down" passage, suggests such metaphysical interconnections among people. In Bailey's introduction, as he recalls his experiences in World War II, his identity expands to coincide with all American soldiers in the Pacific. This merger begins cryptically with the refrain, "*We weren't getting into Tokyo*" (21-23), and develops into a full-blown monologue within Bailey's narration. As The Soldier, Bailey has been present at every Pacific battle, imagines that "the end of the world is blue" (23 passim), feels the horror of Japanese civilians caught in the war, participates in the atomic bombings of Hiroshima and Nagasaki, and worries about the "unborn children" and the "new age" (26) to follow. Bailey encompasses not only every soldier, but also every victim and even unborn victims because he transcends the barriers that usually isolate individuals. He floats free of his well-like isolation, just as the novel's narration allows the characters and its readers to escape theirs.

Characters in this novel are able to cross such boundaries because, unlike Naylor's first three novels, here the characters are not enmeshed in limiting stereotypes. The residents of Linden Hills are trapped by their own conformity to white values of economic success and social status. George and Cocoa in *Mama Day* must struggle with their preconceived, white values of love, courtship, and life. In all three previous novels, Naylor sets her characters against Shakespearean models and, in *Linden Hills*, Dante's *Inferno*.[11] By contrast, in *Bailey's Cafe*, the last of Naylor's tetralogy, Naylor eschews such exterior literary models, and, as Peter Erickson notes, an elaborately bound set of Shakespeare's works is trashed in "a riddance ritual that announces the end of Naylor's artistic apprenticeship" ("Review" 34).

This novel of Naylor's literary independence fittingly ends with the cross-cultural, communal celebration of the birth of Mariam's son.[12] This birth is the occasion for the neighborhood's coming together, but, in keeping with Naylor's and the privileged characters' tough realism, it will not change the world: "Life will go on. Still, I do understand the point this little fella is making as he wakes up in the basket: When you have to face it with more questions than answers, it can be a crying shame" (229). For Naylor to end this novel with a birth is also significant because throughout her fiction births are rare and associated with extreme hardship. In *The Women of Brewster Place*, Lucielia's first child is electrocuted and her second one aborted. In *Linden Hills* Willa Nedeed must watch the corpse of her son as she struggles toward her own psychic rebirth and physical death. In *Mama Day* Bernice Duvall first develops cysts instead of a baby and then her baby dies, and pregnancy for Cocoa Day occurs simultaneously with the nearly fatal spell under which she is placed.

Given this context of difficult pregnancies and births in Naylor's novels, the birth of George at the end of *Bailey's Cafe* is especially miraculous. Not only is he the first child born in this neighborhood, but he is born to a woman whose vagina had been ritually sewn shut. His conception is thus a mystery and a miracle, which strengthens the sense that he is a Christ figure. Mariam's sealed vagina is another well image, in this case a closed well, a well like a tomb, but a well of death transformed into a source of life. With George's birth, Naylor seems to be announcing not only her literary independence but also her literary rebirth.

At the other end of life, deaths in Naylor's novels are also traumatic. Many characters meet violent deaths: Serena, Lorraine, and Ben in *The Women of Brewster Place*, Laurel Dumont and the three Nedeeds in *Linden Hills*, Little Caesar and George in *Mama Day*, and numerous, unnamed suicides in *Bailey's Cafe*.

That birth and death should be so difficult is predicted by the image of the well, which suggests both womb and tomb. Well, birth, and death are mysterious and unavoidable. As Derrida, Morrison, and Naylor intimate, the temptation to ignore such abysses must be resisted and their inevitability acknowledged. In *Bailey's Cafe* Naylor establishes a community of privileged characters who have done just that, who are comfortable with the abysses of a devastating world and therefore are secure in their identities and roles. They endure because they have learned to accept the brutality of African American life in a racialized society and because they have transformed their double-consciousness into an advantage. To that community she brings an assortment of persecuted refugees, each of whom has struggled in vain in his or her well of torment. Together, the privileged proprietors and these waifs transcend their narrow confinements and, along with the novel itself, celebrate a broader community based on openness, tolerance, psychic interconnections, and telling and hearing their life stories. By so doing, they all learn to survive at the rim of the well.

The characters' desire to achieve this social and spiritual community and Naylor's progression in her first four novels toward such an achievement reflect broader cultural concerns. The synthesis of cultures, individuals, genders, and generations at the end of *Bailey's Cafe* embodies an attempt to reestablish the cosmic harmony that characterizes West African religions and philosophies. This world view, in contrast to the Euro-American emphasis on differences and "dissent" as Miss Maple calls it (192), stresses the integration of individual, community, nature, and the supernatural.[13] This novel and the celebration in which it culminates also depict the founding, acceptance of, and consecration of a meaningful African American place and time. The search for place, both literal and figurative, has marked African American experience since the first Africans were brought to Virginia in the seventeenth century. African Americans' assigned places have been in the well at the bottom of American society; as Houston Baker, Jr., contends, they have been consigned to the holds of slavers, then rural cabins, and later urban kitchenettes (136-141). The refugees in *Bailey's Cafe* have been denied not only a place but any meaningful past, since their African past was repudiated by white Americans and since their slave past has often been too shameful to be remembered. As a result of such difficulties, the characters and African Americans are plagued by the problem of establishing and maintaining viable identities: Ellison contends that "Negro Americans are in desperate search for identity" (297), and Barbara Christian urges black women "to define and express [their] totality rather than being defined by others" (*Black* 159).

The occasion of George's birth restores a sense of cosmic harmony to the novel's characters, establishes for them a living and livable African American space, thereby restores a sense of the past and provides hope for the present if not the future, and at the same time strengthens the secure identities of the four privileged characters and offers a basis for positive identity formation for the others. All this can happen because all the characters, as well now as the participating reader, have learned to accept the abyss. Like the inhabitants of the Bottom in Morrison's *Sula*, they have learned that "the presence of evil was something to be first recognized, then dealt with, survived, outwitted, triumphed over" (118).

Endnotes

[1] Elsewhere, I have discussed some connections between deconstruction and African American culture (*Dangerous* 3-25) and some relationships between Derrida and Morrison ("Traces" and *Dangerous* 55-56 and 159-176).

[2] For example, Luce Irigaray exults in women's "disruptive excess" (6), and Rachel DuPlessis celebrates the "both/and vision" of the female aesthetic (276).

[3] Examples of such formulations by African American male theorists include Robert Stepto who praises African American culture for espousing the both/and, or what he calls "modal," perspective (xiii), and Houston Baker, Jr., who attests that "This historic condition outside mainstream American culture forced African Americans to deconstruct, defamiliarize, and signify within the master discourse" (136-141).

[4] For example, Mae Henderson welcomes "the deconstructive function of black women's writing" (135) and the black woman writer's ability "to see the other, but also to see what the other cannot see" (137). Valerie Smith argues that black feminists are ideally situated to insure that the radical discourses of blacks and feminists are not diluted (40-43).

[5] Susan Meisenhelder points out that Miranda's contribution to the community's ongoing, quilt-like, multiple interpretation of itself is to appreciate the male perspective of Sapphira's owner, Bascombe Wade (415).

[6] Catherine C. Ward emphasizes that Ruth Anderson represents a perspective characterized by pure human love (186).

[7] As Ward puts it, the residents "have turned away from their past and from their deepest sense of who they are" (182).

[8] Meisenhelder demonstrates that George as well as Cocoa try unsuccessfully to understand each other and Willow Springs in terms of white myths (405-412).

[9] Naylor's epigraph for *The Women of Brewster Place* applies equally well to Sadie: "What Happens to a Dream Deferred?"

[10] The epigraph is:
hush now can you hear it can't be far away.
needing the blues to get there
look and you can hear it
look and you can hear
the blues open
a place never
closing:
Bailey's
Cafe

[11] For discussions of the Shakespearean models, see Awkward (110), Erickson ("'Shakespeare's Black?'"), Levy (264), Meisenhelder (412), Saunders, Storhoff, and Traub. For analyses of the *Inferno* parallel, see Naylor ("Gloria" 582) and Ward.

¹² Readers who are reading one key down will recognize that this child, George, is the same George who marries Cocoa in *Mama Day* (see *Mama Day* 22 and 131, and *Bailey's Cafe* 228).

¹³ For commentaries on traditional West African world views, see Barthold, Jahn, Mbiti, Roberts, and Smitherman.

Works Cited

Awkward, Michael. *Inspiriting Influences: Tradition, Revision, and Afro-American Women's Novels*. New York: Columbia UP, 1989.

Baker, Houston A., Jr. "There Is No More Beautiful Way: Theory and the Poetics of Afro-American Women's Writing." *Afro-American Literary Study in the 1990s*. Eds. Baker and Patricia Redmond. Chicago: U of Chicago P, 1989. 135-155.

Barthold, Bonnie J. *Black Time: Fiction of Africa, the Caribbean, and the United States*. New Haven: Yale UP, 1981.

Christian, Barbara. *Black Feminist Criticism: Perspectives on Black Women Writers*. New York: Pergamon, 1985.

_____. "Gloria Naylor's Geography: Community, Class, and Patriarchy in *The Women of Brewster Place* and *Linden Hills*." *Reading Black, Reading Feminist: A Critical Anthology*. Ed. Henry Louis Gates, Jr. New York: Meridian, 1990. 348-373.

Derrida, Jacques. *Writing and Difference*. Trans. Alan Bass. Chicago: Chicago UP, 1978.

Du Bois, W. E. B. *The Souls of Black Folk*. New York: Penguin, 1989.

DuPlessis, Rachel Blau. "For the Etruscans." *The New Feminist Criticism*. Ed. Elaine Showalter. New York: Pantheon, 1985. 271-291.

Ellison, Ralph. *Shadow and Act*. New York: Vintage, 1972.

Erickson, Peter. Review of *Bailey's Cafe*. *Kenyon Review* 15 (1993). Reprinted in *Gloria Naylor: Critical Perspectives Past and Present*. Eds. Henry Louis Gates, Jr., and K. A. Appiah. New York: Amistad, 1993. 32-34.

_____. "'Shakespeare's Black?': The Role of Shakespeare in Naylor's Novels." In *Gloria Naylor: Critical Perspectives Past and Present*. Eds. Henry Louis Gates, Jr., and K. A. Appiah. New York: Amistad, 1993. 231-248.

Fowler, Karen Joy. Review of *Bailey's Cafe*. *Chicago Tribune*, 4 Oct 1992. Reprinted in *Gloria Naylor: Critical Perspectives Past and Present*. Eds. Henry Louis Gates, Jr., and K. A. Appiah. New York: Amistad, 1993. 26-28.

Henderson, Mae Gwendolyn. "Speaking in Tongues: Dialogics, Dialectics, and the Black Woman Writer's Literary Tradition." *Reading Black, Reading Feminist: A Critical Anthology*. Ed. Henry Louis Gates, Jr. New York: Penguin, 1990. 116-142.

Homans, Margaret. "The Woman in the Cave." In *Gloria Naylor: Critical Perspectives Past and Present*. Eds. Henry Louis Gates, Jr., and K. A. Appiah. New York: Amistad, 1993. 152-181.

Irigaray, Luce. "The Power of Discourse and the Subordination of the Feminine." *The Irigaray Reader*. Ed. Margaret Whitford. Oxford: Basil Blackwell, 1991. 118-127.

Jahn, Janheinz. *Muntu: An Outline of the New African Culture*. Trans. Marjorie Grene. New York: Grove, 1961.

Levy, Helen Fiddyment. "Lead on with Light." In *Gloria Naylor: Critical Perspectives Past and Present*. Eds. Henry Louis Gates, Jr., and K. A. Appiah. New York: Amistad, 1993. 263-284.

Mbiti, John. *African Religions and Philosophy*. 2nd ed. Oxford: Heinemann, 1989.

Meisenhelder, Susan. "'The Whole Picture' in Gloria Naylor's *Mama Day*." *African American Review* 27 (1993): 405-419.

Montgomery, Maxine Lavon. "Authority, Multivocality, and the New World Order in Gloria Naylor's *Bailey's Cafe*." *African American Review* 29 (1995): 27-33.

Morrison, Toni. *Jazz*. New York: Knopf, 1992.

_____. *Sula*. New York: Bantam, 1975.

Naylor, Gloria. *Bailey's Cafe*. New York: Vintage, 1993.

_____, and Toni Morrison. "A Conversation: Gloria Naylor and Toni Morrison." *Southern Review* 21.3 (1985): 567-593.

_____. *Linden Hills*. New York: Penguin, 1986.

_____. "Love and Sex in the Afro-American Novel." *The Yale Review* 78.1 (1988-1989): 19-31.

_____. *Mama Day*. New York: Vintage, 1989.

_____. *The Women of Brewster Place*. New York: Penguin, 1983.

Page, Philip. *Dangerous Freedom: Fusion and Fragmentation in Toni Morrison's Novels*. Jackson: Mississippi UP, 1996.

_____. "Traces of Derrida in Toni Morrison's *Jazz*." *African American Review* 29 (1995): 55-66.

Roberts, John W. *From Trickster to Badman: The Black Folk Hero in Slavery and Freedom*. Philadelphia: Pennsylvania UP, 1989.

Saunders, James Robert. "The Ornamentation of Old Ideas: Gloria Naylor's First Three Novels." In *Gloria Naylor: Critical Perspectives Past and Present*. Eds. Henry Louis Gates, Jr., and K. A. Appiah. New York: Amistad, 1993. 249-262.

Smith, Valerie. "Black Feminist Theory and the Representation of the 'Other'." *Changing Our Own Words: Essays on Criticism, Theory, and Writing by Black Women*. Ed. Cheryl A. Wall. New Brunswick: Rutgers UP, 1989. 38-57.

Smitherman, Geneva. *'Talkin' and Testifyin': The Language of Black America*. Detroit: Wayne State UP, 1986.

Stepto, Robert B. *From Behind the Veil: A Study of Afro-American Narrative*. Urbana: Illinois UP, 1979.

Storhoff, Gary. "'The Only Voice is Your Own': Gloria Naylor's Revision of *The Tempest*." *African American Review* 29 (1995): 35-45.

Traub, Valerie. "Rainbows of Darkness: Deconstructing Shakespeare in the Work of Gloria Naylor and Zora Neale Hurston." *Cross-Cultural Performances: Differences in Women's Re-Visions of Shakespeare*. Ed. Marianne Novy. Urbana: U of Illinois P, 1993. 150-164.

Ward, Catherine C. "Gloria Naylor's *Linden Hills*: A Modern *Inferno*." In *Gloria Naylor: Critical Perspectives Past and Present*. Eds. Henry Louis Gates, Jr., and K. A. Appiah. New York: Amistad, 1993. 182-194.

Werner, Craig. "Minstrel Nightmares and Black Dreams of Faulkner's Dreams of Blacks." *Faulkner and Race: Faulkner and Yoknapatawpha, 1986*. Eds. Doreen Fowler and Ann J. Abadie. Jackson: Mississippi UP, 1987. 35-57.

Wood, Rebecca S. "'Two Warring Ideals in One Dark Body': Universalism and Nationalism in Gloria Naylor's *Bailey's Cafe.*" Published with permission of the author.

> One ever feels his twoness,--an American, a Negro; two souls, two thoughts, two unreconciled strivings; two warring ideals in one dark body, whose dogged strength alone keeps it from being torn asunder.
>
> -- W. E. B. Du Bois

W. E. B. Du Bois articulates the doubleness that pervades African American literature where characters and texts contend with dual African American and Western traditions. In her fourth novel, *Bailey's Cafe*, Gloria Naylor employs this doubleness to create a text that, paradoxically, fractures perceived reality while it attempts to heal those breaks. Populated by such characters as a religious zealot, a penny-whore, a self-mutilating nymphomaniac, and a black Ethiopian Jew who is "a little off in the head" (143), Bailey's cafe provides a refuge for social deviants whose suffering has led them to the cafe. Naylor's characters exemplify black women's suffering to the extent that even Stanley, a black man, suffers as a woman when he dons a dress to escape the tortures of a summer heat wave. Along with this portrayal of female suffering, Naylor's characters embody Du Boisian doubleness in their universalist and nationalist positions. Naylor places her representative characters in a text that bridges the perceived gap between the European and African American literary traditions by destabilizing the Eurocentric universalist and ethnocentric nationalist frames of reference.

Naylor has qualified herself for this destabilization process by repeatedly signifying on her literary predecessors. Her signifying history dates back to her first novel, *The Women of Brewster Place*, in which Naylor traces the lives of seven women. Peter Erickson has identified the Shakespearean motif in this novel within the "Cora Lee" story where "Naylor matches the comedy of *A Midsummer Night's Dream* with her own mischievous comic mood" ("Shakespeare's Black?" 233). In her second novel, *Linden Hills*, Naylor signifies on Dante's *Inferno* in what Jewelle Gomez rather critically describes as a "literary exercise rather than a groundbreaking adaptation" (8). Finally, Naylor's *Mama Day* returns, full force, to Shakespearean allusion, drawing mainly from *The Tempest* but with *Romeo and Juliet* and *The Taming of the Shrew* playing minor roles (Mukherjee 7).

Naylor does not limit herself to rewriting "classics," though. She also approaches the works of African American authors with an eye for critical revision, an act which Michael Awkward terms revisionary reading (4). Awkward traces the literary antecedents of Naylor's *The Women of Brewster Place* back to Morrison's *The Bluest Eye* and Ellison's *Invisible Man* (39). James Robert Saunders also places Ann Petry's *The Street* on that list of *Brewster* forebearers (2). And Erickson remarks on the similarities between Naylor's third novel, *Mama Day*, and Paule Marshall's *Praisesong for the Widow* ("Shakespeare's Black?" 238).

Naylor continues signifying in *Bailey's Cafe* where her allegorical characters place her novel in the midst of the contemporary universalist and nationalist debate. In this exchange, members of the universalist camp favor a transcendence of race in an effort to achieve human liberation. For universalists, colorless and color-blind humanity defines identity, and ultimately this sense of race-transcending identity can foster the cross-cultural fertilization necessary for liberation from racial boundaries.[1] In contrast to the universalist's downplaying of difference, the nationalist preserves and projects difference to maintain national identity and group solidarity in order to achieve racial equality.[2] In the absence of unifying place that nationhood often implies, black nationalism manifests itself in various cultural forms, and black cultural nationalism has emerged as an ideological counterpoint to the universalist position. The rhetoric of this ideology often encourages the view that blacks and whites are essentially different, and the loss of this essential difference equals a loss of cultural and spiritual identity.

One alternative to universalist and nationalist extremes emerges as a synthesis of these two positions wherein African American cultural difference is maintained within a pluralist universal cultural tradition.[3] Cornel West concludes his essay "The Dilemma of the Black Intellectual" with such a synthesis of the universal and national:

> The future of the Black intellectual lies neither in a deferential disposition toward the Western parent nor a nostalgic search for the African one. Rather it resides in a critical negation, wise preservation, and insurgent transformation of this hybrid lineage which protects the earth and projects a better world. (146)

Out of West's preservation, negation, and transformation comes a position which transcends the rhetoric of possession and lineage. Such transcendence reconciles Du Boisian doubleness through a conservative yet transformative synthesis much like that which Du Bois himself describes in *The Souls of Black Folk*: "The history of the American Negro is the history of this longing . . . to merge his double self into a better and truer self. In this merging he wishes neither of the older selves to be lost" (3).

In *Bailey's Cafe*, Gloria Naylor presents a literary version of Du Bois' synthesis wherein representative characters and canonical conversations combine the universalist and nationalist positions to create a liberating alternative to extremism. Stanley, Jesse Bell, and George represent the universalist, nationalist, and synthesis positions within *Bailey's Cafe*. Stanley attempts to transcend racial divisions, Jesse Bell preserves and projects African American difference, and George simultaneously represents human universals and cultural difference, synthesizing the universalist and nationalist positions. Naylor's responses to Western and African American canonical texts create a dialogue which reinforces her allegory.[4] *Bailey's Cafe* speaks to Geoffrey Chaucer's *The Canterbury Tales*, and Toni Morrison's *The Bluest Eye* to establish a universal and national background, ultimately aspiring to Ralph Ellison's *Invisible Man*, which merges the universal and national. In these conversations, Naylor affirms the canonical nature of these authors' works by re-presenting their structures, motifs, and characters, but she limits this affirmation by critically revising and extending these authors' texts. From these canonical exchanges, Naylor forges a universal/nationalist synthesis in which African American cultural difference has a place within a pluralist universal tradition.

The temporal and geographical settings of *Bailey's Cafe* create an unstable space in which this synthesis may occur. The novel takes place in 1948 and 1949, a transitional period for Americans in general and African Americans in particular. Marking the end of what Cornel West calls the "age of Europe" (*Beyond Eurocentrism* 10), the post-World War II decades were an empowering period for oppressed peoples.[5]   In the United States, this empowerment manifested itself in the development and implementation of integrationist policies. Such overt policy changes did not fundamentally alter the mentality that had justified and maintained racist policies, however. As Winston Van Horne states, "[I]t cannot pass unnoticed that within the bounds of integration a hard color line of racial demarcation persists" (301). Integration did not eradicate racial conflict, and post-World War II prosperity masked persistent racial problems which would erupt in the mid-fifties and escalate during the 1960s.

Naylor not only situates her novel in a transitional American time period, but she also presents conflict in her geographical settings. Bailey's cafe, Eve's boardinghouse, and Gabe's pawnshop--the main settings of the novel--comprise a kind of transitory Bermuda Triangle attracting the hopeless. Unlike the Bermuda Triangle, however, the cafe, boardinghouse, and pawnshop are just "way stations" (159) through which people pass, not in which people remain. The customers arrive from all over the United States and from other parts of the world, but the customer does not go to the cafe; the cafe goes to the customer: Sadie finds the cafe in Chicago, Jesse in New York, Stanley in Pittsburgh, and Mariam in Addis Ababa, Ethiopia. Even Bailey, Eve, and Gabe, who are the constants in this Bermuda Triangle of suffering, find themselves in the fluid universe which Bailey, the main narrator, describes: "When I walk out of this cafe and leave this street, I'm still in San Francisco.   [Gabe is] up in the Caucasus Mountains. And Eve is in New Orleans. You see, it's whatever life we've come from" (222-223). Bailey's street is a liminal zone in which time stands still and place loses its permanence.[6] This temporal and geographical destabilization mirrors the dislocation Naylor's characters experience and the instability of the universalist and nationalist positions these characters exemplify.

Stanley Beckwourth Booker T. Washington Carver represents the universalist position through his integrationist moves toward cultural homogenization. Stanley's name refers to prominent African American historic figures: James Beckwourth, a frontier explorer; George Washington Carver, a renowned scientist and inventor; and--most important--Booker T. Washington, the leading spokesman for measured assimilation at the turn of the century (165).   Following Washington's model, Stanley confronts and attempts to overcome--sometimes covertly--the nationalist concept of identity built upon difference.

Stanley's family history contextualizes his desire to transcend difference. According to Stanley, "I had aunts of all assortments: pure-blooded Yumas; full-blooded Negroes; full-blooded Mexicans; Yuma-Mexicans; Mexican-Irish; Negro-Mexicans; and even one pure-blooded African who still knew some phrases in Ashanti" (171). Stanley's family combines these diverse individuals into a unit which overturns turn-of-the-century stereotypes about minorities in general, and African Americans in particular, through their financial success in southern California's cotton industry. In the face of this diversity and success, Stanley states, "The Americans had no problems with our identities, . . . ; they imported one six-letter word to cut through all that . . . tangle in our heritage" (171)--nigger.

Stanley confronts such reductivist notions of race and identity during his prison sentence and subsequent job search. After the Red Cross' refusal to take his blood donation during World War II, Stanley refuses to fight in that war and is imprisoned for three years as a conscientious objector. As he puts it, "If my blood [isn't] good enough for the Red Cross, why [is] it good enough to be spilled on the battlefield?" (189). While in prison, Stanley and the other CO's succeed in their attempt to desegregate the prison's dining hall, transcending the penal system's policy of foregrounding racial difference. Of course, this success comes at great cost since the prison administration subsequently places Stanley in a cell with a murderer determined to rape his new cell mate. Stanley's role as rape victim in prison prefigures his later role as victim of a racist corporate America.

During his job search, Stanley attempts to overcome the *de facto* segregation of corporate America, but his overt integration tactics fail to secure him a suitable position. Armed with his doctorate degree in mathematics from Stanford University, Stanley searches for a marketing analyst position during a summer heat wave, and his body responds as if he had been whipped, welts running across his back and ringing his neck and wrists (198-199). Although Stanley mentally views universalist integration as a logical goal, physically his body displays the stigmata of black collective memory and rebels against Stanley's attempts to transcend racial differences as he searches for a job.

Stanley contemplates suicide after the mental and physical tortures of his job search, and this personal crisis leads him to Bailey's cafe. Once in this fluid universe, Stanley begins working as a housekeeper in Eve's boardinghouse, a position which allows him covert access to many of the ninety-nine companies that rejected him as a marketing analyst. Ironically, Stanley ultimately achieves financial success at the expense of the white dominated business world since he puts his marketing and housekeeping skills to work by entering jingle contests sponsored by companies such as Chiffon, Fab, Ajax, and Colgate-Palmolive-Peet, winning nearly fifty-thousand dollars in cash and prizes (215). Stanley's success undermines the racism and sexism of the companies he targets since they expect American housewives--code words for white women in the 1940s--to enter their contests, and Stanley fits in neither of those categories. Beneath the racial and sexual liberation lurks the fact that Stanley must use covert methods to achieve his integrationist goals. He gains access to the companies who spurned him through raceless, sexless jingles which can only enter sponsoring companies through their mailboxes. In essence, Stanley's use of a symbolic back door reinforces the white male hegemony of American business.

Naylor reinforces Stanley's problematic universalist position through her signifying on Geoffrey Chaucer's work. Donna Rifkind identifies one of Naylor's canonical sources for *Bailey's Cafe* as *The Canterbury Tales*: "If [*Bailey's Cafe*] reminds you a little bit of *The Canterbury Tales*, it's supposed to: Chaucer's host at the Tabard Inn was Harry Bailly, and Naylor's chorus of tale-telling voices echoes its 14th century ancestor" (28). In addition to Rifkind's associations, structural similarities exist Naylor's and Chaucer's works. Like Chaucer, Naylor presents each character's story in discrete but interconnected narratives that have the headlink-tale-footlink structure. More specifically, Naylor begins each section with an introduction by Bailey--or, on one occasion, his wife, Nadine--

which situates the main character of the section in the Bailey's cafe setting; moves into either a first or third person narrative about the subject; then returns to the original narrator of the section.

While Naylor acknowledges the universal canonicity of Chaucer's work by using it as her structural foundation, such a use necessitates her mastery of Chaucer's text to the degree that she can rewrite it. Naylor must not only master *The Canterbury Tales* as a Western canonical text, but also contend with the strong connections to English themes and geography which mark *The Canterbury Tales* as an English nationalist text. Naylor accomplishes this by African-Americanizing *The Canterbury Tales* through her structural and narratives responses to Chaucer's work.

Naylor begins by revising Chaucer's journey frame. Where Chaucer's pilgrims depart from and return to the Tabard Inn, Naylor's pilgrims reach Bailey's cafe in the midst of their journeys. Framing those journeys is not Chaucer's English landscape, but ever-changing black landscapes in both Africa and America. Bailey describes his place-less cafe as "nothing but a way station, [where] the choices have always been clear: you eventually go back out and resume your life . . . or you head to the back of the cafe and end it" (221). Naylor adds narrative interstitiality to geographic intermediacy when Bailey describes his patrons--"All these folks are in transition; they come midway in their stories and go on" (219)--as though *Bailey's Cafe*, as novel, cannot fully convey each character's entire tale.

Within Chaucer's journey frame, Harry Bailly, the host in *The Canterbury Tales*, instigates a tale-telling contest when he challenges the pilgrims to create stories "*that telleth in this caas / Tales of best sentence and moost solass*" (ll. 797-798). The "instruction" and "entertainment" value of their tales (David 76), evaluated by Harry Bailly, will win the best teller a dinner at the Tabard Inn compliments of the other pilgrims. With this, Harry Bailly not only shows his business savvy--since this ploy ensures his customers' patronage upon their return--but he also demonstrates his power over the entire narrative since he places himself in the role of literary critic, as Alfred David suggests in *The Strumpet Muse* (76).

Gloria Naylor's Bailey also exercises power within *Bailey's Cafe*. Naylor's Bailey acts as a unifying force, though, orchestrating the entire novel much like the lead vocal in a blues set, a role which places Bailey on the threshold between literary and musical forms. In *In the African-American Grain*, John Callahan defines "the pursuit of narrative form [in African American fiction as] the pursuit of voice" (14), and Naylor's repeated use of first person narrators emphasizes the individual nature of that pursued voice. In all but one chapter, Naylor typographically signifies her changing narrators with white space or symbols, creating distance between the narrative voices and emphasizing individual accomplishment and artistic competition.

One exception to this design appears in the chapter entitled "Mary (Take Two)" in which Eve's, Nadine's, and a third person omniscient narrator's voices commingle to tell the story of Mariam, a black, Ethiopian Jew who becomes impregnated by immaculate conception. The combined voices in this chapter subtly reinforce the obvious musicality found elsewhere in the novel, and their simultaneity counterbalances the narrative emphasis on individuality and competition. Naylor's use of embedded second person narration within first person narratives also reinforces this sense of musical community. Narrators such as Bailey, Nadine, Stanley, and Jesse repeatedly call to their audience in second person, expecting their audience's engagement, interaction, and response, and this call-and-response structure reflects what Portia K. Maultsby defines as "[a] salient feature of black music [which] is the conceptualization of music-making as a communal/participatory activity" (195). Naylor signifies on Chaucer's work through geographic and generic re-placement, reconceiving Chaucer within a contemporary, black, urban landscape.

In addition to her universalist deconstruction, Naylor critiques and revises the nationalist frame of reference by presenting Jesse Bell, a cultural nationalist figure who accuses black integrationists of aspiring toward whiteness. Raised in a family of longshoremen, Jesse grows up surrounded by figures of black power. The men demand respect from others--as Jesse puts it, "Nobody messed with colored longshoremen" (119)--and the women have the strength "to make a home for men like that" (120). Jesse's mother demonstrates that strength when her sons "act up"; after looking into their mother's eyes, "they apologized right quick [because] . . . [p]ower knows power" (121), and Jesse inherits that power. Jesse's marriage into the King family of Harlem's Sugar Hill intensifies her African American difference by placing her in an integrationist environment hostile to black power.

The treatment of food on Sugar Hill emphasizes Jesse's nationalist focus on African American history and pride. In his attempt to inculcate whiteness, Uncle Eli, who represents the integrationist attitude on Sugar Hill, insists that the people of Sugar Hill avoid eating what he calls "slave food" (124). Jesse's husband learns Uncle Eli's culinary lessons, finding such food as smothered pork chops, fried catfish, collard greens, biscuits, and oxtail soup, difficult to swallow (124). Upon discovering that her husband does not even know what oxtail is, Jesse introduces him, through food, to his own history. After baking three sweet potato pies and taking a bath in vanilla water, Jesse lies naked in bed and wedges a perfect piece of pie between her legs with her bewildered husband watching: "It was time for the first lesson. Husband, I said, pointing, this is sweet-potato pie. Didn't have a bit of trouble after that. Except it was all the man wanted for dinner for the next month" (124).

Jesse's sexual power fails to stop Uncle Eli from ostracizing her from the King family. One of Uncle Eli's successes in this endeavor appears when Jesse's son refuses to attend his maternal grandmother's ninetieth anniversary "because he [does not] have anything in common with *those people*" (128). When Jesse reprimands him for his elitist attitude, "It might as well have been a dead woman ranting at him. [She] looked into that boy's eyes and saw [her] words were lost, lost" (128). Jesse's refusal to surrender to Uncle Eli's integrationist pressure marks her as an outsider within the Sugar Hill community, one whom even her son will not accept, and her nationalist separation from the Sugar Hill integrationists makes her suspicious of their motives and creates profound distrust and antagonism.

Naylor's extension of Morrison's *The Bluest Eye* reinforces Jesse's equivocal nationalist position. Morrison crystallizes her nationalist views through her characterization of the Breedlove family, demonstrating the effect of white-constructed standards on the black family and calling for a re-centered self-image where black is more than physical beauty. Morrison's narrator describes the family as "relentlessly and aggressively ugly" (34), but their ugliness is not rooted in physical reality:

It was as though some mysterious all-knowing master had given each one a cloak of ugliness to wear, and they had accepted it without question. The master had said, "You are ugly people." They had looked *about* themselves and saw nothing to contradict that statement; saw, in fact, support for it leaning at them from every billboard, every movie, every glance.

"Yes," they had said. "You are right." (34, emphasis added)

The Breedloves never look *at* themselves to determine their beauty. They blindly accept the white supremacist beliefs that white is right and black is not beautiful, and this passive and damaging acceptance signals the necessity for a re-constructed positive self-image which proclaims that black is, indeed, deeply beautiful.[7]

Naylor's characterization of Mary extends Morrison's implicit nationalist call for a redefinition of black beauty. As Bailey describes her, "[Mary] is more than pretty. She's one of those women you see and don't believe. The kind that live just outside the limits of your imagination" (100). Later, Sugar Man, a local pimp, describes Mary in less complimentary terms: "Born to be fucked" (102). Through her reconciliation of external and internal images, Mary escapes the constraints of the sexual objectification Sugar Man articulates and redefines her own beauty.

Mary struggles with the disparity between her external and internal images. Through the eyes of others, Mary sees herself as a sexual object, to be savored by men and envied and feared by women, and this image contrasts against the fact that she views herself as an innocent child. Mary describes this disparity as her dual identity: "She was a whore and I was Daddy's baby" (104), Mary being both "she" and "I." Mary compartmentalizes these identities so completely that, constantly pursued as sexual object, she surrenders "the whore" to "any son of any man . . . [who has] the power to drive away that demon from the mirror" (105). At the same time, she ostensibly maintains a Puritanical distance from this other sexual self. This internal whore/virgin dichotomy disintegrates when Mary realizes that she actually looks forward to sleeping with men and feeling their touch. She becomes the whore-ific image she so despises and must eventually overcome.

Mary confronts this seductive image after her club-footed lover discovers her continuing sexual infidelity and threatens to kill, in front of her, the next man with whom she has sex. Terrified, Mary spends the next two weeks in their apartment, her attention finally resting on her lover's custom-made boots. She describes his willingness to discard boots with the least flaw, and after the second week, Mary mars her own surface as she gouges her cheek with a beer opener. Mary signifies her reconciliation of external and internal images by etching her internal pain on her body, a literal act of defacement that liberates her from her previous image. Like the Breedloves, Mary becomes the ugly image that she sees reflected, her maiming echoing their externalization of self-image.

Where Morrison calls for a conceptual revision of black beauty through her representation of the Breedloves, Naylor extends and refines this nationalist idea by defining external beauty as inadequate without simultaneous recognition of internal beauty. Mary's attempts to reconcile her external and internal images lead to her destructive self-mutilation which paradoxically frees her from the image that repels her, and Mary's paradox parallels Jesse's problematic nationalist stance. While Jesse's drive to maintain cultural difference liberates her from Sugar Hill expectations and imbues her with a certain cultural power, ultimately this nationalist stance alienates her from her family. Like Naylor's response to the universalist position, Naylor critiques the nationalist frame of reference through her equivocal character and canonical responses.

Growing out of Naylor's responses to the universalist and nationalist positions, George represents the synthesis position in *Bailey's Cafe*. George's role as synthesizer precedes his birth, having its roots in his conception in the hills of Ethiopia. According to Beta Israel custom, George's mother Mariam is prepared for her future marriage by being circumcised, and the village midwives sew her up tighter than usual to raise her value as a wife (152). After Mariam's expulsion from the village due to her suspicious pregnancy, she eventually reaches Eve's boardinghouse where Eve discovers that Mariam is still a virgin, and George, an immaculate conception. George not only serves as Christ figure, but he also embodies the connection between African past and American future because of his conceptual geographic history.

George's circumcision ceremony also places George in a global community. Stanley, Bailey, and Gabe play key roles in this ceremony, after which Bailey admits, "[T]hat's what I like the most about Gabe's faith: nothing important can happen unless they're all in it together as a community. After that I felt like this baby was really a part of me" (227). While George's ceremony instigates a transcendence of racial and national difference in which the community unites and welcomes George as a member, it does not offer complete transcendence of difference since only men participate. As Erickson states, "Political and ceremonial discourse is made to seem a largely male affair" ("Canon Revision" 203), and, as such, George's ceremony reinforces existing patriarchal hegemony even as it symbolizes limited racial, national, and religious transcendence.

Gabe and Bailey acknowledge another aspect of George's synthesizing position in *Bailey's Cafe*. Because they believe that a child should not be born into the hopelessness of Bailey's street, Gabe and Bailey discuss the prospects of getting Mariam and George into Israel, the newly-formed Jewish homeland. But Bailey warns:

> People are people. And government is government. And Israel isn't gonna be run any differently from any other country. . . . [I]nside those borders it's the same old story: You got your haves and your have-nots. . . . But above all, the groups who are in power are going to do whatever they can to stay in power. (222)

Just as African Americans are oppressed because of their racial difference in America, so are some Jews in Israel "considered inferior to others because of the type of Jew they are, the color of Jew they are, or whatever" (222). According to Bailey, then, the propensity to define identity based upon difference is a universal characteristic of humankind. Thus, George's anticipated arrival causes other characters to contemplate the synthesis of the universalist and nationalist positions.

Such synthesis of the universal and national also appears in Naylor's revision of Ralph Ellison's *Invisible Man*. Ellison, like Naylor, presents allegorical characters like Dr. Bledsoe and Ras to represent the universalist and nationalist extremes. A subtle and unifying background to the main allegorical production in both Ellison's and Naylor's novels, though, is the blues, a synthesizing force which unites African and European traditions. Alan Lomax describes this dual tradition:

> In origin the blues is bicultural, Afro-American or Afro-European: European in that . . . it is essentially a rhymed couplet set to a compact strophic melody; African in a score of ways--descending cadences, flatted sevenths and thirds . . . , a polymetered relation between voice and accompaniment, and a playful singing style changing role from phrase to phrase. Thus the blues merges two musical languages into an international patois. (3)

Lomax attributes the popularity of this "new language" to the fact that "it speaks of the modern, urban, alienated experience" (3), an experience which Ellison and Naylor present in their synthesized narratives.

Ellison introduces the blues in the prologue to *Invisible Man* wherein he constructs the blues frame of his novel. There, the narrator describes his synesthetic experience of Armstrong's "What Did I Do to Be So Black and Blue," stating, "I not only entered the music but descended, like Dante, into its depths" (9). For the narrator, the blues becomes a place where he can hear, see, and feel the music. He goes on to describe his descent as a move which transports him back in time as he peels away the years layer by layer until he reaches the times of slavery where he sees "*a beautiful girl . . .* [who stands] *pleading . . . before a group of slaveowners who bid for her naked body . . .* " (9). Thus, the narrator experiences aural, visual, physical, and temporal sensations as one blues experience.

Like Ellison, Naylor invokes the blues in *Bailey's Cafe*. Naylor reveals that "the music, itself, formed the songs/chapters in *Bailey's Cafe* . . . where Bailey is [her] bridge or riff to introduce . . . the characters and their songs . . ." ("Mood: Indigo" 502-503). Naylor makes this clear with her section and chapter headings--"Maestro, If You Please . . . , " "The Vamp," "The Jam," and "The Wrap"--which structure the novel as if it were a blues session. Bailey, the lead performer in this session, demands patience as he warns his audience and prepares them for his patrons' songs: "[I]f you're expecting to get the answer in a few notes, you're mistaken. The answer is in who I am and who my customers are. There's a whole set to be played here if you want to stick around and listen to the music" (4). The music Bailey describes resonates through Naylor's text as the blues whose repetition and improvisation structure the work.

Naylor's references to the blues appear before her novel actually begins --in the epigram. Here, Naylor alludes to her use of the blues motif throughout the novel. Like Ellison, she foreshadows the synthesis that will take place in the novel when she repeats the line "look and you can hear it / look and you can hear." The visual and aural synesthesia in these lines is consistent with blues theory since, according to Houston A. Baker,

> The blues are a synthesis (albeit one always synthesizing rather than one already hypostatized). . . . [c]ombining work songs, group seculars, field hollers, sacred harmonies, proverbial wisdom, folk

philosophy, political commentary, ribald humor, elegiac lament, and much more. . . . (5)

Baker's analysis reveals the multi-leveled nature of the blues--a nature that Ellison represents as his character's layered descent into the blues. Naylor offers a similar descent into music as Bailey describes two cafe patrons--Sister Carrie, the "Cornerstone of the Temple of Perpetual Redemption" (32) and Sugar Man, "All-around hustler and pimp" (33)--who ostensibly represent opposite ends of the religious spectrum:

[They] aren't as far apart as they sound. If you don't listen below the surface, they're both one-note players. Flat and predictable. But nobody comes in here with a simple story. Every oneliner's got a life underneath it. Every point's got a counterpoint. (33-34)

Bailey then proceeds to delve below the surface of Sister Carrie's and Sugar Man's words until, far beneath that surface, both characters are singing the same song of pain, despair, and human longing.

Within Naylor's chapters, the recurrence of key patterns and phrases such as *"We weren't getting into Tokyo"* (21-23), *"No man has ever touched me"* (143-145), and *"We won't speak about this, Esther"* (95-99) offers additional examples of repetition and improvisation where the lines become more significant as the stories unfold between each repetition. For example, at the beginning of Esther's story, she describes herself in terms of darkness: "The black gal. Monkey face. Tar. Coal. Ugly. Soot. Unspeakable. Pitch. Coal. Ugly. Soot. Unspeakable" (95). After the first *"We won't speak about this, Esther"* refrain, Esther describes her fears that she will be sent away from her new home--her brother's boss' home--if she tells what her brother's boss does to her in the cellar (96). After the third refrain, Esther reveals that he--her brother's boss--tells her to "[p]lay with her toys . . . as the spiders scratch and spin, scratch and spin their webs in the dark," but she knows that these leather and metal things are not toys, and she understands "that in the dark, words have a different meaning. Having fun. Playing games. Being a good girl" (97). By the end of the fifth refrain, Esther has revealed, by implication, that she spent twelve years of her life satisfying the sexual fantasies of her brother's boss so that her brother would receive favors on the job, and her hopeless situation leads Esther first to Bailey's cafe, then to Eve's boardinghouse, where Esther directly responds to the refrain by speaking the unspeakable and telling her story.

One break in the constant music of Naylor's novel appears at the beginning of Miss Maple's story as Bailey discusses suicides at the cafe. He states, "I can tell if it's gonna be a suicide when the whole thing starts to glow so brightly it hurts your eyes, and the beautiful music gets so dim it hurts your head to strain to hear it" (163). In this instance, Naylor responds to Ellison's use of light throughout *Invisible Man* in which the narrator lives in an abandoned section of a tenement basement that is "warm and full of light" (6), 1,396 incandescent lights to be precise. These lights not only confirm the narrator's existence, but they also imply a host of opposites: non-existence, invisibility, chaos, and death. Ellison's lights embody both existence and invisibility, both form and chaos, both life and death.

Light serves similar ambivalent ends in Naylor's *Bailey's Cafe*. While bright lights herald suicide at one point in the novel, at another point, they announce new life. During George's birth, Eve conjures a dazzling light show and an African setting to ease Mariam's pain. Naylor mitigates the lyricism of this passage, however, by transforming Eve's projection of lights and setting into a factor leading to Mariam's death and George's subsequent abandonment on Bailey's street. Both the lights and setting seem surreal until, in Eve's absence, Mariam's desire for water in which to bathe conjures up "exactly what her childlike mind called up: endless water" (228). Surreality becomes reality as Mariam drowns in this imagined water.

Naylor mixes the surreal with the real, vision with sound, and past with present in her synthetic approach to the characters in *Bailey's Cafe*. Following in the Ellisonian tradition, Naylor re-presents her literary precursors to give her novel both voice and vision, merging the Western and African American literary traditions to signify the creation of a new language that can adequately portray the black urban experience. Through her allegory and signification, Naylor destabilizes the universalist and nationalist perspectives in an effort to construct a liberated view which allows for cultural difference while recognizing that difference within a pluralist universal community.

Endnotes

[1] For related discussions of assimilation see Nathan Glazer's "In Defense of Multiculturalism" in which he argues that despite the contemporary politics of difference, assimilation is a reality. See also "Being Black and Feeling Blue" in which Shelby Steele describes the "integration shock" blacks experience when they move into mainstream American culture.

[2] In his book *National Identity*, Anthony Smith identifies two different conceptions of nations: the Western and the non-Western. According to Smith, the foundations of the Western model of nations are "[h]istoric territory, legal-political community, legal-political equality of members, and common civic culture and ideology" (11). In contrast to this model, the non-Western or "ethnic" model of nations emphasizes "genealogy and presumed descent ties, popular mobilization, vernacular languages, customs and traditions" (12). The fundamental difference between these two models of nations is the tension between civic and ethnic elements (13), and this tension mirrors the tension between universalist and nationalist perspectives where universalism emphasizes integration or assimilation into a civic-based group, and nationalism emphasizes maintenance of an ethnic-based community or nation.

[3] Literary critics such as Charles Johnson and John Barth advocate this synthesis as an invaluable aspect of literary development. Johnson describes this synthesis in terms of the intertextual connections he makes in his writing: "You call it borrowing, I suppose. My intention is somewhat different, a very synthetic technique" (166). On another literary plane, Barth discusses the value of synthesis in terms of producing postmodern literature. Barth states of postmodern fiction that the most promising avenue open to its development lies in neither rejection nor emulation of preceding modernist literary forms; rather, postmodern fiction should develop as "the synthesis or transcension of these anti-theses" (70).

[4] In "Response and Call," Dale E. Peterson offers an analysis of the relationship between Bakhtin's dialogics and African American criticism. According to Peterson,

> the long and the short of it--and by far the most culturally influential side of it--is
> that Bakhtinian discourse analysis presumes that utterances come into the world
> showing and voicing the fact that they are sites of social contestation. Texts
> display themselves as linguistic arenas in which perceptible cultural conflicts are
> acting out or acting up. (764)

Naylor crates such a literary arena through her juxtaposition of the Western and the African American literary tradition.

[5] Lerone Bennett, Jr., outlines the African countries which gained independence during the post-World War II years: Ghana in 1957 (555), Mala and Nigeria in 1960 (561), Sierra Leone

in 1961 (563), Tanzania in 1961 (565), Uganda in 1962 (569), Kenya and Malawi in 1963 (572), and Zambia in 1964 (574).

[6] See Victor Turner's *The Forest of Symbols* and "Liminality and the Performative Genres" for discussions of liminality and its liberating aspects.

[7] See Morrison's "Behind the Making of *The Black Book*" for her scathing critique of the "Black is Beautiful" slogan which she describes as "a reaction to a white idea, which means it [is] a white idea turned inside out, and a white idea turned out is still a white idea" (89). Morrison continues, "The concept of physical beauty as a virtue is one of the dumbest, most pernicious and destructive ideas of the Western world, and we should have nothing to do with it" (89).

Works Cited

Awkward, Michael. *Inspiriting Influences: Tradition, Revision, and Afro-American Women's Novels*. New York: Columbia UP, 1989.

Baker, Houston A., Jr. *Blues, Ideology, and Afro-American Literature: A Vernacular Theory*. Chicago: U of Chicago P, 1984.

Barth, John. "The Literature of Replenishment." *The Atlantic* Jan. 1980: 65-71.

Bennett, Lerone, Jr. *Before the Mayflower: A History of Black America*. 6th ed. New York: Penguin, 1988.

Callahan, John F. *In the African-American Grain: The Pursuit of Voice in Twentieth-Century Black Fiction*. Urbana: U of Illinois P, 1988.

Chaucer, Geoffrey. *The Riverside Chaucer*. 3rd ed. Ed. Larry D. Benson. Boston: Houghton Mifflin, 1987.

David, Alfred. *The Strumpet Muse: Arts and Morals in Chaucer's Poetry*. Bloomington: Indiana UP, 1976.

Du Bois, W. E. B. *The Souls of Black Folk*. 1903. New York: Bantam, 1989.

Ellison, Ralph. *Invisible Man*. New York: Vintage, 1989.

Erickson, Peter. "Canon Revision Update: A 1992 Edition." Review of *Bailey's Cafe*, by Gloria Naylor. *The Kenyon Review* 15 (Summer 1993): 197-207.

_____. "'Shakespeare's Black?': The Role of Shakespeare in the Novels of Gloria Naylor." *Rewriting Shakespeare, Rewriting Ourselves*. Berkeley: U of California P, 1991. Rpt. in Gates and Appiah 231-248.

Gates, Henry Louis, Jr. and K. A. Appiah, eds. *Gloria Naylor: Critical Perspectives Past and Present*. New York: Amistad, 1993.

Glazer, Nathan. "In Defense of Multiculturalism." *The New Republic* 2 Sept. 1991: 18-23.

Gomez, Jewelle. "Naylor's *Inferno*." Review of *Linden Hills*, by Gloria Naylor. *The Women's Review of Books* Aug. 1985: 7-8.

Johnson, Charles. Interview. *Contemporary Literature* 34 (Summer 1993): 159-181.

Lomax, Alan. *Roots of the Blues*. Compact Disc Liner Notes. New World Records, 80252-2, 1977.

Maultsby, Portia K. "Africanisms in African-American Music." *Africanisms in American Culture*. Ed. Joseph E. Holloway. Bloomington: Indiana UP, 1990. 185-210.

Morrison, Toni. "Behind the Making of *The Black Book*." *Black World* 23 (Feb. 1974): 86-90.

_____. *The Bluest Eye*. New York: Pocket, 1970.

Mukherjee, Bharati. "There are Four Sides to Everything." Review of *Mama Day*, by Gloria Naylor. *The New York Times Book Review* 21 Feb. 1988: 7.

Naylor, Gloria. *Bailey's Cafe*. New York: Vintage, 1993.

_____. "Mood: Indigo, from *Bailey's Cafe.*" *Southern Review* 28 (Summer 1992): 502-536.

Peterson, Dale E. "Response and Call: The African American Dialogue with Bakhtin." *American Literature* 65 (Dec. 1993): 761-775.

Rifkind, Donna. Review of *Bailey's Cafe. The Washington Post*, 11 Oct. 1992. Rpt. in Gates and Appiah 28-30.

Saunders, James Robert. "The Ornamentation of Old Ideas: Gloria Naylor's First Three Novels." *The Hollins Critic* 27.2 (April 1990): 1-11.

Smith, Anthony D. *National Identity*. Reno: U of Nevada P, 1991.

Steele, Shelby. "Being Black and Feeling Blue: Black Hesitation on the Brink." *The American Scholar* 58 (Autumn 1989): 497-508.

Turner, Victor. *The Forest of Symbols: Aspects of Ndembu Ritual*. Ithaca: Cornell UP, 1967.

_____. "Liminality and the Performative Genres." *Studies in Symbolism and Cultural Communications*. Ed. F. Allan Hanson. Lawrence: U of Kansas Publications in Anthropology, 1982. 25-41.

Van Horne, Winston A. "Integration or Separation: Beyond the Philosophical Wilderness Thereof." *Race: Twentieth Century Dilemmas--Twentieth-First Century Prognoses*. Ed. Van Horne. Milwaukee: U of Wisconsin System Institute on Race and Ethnicity, 1989. 289-314.

West, Cornel. *Beyond Eurocentrism and Multiculturalism: Volume I: Prophetic Thought in Postmodern Times*. Monroe, [Maine]: Common Courage, 1993.

_____. "The Dilemma of the Black Intellectual." *Breaking Bread: Insurgent Black Intellectual Life*. By bell hooks and Cornel West. Boston: South End, 1991. 131-146.

Interview: "The Human Spirit Is a Kick-Ass Thing"

This exclusive interview with Gloria Naylor and Michelle C. Loris was conducted in New York City on May 29, 1996. Questions for the interview and editing of the material was done by both co-editors, Sharon Felton and Michelle C. Loris. Original material printed with permision of Gloria Naylor.

ML: Do you think your work is political?

GN: I don't think that it is overtly political, but I think that literature is politics; I think that life is politics. And I take political positions all the time but when it comes to my fiction, I don't take political positions because I believe after all is said and done that what I am doing with each book is trying very hard to capture a story . . . to tell a story and to elucidate a life as strongly and as truthfully as I can. But, hopefully, there will be a body politic in what I am doing with each book.

ML: Your work seems to focus on the politics of gender.

GN: I think that you may garner that out of my work. Women's literature in general began to explore the caverns and internal workings of women's lives. I have tried throughout my career to give voice to the voiceless and this hasn't been a conscious decision on my part--that I, Gloria Naylor, will now speak for gay women, will now speak for poor women on dead end streets, will now speak for the middle class women hidden in basements, the basements of life. No, I believe that I am a transcriber of these lives that have always been swirling around in my unconscious, and I have been chosen, in a sense, to give voice to this. What I do is to make myself as ready as I can to do whatever prep work is necessary in order to tell these stories. Now when you see what this has meant for the last fifteen years, what you see is a whole array of stories.

ML: You do present a complex array of women in your stories.

GN: Yes, I thought about that when, as *Bailey's Cafe* began to form that in *The Women of Brewster Place* I was romanticizing the female condition a bit. In *Bailey's Cafe* you see women who are victimizers; in *Brewster Place* the women are mostly victims who are trying to transcend a situation. In *Bailey's Cafe* you see females participating in the acculturation of younger women in ways that I think could be considered oppressive. I think that there was a newness about my feminism when I was writing *Brewster Place*. I was just discovering feminism at Brooklyn College and thinking that if women held the reins, the world would be different. With *Bailey's Cafe* you come through ten or twelve years of seeing women in power often making the same foolish mistakes, making the same expedient choices as men who have been in power have made. And so I say to my-self maybe this isn't a gender thing, maybe it's a human thing.

ML: You said in an interview that your work is female-centered. Would you distinguish that from feminist?

GN: Yes, I do. I define feminism as believing in social, economic, and political equality for all human beings. So a man has the same rights as I have. But to be female centered, I think, is to see the world "gynecologically," to see the world through the eyes of a woman. Women have to operate differently because of the way the power structure is. I think that feminism is a political term and to be female centered is more of a cultural term, a humanist term.

ML: How is the gynecological view different from the phallic view?

GN: Well, the gynecological view is one that is more reflective than active; it's more inner than outer; it's one that doesn't roam as much. I could not envision, for example, with *Linden Hills* two young women doing what those two young men did. Besides the fact that it is a refashioning of Dante's *Inferno* and that I have to have a Dante and a Virgil, when I thought of motion and travel and of adventure, I did not think female.

ML: What do you think accounts for that perception?

GN: The way I was raised, the society in which I came up, the literature I read . . . For example, the Brontës, you know, the furthest that those heroines went was onto the heath. But Melville had his men cross the planet. So there--it's about how we have been bred as far as our literatures, as far as our societies go.

ML: You don't see women as going on adventures or being in motion. Do you see yourself as a woman in motion?

GN: Yes, I've always been in motion from the time I got my driver's license. I was nineteen and I bought an old Dodge Dart and I took that thing on the interstates back in my twenties, you know, when you could go ten hours and not get tired. I always liked the idea of moving, of movement, to me that was a sort of freedom.

ML: That was a departure from the typical idea of female.

GN: Yes, and I don't know why. It wasn't a conscious thing; I just knew that I was restless. When my friends all started to get married, I knew that I didn't want to get married. I didn't know why I didn't want to get married, and I didn't know what I was looking for running up and down those interstates. But I was just searching and I knew the motion, the freedom of it all, would give me an answer. I just knew I didn't want to be still. And I think with the movement and the looking, the looking physically, the looking metaphysically, I came back to what I had been doing when I was eleven or twelve years old . . . and that was writing.

ML: So you write because. . .

GN: I write because I have no choice. I began writing in a sense to save my sanity because I could not in my early years articulate as I can today. So scribbling away in a little diary, writing little snatches of poems and that kind of thing became my way to be human because it meant that I was communicating. Once you cease to communicate, you cease to exist. So writing is my way of living. It's kind of a mission. It's a life's mission to continue to tell the stories.

ML: Can you talk some about your creative process? How you work and write?

GN: Each book has required more and more research. *Bailey's Cafe* was the most recent work until I began *Sapphira Wade*. *Brewster Place* was just an outpouring, a spontaneous kind of outpouring; in a sense my very personal novel. I've had to do intensive research beginning with *Mama Day*. Well, you know, the quartet was there from *Brewster Place*. From this work I had the quartet in my head and it was around *Mama Day* that the realization came that there would be a Sapphira Wade, and that actually this woman had been guiding me. I started out with just very broad sketches with the first novel, a general outline and then I began to fill it in. I heard E. L. Doctorow once give a metaphor for what writing was like and I always liked that metaphor: "writing is like driving from New York to California totally in the night. Your headlights let you see about three hundred feet in front of you, but, three hundred feet at a time, you make the whole distance." Writing is like that: a journey of discovery. I always begin with the title and the first line and the last line. And then I have my notes. But if you are very fortunate you do not end up with what you thought you would end up with. The work takes on its own internal life and grows. That's what I meant before when I said I was a transcriber of stories. You hope that in the process it catches fire and you have to run and catch up. You never even use half of your notes; they are just like little anchors and then you start to free fall. This book (*Sapphira Wade*) will be a little scary because I am free falling into the mind of a woman who is a little bit insane. The characters become real; they are definitely real, more real than real life.

ML: Since you bring it up, can we talk a little about your next book?

GN: Just a little. In the book I am writing now, Cocoa comes back as an old
       woman. It's 2023. This book will be the cornerstone. Always in my head
       Sapphira Wade would be the cornerstone because she has been the
       guiding spirit for now close to twenty years, and now it's time to grapple
       with her. Even when I was back working the switchboard--I was maybe
       twenty-six years old--she came to me, this woman. You know how a
       realization will sometimes bubble up to you. Well, I have someplace on a
       yellow pad a sketch of her picture. I was just sitting sketching and little
       snatches of what will go into this novel came to me then twenty years ago.
       This is the creative force. Sapphira Wade has been with me since way
       back then, although she was never mentioned until *Mama Day*. And now
       it is time that I bring her forth. I have had to do intensive research. I've
       been to Norway and to Africa for this novel. I actually had to physically
       go to the place in order to walk the terra firma . . . to breathe the air with
       this novel. I had to end up in Norway and on the western shores of
       Senegal. I'm going back to 1817 - 1823 in this book and I had to gather
       the material for that time period. And I am writing about two cultures
       neither of which I've had, and I am writing about a gender I've never had.
       So I have been gathering these materials for the last six or seven years.

ML: You are writing about Bascombe Wade as well. This is your first white
       man that you have written about, isn't it?

GN: He was Norwegian. White men weren't invented yet. White was starting
       to be invented in this country at that time but when he comes he will be
       Norwegian.

ML: So you are writing about him as a Norwegian rather than a white man?

GN: Well, to be a white male or female is to be a political definition. You know
       it is a definition of power . . . of privilege and of not being a slave. That is
       how the term evolved; it evolved out of the condition of the Africans who
       had come and of the need to politicize an economic situation. So Black
       emerged meaning what Black means today out of that economic situation
       of slavery. White emerged because you had to define something against
       not being Black. So you are Norwegians, or you are Scots, or Poles, or
       Irishmen, Englishmen, or Italian or Armenian and you became white. So I
       am writing about the meeting of a Norwegian man and a Fulani woman
       and a Choctaw male on the shores of Savannah. They're going off to
       create Willow Springs.

ML: You write about the South. Would you distinguish that from being a
       Southern writer?

GN: Oh yes, I think so, because the whole school of Southern writing means
       that there is a certain style to the writing that I don't think my work falls
       into. I have used the South often as subject matter, but I don't think that
       there is the element of the grotesque or of community, or of the land as a

metaphor. But I have been raised by southerners so I am touched very much by that region and I have my second home in Beaufort, South Carolina.

ML: I'm shifting gears a little here. I was wondering how you would describe the moral vision that your four works exhibit now to date.

GN: People have told me recently that I am a moral writer, that I take moral positions in my work. I believe that my work is saying that the African American community is a diverse people. But there has been this objectification of our identity and objectification is often a denigration of those qualities that compose your culture, be it your skin color, or the way you dance, or raise your children, or whatever. So I think that my work presents to you, the reader, a community of people who are both saints and sinners, who have beauty and blemishes. I don't glorify the African American and say we're all perfect. We are all human beings and that means complexity, that means light and shadow. I would hope that my moral vision has been to present human beings in light and shadow.

ML: You know some of your works have been described as mystical, allegorical, religious. And you were a Jehovah's Witness. How would you describe your religious views now and how might your religious vision show itself in your work?

GN: I consider myself more spiritual than religious, because I don't have an organized religion from which to channel my beliefs in the intangible and in higher powers. But I do know that my religious background shows up in my work. For example, in *Bailey's Cafe* I am retelling classical Biblical figures; I am retelling their stories. And Mariam gives birth to a character whose name is George. And in *Mama Day* George is a Christ figure. He sacrifices himself for love and he dies at thirty-three years old.

ML: So your Christ figure is born in *Bailey's Cafe*?

GN: Yes, because *Bailey's Cafe* predates *Mama Day*. George saved Cocoa and in that way he saved the whole line of the Days, all the women.

ML: You said that you are more spiritual than religious?

GN: Well, yes. In my life that means that there is a belief in something beyond the machinations of flesh and blood and that there is a belief in the intangible, be it love, or be it the creative process, or be it hope.

ML: You once said that people don't write novels unless they have hope.

GN: I used to quote Margaret Atwood as having said that. Then someone told me that it was Flannery O'Connor. In any case, the quote is: "people without hope do not write books." But what I was saying about my spiritual vision as it shapes my work is that I think the transcendence of the human spirit, the power of the human spirit, moves throughout these books, and my hope is that which is transcendent within us will outweigh that which is bestial. We have laws, the government, organized religion all playing a part in helping us balance that tension between the bestial and the transcendent. We also have the arts.

ML: How do you see that relationship between art and morality?

GN: I think that the execution of the artistic in us is a way of sublimating that which is bestial. What was that quote of Shakespeare's--that music calms the savage beast? Everything can be thought of as artistic: the nurturing of life, be it children or plants or animals.

ML: Do you have hope for race relations in this country?

GN: Not within our lifetime. I used to--academically. I don't know if you've read my introduction in *Children of the Night* where I speak about that subject. That was an academic exercise. When I tried to think and to look back over the last thirty years of race relations in America, I realized, it's just thirty years. And that is nothing compared to the time that has gone into creating inequality. To think that thirty years will undo this kind of tangled morass. No, not within our lifetime are we going to see this big thing called race relations ever resolved. What we will continue to have, what we always have had are one-on-ones, and if there are enough of those one-on-ones of people attempting to understand, then maybe we will get a block that lives together, or we'll get a neighborhood that might live together, or a section of the country that might live together, but no, I do not have too much hope for race. Our lifetime is just too short.

ML: I'd like to broach an historical question as it relates to race and *Bailey's Cafe*. Bailey is a World War II veteran and Hiroshima figures prominently. In what ways was the Holocaust in your mind with regard to your fourth novel? Mariam is Jewish . . . Are you bringing together two cultures?

GN: She has to be a Jew because she's giving birth to Christ. The book ends with those two events because those are two of the defining events of World War II and also of the modern age. That these events were two conscious governmental acts changed how we think, how we think of ourselves and our government. In contrast, slavery is a whole different ballgame; slavery is universal. Even talking about African slavery, that was filtered over many centuries. But with the government-sponsored genocide in Japan and Europe, in a very small and concentrated period of time--that's something very different. We've had genocide before; we have genocide right here in this country with the Native American, but that horror took place over a series of decades and with different types of policies. In the World War II era, however, we see man's inhumanity to man that was organized Hiroshima was organized, and the extermination policies of Nazi Germany were organized and methodically executed.

ML: What about relations between the sexes; do you have hope for that?

GN: No, even less. (Laughter). No, let me stop. I think that the definition of gender is slowly changing. And this is where young people could, might carry a part, but you know, I think that the big snakes are creating little snakes. I used to look at the exceptions, you know, like when you see fathers with their children and their baby carriages and they're taking them off to daycare--but those are truly the exceptions to the rule. I think probably what's going on is the status quo where younger people are coming up, young men are coming up to expect young women to assume certain roles. That's what I mean by big snakes creating the little snakes.

ML: That would suggest that you don't foresee change between the genders.

GN: Well, we have had change. Will there be massive change? I don't think there will be within our lifetime; I don't. I used to believe that once women would--sort of--be the vanguard of that happening, that once women got into positions where they could make decisions they could make a difference. But when they've gotten into positions where they *could* make a difference, there were so many other forces that held, that made them conform, either made them conform or they wanted to conform and they have just perpetuated the way things have always been.

ML: Do you think that the way we "mother" our children has changed?

GN: Motherhood? That's changing, I think, to a degree. It has been changing since the post-World War II era. It took a while for the ideology to begin to creep up to the reality. Single mothers began in the workforce in the 1950s and after World War II. Parenting is now changing to include men. I mean, men have always changed diapers and helped with the kids, but now the ideology is catching up with the reality of the fact that our dads did a bit of cooking. Like when one's mother had to be in the hospital to give birth to another child. You know, in those days, they kept women in the hospital for seven days or so. Husbands caved in and did things. I see motherhood expanding in the sense that extended families are important now. And that extended family might not always be a grandparent or an aunt or uncle; extended families could be so many single women with children--a friendship network, a childcare network. Children are being raised now by tribes more so than by a nuclear family. And as an African American, we do not have a matriarchal society. It is definitely a matrilocal society, where women and the idea of mothering is almost central to our community. I can see why mothers would play a part. Also, my own mother--who is here in the house with us today; she's been here for about six months--my own mother was a very strong person throughout my life. As well as my father, but because one's father went off to work in the 1950s, my mother has always been kind of a dominant presence in my life.

ML: In your work would you say that you are equally concerned with race and gender, or are you more concerned with one or the other?

GN: I have never thought about it that way. The two in my mind are interwoven. Like how do you separate being a black woman? I think that when I am in certain situations that it is not my gender that will govern the interactions, it is definitely my race. I think that my race has a more powerful effect upon influencing an environment or shaping a perception of me than my gender. I think the gender is the subtext to text for me as a black woman. In my work, though, it's interesting because these characters don't get made up with formulas like that. If they come out like Lorraine and Theresa in *Brewster Place*, it wasn't a formula, "Black female Lesbians." You start out with the picture of that face with that body in motion and then you go in search of her story.

ML: You know, I was wondering. *The Women of Brewster Place* has been made into a television film, and I think when we met a while back [at Sacred Heart University], you said that *Mama Day* might be made into a film?

GN: You're sitting in One Way Productions and this was designed, this began to film *Mama Day*. Well, now, One Way Productions is doing programming for children which is very nice.

ML: Well, why don't we talk about One Way Productions?

GN: One Way Productions got started as a legal entity in order to bring *Mama Day* to the screen. Where we stand now is here. I finished a draft in December of '95 and that was going to be my last involvement with that work because it's now in the hands of two producer agents who are taking that draft as well as whatever wherewithal they have with packaging to try to make that happen. It moves me into the seventh year of attempting to bring that novel to film, and so I had to then move on. I have to say I have learned the screenwriting process by working by the seat of my pants. But '96 was the year of the novel, and in a way '96 has been the year of the novel in many levels. I've had novel experiences this year.

ML: In the translation from the novel into the screenplay, what do you see happening to your work as it gets transformed from one form to another? Is there anything lost or gained?

GN: Oh, God, yes. You lose a lot because you cannot translate a book to the screen. What you can do is take the basic elements from a book, take the spirit of the book, and then proceed to create a whole new animal because a screenplay calls upon you, the creator, to do different things. One, you're not even dealing with language. For a script, you're dealing with pictures. It is a singular art when one is writing a novel, and a very collaborative art when one is making a film. All these talented people come together. We've done what we had to do and a hell of a lot of praying, because once again, even all of these disparate figures with disparate talents cannot necessarily make the magic happen. It's one of those crazy mystical things; I learned that doing theater. The screenplay's only got the bare bones, the blueprint, of the process. I learned that what will come out of that process will be a film that will reflect the spirit of the novel. You lose an awful lot of characters, you have to invent new situations, disregard other situations altogether. Unless you are going to do voice-overs, you cannot even retain the language that might have enthralled you with a book. But what you want to make is a good film about an old woman on an island somewhere who can work magic with the human soul--and that's what you do. But I'm real comfortable with the cast of characters around me now who are pushing to try to make this happen. We'll see.

ML: So that's how One Way Productions got started. What kind of work does it do now?

GN: Well, now what it does is design work for children. It got shaped into its own mission and our first One Way Production project will be a one-act children's play for the Lincoln Center Institute. We were due to go into production this year, then we had director's problems, so we'll be doing it for the next school year. It's called "Candy." What the Institute does is to bring dance or drama or art or music to the school systems after they have first brought in the teachers during the summer, so that the teachers have a way of integrating whatever the Institute will bring into the school into their curriculum. So that's it's not just a one-shot deal; here we are, kids, goodbye. The teachers have been prepared and the students have been prepared throughout that whole semester for this event, and then it just becomes a part of the whole learning process. So "Candy" is a one-act play that they commissioned us to do.

ML: Can you talk about what some of the personal, the more dominant personal experiences have generated themselves into your art work? For example, *Brewster Place* . . .

GN: I think in those days what that was about was the fact that I was searching for a sense of self, you know, a sense of my female self, and just a sense of personal self with *Brewster Place*. I had always been a great beginner and never finished much of anything, so that I began a ministry that I didn't finish, I had begun a marriage, I didn't finish that, and I had begun school at a late age--at twenty-five, twenty-six years old, and I wasn't sure if I was going to finish that, you know, given my track record. . . So writing *Brewster Place* became number one, one of the first things that I began that I finished. . . finished it simultaneously with getting my undergraduate degree. So that was kind of neat. It also became a way of putting myself into reality, because you know I read voraciously. I just hadn't read books that reflected . . . things that were worthy of my person, my history. So writing it did that for me. I wanted to celebrate what had been invisible.

ML: How about *Mama Day*? What was inside of you that translated out into *Mama Day*?

GN: Oh, my belief in love and magic. That's what that book is about. I saw with my nephew, because he was very ill--terminally ill when he was young--and I saw the power of love literally save his life. And so . . . I know that it can be tangible, that you can cut it and dish it out, you truly can. It has a texture and a weight to it. I know that love can do that, I know that love can heal . . .

ML: An interviewer once asked Albert Camus if there was something in his work that had been overlooked by the critics--a theme or a symbol--something that was really important that had been overlooked. He said humor. Do you think that there is anything that has been omitted or overlooked by the critics or the reviewers in your work?

GN: Well, reviewers and critics are two different things, but I would say with the critics that I would like someday for someone to look at the importance of naming, the whole act of naming, names themselves within my work because that's real conscious when I play certain games with that. I think the naming of characters and what place names play and how they play out. That would interest me to read about my work. And especially I think because I get names first and when you asked me about the creative process the first thing I did were names. Named the book, named the characters, then the other stuff gets filled in later.

ML: Is there anything else you think critics have overlooked?

GN: Well, I am hoping that someday a critic will look at the rhyme scheme in the *Inferno* and then look at the narrative structure of *Linden Hills*. What I did with images, and how I mimicked the rhyme scheme of the original poem with images in my book. That was a conscious design feature. I did it almost all the way through; I think it did fall down a little at the end. The *Inferno* has a *terza rima* rhyme scheme--of A, B, A / B, C, B--and I do that with *Linden Hills*.

ML: How do you imagine literature might change as we reach the twenty-first century?

GN: It already has. I mean, it's not going to be in the form as we know it as far as ink on paper. Literature has gone electronic and I think we'll go even more so. I imagine books being read in virtual reality, where you experience *Moby Dick*, as opposed to actually reading it. I think because the writers of the future will have been born in the electronic age that's going to affect how they think of words on paper. I believe that books will get shorter. I think that images will probably be kinetic and sharper, because of how these children come of age thinking of reality.

ML: Do you think it will affect your work personally?

GN: I'm too old. I'm forty-six and I'm just at the beginning of the television age. I know that working with word processors, I think, has probably affected my work. I'm more verbose than I used to be. But I think I'm too old to be affected by this new wave of technology that other writers will be.

ML: What would you say you would want your achievement to be as a writer? What legacy or influence will you want to leave? You mentioned that at the very beginning of our conversation that "my works are going to be here beyond me" . . .

GN: [long pause]. A couple of things. I would like for people to see how I played with structure and how often the form of the work has been either influenced by the content, or either the content demanded the form of the work. I would like for people to say, well, you know, that she was a little bit of a cutting edge of dealing within a very conventional narrative with some structural avant-garde elements. And so I would like that to be left. Also, I would like it to be said that after all is said and done, that she gave us a world of people . . . that's what I'd like.

ML: Can you tell me about your garden in South Carolina?

GN: I designed it from scratch. I had the stones delivered. Put them in the ground myself. So it's several little raised beds as you move throughout this path and in the middle is a little statuette of a little child leaning over a book and reading. And he's surrounded with strawberries and lilac and thyme, and I call him Sweet Charlie. So you walk into the garden and on either side are these squares and then two long squares and in the middle there's Sweet Charlie, and there are more squares on the other side. And as you move through it with your lettuce and tomatoes and asparagus bed and watermelon bed and . . . 'cause you know you gotta have watermelon growing. All that good stuff like the peas and the sunflowers in the back. Charlie's in the middle with the strawberry bed because the strawberry beds are perennial and my asparagus bed would be perennial. This was my retirement home, so I figured what's done might as well keep going . . .

ML: What does the garden do for you? What does it mean to you?

GN: It reaffirms my belief in creativity and in life. Despite the weeds, the obstacles, those turnips came up. It's about what I do for work. You take a tiny little seed . . . and I have giant marigolds that I grew from seeds. Those seeds came up. And now there are these absolutely gorgeous marigolds. And so what a garden does for me is to say the human spirit is a kick-ass thing. That's what that garden does.

Note: On December 11, 1996, several months after this interview took place, Gloria Naylor informed me that it was not yet time for *Sapphira Wade*, the novel. Ms. Naylor explained that her vision of the meeting of an African woman with a European man to be used as the founding of a country would certainly become a future project, but at this time, Ms. Naylor has begun working on a project entitled *The Men of Brewster Place*. She explained that this new work would be written from the perspective of the men who were on Brewster Place but whose stories could not be written until now.

Michelle C. Loris

Bibliography

Primary Works

"African-American or Black: What's in a Name?" *Ebony* (July 1989): 80.

Bailey's Cafe. New York: Harcourt, Brace, Jovanovich, 1992. Paperback edition, New York: Vintage/Random House, 1993.

"Do You Think of Yourself as a Woman Writer?" Panel discussion with Ellen Gilchrist, Josephine Humphreys, Gloria Naylor, and Louise Shivers. Ed. Willard Pate. *Furman Studies* 34 (Dec. 1988): 2-13.

"Hidden Wealth?" *First Words: Earliest Writing from Favorite Contemporary Authors.* Ed. Paul Mandelbaum. Chapel Hill: Algonquin, 1993. 364.

Linden Hills. New York: Ticknor & Fields, 1985. Paperback edition, New York: Penguin, 1986.

"Love and Sex in the Afro-American Novel." *The Yale Review* 78.1 (Autumn 1989): 19-31.

Mama Day. New York: Ticknor & Fields, 1988. Paperback edition, New York: Vintage, 1989.

"The Myth of the Matriarch." *Life* 11 (1988): 65.

Naylor, Gloria, and Toni Morrison. "A Conversation: Gloria Naylor and Toni Morrison." *Southern Review* 21.3 (1985): 567-593.

"Of Fathers and Sons: A Daughter Remembers." *In Their Footsteps.* Ed. Henry Chase. New York: Henry Holt, 1994. 5-7.

"Power: Rx for Good Health." *Ms.* (1989): 58-60.

"Reflections." *Centennial.* Ed. Michael Rosenthal. New York: Pindar, 1986. 68-71.

"Telling Tales and Mississippi Sunsets." *Grand Mothers: Poems, Reminiscences, and Short Stories about the Keepers of Our Traditions.* Ed. Nikki Giovanni. New York: Henry Holt, 1994. 59-62.

[Untitled]. *Writers Dreaming.* Ed. Naomi Epel. New York: Carol Southern Books, 1993. 167-177.

The Women of Brewster Place. New York: Viking, 1982. Paperback edition, New York: Penguin, 1983.

Secondary Works

Andrews, Larry R. "Black Sisterhood in Gloria Naylor's Novels." *College Language Association Journal* 33.1 (1989): 1-25. In Gates and Appiah.

Awkward, Michael. "Authorial Dreams of Wholeness: (Dis)Unity, (Literary) Parentage, and *The Women of Brewster* Place." *Inspiriting Influences: Tradition, Revision, and Afro-American Women's Novels.* New York: Columbia UP, 1991. In Gates and Appiah.

Bande, Usha. "Murder as Social Revenge in *The Street* and *The Women of Brewster Place*." *Notes on Contemporary Literature* 23.1 (1993): 4-5.

Bellinelli, Mateo, dir. *A Conversation with Gloria Naylor.* Produced by California Newsreel, 1992.

Bonetti, Kay. "An Interview with Gloria Naylor." (audiotape). New York: American Prose Library, 1988.

Bouvier, Luke. "Reading in Black and White: Space and Race in *Linden Hills*." In Gates and Appiah.

Branzburg, Judith V. "Seven Women and a Wall." *Callaloo* 7 (1984): 116-119.

Brown, Rosellen. Review of *Mama Day*. *Ms*. 16.8 (1988): 74.

Carabi, Angel. Interview with Gloria Naylor. *Belles Lettres* 7 (1992): 36-42.

Carroll, Rebecca. *I Know What the Red Clay Looks Like: The Voice and Vision of Black Women Writers.* New York: Crown, 1994. 158-173.

Christian, Barbara. "Gloria Naylor's Geography: Community, Class, and Patriarchy in *The Women of Brewster Place* and *Linden Hills*." *Reading Black, Reading Feminist.* Ed. Henry Louis Gates, Jr. New York: Meridian, 1990. 348-373. In Gates and Appiah.

_____. "No More Buried Lives: The Theme of Lesbianism in Audre Lorde's *Zami*, Gloria Naylor's *The Women of Brewster Place*, Ntozake Shange's *Sassafras, Cypress, and Indigo*, and Alice Walker's *The Color Purple*." *Black Feminist Criticism*. Ed. Barbara Christian. New York: Pergamon Press, 1985. 187-204.

Donlon, Joycelyn. "Hearing is Believing: Southern Racial Communities and Strategies of Story-Listening in Gloria Naylor and Lee Smith." *Twentieth Century Literature* 41.1 (1995): 16-35.

Erickson, Peter. "Canon Revision Update: A 1992 Edition." *Kenyon Review* 15 (Summer 1993): 197-207. Review of *Bailey's Cafe*. In Gates and Appiah.

_____. "'Shakespeare's Black?': The Role of Shakespeare in Naylor's Novels." *Rewriting Shakespeare, Rewriting Ourselves.* Berkeley: U of California P, 1991. In Gates and Appiah.

Fowler, Virginia C. *Gloria Naylor: In Search of Sanctuary.* Twayne United States Authors Series, #660. New York: Simon & Schuster Macmillan, 1996.

Fraser, Celeste. "Stealing B(l)ack Voices: The Myth of the Black Matriarchy and *The Women of Brewster Place*." *Critical Matrix: The Princeton Journal of Women, Gender, and Culture* 5 (1989): 65-88. In Gates and Appiah.

Gates, Henry Louis, Jr. "Significant Others." [Reply to Homans, below]. *Contemporary Literature* 29.4 (1988): 606-623.

_____, and K. A. Appiah, eds. *Gloria Naylor: Critical Perspectives Past and Present.* New York: Amistad, 1993.

Geeslin, Campbell. Review of *Linden Hills*. *People Weekly* (25 Mar 1985):20+.

Glicksman, Marlaine. "Black Like Who?" *Film Comment* 25.3 (1989): 75-6.

Goddu, Teresa. "Reconstructing History in *Linden Hills*." In Gates and Appiah.

Haralson, Eric L. "Gloria Naylor." *African American Writers: Profiles of Their Lives and Works*. Eds. Valerie Smith, Lea Baechler, and A. Walton Litz. New York: Macmillan, 1991. 267-278.

Harris, Trudier. *The Power of the Porch: The Storyteller's Craft in Zora Neale Hurston, Gloria Naylor, and Randall Kenan*. Athens: U of Georgia P, 1996.

Holloway, Karla F. C. *Moorings and Metaphors: Figures of Culture and Gender in Black Women's Literature*. New Brunswick: Rutgers UP, 1992.

Homans, Margaret. "The Woman in the Cave: Recent Feminist Fictions and the Classical Underworld." *Contemporary Literature* 29.3 (1988): 369-402. In Gates and Appiah.

Inoue, Kazuko. "Gloria Naylor's Narrative: Looking Past the Losing." *Language and Culture* 18 (1990): 157-176. In Japanese.

Jones, Robert. "A Place in the Suburbs." [Review of *Linden Hills*]. *Commonweal* 3 May 1985: 283-285.

Kelley, Margot Anne. "Sisters' Choices: Quilting Aesthetics in Contemporary African-American Women's Fiction." *Alice Walker: "Everyday Use."* Ed. Barbara Christian. New Brunswick: Rutgers UP, 1994. 167-194.

Kelly, Lori Duin. "The Dream Sequence in *The Women of Brewster Place*." *Notes on Contemporary Literature* 21.4 (1991): 8-10.

King, Debra Walker. "Reading the 'Deep Talk' of Literary Names and Naming." *Names: A Journal of Onomastics* 42.3 (1994): 181-199.

Korenman, Joan S. "African-American Women Writers, Black Nationalism, and the Matrilineal Heritage." *College Language Association Journal* 38.2 (1994): 143-161.

Kort, Michele. "Lights, Camera, Affirmative Action." *Ms.* 17.5 (1988): 55.

Kubitschek, Missy Dehn. *Claiming the Heritage: African American Women Novelists and History*. Jackson: UP of Mississippi, 1991.

_____. "Toward a New Order: Shakespeare, Morrison, and Gloria Naylor's *Mama Day*." *MELUS* 19.3 (1994): 75-90.

Leonard, John. "Character Building." *New York* 22.12 (20 March 1989): 76-77.

Levy, Helen Fiddyment. "Lead on with Light." *Fiction of the Home Place: Jewett, Cather, Glasgow, Porter, Welty, and Naylor*. Jackson: UP of Mississippi, 1992. 196-222. In Gates and Appiah.

Lynch, Michael F. "The Wall and the Mirror in the Promised Land: The City in the Novels of Gloria Naylor." *The City in African-American Literature*. Eds. Yoshinobu Hakutani and Robert Butler. Madison: Fairleigh-Dickinson UP, 1995. 181-195.

Matus, Jill L. "Dream, Deferral, and Closure in *The Women of Brewster Place*." *Black American Literature Forum* 24.1 (1990): 49-64. In Gates and Appiah.

Meisenhelder, Susan. "'Eating Cane' in Gloria Naylor's *The Women of Brewster Place* and Zora Neale Hurston's 'Sweat'." *Notes on Contemporary Literature* 23.2 (1993): 5-7.

Montgomery, Maxine Lavon. *The Apocalypse in African-American Fiction*. Gainesville: UP of Florida, 1996.

Mukherjee, Bharati. Review of *Mama Day*. *New York Times Book Review* 21 Feb. 1988: 7.

Novy, Marianne. *Engaging with Shakespeare: Responses of George Eliot and Other Women Novelists*. Athens: U of Georgia P, 1994.

O'Conner, Patricia T. Reviews of *Linden Hills*. *New York Times Book Review* 23 March 1986: 52, and 7 Dec. 1986: 84.

O'Connor, Mary. "Subject, Voice, and Women in Some Contemporary Black American Women's Writing." *Feminism, Bakhtin, and the Dialogic.* Eds. Dale M. Bauer and Susan J. McKinstry. Albany: State U of New York P, 1991. 199-217.

Olson, Patricia. Review of *Mama Day. Christian Century* 105.34 (1988): 1047.

Palumbo, Kathryn. "The Uses of Female Imagery in Naylor's *The Women of Brewster Place.*" *Notes on Contemporary Literature* 15.3 (1985): 6-7.

Pearlman, Mickey. "An Interview with Gloria Naylor." *High Plains Literary Review* 5.1 (1990): 98-107.

_____, and Katherine Usher Henderson. *Inter/View: Talks with America's Writing Women.* Lexington: UP of Kentucky, 1990. 23-29.

Perry, Donna. "Gloria Naylor." *Backtalk: Women Writers Speak Out.* New Brunswick: Rutgers UP, 1993. 217-244.

Puhr, Kathleen M. "Healers in Gloria Naylor's Fiction." *Twentieth Century Literature* 40.4 (1994): 518-527.

Pullin, Faith. Review of *Mama Day. Times Literary Supplement* (3 June 1988): 623.

Ranveer, Kashinath. *Black Feminist Consciousness.* Jaipur: Printwell, 1995.

Rao, Eleonora. "'This Island's Mine, by Sycorax My Mother': *The Tempest* in *Mama Day* di Gloria Naylor." *Shakespeare e la sua eredita.* Ed. Grazia Caliumi. Parma: Zara, 1993. 271-279. In Italian.

Reckley, Ralph. "Science, Faith, and Religion in Gloria Naylor's *Mama Day.*" *Twentieth-Century Black American Women in Print: Essays by Ralph Reckley, Sr.* Ed. Lola E. Jones. Acton: Copley, 1991. 87-95.

Russell, Sandi. *Render Me My Song: African-American Women Writers from Slavery to the Present.* New York: St. Martin's, 1990.

Sandiford, Keith A. "Gothic and Intertextual Constructions in *Linden Hills.*" *Arizona Quarterly* 47.3 (1991): 117-139. In Gates and Appiah.

Saunders, James Robert. "The Ornamentation of Old Ideas: Gloria Naylor's First Three Novels." *The Hollins Critic* 27.2 (April 1990): 1-11. In Gates and Appiah.

Showalter, Elaine. *Sister's Choice: Tradition and Change in American Women's Writing.* Oxford: Clarendon, 1991. 38-40.

Smith, Barbara. "The Truth that Never Hurts: Black Lesbians in Fiction in the 1980s." *Wild Women in the Whirlwind: Afra-American Culture and the Contemporary Literary Renaissance.* Eds. Joanne M. Braxton and Andrée Nicola McLaughlin. New Brusnwick: Rutgers, 1990. 213-245.

Stanford, Ann Folwell. "Mechanisms of Disease: African-American Women Writers, Social Pathologies, and the Limits of Medicine." *NWSA Journal* 6.1 (1994): 28-47.

Tanner, Laura E. "Reading Rape: Sanctuary and *The Women of Brewster Place.*" *American Literature* 62.4 (1990): 559-582. In Gates and Appiah.

Taylor-Guthrie, Danille, ed. "Gloria Naylor and Toni Morrison: A Conversation." *Conversations with Toni Morrison.* Jackson: UP of Mississippi, 1994. Reprint of *Southern Review* interview.

Traub, Valerie. "Rainbows of Darkness: Deconstructing Shakespeare in the Work of Gloria Naylor and Zora Neale Hurston." *Cross-Cultural Performances: Differences in Women's Re-Visions of Shakespeare.* Ed. Marianne Novy. Urbana: U of Illinois P, 1993. 150-164.

Wagner-Martin, Linda. "Quilting in Gloria Naylor's *Mama Day.*" *Notes on Contemporary Literature* 18.5 (1988): 6-7.

Wallinger, Hanna. "Gloria Naylor's *Linden Hills*: The Novel by an African American Woman Writer and the Critical Discourse." *Moderne Sprachen* 37.3 (1993): 172-186.

Ward, Catherine C. "Gloria Naylor's *Linden Hills*: A Modern *Inferno.*" *Contemporary Literature* 28.1 (1987): 67-81. In Gates and Appiah.

Warren, Nagueyalti. "Cocoa and George: A Love Dialectic." *SAGE: A Scholarly Journal on Black Women* 7.2 (1990): 19-25.

Wells, Linda; Bowen, Sandra E. (reply); Stutman, Suzanne (reply). "'What Shall I Give My Children?': The Role of Mentor in Gloria Naylor's *The Women of Brewster Place* and Paule Marshall's *Praisesong for the Widow.*" *Explorations in Ethnic Studies* 13.2 91990): 41-60.

Wickenden, Dorothy. Review of *The Women of Brewster Place*. *The New Republic* 187 (6 Sept. 1982): 37-38.

Winsbro, Bonnie. "Modern Rationality and the Supernatural: Bridging Two Worlds in Gloria Naylor's *Mama Day.*" *Supernatural Forces: Belief, Difference, and Power in Contemporary Works by Ethnic Women*. Amherst: U of Massachusetts P, 1993. 109-128.

Index

Achebe, Chinua, 58

African-American, 4, 9, 44, 57, 80, 86, 88, 90, 94, 96, 143, 156, 165, 167, 175, 183, 187, 195, 209, 212, 214, 219, 220, 226, 236, 244, 257

African-American authors, 1, 3, 11, 153, 166, 178, 200, 240

African-American novel, 153

Aidoo, Ama Ata, 13ff

Alcott, Louisa May, 11, 129, 130, 141

Alcott, Winston [Linden Hills], 4, 53, 71, 78, 83, 92, 93, 95, 99, 101, 104, 106

American Book Award, 1

Anderson, Ruth and Norman [Linden Hills], 73, 90, 96, 227

Andrews, George [Mama Day], 7, 56, 59, 113, 114, 115, 120, 123, 125, 131-143, 148, 149, 152, 155, 160, 161, 162, 163, 164, 169-174, 180, 181, 183-187, 216, 219, 222, 227, 236, 247, 257

Anowa, 13, 14, 16, 17, 21, 22

Atwood, Margaret, 257

Bailey [Bailey's Cafe], 8, 188, 212, 213, 214, 220, 229, 231

Bailey's Cafe, **187-252;** 2, 6, 8, 9, 11, 164, 165, 187, 188, 192, 193, 194, 198, 199, 201, 210, 211, 215, 219, 220, 222-225, 229, 235, 236, 238-244, 247, 248, 250, 251, 252, 254, 255, 257, 258

Baldwin, James, 3

Baker, C. C. [The Women of Brewster Place], 43, 46, 49, 228

Baker, Houston, 58, 156, 157, 176, 236, 237, 238, 248, 251

Barthes, Roland, 167, 176

baseball, 212, 213, 214, 221, 223

Beloved, 34, 36, 59, 193

Ben [The Women of Brewster Place], 3-4, 43, 207

Benston, Kimberly W., 159, 163, 165

Berg, Christine G., 98-111

black cultural nationalism, 11, 211, 213, 214, 218, 219, 223, 224, 240, 245, 247

blues singers, 5, 45, 85

The Bluest Eye, 240, 241, 245, 251

Bobo, Jacqueline and Ellen Seiter, 26-42

Bone, Robert, 65, 74

Boyd, Nellie, 76-80

Brewster Place [as setting or place], 3, 23, 42, 43, 47, 48, 227

Browne, Kiswana [The Women of Brewster Place], 10, 13, 14, 15, 17, 18, 21, 31, 37, 44, 46, 90, 207

Browngirl Brownstones, 13, 16, 17, 20, 21

About the Editors

SHARON FELTON is a specialist in modern and contemporary American and British literature and women's writing. She has been an Assistant Professor of English at the Waterbury campus of the University of Connecticut and at Austin Peay State University. She is the editor of *The Critical Response to Joan Didion* (Greenwood, 1993) and has published articles and reviews in *The Hollins Critic, Connecticut Review, American Literature, Modern Fiction Studies, Studies in Short Fiction*, and other journals.

MICHELLE C. LORIS is a Professor at Sacred Heart University, where she teaches American Literature, Women's Studies, and Psychology. She holds doctorates in Modern American Literature and in Psychology and is the author of *Innocence, Loss, and Recovery in the Art of Joan Didion* (1989). She has published articles on psychology and on a wide range of authors, including Willa Cather, Saul Bellow, Toni Morrison, Kurt Vonnegut, and Edmund Spenser.

ISBN 0-313-30026-7

90000>

EAN

9 780313 300264

HARDCOVER BAR CODE